NEW THOUGHT RELIGION

A Philosophy for Health, Happiness, and Prosperity

Other Books by the Same Author

Milton And Servetus
The Theory of Logical Expression
The Modernity of Milton
The Plaster Saint
The Religion of the Occident
Wanton Sinner
Church Wealth and Business Income
The Essene Heritage
The Great Tax Fraud
The Churches: Their Riches, Revenues, and Immunities
Praise the Lord for Tax Exemption
When Parochial Schools Close
Tax Revolt: U.S.A.!
The Federal Reserve and Our Manipulated Dollar
The Religious Empire
The Story of Christian Origins
How to Defend Yourself against the Internal Revenue Service
The Essence of Jefferson
How to Establish a Trust and Reduce Taxation
The Essene Christian Faith
How You Can Save Money on Your Taxes This Year
The Continuing Tax Rebellion
The Best of Martin A. Larson
The IRS vs. The Middle Class
Jefferson: Magnificent Populist
How to Live a Productive Ninety-Year Life
Tax Revolt: The Battle for the Constitution
New Thought: A Modern Religious Approach

NEW THOUGHT RELIGION

A Philosophy for Health, Happiness, and Prosperity

by
Martin A. Larson

Philosophical Library
New York

Library of Congress Cataloging in Publication Data

Larson, Martin Alfred, 1897-
  New Thought religion.

  Rev. and updated ed. of: New Thought, or, A modern
religious approach.   1985
  Includes bibliographies.
  1. New Thought.   I. Larson, Martin Alfred,
1897-   .   New Thought, or, A modern religious
approach.   II. Title.
BF639.L384   1986   289.9'8   86-16947
ISBN 0-8022-2525-x
ISBN 0-8022-2527-6 (soft cover)

CONTENTS

INTRODUCTION

The reader will understand that New Thought is a basic attempt to reinterpret the conventional dogmas of historic religion. As my old friend Charles S. Braden emphasized in his *Spirits in Rebellion*, published in 1963, its spokesmen were and are actually in rebellion, even though they regard themselves as the true proponents of original Christianity. And there certainly have been conflicts and persecution: Michael Servetus, who, so far as I know, was the first to proclaim the theology and Christology which lie at the core of New Thought, was burned at the stake in Geneva, Switzerland, in 1553, under the dictatorship of John Calvin. When Swedenborg adopted a similar theology shortly after 1745, he did not dare make himself known as the author of his books on religion, all of which were published in Latin anonymously and at his own expense in foreign countries. When his authorship finally became known, this man, then about eighty years of age, was forced to leave Sweden under the threat of punishment; an attempt was even made to have him committed to an insane asylum. Almost 150 years elapsed before his greatness was recognized and he was given a state funeral at Upsala Cathedral; but even then his massive lucubrations and startling innovations in the religious field were completely ignored.

However, in the United States, a more congenial and freer religious climate was established by our Founding Fathers; under the concepts of church-state separation and freedom of conscience, dissidents could not be prosecuted after 1790 for deviations from generally accepted dogmas. This situation developed, not because of religious tolerance, but because a great variety of religious groups had come to this country in search of liberty and the freedom to worship according to conscience. Had any one of these been numerous or powerful enough to establish itself as a state church, there is little doubt that the bigotry prevalent in Europe would have been transferred to these shores; and in some places, especially in Virginia (Episcopalian), Massachusetts (Presbyterian), and Maryland (Roman Catholic), attempts were made to enforce religious uniformity under the coercive power of the government. However, reluctantly enough, since all were national minorities, the members of these diverse groups agreed that it would be better for themselves to be free of control from others or the state, even if the condition of such liberty had to be based on a surrender of judicial power or any expectation of support from the public purse. Thus, the First Amendment to the Constitution declares that "Congress shall make no law respecting an establishment of religion or prohibiting the free exercise thereof." In short, every denomination would have complete freedom to worship as it pleased, but must be completely private, self-dependent, and without coercive power over others. The same applies to every individual.

Although the various sects projected certain distinct differences, none denied or questioned such doctrines as the Trinity, the Virgin Birth of Jesus, his bodily resurrection and ascent into heaven, his death as an atonement and sacrifice for a humanity otherwise lost in original sin, the existence of a physical heaven and hell, the necessity of holy communion, and the belief that Jesus would one day return to earth to conduct the Last Judgment and inaugurate the Kingdom of Heaven or, as an alternative, awaken those who had died in the faith and transport them into the celestial realms. There were also other historic dogmas which were generally accepted among the otherwise warring sects.

Dissidents could no longer be sent to prison or the stake, but the churches nevertheless could and did exercise great influence upon public opinion. Even such men as Thomas Jefferson strictly forbade private correspondents to divulge the contents of personal letters which discussed religion; and this was true even during a time when only a minority of the people professed any religious commitment at all—as was the case at the beginning of the nineteenth century. So fierce and powerful were the clerics that they could publicly proclaim that Jefferson was the Antichrist in the White House.

Furthermore very nearly all the schools, and especially the institutions of higher learning, had been established by religious denominations and were operated by them well into the 1800s. The University of Virginia, which opened its doors to students in 1824, was, I believe, the first to declare itself a secular institution that would regard religion as an historic phenomenon to be studied objectively rather than as a dogma to be inculcated into the minds of students as infallible truth.

When the deist-rationalist Thomas Paine published *The Age of Reason* about 1795—rejecting the Bible as a human document filled with error—it was read avidly and widely; however, the condemnation to which Paine was subjected was so effective that even children followed him in the streets and threw stones at him; and when he died, his enemies dug up his bones and scattered them to the four winds.

When New Thought emerged on these shores, such early proponents as Warren Felt Evans and Phineas Parkhurst Quimby did not lay themselves open to such assaults. Like Swedenborg, they accepted the Scriptures and proclaimed them to be divine revelations; but they denied their literal meanings by a method called Spiritual Interpretation, by which they discovered new and different connotations in countless passages; and, by this technique, they abolished the basic doctrinal structure of historical or orthodox religion and supplanted it with a new and differing body of faith and belief. All this is the subject of this book; and we wish merely to say at this point that this has been the prevailing method of New Thought. The Bible is accepted as the Truth, but with meanings which vary from those held by the "orthodox" or from literal meanings. New Thought has, therefore, in a sense and in its own way, accomplished an objective somewhat similar to that of the deists or the rationalists.

It should be noted also that a number of famous men not specifically identified with religion as such adopted and proclaimed a New Thought ideology: among these were the Brook Farm group, Ralph Waldo Emerson, and Henry James, Sr. Such individuals as Samuel

Taylor Coleridge and the Brownings were Swedenborgians and proponents of New Thought. When Quimby began his practice of mental healing, he was called a charlatan; but he returned at least as good as he received, and his success placed him on a pedestal from which he could not be removed. The same was true of the Swedenborgian minister, philosopher, healer, and author Warren Felt Evans.

When Christian Science began achieving its extraordinary success, it was attacked bitterly, not only by the clergy and the medical profession, but also by objective scholars and disillusioned ex-members; and it was torn by internal dissensions, as we will show in a subsequent chapter.

However, it was not long before a number of very gifted individuals began publishing books proclaiming the principles of New Thought in an atmosphere of complete freedom. Although their writings were extremely popular—Ralph Waldo Trine's *In Tune with the Infinite* sold millions of copies and exercised enormous influence—they made no attempt to establish any organizations. Such teachers as Emma Curtis Hopkins conducted two-week seminars attended by a thousand students in various cities—each of whom paid fifty dollars—but she never tried to create a church organization. Nevertheless, she was extremely influential upon the Fillmores, Nona Brooks, and Ernest S. Holmes, all of whom did create the basis for churches. But even these people did not originally intend to do so; when churches came into existence among their followers, this was almost by accident or by spontaneous and popular demand.

Although one could collect a small library of books which criticize or condemn Christian Science, I know of very few which attack the modern New Thought movement or any of its proponents. For one thing, these people welcome debate and discussion and stand ready at any time to meet any adverse opinions head on in public or in private; they utilize skillfully many passages in Scripture which are in agreement with their philosophy. Probably most important of all, those who are in basic disagreement find it advantageous to ignore the movement as if it did not exist. Moreover, today it is obvious that thousands of ministers who belong, for example, to churches which are members of the National or World Council of Churches have accepted as their own—perhaps in private—some of the New Thought theses. Thus they cannot, in good conscience, attack them; and even though they do not publicly endorse them, they do not condemn what they have accepted in their own hearts. How many Lutheran, Methodist, or Presbyterian clerics today really believe that the great bulk of the human race is condemned to everlasting torture in hell simply because that is its predestined fate? How many Episcopalians actually accept their Thirty-Nine Articles as a personal creed? Thus, the principles of New Thought have penetrated many other religious communions and have ameliorated their teachings and humanized their theology.

We should note, therefore, that the influence of New Thought extends far beyond the membership of its own churches. Unity, for example, sent out 85,000,000 pieces of mail in 1984, only a small portion of which went to its 425 churches, which have perhaps 95,000 members. Such popular writers and preachers as Norman Vincent Peale and Robert Schuller belong definitely in the New Thought cycle. Secular writers such as Dale Carnegie and Maxwell Maltz, author of *Psycho-Cybernetics,* which is very popular in New Thought circles, should be classified in the same category.

Nor is this by any means all. A great many writers, many of them popular in New Thought, continue to write one book after another, some of which have sales running into the hundreds of thousands.

We should note that Charles Braden's *Spirits in Rebellion,* found almost everywhere in New Thought churches, published in 1963, has the same attitude and purpose which we have striven to maintain in this study: that is, complete objectivity, without bias or prejudice of any kind, for or against anyone or anything. However, even as his book was an important update over Horatio Dresser's *History of New Thought* (1919), so do we believe that a new work should now be available to the public. There are some differences in approach between the present study and Braden's: his was written about twenty-five years ago, and tremendous developments have occurred since then; he did not go back as far as we do in the treatment of sources; and he focused largely upon the historical events and personalities involved, whereas our principal attention is given to the teachings of New Thought theorists, teachers, and organizations.

Nor is any attempt made here to summarize most of the existing New Thought literature or authors. A special collection of such works in the Unity Library contains about 8,000 volumes; Science of Mind in

Los Angeles has a similar collection. An entire lifetime would scarcely suffice to study and analyze all of these. We believe, however, that we have presented an acceptable cross-section of what is most important and representative in all New Thought.

I am not aware of any other work now available which does the same. It is my hope that this will be accepted in and out of the New Thought movement as an adequate analysis and summary of what it is attempting to accomplish. Incidently, this edition is an updated revision of *New Thought: A Modern Religious Approach*, published in 1985.

Martin A. Larson

Chapter I

MICHAEL SERVETUS VILLANOVANUS

The day was October 27, 1553; the place the central square in Geneva, Switzerland; the action consisted in the slow burning at the stake of one of the most brilliant and creative minds of the entire Renaissance period: the Spanish scholar and theologian Servetus. But let us present a brief background for this event.

Michael Servetus had written several books dealing with geography and medicine; he had been a professor and had distinguished himself by the bold originality of his thought. But much more, he had dared to question and deny the principal foundation on which conventional or orthodox religious dogma was based—the Trinity of persons in the deity. In 1531, he had published, anonymously, a small volume in medieval Latin entitled *De Erroribus Trinitatis in libri septem* (*The Errors of the Trinity in Seven Books*). Since he took no responsibility for this at the time, he seems to have escaped detection or subsequent punishment. In 1553 he published a much larger tome called *Restitutio Christianismi* (*The Restitution or Restoration of Christianity*), in

1

which he condemned the existing religious power structures, both Catholic and Reformation, as corruptions of true or original Christianity. For this he was arrested on April 4th of that year and confined to prison in Milan, Italy. It appears that an old classmate was the warden and left the rear door open, through which he escaped on April 7 and fled north to Switzerland; whereupon he was condemned to burn at the stake by the Inquisition on June 4th, in absentia.

On his arrival in Geneva, where John Calvin reigned as dictator, he was arrested on August 13th, brought to trial on the 15th, and condemned to burn by slow fire on the 17th, a sentence which was carried into execution on October 27th.

However, it was not the heavy and difficult *Resititutio* (in which the author described the circulation of the blood long before anyone else had done so) but the *De Erroribus* which circulated widely and became influential; this was printed by the underground press in the Netherlands and made a very significant impact upon the theological thought of the period. Although it was extremely dangerous to be found with a copy of this explosive treatise, a great many were certainly printed; it circulated far and wide, and influenced many individuals of stature.

In my study of John Milton many years ago, I found the subject for my Ph.D. thesis in his theology, which, I finally concluded, probably had its principal source in Servetus. It was obvious to me that Milton did not accept the prevailing doctrine of the Trinity; instead, he conceived of the godhead as a universal entity with differing aspects or manifestations: not three distinct persons, or, in fact, any persons at all, but functions or activities, instead. As the basis for his universe, he postulated a unified substance which is God himself; however, there are three aspects in this basic reality. God the Father is the material of the cosmos; God the Word the energic force therein, its power of action, creation, effectual strength; God the Spirit simply its illumination, vitality, irradiance. Ideas similar to this are found in *Paradise Lost*, but even more definitely in the heretical *De Doctrina Christiania*, written in Latin and only translated many years after Milton's death.

We should note that in the early centuries while Christianity was spreading throughout the Graeco-Roman Empire, multifarious theological and Christological heresies flourished before the basic dogma of the Church, first expressed in the Apostles' Creed, was finally frozen into what became known officially as the Athanasian Creed, adopted in 325 at the Council of Nicaea, which declares in part:

> ...we worship the one God as a Trinity, and the Trinity as a Unity...for there is a person of the Father, another of the Son, another of the Holy Ghost.... The Father is infinite, the Son infinite, the Holy Ghost infinite.... So the Father is God, the Son is God, the Holy Ghost is God [all consubstantial with each other]; and yet they are not three Gods, but one God...all three persons are co-eternal one with another; and co-equal.

When this became the official dogma, every diverse opinion was punishable by exile or death, under the union of church and state established under Constantine.

Among the early heresies, we find the Arians, the Semi-Arians, the Photinians, the Marcellians, the Apollinarians, the Nestorians, the Monophysites, the Monothelites, the Patripassians, the Eutychians, and various others; but there were none among all these with anything closely resembling the concept developed by Servetus even at the age of twenty-two.

There were other outstanding heretics contemporary with Servetus, principally Leilius Socinus (1525-1562) and his nephew Faustus Socinus (1539-1604), who fled to Poland, where he developed a doctrine similar to that accepted much later by Joseph Priestley and the Unitarian Church. However, the concepts of Servetus were not only different from all others, but entirely original; they may, briefly, be summarized as follows:

The universe—the Cosmos—should be recognized as the all-existing or universal and omnipresent God, in which or whom persons or divisions are impossible. God is a Unity; He is identical with all existence. But this vast reality expresses itself on three planes, by three manifestations, in three aspects. As the Father-God, the deity constitutes the substance of the universe; as the Word, or Son, the energy or creative force which exercises its power throughout the whole; and as Holy Spirit, the light or illumination without which no life could seek its fulfillment. Basically, all this is good—beneficent; the three aspects exist in the universe as whole, in every living thing therein, animate or inanimate, in every creature that walks, flies, swims, or crawls; in every tree, flower, and shrub; in fact, even in every grain of sand. It is from this Central Power which enlivens all existence that man derives his nature; and, since the universe and everything in it is God, and all things therein are expressions of this deific source, man also is divine.

In this unific universe, duality is impossible. Evil, being a mere negation, has no actual or substantive existence; it is comparable to darkness, which is nothing in itself, but only the absence of light.

This was a concept with tremendous potential; and, although it was a long time before the concepts of the lonely man who died in Geneva in 1553—proclaiming that he would gladly recant if he could be shown by Scriptural authority that he was in error—received general recognition, we should realize that he was the first who gave ideological expression to the gospel of New Thought, which is now spreading all over the world as a philosophy of human divinity, a religion of well-being for humanity, and a reconstruction of the creeds and dogmas that ruled much of the world for centuries but that are now gradually losing their grip on the human psyche.

Just four hundred years after Servetus was burned, the Presbyterian Church erected a monument in his memory on the spot where he died. Surely, we can join in offering an accolade of honor to this heroic martyr.

Chapter II

SWEDENBORG: THE FOUNTAINHEAD

I. AN AMAZING PERSONALITY

Among most people, even the educated, the name of Emanuel Swedenborg evokes only a curious smile, or no response at all; for he is generally unknown or regarded simply as a self-deluded dreamer—or, perhaps, a literal madman—who could not possibly have left any serious or permanent imprint upon the sands of time.

The fact is, nevertheless, that this man has exercised enormous influence, direct and indirect, upon the moral, religious, and intellectual development of the Western world. More than anyone else, he was the catalyst that shattered the age-old creeds and dogmas of medieval and Reformation Christianity and thereby ushered into being, not only the potent ideology known as New Thought, but also many of the elements which have become increasingly conspicuous in the various large and powerful denominations.

Emanuel Swedenborg is surely without parallel in the modern world: for more than thirty years he was a civil servant who performed all the duties of his office faithfully, meanwhile producing scientific and philosophical treatises, vast in scope and astonishingly creative in content. He was an indefatigable scholar who labored without fanfare and got little public notice. He lived a long and, for the most part, seemingly unruffled existence. Approaching the age of sixty already with immortalizing accomplishments behind him, he embarked upon what was to be his overwhelming mission in life, in which he continued for more than twenty-five years: the reconstruction of the dogmas and practices of the existing churches and religious organizations.

Little could the ordinary observer suspect what was going on in the mind of this cultivated man, an inveterate bachelor whose white wig was sometimes awry, who lived frugally and labored incessantly, composing religious works in Latin and publishing in a foreign country. Under this protective covering, he proclaimed his condemnations and enunciations of individuals and religious organizations, as well as their ethical practices and motivations. It was many years before the contents of his lucubrations were identified as his; and secretiveness was indeed important. When his teachings began to circulate and gain disciples in Sweden, he barely escaped commitment to an insane asylum, in spite of his extraordinary achievements, his noble family, and his venerable age. When death came to him in 1772 at the age of eighty-four, it was in obscurity and in a foreign land. It took his countrymen almost 140 years to recognize his greatness; and even when honor was paid him, after his remains were restored to his native land and enshrined among the great, this was not a tribute to the theologian or religious reformer, but only to the scientist and philosopher.

It is impossible accurately to estimate the intensity or the extent of the Swedenborgian influence upon individuals, churches, movements, or thinking in general. The *World Almanac* of 1964 lists only 58 Swedenborgian congregations with 5,705 members in the United States; but this measures only a minute fraction of his total impact. It is certain that the number, quality, and variety of major minds which have been fascinated by the Swedish seer are indeed impressive. Some may be surprised to learn that Helen Keller, whose book, *My Religion* enjoyed wide popularity, was for many years a devout and fervent communicant of the New Church. Thomas Carlyle was deeply impressed by Swedenborg's philosophy and his *Sartor Resartus* is drenched in it. Henry James, father of the novelist of the same name and his famous brother, William, was a devoted Swedenborgian theologian who transmitted much of his thinking to his renowned sons. In a private letter, now in the library of the Swedenborg Society of London, Coleridge conferred the highest encomiums upon the Swedish theologian and declared that he devoted all the time he could spare to a study of his works. Such men as Tennyson, Patmore, Ruskin, Drummond, O. W. Holmes, Thoreau, Goethe, Heine, and others of comparable stature absorbed the Swedenborgian ideology to a great degree and served as transmission belts by which it became an integral element in Western culture. Mark Twain's *Captain Stormfeld's Visit to Heaven* is a Swedenborgian fantasy. The Brownings, especially Elizabeth Barrett, referred to themselves as "we Swedenborgians." Balzac, a devoted student, wrote concerning Swedenborg: "His theology is sublime, and his religion the only one a superior mind can accept."[1]

In this analysis and appraisal, we shall stress only those elements in Swedenborg which have been widely accepted and have exercised great influence; we simply do not consider it germane to our research to delve deeply into much that is found in him, such as his travels to other planets, his conversations with the departed, and his various visits to the world of spirits.

Swedenborg's ideas made deep inroads into American culture through the socialist-liberal-Unitarian coalition which established the communal experiment known as Brook Farm, near West Roxbury, Massachusetts, in 1841, in which the Channings were the prime movers. In 1844, this became a Fourierist phalanx, in which, in addition to the three Channings, we find such individuals as Albert Brisbane, Horace Greeley, Charles Dana, Margaret Fuller, Adin Ballou, George Ripley, Parke Goodwin, James Russell Lowell, John Greenleaf Whittier, and Henry James, Sr. However, as Fourierism began to subside after 1845, a new development emerged at Brook Farm; its leaders, especially Charles Dana and William H. Channing, became ardent Swedenborgians; if they could have created an American state religion, it would have been Swedenborgianism.

The penetration of this theology into Unitarianism is further illustrated by the case of Theodore Parker, upon whom the mantle of William E. Channing fell after 1842. Parker repeatedly addresses his impersonal deity in terms which could have had no source other than the cosmology of Swedenborg. "Thou Central Fire, the Radiant Light of All," he exclaims in passages which equate the Great Sun with God. In another, after setting forth the doctrine of universal influx, he declares: "Thus it is that human souls communicate with the great central Fire and Light of all the world, the Lodestone of the Universe, and thus recruit their powers, grow young again, and so are blessed and strong."[2] The sermons and prayers of Parker are studded with Swedenborgian concepts, which have thus, and through the writings of William H. Channing and Ralph Waldo Emerson, become an integral element in all Unitarian thinking—and, to a lesser extent, in the thinking of many educated Americans.

The influence of the Swedish seer and sage on modern thought, culture, and religion is summarized by Emerson in his essay on Swedenborg: "This man, who appeared to his contemporaries as a visionary...begins to spread himself into the minds of thousands.... A colossal soul, he lies vast on his times, uncomprehended.... The most remarkable step in the religious history of recent ages is that made by the genius of Swedenborg.... These truths, passing out of his system into general circulation, are now met with every day, qualifying the views and creeds of all churches and of men of no church."[3] And this is the simple truth: for his ethics and metaphysics have modified profoundly the thinking of millions who have never even heard his name. Taken as a whole, his mind was one of the most capacious that has ever appeared on this planet.

A number of years ago, a Believe-It-Or-Not Ripley cartoon[4] summarized Swedenborg's activities and achievements as inventor, botanist, zoologist, chemist, assayer, machinist, cabinetmaker, bookbinder, lens grinder, musician, organist, legislator, psychist, clockmaker, linguist, hydrographer, editor, poet, legislator, mining engineer, and publisher. He was an authority on blast furnaces, glass manufacture, and termite control; the author of the first Swedish textbook in algebra, and a practical innovator in educational theory. He devised the first threshing machine; and he made detailed sketches of many inventions, some of which have long since come into common use. Early in life, he calculated an elaborate method for determining the earth's longitude by the lunar orbit. As a member of the Riksdag, he was a diplomat, a financier, a political economist, a practical statesman; and he was an advocate of peace among the nations, urging his own in that direction. He was a mathematician, astronomer, metaphysician, and neuro-physiologist. He could easily qualify as a medical expert. His acute and voluminous studies in anatomy were so advanced—especially those on the brain—as to be incomprehensible to his contemporaries. Among other things, he discovered the function of the ductless glands and the fact that the brain animates sychronously with the lungs; and he made important discoveries concerning the circulation of the blood. He was the first to explain the nature of the Milky Way and to promulgate the Nebular Hypothesis, later elaborated by LaPlace. In geology, cosmology, physics, metallurgy, minerology, and smelting technology his contributions were immense and practical. He added substantially to knowledge concerning atomic theory and the science of radioactivity. He was the first to investigate the meanings of dream-symbolism and to describe the three levels upon which the human psyche operates, later elaborated by Warren Felt Evans and eventually called the Id, the Ego, and the Superego by Sigmund Freud. He produced an ear-trumpet and an airtight, hot-air stove; and he is the father of the decimal system of coinage. He advocated Swedish industrializiation as a means toward domestic prosperity and independence for Sweden. He did everything possible to advance intellectual, political, and religious libertarianism, as well as a completely republican form of government fully two generations before the French and American revolutions. He did not merely touch upon all these: he wrestled with the problems involved and offered workable solutions, many of which have since been accepted and implemented.

But most of all he was a religious reformer and innovator, the most extraordinary revealer in all history, and it is this phase of his activity which concerns us here. He is the grand fountainhead of a variety of deviationist religious movements, and, specifically, the grandfather of New Thought. In the vast expanse of his writings (Emerson calls him a mastodon of literature), single details have proved so pregnant with creative power as to become the source of cults and sects; each can take what it chooses and ignore the remainder.

Every widespread movement or philosophy has originated with some great and independent thinker. This does not imply that all the elements derive from one towering intellect; but it does mean that he has organized existing materials, added certain elements of his own, and given the whole a distinctive formulation. What Pythagoras did for ancient religion in the Western world, Marx for socialism, Darwin for the theory of evolution, and Freud for psychoanalysis, Emanuel Swedenborg did for various religious movements, but especially for the metaphysical system known as New Thought, the religion of health, happiness, prosperity, and human well-being, which purports to be as factual and demonstrable as a laboratory experiment. By combining accepted doctrine with his science and philosophy, Swedenborg accomplished a revolution in Christianity—which had also been the aim of the martyred Servetus Villanovanus.

II. HIS OUTWARD LIFE

1. *The Swedbergs.* Emanuel was born in Stockholm on January 29, 1688. Most of those who have founded religious cults have been persons of little or no education; some have been totally illiterate. Quite different, however, was this remarkable innovator, for his education was the most elaborate possible in his day. His father, Jasper Swedberg, was born in 1653, and became a professor at Upsala University in 1692, Dean there in 1694, and Bishop of Skara in 1702, in which capacity he continued until his death in 1738. In 1719, the family was ennobled and given the name *Swedenborg*. Both of Emanuel's grandparents had engaged in successful mining operations, and from them he received substantial bequests. And so we see that the families of the avid young student combined affluence with the best current learning and the most respectable ancestry.

2. *The Youthful Years.* At the age of eleven, the precocious child matriculated at Upsala, where René Descartes had lit the torch of freedom shortly before he died of pneumonia in 1650. Emanuel entered as a student of philosophy, which at that time included the physical sciences. After ten years, he graduated in 1709, having mastered a classical education in which the Graeco-Roman authors became his mentors and Latin as familiar as his mother tongue.

3. *Assessor, Scientist, and Philosopher.* Through the good offices of a friend, in 1716 King Charles gave the twenty-eight-year-old Swedenborg an appointment as Assessor of the Board of Mines, a position

in which he continued until June 17, 1747, when he retired to devote the remainder of his life to his mandate as revealer-extraordinary.

During the Assessorship years, he published his *Motion and Position of the Earth and the Planets*, a *Work on the Principles of Natural Philosophy*, and an opus called *Principia, On Iron, and On Copper*. The first part of this last work is Swedenborg's basic contribution to cosmology, in which the Nebular Hypothesis is for the first time clearly stated,[5] and in which he advances the theory that the universe is a mechanism governed throughout by mathematical law.[6] He declares that atoms are actually entities of energy and activity; and thus anticipates the modern concepts of electrons, protons, and neurons. In the second and third work, he performs a signal service in the field of smelting and metallurgy. He gathers from innumerable sources all existing knowledge concerning these industries and publishes it for all to read.

The year 1734 marks the culmination of one phase of his development, for at this point his overriding interest in science as such came to a close and he sought wider horizons in the realms of metaphysics. With the publication in that year of his treatise *The Infinite*,[7] he began an intensive search for the human soul, which was to dominate his interest for ten years. In the hope of discovering this elusive entity, he became an authority on anatomy. His first major work in this field was the ponderous *Cerebrum* (written 1738-40) which was followed by a number of other extensive works.

Swedenborg was so far in advance of his age in the knowledge of anatomy that a century had to elapse before the scientific world could understand his contributions. Then, at last, it was realized that here was the man who had cleared the way for future research, not only in this field, but also in metallurgy, psychology, cosmology, physics, chemistry, and various other scientific disciplines.[8]

4. *Heresy, Conflict, and Persecution*. The small volume *The Worship and the Love of God* (1745) signaled Swedenborg's transition from philosophy to theologian and revealer. We should note that the publication of any religiously unconventional ideas, even in Latin, was proscribed in 1750. Only in 1766 did he admit responsibility for his writings by affixing his name and humbly describing himself as the Servant of the Lord Jesus Christ. His first Swedish disciples, obtained

in 1765, were subjected to the severest strictures.[9] Another convert was defrocked, declared insane, and sent to prison.[10]

The most bitter experience of Swedenborg's life was his persecution for heresy at the age of eighty-two. The storm first broke in Gothenburg, where one disciple had written a favorable review of *The Apocalypse Revealed*, and where another had published a volume of *Household Sermons* surcharged with Swedenborgianism.[11]

Once this new doctrine began competing for popular support, it engendered the fiercest hostility among the established clergy. Olaf Ekebom, Dean of the Consistory of the Lutheran Synod and an archenemy of the New Church, declared that Swedenborg's teachings were "corrupting, heretical...diametrically opposed to God's Word ...full of the most intolerable errors...."[12] When he added that the Christology was Socinian, Swedenborg retorted that such a statement constituted "a cursed blasphemy" and that "the Dean's opinion may be taken for the flood which the Dragon cast out of his mouth after the Woman, to drown her in the wilderness."[13]

A shipment of books from England for distribution among members of the Diet was confiscated by the customs agents. Bishop Filenius, a nephew-in-law of the author, who had caressed his old relative upon his return, led the movement to proscribe his writings; and the enraged Swedenborg called the cleric a modern Judas Iscariot.[14]

In December 1769, Bishop Lambert charged that Swedenborg's writings were "plentifully tinged with Mohammedanism,"[15] because of his lush descriptions of connubial bliss in heaven in *Conjugial Love*, which also permitted concubinage under certain conditions. A movement was instigated to put him away as a lunatic. On January 2, 1770, the Royal Council forbade all circulation, reviews, or translations of his writings; and it called upon the Consistory to make an exact and detailed report of all errors and heresies lurking in them. It would seem, however, that this was too great an undertaking, for this body never complied with the behest.[16]

Drs. Beyer and Rosén wrote astute and spirited defenses in which they maintained that Swedenborg's teachings were based entirely upon authentic interpretations of Scriptures, but to little avail. When the report reached him that his two foremost disciples were not only to be deprived of office and livelihood but also banished, he issued an eloquent and denunciatory letter to the Royal Council. This, at least, had the effect of bringing an informal decision that the sage himself was to remain inviolable. Furthermore, his heresies were formulated so subtly, and often were so much in conformity with emerging philosophy and morality, that it was difficult to make out a decisive case against him. Actually, those who accepted the Bible *literally* had been much reduced in number and influence; and few were prepared to defend the true implications of many of its precepts.

5. *Condemnation and Departure.* Nevertheless, on April 26, 1770, the Royal Council "totally condemned, rejected," and forbade the dissemination of Swedenborgian literature or doctrines.[17] The argument that they were in agreement with Scripture was brushed aside with the declaration that no individual could repudiate the Augsburg Confession.[18] Dr. Beyer was prohibited from teaching theology and Dr. Rosén was warned not to intermix any novelties in the study of Terence and Cicero.[19]

Swedenborg complained bitterly in a letter to the King (May 25, 1770) that he had "been treated as no one has ever been treated before in Sweden since the introduction of Christianity...."[20] On July 23rd, he declared that his "trial had been the most important and the most solemn...during the last 1700 years, since it concerned the New Church which is predicted by the Lord" in the Scriptures.[21]

Since the authorities could not lay their hands on the person of the venerable seer, it was their devout hope that he would not embarrass them by his presence. In this, at the age of eighty-two, he accommodated them, for he soon left for Holland and England, never to see his home again.

On December 7, 1771, the Royal Council referred the prosecution of Swedenborg's doctrines to the Gothic Court of Appeals, which, after three years, shuttled it to Upsala University for a study of his writings. However, this proved too great a task for them also, and no report was ever submitted.[22]

6. *After Death, Triumph!* Soon after Swedenborg's death on March 29, 1771, an organization consisting of substantial individuals was formed in England to translate and publish his theological works and to promulgate his teachings. It was, however, many years before his own countrymen began to comprehend even the scientific achievements of the saintly iconoclast. It was not until April 7, 1908,

that the Swedish Government dispatched a cruiser to retrieve his remains; on May 13th, amidst resplendent ceremonies, the bones of the sage found a final resting place among the immortals in the Cathedral of Upsala. The city was decked in flags and memorials; there was a long procession, led by his family descendants, who were followed by representatives of many Swedish and foreign scientific organizations. The students of the University proceeded up the long aisle singing, and dipped their banners as they passed the coffin of the incomparable heretic. It was an hour of majestic solemnity unparalleled in the annals of the nation, and every eye offered its generous tribute of tears.

III. HIS INTELLECTUAL AND SPIRITUAL LIFE

1. *Early Accomplishments.* In 1718, Swedenborg devised a means by which Charles XII was able to transport five brigantines fifteen miles overland in a single day.[23] On another occasion, we find him laboring on a project to build a canal from Stockholm to Gothenburg, which became the basis for the great Göta Canal, still in operation, complete with locks, constructed a generation later.[24]

When Charles XII died in 1718, an era in Swedish history came to an end. As a result of his military adventures, a ruinous inflation had developed and Sweden was bankrupt. Then Swedenborg memorialized the Riksdag in a closely reasoned thesis in which he declared that a sound currency was essential in the international market. He was the first who advocated the financial policies which his country pursued thereafter.[25]

In 1725, the young man, now ennobled, memorialized the Riksdag again, this time with an essay he called *The Balance of Trade*. He declared that Sweden should industrialize, establish its own manufacturing plants, and thus be able to offer superior products in the competitive market.[26]

2. *The Statesman.* In 1734, a political crisis arose. Swedenborg argued convincingly that his country should maintain peace and had everything to lose and nothing to gain by war; that it should husband its resources and encourage mining, metallurgy, and manufacture,

thus embarking upon the ways of international amity in a solid, industrialized economy.[27]

3. *The Nebular Hypothesis*. In 1765 Immanuel Kant advanced in part the Nebular Hypothesis, which was perfected by LaPlace in 1796, and which offers an explanation for the origin of the solar system. However, Swedenborg had already clearly set forth this cosmological theory in his *Principia* in 1734, and again in his *Worship and the Love of God* in 1745.[28] According to this, our solar system—together with the planets—came into existence when, by the force of gravity, the central nebula threw off masses which, by centrifugal force, separated into the form of rings and gave birth to the orbiting lesser suns with their satellites. This scientific theory is crucial in Swedenborgianism, for without it, his theology, his theory of influx, and various other distinctive religious doctrines would never have been developed.

4. *Revelatory Claims*. However, Swedenborg is now best known as seer and revelator, and his claims in this regard were indeed immense. "It has pleased the Lord," he wrote, "to prepare me from my earliest youth to perceive the Word...."[29] He was much given to introspection and religious meditation. This development reached its culmination in a traumatic experience at Delft, Holland, on Easter Day, April 5, 1744, and on the succeeding night at the Hague, all of which is recorded in detail in *The Journal of Dreams*, never intended for any eyes but his own. This document was finally translated at Bryn Athyn, Pennsylvania, in 1918, where it was printed and later published. It may now be obtained from the Swedenborg Foundation in New York.

When he wrote the description of his Illumination, Swedenborg was in a state of superinduced fantasy: "I had in my mind and body the feeling of indescribable delight, so that had it been in any higher degree, my whole body would have been, as it were, dissolved in pure joy.... I was in heaven and heard speech which no human tongue can utter...."[30]

It is clear that we have here a psychological condition in which the subject could see great visions and hear strange voices. Half an hour after he went to bed on the evening of April 6th, he heard a great roar as of a mighty hurricane, was seized with a powerful trembling, and sensed a holy presence, which caused him to fall upon his face. "It was," he wrote, "a countenance of a holy mien" such as he had "while He lived on earth...I awoke with trembling." He continued, "And so I said, 'It was Jesus Himself.... Our Lord has been willing to show such grace to so unworthy a sinner.' "[31] Note here the word *grace*, later banished from his theology and vocabulary.

5.   *Prophet and Revelator.* The *Journal* established beyond doubt that these experiences were dreams only, but the psychological effect was permanent and supreme. From this time forward, Swedenborg was a different man, for he had received his divine mandate. "If you only knew what grace I am enjoying...."[32] he exclaimed rapturously. In 1771, at the age of eighty-three, he wrote to the Landgrave of Hesse-Darmstadt: "The Lord our Savior foretold that He would come...and institute a New Church.... But as He cannot come again into the world in Person, it was necessary that He should do it by means of a man, who should not only receive the doctrine of that church by his understanding, but also publish it by means of the press; and as the Lord had prepared me for this from my childhood, He manifested Himself in Person before me, His servant, and sent me to do his work.... I declare in truth that this is so."[33]

6.   *The Vision Grows.* The only actually authentic description of his Illumination is that written by Swedenborg himself in *The Journal of Dreams.* How this was elaborated and how his theology evolved becomes apparent as we study his own later versions of that event. The description of it given to Dr. Beyer shows not only that the vision grew more gorgeous with time, but also that the prophet added various things unrecorded in the *Journal.* "The information respecting the Lord's personal appearance...in imperial and majestic light, seated near his bed while He gave Assessor Swedenborg his commission, I had from his own lips...."[34]

At all events, by 1748 Swedenborg was irrevocably committed as the Great Seer, the Unique Revelator, the man appointed by the Lord himself to establish the New Chruch.

7.   *The Preparation.* Swedenborg spent three years compiling his own cross-indexed concordance of the Bible, so that he could find instantly any desired passage.[35] He also composed a spiritual intepretation of the Lord's Prayer, phrase by phrase,[36] for the purpose of showing that it was really a prophecy of the coming kingdom of the Lord. He also prepared *The Hieroglyphic Key,* [37] in which he

explained how the Scripture must be understood in its spiritual sense, a method generally applied throughout the New Thought movement.

In spite of rationalistic explanations, the intensity of Swedenborg's emotional experience can neither be questioned nor over-estimated. The *Journal* establishes beyond doubt that his visions of 1744 were often accompanied by violent tremors and prostrations. On a later occasion, he remained in a trance-like state for more than three days, which he described in great detail in *The Apocalypse Revealed*.[38] On another, we are told that this condition continued for more than three weeks, during which he took practically no nourishment.[39] Once, in 1748, he went through the experience of dying and being resurrected, which he described fully in *The Spiritual Diary*.[40]

8. *The Inner Dynamics.* History is studded with individuals who created revolutionary ideas or techniques even at the price of poverty, ridicule, persecution, personal destruction, and even death at the stake. We can only say that such personalities are driven by an overwhelming compulsion which forces them to continue their work, against all odds. The fact, therefore, that the usual human motives were absent by no means proves that Swedenborg's claims were based upon objective reality. His purpose was nothing less than to transform and recreate the ethics, philosophy, and religion of the Western world; and such a motive can be sufficient to drive a man of great genius into the most unconventional persuasions and activities.

We believe that Swedenborg elaborated his revelations for the purpose of mounting his assault upon the bastions of orthodoxy, and that their reality or unreality is relatively immaterial in the system itself or to the convictions of the devout Swedenborgian communicant, for much of what is essential to the faith is quite independent of the prophet's revelatory claims.

9. *Whence Came These Novel Doctrines?* Much that we find in Swedenborg was quite original, for we search in vain for definite predecessors. However, we note also that he often refers to the diabolical heresies of Arius and Socinus, from whose Christology his differs sharply; but he never refers to Servetus or Sabellius, whom he must have understood thoroughly, and with whom he had much in common.

10. *The Corpus of Theological Literature.* Of the thirty volumes of basic theological works containing some 20,000 pages, twelve are

known as the *Arcana Coelestia*, written between 1748 and 1756; six as *The Apocalypse Explained* (1758-59); and two as *The Apocalypse Revealed* (1766). These twenty volumes, which constituted his key to the Scriptures, are line-by-line commentaries or spiritual interpretations of Genesis, Exodus, and Revelation, covering every phase of theology and religious doctrine and practice. His principal remaining works, some of them much more widely read than the preceding, are: *Heaven and Its Wonders, and Hell* (1758), *Divine Love and Wisdom* (1763), *Divine Providence* (1764), *Conjugial Love* (1768), and his final summary of doctrine, *The True Christian Religion* (1771). Various shorter disquisitions are now available in *The Four Doctrines* (1763) and the *Miscellaneous Posthumous Theological Works*.

11.   *A Unique Achievement*. Whatever else we may say about Swedenborg, we must admit that he is unique. His thought is a vast and generally consistent system dealing with ethics, philosophy, metaphysics, cosmology, Christology, theology, anthropology, eschatology, regeneration, redemption, practical conduct, health, happiness, temporal success, and eternal well-being—and it was indeed novel in the extreme. We may also add that his theological synthesis constituted a fully rounded structure which, presented as a spiritual intepretation of Scripture, mounts a devastating assault upon the old and accepted citadels of orthodoxy; and, if accepted, reduces them into one stupendous ruin.

IV. THE SWEDENBORGIAN SYSTEM AND SYNTHESIS

A. *The Spiritual Revelation*

1.   *The Word Divine*. Swedenborg's vast system of doctrine purports to rest solely upon the Christian Scriptures. "It is impossible," he declared, "to derive a single theological truth from any other source...."[41] And "man has no knowledge of...the other world except from revelation...."[42] The Word, however, has an internal or mystical meaning, an arcanum[43] which "lies hidden in every detail" thereof.[44] In its literal meaning, the Word is often trivial, immoral, illogical, and even repulsive: this could not be unless it concealed divine mysteries.[45]

Despite various passages in the Bible, Swedenborg says that God is never angry, never repents, never leads anyone into temptation, never tortures the damned, and never predestines the innocent, or even the wicked, to eternal damnation.

The spiritual interpretation of Scripture often yields surprising meanings. When, for example, Genesis speaks of the Great Flood, this simply signifies an influx of evil spirits which suffocated the people.[46] When Jesus speaks of treading on scorpions, he refers to "murderous persuasions."[47] Adultery means the corruption and falsification of Scriptural truth,[48] an interpretation adopted by Mary Baker Eddy in her controversies with opponents. Swedenborg was also moved to revise Matthew 5:28 to make it read: "Whosoever looketh on *the woman of another* to lust after her, hath committed adultery with her already in his heart."[49] When, however, the literal meaning agreed with his exegesis, he was quite willing to accept it; for example, when the Fourth Gospel states that the Son and the Father are one, this proves conclusively that a trinity of persons is anti-Scriptural.[50]

2. *A Cult Is Born.* And so Swedenborg declared that the Scriptures "down to the smallest jot, are Divine" and "dictated by the Lord...."[51] But since no new cult can come to birth except on the basis of a new or at least a supplementary revelation, it became mandatory for him to supply such an authority. And so, with what seemed to his contemporaries a staggering effrontery, he proclaimed that it had been given to him alone to understand the ancient revelations in their true, internal and spiritual sense.

B. *Dismantling the Old*

1. *Everything Condemned.* Before the ground could be cleared for the establishment of the New Church, the old structures had to be demolished. Swedenborg, outwardly so calm and gentle, was filled with a fierce animosity toward almost everything and everyone around him—especially in the religious realm. At least he was impartial: almost nothing escaped his vitriolic pen. The intensity of this spirit in rebellion is to be measured by the extent and bitterness of his condemnations. He gazed with loathing and contempt upon the various churches, creeds, dogmas, rituals, and disciplines which filled the world around him. There is no bar, he declared, against the redemp-

tion of moral pagans[52]; they are never condemned because they lack the Christian Scriptures or sacraments.[53] It is not a person's creed, doctrines, or belief, but rather his moral propensities that enable any individual to achieve salvation.

2. *Protestants.* Swedenborg had nothing but contempt and condemnation for the Protestant sects in general; and his animosity toward the Lutherans and others whom he called the Reformed intensified as he suffered persecution. Although he credited the Reformation with certain virtues, he never forgave the "leading Reformers, Luther, Melanchthon, and Calvin" because they "retained all the dogmas concerning the Trinity of persons...the origin of sin from Adam, the imputation of the merit of Christ, and justification by faith alone, as they had been held by Roman Catholics...."[54] The "Great Red Dragon" of the Apocalypse, we are told, "signifies those in the church of the Reformed who make God three and the Lord two, and who separate charity from faith...."[55] The Reformed have thus taken the Mark of the Beast,[56] mentioned in Revelation, and worship it.[57] The only virtues of the Reformation consisted in making the Word available to the people and in rejecting altogether "the dogmas that have proceeded from the Papal Consistory...."[58]

3. *Roman Catholics.* During his first journey through France, Swedenborg was outraged by the social conditions of the people and by the common practices of the Catholic hierarchy. "Everywhere," he wrote, "the convents, churches, and monks are the wealthiest and possess most land. The monks are fat, puffed up, and prosperous ...lead a lazy life...."[59] He was filled with contempt at such frauds as the bones of the Three Wise Men at the Cathedral of Cologne and the "relics near the altar" in St. John Lateran, represented as being the "heads of Peter and Paul, under a rich tabernacle or shrine."[60]

Roman Catholicism, declares Swedenborg, is only a Christianized "paganism, where the images of sanctified men are exhibited for adoration...."[61] and which "is simply and foully idolatrous...."[62] Catholics have committed a sacrilege in exalting "Mary...a goddess or queen over all their saints."[63] Another of their infernal heresies consists in teaching that they have "the power to let into heaven and shut out from heaven whomsoever" they will[64]; the power to do this was, however, not given even to Peter.[65]

In this world, the popes demand veneration, and plot to rule tyrannically over all men[66]; the papists call the pope "the Lord's Vicar and thus they make him god upon earth...."[67] Dominion, not salvation, is the purpose of their decrees.[68] They have profaned "the Lord's Divine authority by transferring it to themselves."[69] They have adulterated every "truth of the Word and thence of every holy thing in the church"[70]; papal bulls have displaced the holy Scriptures.[71] "Purgatory...is purely a Babylonish fiction for the sake of gain...."[72] The dominant objective of the Roman Catholic priesthood is to become the supreme lords of the whole world and to reduce all others to the most abject slavery.[73]

These merchants of Babylon, mentioned in the Apocalypse, are "the greater and the lesser in rank in that hierarchy who through dominion over the holy things of the Church strive for Divine majesty and super-regal glory...."[74] The Catholic Church has grown rich and mighty "by threats and terrors, especially in regard to purgatory, into which everyone is to come...."[75]

Is it any wonder, after all this and much more, that Swedenborg should have nightmares in which his enemies assailed him screaming: "Drag him forth, crucify him, crucify him; go, go all of you see the great heretic, and amuse yourselves with him."[76]

C. *Historic Christianity*

1. *The Original and the Hellenic Reconstruction.* The Synoptic Gospels proclaim a forthright synthesis of communal ethics based on personal renunciation, in which Jesus was the god-man who died as the supreme sacrifice for the sins of humanity in order to accomplish the salvation of those elect men and women chosen for this glorious destiny; they proclaimed an eschatology which declared that Jesus would one day return in power to conduct the Last Judgment and establish the Kingdom of Saints on earth, and a soteriology which involved worldly renunciation.

When, however, these pristine doctrines appeared in the Gentile world, they underwent a profound Hellenization in the Pauline literature and in the Fourth Gospel. Here the Christology becomes mystical, an elaborate theological concept in which Jesus is the Word, a pre-existing deity. Everlasting torture in hell is no longer proclaimed.

Saintly poverty is replaced by private enterprise and charity, and there is no ethical imperative for renunciation. There is no Last Judgment or Kingdom of Saints. Only the doctrine of a vicarious atonement remained intact.

2. *Catholicism*. Pauline Hellenization constituted indeed a basic revision, but Catholicism went far beyond this. For it drew heavily upon Monachism, Manichaeism, and Mithraism, as well as the cults of Isis, Adonis, Orpheus, and Eleusis in order to become the universal, or catholic, communion.

3. *The Reformation*. The paramount purpose of the Reformation was to break the stranglehold of the feudal Catholic hierarchy upon a northern economy struggling for freedom to develop into free enterprise and competitive production. It stripped from Catholicism many of its excrescences; but it returned, not to pristine Christianity, but rather to the Hellenized form found in Paul and the Fourth Gospel. In addition, it retained the dogmas of the Trinity, Original Sin, the two natures of Christ-Jesus, the creation of the world out of nothing, an indeterminate but sometime expected literal Parousia, as well as several other tenets not clearly enunciated in the original Gospels.

D. *The Cosmological and Theological System*

1. *The Central Sun*. Swedenborg's theological cosmology is precisely that of the *Principia*, written many years before his Illumination. At the center of the universe is a great sun, or primary substance, the parent of all the other celestial bodies, which are derivative from this original source and move about it in orbital circuits. There are thousands, perhaps millions, of these secondary suns, of which ours is one, each of which has its own primary and secondary satellites. The primary sun is the ultimate source of light, heat, vitality, life, and existence in the universe; the derivative suns are pure fire and their function is simply to relay the life-giving force proceeding from the original creator to the lesser bodies and to all creatures who may live upon them.

2. *God and the Central Sun*. God, or the Lord, is equated with the central sun of the universe; he is, therefore, not only the fountainhead of all that lives or exists, but is also identical with all substance or

existence. "There is only one substance," he states, "from which all things are, and the sun of the spiritual world is that substance."[77] "Creation must...be wholly ascribed to the sun of the spiritual world...a living force...."[78] "The Lord from eternity...created the universe and all things therein from himself and not from nothing."[79] Since "God is omnipresent,"[80] we read, his absence from "man is no more possible than the absence of the sun from the earth through its heat and light."[81] "There is only one fountain of life, and all life is there-from.... Creation is the continuous operation of this vital force."[82] "There is only one life, and whatever things live, live from that life...the Lord is that Life itself...."[83]

3. *No Providence.* God, then, is the source of light, heat, life, vitality, and generative power, which are omnipresent and flow into every object which exists. This was the central thesis of Michael Servetus, and the basis of his unitarian theology. The Swedenborgian God cannot be influenced, persuaded to grant any special favors, or listen to individual pleas:[84] for he is not a personality, he is the creative force, the cosmic law, the universal substance. We find no vestige of an orthodox providence in Swedenborg, or one known to historical Christianity, not one word concerning supplication to the deity or its efficacy as a solution for the ills or the problems of humanity.

4. *The Trinitarian Dogma.* As we have noted, during its early centuries, Christianity was subdivided into many sects, all of which were suppressed after the union of church and state was effected under Constantine, when any rejection of the Athanasian Creed received the most condign punishment. Swedenborg, however, declared, "A Trinity of persons from eternity is not only above reason, but opposed to it."[85] "How can the divine essence," he demands, "which is one, the same, and indivisible, fall into number, hence be either divided or multiplied?"[86] "The Athanasian Faith is such as to be incomprehensible, and thence incredible, and likewise contradictory."[87] "The heresies, from the first ages to the present day, have sprung up from no other source than from the doctrine founded in the idea of three gods."[88]

Instead of a trinity of persons, he continues, there is one of operations or attributes: "These three, Father, Son, and Holy Spirit, are Three Essentials of One God, since they are One, as soul, body, and operations with man are one."[89] "The Divine Itself," we read, "is the

Trine.... This Trine itself, and the one Divine, is the Lord."[90] And again: "By three persons I understand three Divine attributes going forth, Creation, Redemption, and Regeneration; and that these are attributes of one God...."[91]

5.   *The Impersonal God.* Swedenborg ridicules those who think of God as someone who can be seen or on whose right hand the Son might be seated.[92] He is certainly not "an old man, holy, with a gray beard."[93] The Christ is a power, not a person or a personality.

God, then, is the uncreated, impersonal, and basic substance of the universe, which is revealed successively as Creator, Redeemer, and Regenerator, which are the triune attributes or operations of the unitarian God.

E. *The Major Derivative Doctrines*

1.   *Divine Penetration or Influx.* According to the Doctrine of Influx, a vitalizing power flows constantly and universally from the central life-giving force into everything that exists. Without this, there could be no health, moral or physical, in any living creature. "God alone is life," says Swedenborg; and, employing almost the very words of Servetus in his *Erroribus*, he continues; "It follows without question that from His life He gives life to every man...as...the sun of the world with its whole essence, which is heat and light, flows into every tree, every shrub and flower, every stone...each object draws its own portion from the common influx...he gives it to all, and to man the ability to take either little or much."[94] Birds and beasts derive their skills[95] and bees their wisdom[96] from this influx. Without it, man "would instantly fall down dead."[97] Were it not for this cosmic vitality, the whole universe would become, as it were, an infinite corpse.

2.   *The Departure into New Thought.* The Doctrine of Influx marks the point of departure into New Thought, the metaphysical system of philosophy and religion in which the ancient creeds and dogmas are no longer valid; for, in this, God, made manifest in Christ, becomes the life-force which animates the cosmos. Every living being in it, and especially the apex of creation, Man, needs only open the sluice-gates of his mind-soul to allow this natural force to flow in and possess him. All this is declared a universal and scientific reality: it is

neither mystical nor mysterious; it is all around us, and presses upon us for admission. A religion built on such premise therefore purports to be as completely demonstrable in discipline and as certain in its assumptions, operations, and results as any empirical science, verifiable by repeated experiment.

3. *Freedom of Choice.* In the Swedenborgian metaphysics, each human being is a moral receptacle, seeking to absorb whatever fosters his own basic love. Good as well as evil can exist in man; there is freedom and moral responsibility because everyone has the capacity "of perceiving whether a thing is so or not so"; he has this power because of the influx from the spiritual world.[98]

Since man is thus endowed with perceptional cognition, he has the power to choose good or evil, and, by so doing, determine what his moral nature will be. "Man has the freedom to think what is good or...what is evil. This freedom the Lord never takes from anyone, for it belongs to his life and is the means of his reformation."[99]

4. *The World a Replica by Correspondence.* The Doctrine of Correspondences was first developed in *The Animal Kingdom* (1740); it means that our world is a copy of the eternal and spiritual,[100] somewhat as in Platonism. This extends, however, also into the realm of ethics. "A man," we read, "who is in correspondence, that is, who is in love of the Lord and charity toward his neighbor...is also a little heaven in human form...."[101] Again, "man is so created as to be an image of heaven and an image of the world, for he is a microcosm."[102] And so we have countless millions of immortal but finite creatures in the world, every one of which is a replica of the cosmos, which is God or the Grand Man. In short, man is an individualized expression of the divinity.

5. *The Origin of Evil.* "Hereditary evil did not come from Adam and his wife Eve by their eating of the tree of knowledge...."[103] "Everyone who commits actual sin develops an evil nature which" is never dissipated "except in those who are being regenerated by the Lord."[104]

This anthropology was anathema to the theologians of the Reformation because of two basic deviations. The first is that the evil in men here emphasized is not the ineradicable Original Sin which lies at the center of Pauline and Reformation doctrine; it is only an acquired propensity, for which "no man ever suffers punishment...."[105] and which can be eliminated by the aid of the divine influx available to everyone. The second deviation was even more fundamental, for it postulated a regenerative process which results from voluntary conduct wholly independent of the Vicarious Atonement. In Swedenborgianism, there are no elect and no reprobates; God has predestined no one to damnation. "He loves the universal human race and desires eternally to save every member of it...." "No one has ever been predestined to hell...."[106] The God of Swedenborg is one of beneficent justice.

F. *The Redemptive System*

1.   *The Atonement*. All orthodox denominations have agreed that Jesus was the divine God-man who died as an atonement for the sins of humanity and whose sacrament must be consumed for redemption. By rejecting this dogma, the Christology of Swedenborg underwent a drastic reconstruction. The doctrine that salvation is accomplished through faith or a vicarious atonement, he declared, is "no religion" at all, but mere "emptiness and vacuity"[107] because it would be a "reformation and regeneration without means...."[108] "Be it known that no one is purified by the Lord's passion on the cross, thus by his blood..."[109] The "Lord did not come into the world to propitiate the Father and to move Him to mercy, nor to bear our iniquities and thus to take them away, nor that we might be saved by the imputation of His merit...."[110]

And here lies the very heart and core of all New Thought and of the Swedenborgian heresy and doctrine.

"The Lord Himself came into the world and became Man...to...the end that...He might" teach and instruct mankind principles of salvation.[111] Thus, Jesus did not die as a sacrifice, but was, instead, the Great Exemplar, as the Gnostic Marcionites declared, or the Way-Shower, as we are told in New Thought literature.

2.   *The Integrity of the Will*. The Catholic and Reformation councils, declared Swedenborg, hatched "one after another direful heresies based upon...man's impotence in spiritual things and also that most pernicious heresy, predestination...all of which imply that God is the cause of evil, or that he created both good and evil."[112] Swedenborg emphasizes "that it would be impossible for any good to be rooted in man except in his freedom,"[113] which enables "every man...to desist

from evil, because He [the Lord] gives him to will and to understand...
By this the Lord brings man into a state of conjunction with Himself,
and in this...reforms, regenerates, saves him."[114] This is accomplished
by the divine influence, available to everyone, which can transform his
nature into the divine.

Should God, however, manifest his power by miracles in order to
persuade, these would "close the internal man, and deprive him of all
that free will, through which he is regenerated."[115] God could easily
decree that all should be saved, but this would be an ethical perversion
comparable to universal damnation without guilt. Since compulsion
does not reconstitute the will, signs, miracles, visions, threats of future
punishment cannot regenerate.[116] "If man," continues Swedenborg,
"could have been reformed by compulsion, there would not be any
man in the universe who would not be saved; for nothing could be
easier for the Lord than to compel men to fear him, to worship him...."
But worship under compulsion has no value whatsoever.[117]

3. *Conventional Doctrine of Redemption.* Swedenborg rejected
summarily the Pauline, Augustinian, Lutheran, and Calvinist doctrines, according to which "man is so utterly corrupt and dead to good
that...there does not abide in his nature...even a spark of spiritual
strength by which...to understand...or do anything toward his own
conversion...in the smallest measure."[118] All this, he concluded, "is at
this time a fiery flying serpent in the church, and by it religion is
abolished, security reduced, and damnation imputed to the Lord...."[119]

4. *True Basis for Redemption.* How then *does* regeneration take
place? We read that it is only necessary to live a truly ethical life, obey
the Commandments, observe the civil law, and live a life of charity and
neighborly love; but we must do this because it is in accord with our
internal will and *not because of expediency or external pressure of any
kind.* In short, good ethics practiced from internal choice constitutes
the highest religion, which merely directs that we should love our
neighbor as ourselves, and do unto others as we would have them do
unto us, because this is our basic nature. "Everyone who makes these
commandments the principles of his religion becomes a citizen and an
inhabitant of heaven...."[120] Heaven, therefore, is a state of mind.

5. *The Ethical Highway to Heaven.* It is quite possible for anyone
who sincerely desires regeneration to abhor what is prohibited by the
law.[121] Actually, "it is not so difficult to live the life of heaven as some

believe," for, as "a man accustoms himself" to think ethically, "he is
gradually conjoined to heaven...."[122] By making his desires for righteousness paramount, man begins the slow and arduous process of
regeneration.[123] "In the measure in which the spiritual internal and
heaven are opened to man, the natural internal is purified...by
degrees...."[124] "Every man may be regenerated...." If he is not saved, it
is "because he does not cooperate."[125]

6.   *What Is True Charity*? Regeneration, then, can result only from
a life actuated by a love of God and charity for one's neighbor.[126] But
then the question arises: how is love of God to be expressed? And what
constitutes a life of charity toward one's neighbor? And finally, who is
my neighbor?

Brushing aside the precepts of the theologians and of various popular religions, Swedenborg declares that the enjoyment of material and
intellectual pleasures and well-being is compatible with the practice of
a true Christ-religion; the health, prosperity, and ultimate happiness of
the individual, therefore, emerge as wholly permissible, even laudable,
objectives. This revolutionary transformation was accomplished largely through a system of ethics which glorified science, self-reliance, free
enterprise, private property, personal integrity, and individual responsibility; and which requires of each and every one that he care for
himself, practice the Golden Rule, and contribute to society at least as
much as he receives from it.

If charity to the neighbor is paramount, who then *is* my neighbor?
"The collective man—that is, a community smaller or greater—and
composite man formed of communities—that is, one's country is the
neighbor that is to be loved," declares Swedenborg.[127] And again, "the
objects of charity are the individual man, a society, one's own country,
and the human race; and all men are the neighbor...."[128] True religion
consists in activity useful "to the neighbor, from affection and
delight."[129] The ethical religion of Swedenborg may be summed up in
these words: "All religion is of the life, and the life of religion is to do
that which is good."[130]

"The charity that comes from a selfish or worldly end...is not charity," but only that which "regards as its end the neighbor" and "the
general good...."[131] "In common belief, charity is nothing else than
giving to the poor, relieving the needy, caring for widows and orphans,
contributing to the building of hospitals, infirmaries, asylums,

orphans' homes, and especially of churches...."[132] "Some think that if good works must be done for the sake of eternal life, they must give to the poor all they possess, as was done in the primitive church, and as 'the Lord commanded the rich man....' "[133] In Swedenborg's ethical system, however, no error could be greater than this.

"The poor," he says, "come into heaven, not on account of their poverty, but because of their life.... Moreover, poverty leads and draws man away from heaven just as much as wealth does."[134] Many of the poor are not content with their lot, but believe riches to be blessings, and when they do not get them "harbor ill thoughts about Divine providence...."[135]

True charity requires that all be socially productive. "No man is wise or lives for himself alone, but for others also.... Living for others is being useful. Uses are the bonds of society; these bonds are as many as there are good uses, and in number uses are infinite."[136] And further, "every man must make provision for himself so as to have the necessaries of life, as food, clothing, a place to dwell in, and other things...and this not only for himself, but also for his family, and not only for the present time, but also for the future. Unless each person procures for himself the necessaries of life, he cannot be in a state to exercise charity toward the neighbor, for he is himself in need of all things."[137]

We live a life of true charity when we deal justly and honestly with every man, contribute more to society than we take in return, do useful and productive work constantly and competently, and live self-reliantly without aggression toward anyone.[138] "Magistrates and officers" practice charity "if they discharge their respective functions from zeal for the common good...."[139] Conducting a business honestly is a life of charity,[140] as is fighting a defensive war.[141] Making a fortune in the production and distribution of honest merchandise may well be the highest form of charity.[142]

7. *The Riches of Holiness.* Wealth, prosperity, honors, material well-being, beauty, and pleasure in this life are, then, not merely permissible; they are acceptable in the highest degree—the proper objectives of the truly religious life. It is precisely this ethical concept which separates Swedenborg and New Thought as a whole from the historical Christian disciplines. "Truth is falsified," he continues, "when it is said that no man can enter heaven except one who has...reduced himself to miseries."[143] "Riches and wealth are hurtful" only

when used for evil purposes.[144] Did not Jesus say that he came that we might have a more abundant life?

Swedenborg warns, however, that there are wicked individuals who persuade themselves that their own personal advantage and aggrandizement constitute the common good.[145] Anyone who desires power and wealth so that he can reduce his fellows to servitude "murders them in his heart,"[146] and can never breathe the pure atmosphere of heaven.

G. *Eschatology*

1. *The Last Judgment*. Never before had any professed Christian publicly denied that there would one day be a great Parousia in which Christ-Jesus, surrounded by myriads of angels, would appear in the earthly sky, descend to earth, and there conduct the Last Judgment and so receive his saints. But, according to Swedenborg, all this was a purely spiritual event, to be followed by the institution of the Church of the New Jerusalem which he was founding. There would never be another judgment.

2. *The Spiritual Man*. Imagine a being who is pure spirit, yet identical in every essential to what he was as a man on earth: this is the Swedenborgian entity, the immortal. Emotionally, intellectually, morally, and anatomically, he is a replica of his former self.[147] "A spirit or an angel...has a similar face, similar body...in a word, he is a man in external form altogether like a man of the world...interior viscera of the body are similar...conjugial love is also similar with all its effects...."[148]

This may be the source, not only of the metaphysics of New Thought in general, but also of its basis for a theory of sin, sickness, disease, healing, and well-being. Since the mind is the true essence of man and the only aspect which is real or permanent, it follows that the body is only a temporary integument, the portion of man which at death, as it is called, fades as a dream, leaving the reality. Although Swedenborg never taught the unreality or non-existence of matter or the physical body, we can understand how one who failed to understand this fully might leap to this conclusion by studying him only cursorily, and conclude also that the body has no actual existence and that, therefore, all sickness and disease are pure delusions, errors of the mortal mind. According to Swedenborg, heaven and hell begin here in human beings in this life, for both are conditions of the psyche. "Hell did not originate in any devil...cast down from heaven, but both heaven and hell are from the human race...."[149]

3. *Man in the Spirit-World.* According to Swedenborg, the transition to immortal life is rapid, easy, and without shock. "Every man after death becomes a spirit...." When he "comes into the spiritual world, which for the most part takes place the third day after he has expired, he appears to himself in a life similar to that to which he had been in the world...."[150] "From which it is plain that death is but a continuation of life and is only a transition."[151]

When a man becomes a spirit, every virtuous or immoral act committed in his former life will have contributed to the formation of his character.[152] His ethical constitution has been formed for eternity, and he must continue according to his dominating love or desire. Again and again it is emphasized that whatever he had become on earth is taken with him into the other world.[153]

4. *Heaven and Hell.* In Chapter V of *Divine Providence*, Swedenborg explains much of his meaning of heaven and hell. Every person's psyche operates on differing levels, the conscious and the subconscious; and everyone has the power to accept good or evil thoughts, which are relayed into the lower or hidden self. By rejecting evil and accepting good—because doing so is his true nature—man achieves a virtuous life; in short, he creates a heaven within. If, on the other hand, he accepts evil thoughts, which emanate in evil deeds, he creates an inner hell, which becomes his real self. Thus, heaven and hell are states or conditions of mind—a concept which has permeated and is basic in New Thought.

5. *Sex and Marriage.* We are told that when the blessed enter the world of spirits, they will find permanent partners with whom they will enjoy delightful intercourse.[154] Those who condemn marriage in this world are excluded from heaven; and we are told that chastity does not consist in abstinence[155] but in faithful conjugal love.[156] We read that "those who have lived in a chaste love of marriage" experience ineffable delights throughout eternity.[157]

H. *Spiritualism*

We can also say with a fair degree of certainty that Swedenborg was the primary source and the father of the modern spiritualist movement, which became one of the more important American cults in the 19th century, but which has now declined to the point of being little more than a mere fad. "Spiritualism is Swedenborgianism Americanized," wrote John Humphrey Noyes in his *History of American Socialisms*.[158]

I. *Disease and Health*

1. *The Temporary Integument.* Swedenborg's assumption concerning man as a substantive mind-essence leads directly to his theories concerning health and disease. Since the body is only the temporary abode of the real self, which is mind or spirit, it follows that nothing of serious consequence can attack or injure this exterior. Sickness does indeed exist, but it is simply a malady which, because of sin or error or a failure of understanding, attacks the temporary or unreal man; the spiritual man can have no cognizance of disease.[159] It is true that, while man remains in this world, his "faculty of sensation" is manifested in the body, but even then it is only "the spirit that sensated."[160]

2. *The Metaphysics of Health.* Swedenborg once refused any medicine for pain, saying that it was caused by a certain hypocritical spirit which would soon depart.[161] He declared that apparently physical ailments are only the concomitants of the sins we permit to infest our minds. He declares that "diseases...correspond to the cupidites and passions of the lower mind [the Id]...for the origins of disease are, in general, intemperance, luxury of various kinds, mere bodily pleasures, as also feelings of hatred, revenge, lewdness, and the like, which destroy men's interiors; and when these are destroyed, the exteriors suffer and drag men into disease, and so into death."[162] "Diseases" result "from excessive indulgences of various vices...from lascivious practices and from worry and anxiety about the future.... These things vitiate the blood; and when this is vitiated, they obstruct and choke up the very small vessels... wherefore diseases break out."[163] Thus Swedenborg fully recognized the psychosomatic nature of much disease,

which, he declared, may be cured by spiritual means "because the power of the Lord is infinite."[164]

3. *Disease Is Sin and Error.* Thus Swedenborg was the first to proclaim that maladies result from evils, errors, or the destructive emotions which infest the mind. When we open our emotional and intellectual sluice-gates (the will and the understanding) for the divine influx to enter, we experience a healing regeneration which combats and overcomes sin and sickness. Since the divine influx is universal, no one can possibly refuse its benefits except through perversity or error, which thus become synonymous with sin. And since this truth can be demonstrated as in a laboratory, it becomes a scientific instead of a mystical process; we have, therefore, at last an empirical religion—in short, a scientific Christianity.

4. *Sickness and Death.* Swedenborg sometimes utilized his anatomical knowledge to illustrate the nature of physical maladies. "As death is from no other source than sin, and sin is all that which is contrary to Divine Order, therefore evil closes the very smallest and most invisible vessels.... Hence come the first and inmost obstructions ...into the blood. When this vitiation increases, it causes disease, and finally death. If, however, man had lived a life of good, his interiors would be open to heaven, and thus to the Lord; and so too would the very least and most invisible little vessels.... In consequence, man would be without disease, and would merely decline to extreme old age...when the body could no longer minister to his internal man or spirit, he would pass without disease out of his earthly body into a body such as the angels have, thus out of the world directly into heaven."[165]

The Christ-Power, then, of the Lord, when permitted to enter drives away every sin and disease. Sickness is caused by physical indulgence, lustful desire, or ethical and doctrinal error carried into the human viscera by evil agencies, which thus debilitate the whole human organism.

J. *The Church of the New Jerusalem*

1. *The Great Mission.* This brings us to the crowning achievement of Swedenborg: his proclamation of the Second Coming, the Parousia

so long awaited by the Christian churches. This constitutes his interpretation of Revelation, and particularly of certain passages in Chapters 12 and 21 relating to the woman crowned with twelve stars and the
holy city Jerusalem descending out of heaven. It was because of this
that his communion is sometimes known as the Church of the New
Jerusalem.

His mission, as already noted, was nothing less than the complete
restitution of religion. In 1769, he published *A Brief Exposition of the
Doctrine of the New Church*, in one extant copy of which these words
are inscribed in his own hand: "This book is the advent of the Lord,
written by command."[166]

2.   *What Is the New Jerusalem?* "The prevailing opinion in the
churches...is that, when the Lord shall come for the Last Judgment, He
will appear in the clouds of heaven with angels and the sound of
trumpets; will gather together all who have died; will separate the
wicked from the good; and...will create a new visible heaven and a new
habitable earth, and...send down upon the earth the city called the
New Jerusalem built according to the description of it in the Apocalypse...."[167] All this, however, was incorrect. "*A Woman clothed with
the sun and the moon under her feet* signifies...the Lord's New Church
which is about to be on the earth, which is the New Jerusalem"[168]; "by
the crown of twelve stars upon the head of the Woman, the wisdom
and intelligence of the New Church is signified."[169] The Little Book
means the doctrine of the Lord.[170]

3.   *The Red Dragon.* Swedenborg declared "that this 'Woman'
signifies the New Church, which is to be established by the Lord after
the end of the church now existing...."[171] "From this," he declares, "it is
clear that 'the dragon persecuting the Woman'...signifies" those who
"reject and revile the Church which is the New Jerusalem, because it
has the doctrine of life."[172] When we read that the serpent cast out a
river of water after the Woman, this "signifies crafty reasonings...re-
specting justification by faith alone...."[173]

4.   *The Church Everlasting.* And so the mandate had fallen upon
Swedenborg to reveal the doctrine of the New Jerusalem, and thus to
establish the New Church,[174] without which no "flesh can be
preserved."[175]

This church is "to endure for ages of ages, and is thus to be the crown
of all the churches that have preceded...."[176] It "will endure to eter-

nity"[177]; it "succeeds" all previous ones, and "will never undergo consummation."[178]

And so Swedenborg extends "an invitation to the whole Christian world to enter this church...."[179] However, only those who practice its ethics and accept its doctrines can qualify. "No others are received," he says, because "those who do not believe them and live thus are not in accord with the life of heaven."[180] And so the new saints will for the time being be few in number, because "the former church is become a wilderness...."[181] In his eighteenth letter to Dr. Beyer (dated April 30, 1771) Swedenborg discussed his forthcoming *True Christian Religion*. "I am certain," he stated, "that after the appearance" of this book, "the Lord our Savior will operate both mediately and immediately towards the establishment throughout the whole of Christendom of a New Church based upon this 'Theology.' "[182]

K. *No Mass Communion*

1. *The Conservative Prophet.* Swedenborg's message was beamed primarily toward the members of that emerging class of men and women able to achieve success ethically, according to the prevailing codes; it was not intended for the lazy, the unambitious, the stupid, the starving, the poverty-stricken, the social failures, or those who refuse to prepare themselves by study and otherwise for success in life.

Swedenborg lauded comfort and wealth and condemned every kind of charity which takes the form of gifts, handouts, or maintenance for any human being who will not strive to support himself. Every person must be socially useful and productive or he has no right to enjoy life in an organized community. Society is not in debt to the individual; it is the reverse. And here Swedenborg proclaims the philosophic basis for the ethical standards which have dominated the New Thought movement.

2. *The Price of Redemption.* When Swedenborg declared that an ethical life and obedience to the civil law could lead to spiritual regeneration, he laid the basis for a communion founded in ethical-temporal imperatives. Furthermore, his rejection of the atoning, sacrificing savior, which is the core and essence of historical Christianity, creates a deep, wide chasm between his followers and the orthodox.

And since his religion requires in practice that man regenerate himself with the aid of an influx equally available to everyone, it places upon the communicant the requisite of personal responsibility.

3. *The Wrath of the Orthodox*. To the established clergy, the far-reaching innovations of Swedenborg were like hideous specters charging upon them from the darkness. No wonder that their reaction became violent when these new doctrines were offered as the basis for a competing popular communion and when they heard themselves denounced as the Red Dragon of the Apocalypse. They accused Swedenborg of twisting the Scriptures to suit his whim in what he called a spiritual interpretation, of being personally dishonest or actually insane because of his revelatory claims, of having no standards beyond his personal opinions, of adducing no proof for his fantastic "revelations," of offering bait that smacked of Mohammedanism and unbridled licentiousness.

4. *Assailed or Ignored*. However, Swedenborg smote his opponents in many vulnerable spots; and, in due course they absorbed far more of him than they would ever admit. While his Latin tomes lay unread they ignored them and him, but they unleashed a hurricane of frenzied assault when his first followers preached his doctrines in the vernacular. Finally, when it became clear that his permanent sect would be limited to a small number of persons (mostly intellectuals and therefore harmless), they could again regard this last, great, and original Christian theologian with benign toleration and dismiss him with a sneer.

L. *The Denouement*

1. *Health, Happiness, and Prosperity*. We know that Swedenborg and some of his disciples hoped that the existing communions would accept his reconstitution of Christianity as a definitive revelation the purpose of which was (1) to declare God's will and explain the destiny of mankind; (2) reveal the true nature of the life eternal; (3) disclose the truth concerning the Last Judgment, the Second Coming, the Parousia, the nature of the deity, the true regenerative process, etc.; and (4), most important of all, accomplish a complete reconstitution of the Christian system and religion.

2. *A Difficult Problem*. After everything else has been said con-

cerning Swedenborg, the researcher is faced with a knotty question: was he totally sincere, or were his pretensions to revelation, conversations with the dead, journeys to the world of spirits, etc., wholly or partially a mere technique to accomplish certain practical objectives? This is no mere academic matter, nor one to which a ready or conclusive answer is readily available. And, should we admit his sincerity, what can be offered in the way of explanation that will satisfy the unbelievers?

Let us note that his 1744 Illumination, as explained in his *Journal of Dreams*, was definitely only a dream, but that in subsequent years it became to him an objective reality. Is it impossible or even unlikely that intensive thought and brooding over this experience persuaded him in due course to accept it as an actual fact?

It would seem that an acceptable hypothesis can be offered of the whole Swedenborgian syndrome. We believe it possible that the trances into which he entered from time to time (one of which was said to have lasted three weeks) were really states of self-hypnosis, now an officially recognized condition. The mind is a mysterious entity: we know that hypnotized individuals can talk, walk, answer questions with lucidity, reveal their most secret thoughts, travel to distant places, perform astonishing physical feats and, upon awakening, retain no memory of this. Perhaps Swedenborg's self-hypnosis was of somewhat different character and his experiences were so deeply etched into his consciousness that he remembered vividly everything he had imagined.

If we accept this or a similar hypothesis, an entirely new light illumines the entire Swedenborgian complex. We know that since early childhood he had been subject to extraordinarily emotional and psychotic experiences. We know also that these became more intense, culminating in the 1744 Illumination. From that time forward, such experiences may have become routine with him and constituted a continuous state of mind which enabled him, with complete sincerity and total commitment, to go forward with the monumental revelatory labors which filled the last twenty-seven years of his life.

3. *The Originality of Swedenborg.* There may be those who will say that the theology and other teachings of Swedenborg had been part and parcel of the intellectual heritage of the Western world long before his day. But we must reply that such persons are quite mistaken. For his entire system is not only homogeneous and interdependent in its parts, it is also inseparably bound up with the Nebular Hypothesis

(which belongs to him alone) and could have originated only in the mind of one who applied this to Christian dogma and tradition. His theology stems from his physical, cosmological, and anatomical science; his religious doctrines came into existence only when conventional Christianity was distilled in the alembic of his metaphysics.

M. *The Specific Contributions*

What then were the creative Swedenborgian concepts which have exercised a wide influence upon Western religious ideology and which are now central in several significant American denominations?

Among the more important, we may list the following:

(1) that God is impersonal and unitarian, the life-giving force which exists in the universe and which is shared by every creature that inhabits it; God, in fact, is the substance of the cosmos;

(2) that no one is redeemed by the vicarious atonement of a god-man, but that every human being may create in himself, by ethical conduct that he is free to embrace or reject, a character which will achieve regeneration and happiness;

(3) that the Bible is throughout the Word of God, but that it possesses a spiritual sense which cannot rightly be understood except through an inspired interpretation which reveals its true significance, often quite at variance with its literal meaning;

(4) that the human psyche exists and operates on different levels comparable to the Freudian Id, Ego, and Superego;

(5) that if we practice the best ethical code of our own society, there need be no fear of punishment hereafter;

(6) that productive activity, both intellectual and material, is the highest ideal of the ethical man;

(7) that the neighbor is all mankind and that we best express our love for him in performing useful and reciprocal services;

(8) that the highest charity consists in dealing honestly with our fellow men and in doing our work well at all times, and that the comforts of life may be enjoyed and wealth obtained by methods completely just and virtuous;

(9) that the pursuit, possession, and temporal enjoyment of material comforts and even luxuries are highly laudable so long as these are

obtained through honest service to our fellows or the creation of social wealth, and so long as the money so gained is not the sole or the principal objective;

(10) that the Second Coming consists simply in the proclamation of reconstituted Christianity and that the New Jerusalem, of which we read in Revelation, is that reconstituted church;

(11) that the Last Judgment and the Parousia are purely spiritual events, consummated without the cognizance of the people on earth;

(12) that there is a universal, vitalizing, and beneficent influx or emanation from God—the central sun of the universe—which, if we allow it to flow into ourselves, fills us with vigor, health, and moral virtue;

(13) that the failure or refusal to accept this divine influx is simply a failure on the part of our understanding or a misuse of our free will; thus, sin is really only a form of error or ignorance;

(14) that all sickness and disease, whether mental or physical, are caused by lustful thoughts, evil desires, or corrosive hatred, which destroy a person's peace of mind and, transferred to the bodily functions, bring on many forms of malady and illness;

(15) that much sickness may be cured and eliminated from the body by permitting the divine influx to permeate our beings entirely;

(16) that both heaven and hell exist within us as subjective states, which are simply transferred to the next life at the transition called death;

(17) that the punishments which ultimately overtake the wicked are self-inflicted; and,

(18) all this being true, that a scientific religion is demonstrably possible that has as its objective the well-being, health, happiness, success, and prosperity of its communicants.

Emerson, who was a Transcendentalist, called Swedenborg a mystic; and we should recognize that this system as well as that of New Thought in general is based upon an element which may be called mystical and which makes it unique, constitutes its principal religious basis, and sets it apart from all other faiths. For it holds that the universe is instinct with life, energy, and power, which is equated with God and which gives vitality to all that lives and reaches all human beings to whatever extent they avail themselves of it. Thus, in spite of all New Thought claims to scientific truth and demonstration, this all-embracing concept must rely on faith for its total acceptance; and this places the entire movement within the parameters of what is properly called religion rather than in the realm of science. Other features of Swedenborgianism and New Thought are cognate with this fundamental thesis, but could be found, to a greater or lesser extent, in other systems of belief, and could be considered philosophic truth, rather than religious dogma. And yet every intelligent person must admit that there is a vast energy and power which pervades the cosmos and which is expressed as forms of heat and light, much of which is beyond the mastery of mere science.

V. THE SWEDENBORGIAN CHURCH
IN THE UNITED STATES

Although the influence of Swedenborg has permeated not only the New Thought movement but even, to a lesser extent, society at large, the New Church or the Church of the New Jerusalem has always consisted of a rather small number of highly dedicated members. Those who accept *all* of Swedenborg remain comparatively few, while those who accept portions of his teachings, consciously or not, are to be counted in the millions.

Not only is the Swedenborgian membership *per se* quite small, but it is divided into two divisions in the United States: The General Church of the New Jerusalem and the General Convention. A handsome volume entitled *The New Church in the New World*, written by Marguerite Block, first published in 1932 and now available from the Swedenborg Foundation in New York, details the history of both divisions down to 1932. First organized in Philadelphia in 1817 by delegates from seventeen societies, they had a membership of 350, and grew to 500 in 1830, 1,450 in 1850, 4,150 in 1870, and 5,272 in 1890.

The Swedenborgian churches were full of controversy, almost from the beginning. For years preceding 1890, while "liberalism" was growing in the Convention, another group was taking form which emphasized the infallibility and inerrancy of Swedenborg's writings, stressed the need and importance of education, and insisted on a literal interpretation of certain passages in *Conjugial Love*. Seven congregations organized themselves *within* the Convention in 1883 as the General Church of Pennsylvania; however, as the friction increased, they seceded in 1890 with 347 members—six percent of the total—and called themselves the General Church of the New Jerusalem or the Academy Movement, with headquarters at Bryn Athyn, just outside of Philadelphia. In 1900, there were 560 members, and the magazine *New Church Life* was established. In 1910, there were 941 members; in 1920, 1,415; in 1930, 2,012, of whom 1,112 were in the United States. The *Yearbook of American Churches* gives the membership as 2,028 in 1966 and 2,143 in 1971. The December 1985 issue of *New Church Life* gives a complete report concerning church membership and operation. In 1984, its revenues totalled $2,905,345, its expenses $2,325,417, with a balance of $22,446,259 on hand at the end of the year. It had a membership of 3,879 of whom 2,725 were in the United States. It had churches in Australia, Canada, England, and Africa. It had three members of the clergy ranked as bishops and eighty-three as pastors; it had twenty-two Societies (the largest category), thirty churches, and thirty groups, of which fifteen were in foreign lands. Today, it has a magnificent center at Bryn Athyn, including a seminary, other schools, administration buildings, and a library—which even in 1932 possessed 46,000 volumes.

However, we find that while the General Church has grown significantly, the Convention has had an entirely different development. For some time after the split the Convention was much larger than the General Church; in 1900, it reached its peak with 6,926 members, which declined to 6,582 in 1920 and 5,805 in 1930. The 1969 *Yearbook* credits it with 4,450 members in 1967, but the 1983 issue notes only 1,820 members in 1981.

The Convention publishes a magazine of long standing called *The Messenger*. For many years, it operated a Theological School at Cambridge, Massachusetts, but in 1965 this was moved to Newton and its name was changed to the Swedenborg School of Religion.

Thus, in 1983 and 1984 the two divisions in the United States had nearly 6,000 members. In 1985, the English Conference, including New Zealand, had 1,861 members. We estimate, therefore, that true receivers organized in Societies and churches may number between 8,000 and 9,000. In addition, however, there are many who consider themselves Swedenborgians who belong to no organized group. And then there are millions who accept parts of Swedenborg, and other millions who have been influenced by him in one way or another.

Chapter III

PHINEAS PARKHURST QUIMBY

I. THE FORERUNNERS

1. *Franz Anton Mesmer*. Mesmer was an Austrian (1735-1815), born at Weil, near Lake Constance, Switzerland. Turning to the practice of medicine in Vienna, he advanced the theory that there is a cosmic fluid (somewhat similar to the Swedenborgian influx) which originates in the solar system and affects every living organism in the universe. Year after year, he continued his search for new and scientific explanations of health, disease, and the invisible forces of the cosmos. In 1774 a case came to his attention in Vienna in which a piece of magnetic iron was said to have cured a patient of stomach disorders. He thereupon obtained several such instruments and applied them to the throat, the heart, and other organs, in some instances achieving remarkable results.

Persuaded that the magnetic instruments had the power to heal, Mesmer set up a large facility in 1774, where he had his patients join hands while they bathed in water magnetized by steel rods. His fame and practice grew by leaps and bounds. Hundreds of wealthy patients testified that they had been cured as a result of their hypnotic trances.

Then suddenly and quite by accident, he discovered that his magnetized objects, which he had thought transmitted the healing fluid to the patient, were without force and therefore unnecessary. He found that his cures could be accomplished just as well without them. Persuaded that the power to transmit the cosmic fluid lay in himself, he renamed this *animal magnetism*. In order to facilitate the transfer of healing power to the patient, he utilized manipulation: like the first Apostles, he cured by the "laying on of hands." His touch led to the same results as had previously been accomplished by the use of the magnet, and he declared that the cosmic fluid, flowing through himself, streamed into the patient and restored his health.

However, the medical establishment turned out to be a bitter enemy, and when a patient suffered a relapse, Mesmer was driven from Austria and took refuge among the French.

During the years following his arrival in Paris in 1778, Mesmer once again became popular and famous: Madam de Pompadour and Marie Antoinette were among his clients. He established a hospital where, for five years, patients from all walks of life were received and treated.

Mesmer still did not understand what he was doing, for the trance-like state into which he placed his patients was actually hypnotic. In the emotional purgation which accompanied this condition many experienced relief from nervous and other maladies. The patients sat in a circle, touching hands. One by one, they subsided into a hypnotic state or trance, after which, when awakened, many declared themselves healed.

In Paris, however, as in Vienna, there were skeptics and powerful enemies. A commission was set up to investigate the nature of this "animal magnetism." It concluded that it had no objective existence and thus could not possibly serve any useful purpose. It also declared that any effects which might be observed resulted merely from a stimulus of the imagination and were therefore completely fraudulent.

In 1794, friendless and penniless, Mesmer fled to Vienna, and thence to Frauenfeld, Switzerland, where he continued to practice in obscurity for more than twenty years until his death at eighty-two; even then, he was not aware of the controversies raging over his theories among his disciples and epigones.

2.   *The Count de Puységur.* It was not long before many sprang to

Mesmer's defense, and his disciples multiplied; in fact, they became nothing less than a cult. Obviously there was present in his therapy some kind of active force, even if this could not be detected by the senses or weighed in a mechanical balance. It was found to be not one whit less potent whether it operated through the body or through the imagination.

It must be admitted, however, that Mesmer himself did not comprehend the nature of his therapy. It is therefore ironic that his name is still attached to a psychic phenomenon which a disciple of his, the Count Maxime de Puységur, was the first to understand or control. Quite by accident, like so many other great discoveries, while practicing the Mesmeric technique, he discovered that one of his entranced patients, a simple, healthy, young peasant, could perform extraordinary feats while sleepwalking. The practitioner's amazement became still greater when he found that his subject could answer questions with complete lucidity while entranced, but had no memory of such conversation upon awakening. The Count's conquest of psychic phenomena was still further advanced when he found that he could, at will, plunge his subject into, or awaken him from, this strange sleep, and that he could accomplish identical results with others.

Nor was this all: the Count concluded that while his medium was magnetized, the latter could read the thoughts of the people about him, travel in spirit to distant places, diagnose the symptoms of the sick and the diseased, place his hands on the parts of the body where pain existed, and, finally, prescribe drugs and other remedies for any malady.

This procedure became known as Mesmerism although Mesmer had nothing to do with it. The discovery of Puységur was let loose in Europe and later in America. A horde of practitioners used this new technique, which was a form of mental healing, although not so recognized.

3. *James Braid.* It remained for James Braid (1795-1860), a Scottish surgeon who practiced in Manchester, to demonstrate in his book *Neurohyponology* (1843) that there is no such thing as a cosmic fluid and that Mesmerism is a purely subjective force, which he called *hypnotism.* At first he believed that the subject was put to sleep by the use of a mechanical object, such as a glass ball. Gradually, however, he understood that the condition was induced by the power of suggestion.

At about the same time that Quimby was making the same discovery in America, Dr. Braid became aware that a subconscious mental level exists, which he called "double consciousness," an understanding of which finally led to the Freudian analyses of the ego, the id, and the superego.

Mesmerism cut a wide swath in its day. A whole cult of healing sprang up, with many practitioners and thousands of clients. The standard technique was simple enough: the Mesmerizer traveled about with a colleague, one who could easily be entranced. In this state, it was proclaimed that the medium was clairvoyant; could read the thoughts of people near or far away; travel in spirit to distant places; describe minutely what was there; diagnose the diseases of all who submitted themselves for analysis; and prescribe cures for every malady.

4. *The Swedenborgian Healers.* In 1812, the Swedenborgian Society in Sweden conducted elaborate spiritualist therapeutic experiments based upon a subjective therapy quite similar to the technique used by Quimby toward the close of his Mesmeric period. Spiritualism became so popular that at one time it had hundreds of congregations. Thus the "fad" of Mesmeric healing passed away and was replaced by Swedenborgian spiritualism. Nevertheless, the Mesmeric movement furnished the original impetus and the connecting link by which an extraordinary American created the foundations for the superstructure of New Thought.*

II. QUIMBY'S OUTWARD LIFE AND CAREER

1. *Who and What Was He?* Phineas Parkhurst Quimby, who is generally recognized as the first great exponent of New Thought in America, was born in Lebanon, New Hampshire, in 1802; his family soon moved to Belfast, Maine, where he spent an uneventful boyhood. In due course, he became a clockmaker; and it was said that his products were so excellent that some of his clocks were still in good working order a century later.

Among therapeutic practitioners, he is probably unique. He had undergone little intellectual discipline and had no scientific training, but was a sincere and determined man with an extraordinary bent for

---

*The preceding material is taken from many sources, chiefly Stephan Zweig's *Mental Healers* and Margaret Goldsmith's *Franz Anton Mesmer.*

originality. For authority in general he had only supreme contempt; and, since he was burdened neither with erudition nor with tradition, he played fierce havoc with the conventional judgments and beliefs of the past. Perhaps his outstanding characteristic consisted in a constant search for truth, an all-pervasive skepticism concerning accepted doctrines, a relentless rejection of popular conceptions, a capacity to turn all things into something resembling their opposites, and an intransigent enmity toward vested interests and respectabilities. He declared that ninety percent of all beliefs are erroneous.[1]

He was a plain, simple, humble man; but his dark piercing eyes could penetrate and transfix, and his convictions were contagious. He was utterly selfless; he so gave himself to the service of his patients that he sacrificed his own life for them. What was more serious, this left him no time to organize his philosophy, or to prepare others to practice his technique.

2. *Quimby's Own Healing.* Quimby's first great experience came in 1833, when he was thirty-one, which he described in an article written in 1863, first published by Julius A. Dresser in 1887 as part of a lecture called *The True History of Mental Science*.[2] "I was very sick," he wrote, "and was considered fast wasting away with consumption. At that time, I became so low that it was with difficulty that I could walk.... My symptoms were those of any consumptive, and I had been told that my liver was affected, and my kidneys were diseased, and that my lungs were nearly consumed. I believed all this, from the fact that I had all the symptoms, and could not resist the opinions of the physicians while having the proof with me. In this state, I was compelled to abandon my business, and, losing all hope, I gave up to die."[3]

However, when told that riding horseback might cure him he took a ride in a carriage, after which all the symptoms vanished. He was thus convinced that the disease had no reality except in his belief.

Physical maladies, however, or at least a belief in them, continued to plague Quimby. He had pains in his back, supposedly caused by his partially consumed kidneys. He was also told that he had ulcers on his lungs. "Under this belief," he wrote, "I was miserable enough to be of no account in this world. This was the state I was in when I commenced to Mesmerize. On one occasion, when I had my subject asleep, he described the pains I felt in my back...and he placed his hand on the spot where I felt the pain. He then told me that my kidneys were in a very bad state, that one was half consumed.... This was what I believed to be true, for it agreed with what the doctors told me, and with what I suffered.... I asked him if there was any remedy. He replied, 'Yes...and you will get well....' He immediately placed his hands upon me...and from that day I never have experienced the least pain....

"Now what is the secret of the cure? I had not the least doubt but that I was as he described; and if he had said, as I expected...that nothing could be done, I should have died in a year or so. But when he said that he could cure me...I discovered that I had been deceived into a belief that made me sick. The absurdity of his remedies made me doubt the fact that my kidneys were diseased...."[4]

3. *French Mesmerists in America.* Mr. Du Commun, a pupil of Puységur, first introduced the Mesmeric therapy into the United States in 1829. He was followed in 1836 by the renowned Charles Poyen, who, accompanied by his medium, lectured and practiced in New England, where his entranced colleague diagnosed the diseases and maladies of those who applied for treatment and prescribed drugs to alleviate and cure their diseases. Fascinated by this "science," Quimby became a Mesmeric healer.

4. *The Progressing Doctor.* Beginning with 1836, Quimby's life divides into three periods: (1) the Mesmeric (1836-47), when, as an itinerant hypnotist, he travelled from place to place; (2) the intermediate phase of experimentation and discovery (1847-59), during which he set up what might be called temporary clinics in various towns; and (3) the period of maturity (1859-65), with an office in Portland, Maine, where he committed his ideas to writing and began to obtain disciples and command serious attention.

The following excerpt from the *Bangor Democrat* (April 1843) is the first public discussion of Quimby's work which has come to our attention. "Mr. Quimby of Belfast has visited here by invitation.... He has with him two young men, brothers, one twenty-three and the other seventeen. They are clairvoyant subjects.... The young man was magnetized by Mr. Quimby, when one of our citizens was put in communication with him. In *imagination*, he took the boy to St. John, New Brunswick, before the New Custom House....

"The gentleman says no one knew where he proposed to take the boy: the boy had never seen the building, and yet he described it...accurately.... This gentleman's word is not to be questioned...."[5]

Since we hear no more of these two brothers, Quimby must shortly have replaced them with the nineteen-year-old Lucius Burkmar, the medium who continued as his colleague until 1847, and who, while "magnetized," possessed, according to Quimby's own testimony, not only clairvoyant power, but also the ability to read the thoughts of any person in proximity, see through solid matter, travel in spirit to distant places, be in two locations at the same time, detect and diagnose diseases, and, finally, prescribe cures for every malady.[6]

The fame of Quimby and Lucius grew apace; and, although ministers and medical practitioners called Quimby a charlatan, his popularity increased and many credited him with extaordinary cures. Lucius himself kept a journal, beginning in December 1843, in which he wrote that some of Dr. Quimby's cures, performed through magnetism, were actually miraculous.[7]

Toward the end of the Mesmeric period, however, Quimby began to suspect that his success depended very little either upon the diagnosis of Lucius or the drugs he prescribed. We must point out that the Mesmeric therapy was not intended as any form of mind-healing, but only as the most reliable diagnosis possible of ordinary disease. The discovery which Quimby was now about to make was therefore momentous: he was the first to proclaim a system of healing dependent entirely upon mental processes.

"When I Mesmerized my subject," he wrote later, "he would prescribe some simple herb that would do no harm or good of itself. In some cases this would cure the patient. I also found that any medicine would cure if he ordered it. This led me to investigate the matter, and arrive at the stand I now take: that the cure is not in the medicine, but in the confidence" of the patient in "the doctor or medium."[8]

This belief ripened into conviction when Lucius ordered drugs costing twenty dollars, which was more than the patient could afford. However, when a simple herb was substituted, the patient "got well."[9] From this experience Quimby finally concluded—as had no other Mesmerizer—that his cure depended, not on the diagnosis, the clairvoyance, or the prescriptions of his medium, but upon the force, power, or dominance exercised by the practitioner, which filled the patient with confidence in the healer and the expectation of recovery. The whole process thus became subjective; and Quimby leaped to the conclusion that sickness and disease have no reality except as they are created by the mind.

With no further need for Lucius, Mesmerism, or placebos, Quimby discovered that he was himself as clairvoyant in the waking state as

Lucius had been when "magnetized"[10]; he could read the thoughts of his patients, be in two places at the same time, perceive phenomena without the use of the bodily senses,[11] and take upon himself the physical symptoms of his patients.[12]

5. *Experimentation and Writings*. And so Quimby set forth upon the second phase of his career, which continued for twelve years, during which he experimented ceaselessly until he was convinced that he had indeed discovered an infallible scientific method by which to achieve universal health and happiness.

When Horatio W. Dresser published *The Quimby MSS* in 1921, a vast lode of knowledge concerning the origin of New Thought was at last made public, even though only 101 of the 311 articles written by Quimby were included. Some valuable material, however, had already been given the world in 1895 when Annetta Gertrude Dresser published *The Philosophy of P. P. Quimby*.

6. *The Impact of Swedenborg*. We know that Quimby studied Berkeley between 1843 and 1847,[13] and probably encountered the works of other idealist philosophers. We feel sure that he discovered Swedenborg,[14] who left a definite influence upon his thinking. It is also possible that Quimby came into contact with Brook Farm after its leaders became Swedenborgians; and we believe that this philosophy was the catalyst which transformed Quimby from a Mesmeric practitioner into a self-proclaimed mind- and faith-healer, utilizing a technique and vocabulary essentially taken from this source. It must not be supposed, however, that he was a mere copyist; every element reproduced by him from preceding sources was always stamped with a peculiar originality when it re-emerged from the Quimby alembic.

7. *The Advertising Therapist*. From 1847 to 1859, then, the tireless, searching Quimby went from town to town offering mental therapy through the power of faith. He distributed a brochure in 1855 which repudiated the Mesmeric technique and which read in part: "Dr. P.P. Quimby would respectfully announce...that...he will attend to those wishing to consult him in regard to their health, and, as his practice is unlike all other medical practice, it is necessary to say that *he gives no medicine and makes no outward applications*, but simply sits down by the patients, tells them their feelings and what they think is their disease. If the patients admit that he tells them their feelings, etc., then his explanation is the cure; and if he succeeds in correcting

their error, he changes the fluids of the system and establishes the truth or health. *The truth is the cure.*"

When people consult a regular physician, the flyer continues, "five or ten dollars is then paid, for cure of some disease they never had, nor ever would have had but for the wrong impression received from these quacks or robbers...." The doctors have in mind only their "own selfish objects—to sell their medicines. Herein consists their shrewdness, to impress patients with a wrong idea, namely that they have some disease. This makes them nervous and creates in their minds a disease that otherwise would never have been thought of. Wherefore he [Quimby] says to such, never consult a quack: you not only lose your money, but your health.

"He gives no opinion, therefore you lose nothing. If patients feel pain, they know it, and if he describes their pain he feels it and in his explanation lies the cure....

"There are many who pretend to practice as he does, but when a person, while in 'a trance,' claims any power from the spirits of the departed, and recommends any kind of medicine to be taken, internally or applied externally, beware! believe them not, 'for by their fruits ye shall know them.' "[15]

8. *A Settled Practice.* In 1859 Quimby set up a permanent office in Portland, Maine, to which came those who were sick in body and tortured in mind. He sat down by them, and took upon himself the sins, the errors and the maladies of his patients, all of which, by some mysterious process or principle, passed from their bodies into him. He did not ask them to describe their pains or their symptoms; and when he succeeded in explaining theirs in terms they could not gainsay, *this was the cure.*

Quimby states that during his ministry, as it should be called, he treated 12,000 patients[16]; and he declared that during the Portland period, he administered to 500 every year.[17] Few indeed sought him out except as a last resort; only when all else had failed, and then often amidst the hoots and sneers of enemies and skeptics, did many of his clients drag their weary feet over his threshold. Some had been ill for years, their maladies beyond all aid or diagnosis. Yet by the dozens and the hundreds they were restored to health, and went their way rejoicing, proclaiming the wondrous power of Phineas Parkhurst Quimby, to cure as no man had cured since Jesus of Nazareth had healed the halt, the blind, the scrofulous, and those bedridden with ailments unknown.

At the close of 1865, he returned to Belfast to recuperate from exhaustion; but he was completely worn out, and died in January 1866.

III. QUIMBY'S RELIGIO-PHILOSOPHICAL SYSTEM

1. *The Simple and Central Problem.* It must be recognized that Quimby's system was limited in scope; beyond a few convictions basic to this therapeutic system, his metaphysical concepts were blurred and sometimes inconsistent. He was no Swedenborg; and he never came to grips with many questions which lie close to his principal thesis. It is difficult to discover just what he *did* believe in regard to matter, the human soul, or what takes place after death. Concerning all this, we have hints only.

Quimby's conviction focused upon a single point: that the science of health is also the science of life and happiness. Although the question of health was significant to Jesus, Swedenborg, and the Shakers, for all of them this was only one among various facets in the life-complex. To Quimby, health was the *ne plus ultra*: ninety percent of all people, he maintained, suffer from some kind of malady; and if we could only rid the world of this suffering, a human paradise would ensue. His indictment against the clergy is not so much that they teach false doctrine as that they fill the world with sickness and disease.

Quimby's efforts are therefore directed to the achievement of perfect happiness through the science of health, which is identical with the Science of Christ, or Christian Science.

2. *Theology and Christology.* Quimby's references to God are often negations or abstractions. "God," he says, "is spirit and not a man";[18] and there is no personal god.[19] Again, God is a principle,[20] without form or sex,[21] which has never spoken;[22] God is the only reality, [23] and everlasting essence, existing without matter.[24] God is Science,[25] the principle which Jesus taught as the Christ.[26] The reality which is Man is also God,[27] and all men and women are part and parcel of deity.[28] The gods of all existing creeds and religions have been

created by men[29]; the Calvinist God, in particular, is a terrible tyrant,[30] worthy only of being cursed.[31] On the contrary, the true God is benevolent, and could, therefore, never have created disease.[32]

"I must," says Quimby, "make the reader detach his senses from a god of man's belief and attach them to this invisible Wisdom which fills all space, and whose attributes are all light, all wisdom, all goodness and love, which is free from all selfishness and hypocrisy, which makes or breaks no laws, but lets man work out his own salvation; which has no laws and restrictions, and sanctions men's acts according to their belief, and holds them responsible for their belief, right or wrong, without respect to persons."[33]

Quimby's Christ-Science, inseparable from his Christology, is more elaborate and distinct than his theology. This Science of Life and Happiness was, he says, founded by Jesus Christ [34] and is the only true religion.[35] When this is established, it will take the place of all other sciences[36]; it is eternal life in Christ[37]; it is Divine Wisdom reduced to self-evident propositions[38]; and it is therefore universally demonstrable, like a mathematical equation. Jesus put intelligence, not in matter, but in Christ, or Science[39]; all those subversions of his doctrine which now pass as religion must one day give way to Truth,[40] which is the Christ-Science,[41] and which anyone can learn.[42] Finally, it is the only Key to Heaven.[43]

3. *The Healing Christ-Science.* The core of Quimby's system is, then, that all diseases may be cured by an exact science, which was that of Jesus Christ. We know, says Quimby, that Christ healed scientifically because "there can be no such thing as accident with God; and if Christ was God, He knew what He was doing." When he was accused of curing disease through the aid of the Evil One, "he said, 'If I cast out devils or disease through Beelzebub or ignorance, my kingdom or science cannot stand; but if I cast' " them out " 'through a science of law, then my kingdom or law will stand, for it is not of this world.' When others cast out disease, they cured by ignorance of Beelzebub, and there was no science in their cures, although an effect was produced; but not knowing the cause, the world was none the wiser for their cures."[44]

Quimby proclaimed that he practiced this Christ-Science and healed as Jesus healed[45]; and in so doing, was simply emulating the original disciples, whom Jesus commissioned to do the same.[46] Jesus certainly had a science which could be taught, and thus practiced by others[47]; and Quimby's truth was the Truth of Christ.[48]

This Christ-Science, first taught 1800 years before, [49] was the same that enabled Quimby to heal the sick.[50] Believing in Jesus Christ,[51] he practiced the same science, which is simply the Wisdom of God,[52] and the practical religion of Jesus.[53] This "Christ," says Quimby, "whom you think is Jesus, is the same Christ that stands at the door of your dwelling or belief, knocking to come in and sit down with the child of Science that has been led astray by blind guides into the wilderness.... To be born again is to unlearn your errors and embrace the truth of Christ; this is the new birth, and it cannot be learned except by a desire for the truth, that Wisdom that can say to the winds of error and susperstition, 'Be still!' "[54]

Although Quimby declared that he had "no belief in religion of any kind...." he stated that Jesus was the only true prophet that ever lived on this earth[55]; that he is the bread of life and happiness, which we should eat; that Christ or Science is the body of that Christ of which we may partake[56]; that the Christ in Jesus is eternal life, or Science[57]; and that Man, when reborn in Christ, is himself this Science, which is also the Wisdom of God.[58] The Christ of Jesus, who was crucified by the priests and the doctors of his day, is still being crucified by the priests and doctors who mislead and delude the blind.[59] This Christ-Science or Science of Life, as Quimby calls it again and again, "is shown in the progress of Christian Science...."[60] and is the most precious thing on earth; for those who find it it will be resurrected into eternal life, which is Christ, or Science.[61]

4. *The Gnostic Christ.* Quimby's Christology is basically the same Gnostic concept which we find in Shaker doctrine, in Swedenborg, and in many ancient cults. Christ was simply a spirit which, for a time, occupied the flesh-and-blood body known as Jesus. At the crucifixion, Christ remained what he had been before; and, when he appeared to his disciples, this apparition was simply clothed in a condensation of a spiritual body.[62] Jesus and Christ are, therefore, different identities[63]; Jesus was a man, just as we are; he had a natural body of flesh and blood like ours.[64] Christ is God, the unseen principle in Man.[65] Christ is a power which has appeared intermittently in all ages.[66] Jesus was therefore only the oracle, but Christ was the Wisdom of God.[67]

Understanding the difference between Jesus and Christ, says Quimby, is the key to the understanding of all religion. The construction given their relationship by the Church makes our life one thing and our religion another. Jesus created a Science which "separates us from the world of sin and death and brings life and immortality.... Ignorance of Christ or Science put 'Jesus' and 'Christ' together and said 'Jesus Christ...!' "[68]

The power of Jesus was the Christ within him,[69] which is health, as Health is Heaven[70]; again, Christ is the heavenly man of Science,[71] who is in each and every one of us.[72] He is the Science of Health[73]; to accept him is to have Christ within us,[74] which is the Christ-Truth available to all; and which, for example, when exhibited through the man Franklin, was called electricity.[75]

5. *Creeds, Priests, and Medicine Men.* The great absurdity in the Christian churches, says Quimby, is the requirement that their communicants believe, on pain of everlasting damnation, that the man Jesus was Christ and a member of the tripersonal Trinity, that he died on the cross, that he rose from the dead, and that he went to Heaven to sit at the right hand of God. And so man's salvation is made to depend upon accepting such a false and ridiculous creed.[76]

Those who teach that Jesus came to save mankind from damnation after death are teaching a grievous error[77]; in fact, he never taught any doctrine concerning another world;[78] and he certainly never believed that his natural body would rise from the dead.[79] He came to destroy death and the devil[80]—that is, disease and error; he was opposed to all forms and ceremonies[81]; he had no "religious" opinions, as such[82]; and he cured simply by changing the minds of those afflicted with maladies.[83]

Quimby's condemnations of the clergy are the most ferocious found in his writings. It would not be amiss to say that his health mission consisted primarily in freeing his patients from the diseases created in them as a result of the fears resulting from priestly threats of eternal torture. In his essay "The Senses and Language," he explains that since, in primitive society, it was necessary that someone interpret the phenomena of nature, certain persons were appointed for that purpose; and so priests and prophets arose, who had to be supported by taxation. As the tribes grew into nations and kingdoms, the priests seized political power also; and since the priesthood was founded on superstition, inventions of all kinds were devised to keep the people in ignorance. As scientific truths were discovered, these were kept in concealment so that any chemical or mechanical advance might be passed off as a gift through the priests from heaven. When astronomy was developed, they kept it as their own, and all their calculations were made, not as a science for the benefit of the people, but as a divine revelation.[84]

Priests, said Quimby, are "fake-guides" who have subverted the Scriptures[85]; they have stolen the teachings of Jesus and engrafted them upon a system of their own. After these deceivers arrogated to themselves the role of revelators, "another swarm of hungry dogs, called doctors, who invent diseases..." came along to devour an additional portion of what the people produce.[86] Superstition, religion, and slavery have always gone hand in hand[87]; they have conspired to rule and ruin[88]; and have filled the earth with error, ignorance, and disease.[89] Religion, law, and medicine are the actual Christian Trinity: "I will introduce a priest, a doctor, and the law as the Godhead, for these three are equal in power. Religion is the father, medicine is the son, and law is the Holy Ghost...."[90] Every creed serves only as an instrument by which one set of liars, charlatans, and impostors seek to replace another.[91] Priests have created a fictitious world in the hereafter filled with torment and despair, in order to terrify their victims and fill their own pockets.[92] Priests and religion crucified Jesus[93]; and priests have always made violent and bloody persecution the highest virtue.[94] They have twisted the teachings in the Book of Revelation for their own ulterior purposes; they want people to have creeds, but never understanding.[95] To the priest, an infidel is simply anyone who will not accept his peculiar interpretation of the Bible.[96] Religion is literally a disease, invented by humbugs.[97]

Many are driven insane or are afflicted with all manner of disease because of the deceptions and terrors of religion[98]; countless persons are sick because of this all their lives.[99] Religious sects fight like maniacs to establish their own false and degenerating opinions[100]; and when they obtain proselytes, these victims are filled with torments.[101] Thus religion, which should be a source of consolation, brings sickness and despair.

Prayers offered in Christian churches are a travesty: for they are pleas for what is not deserved, or for what can only be harmful to others, as in the North and the South during the Civil War.[102]

The great exploiters of mankind, says Quimby, are the priests, the doctors, and the politicians. The people have given their souls to the priests and their bodies to the medicine men[103]; and these two professions have destroyed both body and soul.[104] Like the robbers from the beginning,[105] condemned by Jesus, these have gained domination over the masses[106]; by working together,[107] they have become the worst enemies of humanity.[108] In their hands men are mere pawns[109] who have become impoverished through their machinations.[110] There are now more diseases than ever before[111] because the opinions and teachings of the priests and doctors create ninety percent of the miseries and maladies which infest the human race.[112] Priests invent fears and doctors invent sickness[113]; "disease was conceived in priestcraft and brought forth in the iniquity of the medical faculty."[114] Together, they cause "more misery than all other evils" combined.[115]

Priests and doctors, of course, had nothing but contempt and condemnation for a man like Quimby.[116] "I am hated by some," he wrote, "laughed at by others, spit upon by the doctors, and sneered at by the priests, but received into the arms of the sick who know me."[117] He declared that he could restore more people to health during a lecture than all the clergymen and doctors in the whole state of Maine.[118]

In all ages, continues Quimby, deceivers exploit the people beyond endurance; and this is why periodic revolutions are inevitable.[119] After the priest and the medicine men have taken their pounds of flesh, the politicians, who always pretend to love the people and the poor, seize what is left.[120]

"The religious belief," says Quimby, "prepares the mind for the medical belief, one based on old superstitions; this gets the mind worked up like mortar, and then the doctor or potter molds the mind into disease."[121] Since the doctor would have no income or occupation if health were universal, it is to their interest to create ninety percent of all diseases.[122] When a man or woman is freed from the terrors inculcated by priests and doctors, the victim, in a real sense, is resurrected from the dead.[123]

Quimby and the genesis of New Thought can be understood only in the context of mid-nineteenth century religious dogma. The official doctrine in various large denominations, especially the Reformed, Lutheran, Calvinist, and Congregational-Presbyterian, declared that the ninety-nine percent of the human race which had not been chosen by God before the foundation of the world to constitute the community of Elect Saints would be tortured eternally in hell fire. Hapless men and women cowered and trembled in terror before the face of an angry God, who without the slightest compunction or compassion, and in the course of simple justice, would plunge into everlasting perdition those upon whom he had not conferred a full measure of prevenient grace. Countless individuals spent much of their lives brooding over this frightful destiny.

The first thing Quimby wanted to know, therefore, was the religious belief and background of his patient. The awful thing about religion, he said, was its absorption with creeds, rewards, and punishment,[124] because of which society was submerged in poisons and diseases which cause even the mother to transmit them to her children.[125]

"I went to see a young lady during the Miller excitement [1843-44]," he wrote. "She was confined to her bed, would not converse with any person, lay in a sort of trance with her eyes rolled up in her head, took no notice of any person; the only thing she would say was that she was confined in a pit, held there by a large man...and she said to me, 'I shall never die, nor ever get well.' She had been in this condition for one year, refused all nourishment, and was a mere skeleton at the time I went to see her...in about an hour I saw the man she had created, and described him to her, and told her that I would drive him away. This seemed to frighten her for she feared for my safety. But when I assured her that I could drive the man away, she kept quiet. In three hours, she walked to the door, and she recovered her health. I could name hundreds of such cases, showing the effect of the mind upon the body."[126] Here Quimby definitely recognizes the psychosomatic nature of his therapy.

We see, therefore, that in addition to the conscious practice of psychosomatic healing, Quimby believed he could read the thoughts and visualize the idea-images of his patients. He believed also that his curative powers were intimately related to the empathy he felt with his patients.[127] A constant stream of sufferers came to him who were sick of worry[128] since they were persuaded that God had predestined them irrevocably to everlasting torture.[129] One was so ensnared by her beliefs that, rather than surrender them, she wished to die of her disease; some were convinced that they had committed the unpardonable sin.[130] Some suffered actual paralysis as a result of the religious doctrines preached to them.[131] Getting religion, he declared, is the prelude to misery; and he delineated the process by which an innocent and happy young woman is converted, gets religion, becomes miserable, and, in due course is filled with weird diseases.[132]

6. *Quimby's Technique.* Whenever, therefore, these sufferers came to Quimby, he began by explaining that God is benevolent, that he loves all members of the human race, that he has condemned no one to hell, and, most of all, that he never created any disease.[133] Quimby's method was essentially psychoanalytic, the one used by Freud and his successors, by which they removed neuroses through the discovery and explanation of their origin. Horatio W. Dresser explains that "what Quimby taught was that false ideas and mental imagery causing the disease were directly impressed on the plastic substance of the mind, which included what we now call the subconscious."[134]

Quimby offered himself simply as "a teacher of Christ, or Science...."[135] Jesus was to the Christ precisely what Quimby was to the Christ-Science.[136] Jesus and Quimby both taught the wisdom that destroys death and the devil[137]; and since God, as the Wisdom of Science, is in Quimby, he and God are one, even as the Son Jesus was one with the Father.[138]

Quimby was accused of making himself equal to Jesus[139]; but this was a misconception due to the fact that people think of Jesus the Christ as a single entity, when, as a matter of fact, Jesus was simply a human being who, like Quimby, was filled with the Science of God, or the Christ-Spirit. Quimby was also accused of interfering with the religion of his patients,[140] a charge he readily accepted, since religion was the basic cause of their maladies. And he asserted: "It is necessary to say that I have no religious belief,"[141] only a God-Wisdom properly called the Science of Christ. Since correct or scientific beliefs lead to heaven, and false or "religious" beliefs create the hells of mankind,[142] it is his principal objective to eradicate from the minds of his patients every vestige of orthodox dogma, especially that which requires suffering on earth to merit the joys of heaven.[143]

7. *The Superior Feminine.* In evaluation of Woman—the Female Principle—Quimby served as a transmission belt between the Shakers

and Mary Baker Eddy. Of the two elements which constitute Man,[144] the female has always been the higher; spiritual wisdom has always been transmitted through her. Man as male, or Adam, was of the earth, earthy; yet there was in the man also "this Science in the form of a rib, of this higher power," known as "Woman."[145] Women are more elevated and scientific than men[146]; they would, if they had the power, soon rid the world of priests and doctors [147]; and in the future, Woman will be the teacher of health and happiness.

IV. THE QUIMBY THERAPY

1. *Treatment and Cure.* If Quimby's therapeutic technique was basically psychoanalytical,[148] his cure, in the majority of cases, was a parareligious experience.[149] "The question is often asked," he notes, "why I talk about religion and quote Scripture while I cure the sick. My answer is that sickness being what follows a belief, the belief contains the evil which I must correct. As I do this, a chemical change takes place. Disease is an error the only remedy for which is the truth. The fear of what will happen after death is the beginning of man's troubles, for he tries to get evidence that he will be happy, and the fear that he will never arrive at happiness makes him miserable."[150] In short, the fear of hell is the basic cause of sickness and disease.

When a woman unable to walk was brought to him, he made the following typical analysis: "Your belief is the sepulchre in which your wisdom is confined.... Your opinions and ideas are your garments and the truth is the Holy Ghost or angel which will roll away the stone and heal your grief. The God in you will burst the bonds of your creed and you will rise from the death of your belief into the truth. You will then walk into the sitting room, and the friends will start as though you were a spirit.... You will leave the body of belief and take that of Science and rise into health. This is the resurrection from the dead."[151]

Quimby said that he was not superior to other men, except as he had learned to use the wisdom of God, or the Christ-Science.[152] When called a harmless humbug,[153] who relieved the nervousness of a few patients,[154] Quimby replied that he had enabled hundreds of those long bedridden to rise again into excellent health,[155] that he had enabled the lame to walk—a fact to which the canes and crutches left in his office bore eloquent testimony.[156] He had not only caused the dumb to speak,[157] he could also teach others to cure by his method.[158] Some there were who said that he cured by the aid of the devil; to which, like Jesus, he replied that a house divided against itself cannot stand.[159]

2. *Mind and Matter.* At the base of Quimby's metaphysics was his belief that mind is Spiritual Matter.[160] He found, he says, that "*if I really believed in anything, the effect would follow whether I was thinking of it or not.*... I found it could be condensed into a solid and receive a name called 'tumor,' and by the same power under a different direction it might be dissolved and made to disappear."[161] In another passage, he elaborates: "After I found that mind was spiritual matter, I found that ideas were matter, condensed into a solid called disease...."[162] He emphasized, however, that there is neither wisdom nor intelligence in matter.[163]

We read that the human body or "natural man" is merely a dense shadow of reality or substance, condensed into matter.[164] The body is a house for the mind[165]; but it is error to postulate a duality of body and soul,[166] for Man is an individual entity. When the body grows old, it withers away, and, like a tree, simply decomposes,[167] and mingles again with the visible condensation of mind which is the universe.

Quimby was certain that one human mind could directly affect and influence another. "It is an undisputed fact," he declared, "that persons affect each other when neither are conscious of it. According to the principle by which I cure the sick, such instances can be accounted for, and it can be proved beyond a doubt that man is perfectly ignorant of the influences that act upon him, and being ignorant of the cause, is constantly liable to the effect."[168] There is, therefore, constant, even though unconscious, mental intercommunication[169]; and for this reason diseases which afflict children are actually the result of the unconscious influence of community opinion.[170]

The Natural Man, or the body,[171] says Quimby, is simply the tenement occupied temporarily by the real man, which is the invisible, spiritual reality.[172] Man, therefore, has an identity entirely independent of matter.[173] The senses are independent of the body[174]; and, together with all the faculties of man, they will continue intact when the body is laid aside.[175] This spiritual body, which has an identity separate from the natural, [176] was something that Quimby could see[177] and with which he could converse.[178]

3. *Disease: The Self-Created.* Diseases, says Quimby, are lies which make us ill—smallpox and kinepox are such lies.[179] Water will poison us, no matter how pure, if we believe it to be toxic.[180] Disease is a self-imposed prison, which makes of the victim, as it were, a helpless stranger in an alien land.[181]

"Disease," continues Quimby, "is the natural result of ignorance and error governed by discords of the mind." Bronchitis is like a belief in witchcraft[182]; and the belief in witches at Salem was no more of a superstition[183] than a belief in the efficacy of vaccination.[184] A disease is comparable to the misery caused by the loss of $10,000, the recovery of which is the cure.[185]

To illustrate how error creates disease, Quimby describes the onset of bronchitis and the subsequent pneumonia. It comes like a cloud which presages rain or storm. "So in your belief you...are shaken, the earth is lit up by the fire of your error, the heat rises, the heaven or mind grows dark.... At last the winds or chills strike the earth or surface of the body, a cold clammy sensation passes over you."[186] And so the bronchitis develops into pneumonia and consumption, and the victim dies. In the same way, fear creates the malignancy called cancer.[187]

4. *Exorcising the Devil.* Unfortunately, most people accept as truth what is nothing but error and this is "the evil that dwelleth in us" which "comes from the knowledge of this world.... To separate us from the error...is to explain the false idea away and then all sorrow will pass away...like a dream or a nightmare..."[188] Since sickness is merely an evil infestation,[189] diseases are cured when devil-error is cast out.[190]

5. *Chemicalization of the Body Fluids.* Quimby's theory of disease and its cure involves his teaching concerning changes in body fluids which take place as disease originates, grows, or disappears. "The mind is the name of the fluids of which your body is composed, and your thoughts represent the change of the fluids or mind...."[191]

In one essay, Quimby explains how the patient, under the influence of the medical profession, creates his disease and destroys his own happiness. "A chemical change in the fluid of the system takes place," we read, "and you condense them into a phenomenon corresponding with your plan." In order to "destroy the disease, I convince you that what the doctor said was an idea gotten up by error, not knowing how to account for some little disturbance...you were led astray into the darkness of heathen superstition where all kinds of evil spirits and diseases dwell in the brain of man."[192]

"Disease," repeats Quimby, "is what follows the disturbance of the mind or spiritual matter."[193] And "mind," we note, is the body fluid or "a spiritual matter which, being agitated, disturbs the spirit. This disturbance contains no knowledge of itself, but produces a chemical change in the fluids of the system."[194] Every phenomenon observed in the natural or temporary man is only a reflection of his spiritual entity; and when "death" occurs, nothing happens except that the essential man, retaining all the senses, faculties, and qualities of his earthly manifestation, sheds his material chrysalis and begins his permanent existence.[195]

As disease injures the mind or the body fluids, "chemicalization" takes place, a process which is simply reversed when healing follows; when an impression is made upon the mind, "I found that by the power of my own mind I could change the mind of my patient and produce a chemical change in the body, like dissolving a tumor."[196] Again: "All effects produced in the human frame are the result of a chemical change of the fluids with or without knowledge...."[197] Matter exists, says Quimby, "only as it is spoken into existence...." And as a man's belief changes, "the matter or opinion will change, and when a chemical change takes place, the mind or opinion will be destroyed and truth or Science takes its place.... When man arrives at that, then death will be swallowed up in Science."[198]

The word "consumption," he says, "is of itself nothing to the person who has never heard of it. To make it is to create the opinion or building and then reduce it to an idea. So matter in the form of words is so arranged as to make the idea in the opinion. While the opinion is forming in the mind, a chemical change is going on, and the matter is held in solution till it is condensed into a form according to the pattern given by the direction of the mind...."[199]

6. *The Power of Faith.* Following his Mesmeric period, Quimby came to understand fully a therapeutic element which perhaps no one had ever explained before: the importance of suggestion and the confidence of the patient in his healer. "Your faith is what you receive from me..."[200] he wrote to one patient. He emphasized that the afflicted

person must wish to recover; believe healing to be possible; have implicit faith in the physician; and be ready to abandon old religious terrors and beliefs. Even as Jesus told the sick that their faith had made them whole, so Quimby told his patients that what he gave them was the moral certainty that they could and would be healed. For beliefs, he said, act upon the mind, and can produce a salubrious chemical change[201]; and he was sure that the doctor, by talk alone, can accomplish this transformation in the mind, the fluids, or the spiritual matter of the patient.

7. *The Mystery of the Sub-Conscious.* After studying Berkeley, Swedenborg, and others, Quimby gradually concluded that nothing of a Mesmeric nature passes from one body to another.[202] Nevertheless, the hypnotic trance continued to fascinate him for a time: "I once put many persons into this state," he wrote later; "a mesmerized subject is all that any person can be in a waking state; at the same time, he is another person, separate from his earthly identity. He can feel, fly, walk, and pass into the sea and describe things lost. He can find things that he knows not of in another state.

"Now where and what was this invisible something that could pass in and out of matter? What is this clairvoyance? It is the mystery or power that has troubled the wisdom of the world to solve.... To understand the phenomenon is to go back to the First Cause and see what man was."[203] What was this but the Swedenborgian separate spiritual self or body?

V. THE SWEDENBORGIAN INFLUENCE

1. *How Quimby Used His Sources.* After Quimby repudiated Mesmerism as well as Berkeley's idealism, he began an intensive study of the healing technique described in the Synoptics, and he utilized the Swedenborgian interpretation of Scripture. Capitalizing on the universal acceptance of Jesus as the savior, he transformed the Christ of the Gospels into a most unconventional redeemer.

He took from his sources—particularly the Bible—only what he actually wanted and then he interpreted it according to his needs. It is certainly true that ideas may be original in a second appearance; however, the similarities between Quimby and Swedenborg are too many, pervasive, striking, exclusive, and characteristic to be written off as mere coincidence, especially since we know that he had "discovered" Swedenborg, who was in great vogue at the time. We do not mean that Quimby was a mere disciple of the Swedish revelator; but we must note that when he formulated his belief or "creed," he did so almost in the very words of Swedenborg. "My religion," he declared, "is my life, and my life is the light of any wisdom I have."[204]

2. *The Psyche and Absent Healing.* The Mesmerizers had no explanation for the mysteries of the psyche; but Swedenborg had solved the problem for Quimby by equating mind with spiritual matter, the essential man; this reality, now obscured by the body, has powers and qualities as yet uncomprehended. The spiritual man can leave the natural body, converse with unseen persons, and read the thoughts of others. Clairvoyance, then, is a natural function of the spiritual man. Conquest over disease becomes possible for those who master this science, and then it ceases to be a mystery.

Since the Swedenborgian Spiritual Man is not restricted by place or time, Quimby found he could practice "Absent Healing," which has always been standard procedure with Christian Scientists. Quimby declared that when Jesus cured the centurion's servant, he became clairvoyant and utilized this technique. Julius Dresser, who said that he was cured of "typhoid pneumonia,"[205] declared that Quimby had healed many patients whom he had never seen and who lived far away.[206] Quimby wrote patients that he would visit them *in spirit* at specified times, when they would experience relief from their maladies, and finally achieve complete recovery.[207]

To one patient he wrote: "when you receive this letter...I think you will feel better. Sit up straight. I am now rubbing the back part of your head.... I am in this letter, so remember and look at me...."[208]

To another he wrote: "Perhaps you cannot see how I can be sitting by you in your house, and at the same time be in Portland.... If you understood, you would not doubt that I am now talking to you.... So I shall try to convince you that, although I may be absent in the idea or body, yet I am present with you in mind...."[209] To still another he wrote that because he had thirty patients on his hands, he could not leave "in person," but would nevertheless give a treatment for a stomach ailment; for remember that "I am in this letter and as often as you read this and listen to it you listen to me."[210] On a certain Sunday, between the hours of eleven and twelve, he visited in spirit one woman patient who had been bedridden for nine months; and at that hour, she arose, walked into the dining room, and in short, recovered her health completely.[211]

3. *The Spiritual Man.* The "natural man," says Quimby, "never can understand the things of the Spirit; for all these are governed or created in the heavens or spiritual world...."[212] Although its exact locality is a "mystery,"[213] there is no doubt that he accepted its factual existence. He explains that "in the spiritual world there are things as they are in the natural world that affect us as much, but these are not known by the natural senses...."[214] Ideas, he says, have a *real* existence in the spiritual world as well as in the natural.[215] And again: "As the degrees from total darkness or ignorance are progressive, they embrace all kinds of talent, like teachers from the lowest classes of this world to the highest of the spiritual world. All science to the natural world is looked upon as mystery, witchcraft, sorcery, etc., because the natural world cannot use anything beyond itself."[216] Near the close of his career, he wrote: "I think now that I have succeeded so that any person of ordinary talent can see" that my teaching "is the key to unlock the mysteries of the spiritual world."[217]

4. *Death and the Resurrection.* Quimby's son, George W., wrote concerning his father: "although not belonging to any church or sect," he had "a deeply religious nature, holding firmly to God as a first cause, and fully believing in immortality and progression after death.... An hour before he breathed his last, he said to the writer: 'I am more than ever convinced of the truth of my theory. I am perfectly willing for the change myself, but I know you will all feel badly; but *I* know that I shall be right with you, just the same as I have always been. I do not dread the change any more than if I were going on a trip to Philadelphia.' "[218]

Quimby believed, he said, in another world, but not as the clergy do[219]; but when we try to determine his exact meaning, we have no definite answer. Rising from the dead means simply "*a resurrection from an error into truth.*"[220] Jesus never meant that his body would live again[221]; what appeared to his disciples was only a condensation of his spiritual entity[222]; and all "he meant was that his senses should rise from the dead or the error of the people who believed that the senses are a part of the idea called body."[223] At the transition called death, "life rises to that happy state where death, hell, disease, and the torments of existence find no place, from whence no traveler ever returns, but where man knows himself."[224]

Nowhere is Quimby more Swedenborgian than in his concept of death, which, he says, "does not change us at all. We are just what we were before. If we have any ideas which make us unhappy, we still have them."[225] Death is a painless and even unconscious transition or transferral in which all that was before continues.[226]

"Christ," says Quimby, "lost nothing by the change" called death. "Every person rises from the dead with their own belief; so to themselves, they are not risen and know no change, and the dead, as they are called, have no idea of themselves as dead."[227] When Jesus appeared to his disciples after the crucifixion, "they thought he was a spirit, for they believed in spirits, but Christ Himself was the same Jesus as before... when you think a person dead he is dead to you, but to himself there is no change, he retains all the senses of the natural man, as though no change to the world had taken place. This was what Jesus wanted to prove."[228]

5. *The Spiritual Interpretation of Scripture.* The fact that a man who previously had shown no interest in religion or the teachings of Jesus should suddenly, upon contact with Swedenborg, become so intensely absorbed in these, adopt many concepts strongly reminiscent of the Swedish seer, and embrace that savant's method of interpreting the ancient texts, points persuasively to direct influence. Quimby declares that the "Bible is spiritual truth illustrated by literal things, but religious people follow the shadow or literal explanation and know nothing of the true meaning."[229]

As with Swedenborg, and later with Mary Baker Eddy, almost every page of Quimby is studded with restatements of Scripture which illustrate the method. Nothing means what the words say; in fact, many of them are given interpretations which seem to have little relevance.

When Jesus told the rich young man that he must sell his possessions and distribute them among the poor, he meant that the questioner should repudiate his Judaistic doctrines and accept those of Jesus.[230] According to another passage, he meant that he should "go and give your ideas away and follow the Science, or Me."[231] When he said that he would rise from the dead, he meant only that even if his flesh and blood were destroyed, the knowledge of them would remain, and this knowledge would create another body.[232] When the rich farmer said he would build larger barns to store his grain, he meant that he would "dress up and go into more educated society, among the literary and enjoy himself."[233] The Kingdom of which Jesus spoke and which came down to the natural man was the stone, or Science, which the builders, or error, rejected and which had become the head of the foundation in the new Science of Life.[234] The new heaven and the new earth of Revelation will be the new world, free from error, which will exist when the fire of science has destroyed all bigotry, disease, and superstition.[235]

Science is "the New Jerusalem that came down from heaven," which may also be "called the kingdom of heaven."[236] When Jesus said that the Scribes and Pharisees placed burdens upon the people, he was speaking of diseases and false opinions.[237] When he spoke of his Kingdom, he meant his Christ-Science.[238] When the Samaritan woman said that she had had several husbands, this signified that she had embraced different religious creeds in the past "and as each was destroyed by her wisdom, she became a widow."[239] When Jesus told the fishermen who became his disciples to throw away their nets, he meant that they should discard their old creeds.[240]

6. *Summary*. We find, therefore, that Quimby's concepts of death, the natural and spiritual man, the moral progression which continues before and after "the change," the nature of the body and its relation to disease and health are definitely Swedenborgian, as was his belief that he could travel to distant places as to his spirit. Quimby's impersonal theology, his libertarianism, and his pursuit of temporal health and happiness as supremely laudable objectives are thoroughly Swedenborgian; and we should certainly realize that except for the Swedenborgian concept of spiritual matter and the spiritual man, which constitutes the core of Quimby's metaphysics and the basis for his therapy, his whole system would have been without foundation and his great contribution to New Thought would have been impossible.

VI. THE EVALUATION OF QUIMBY

1. *Quimby's Discovery of Psychic Levels*. Quimby definitely comprehended the psychological factors which operate through the emo-

tions which the Freudian school was one day to lay bare. He discovered that man has two levels of mind or consciousness; his "reason" is active on the upper level, but his beliefs are active on the lower, or the subconscious.[241] "This shows," he declares, "that every man has two selves, one acknowledged by the natural man, the other by the spiritual man."[242] Elsewhere, he says that "the mind is the medium of a higher power independent of the natural man.... As our bodies are the machine to be moved like the locomotive, and our mind is the steam, the whole must be kept in action by a power independent of itself.... These two powers govern the mind and body as the engineer governs the steam engine."[243]

Whatever Quimby may have meant by science, Spiritual Body, the Real Man, etc., it is certain that he grasped clearly the fact that the Mind of Man, even though a unity, exists and operates on different psychic levels which have their own peculiar functions and nature. Like the later psychoanalysts, he had a deep sympathy with his patients: he did not judge—he sought only to understand and heal, first the mind, and then the shadow, the mortal coil. With him, sin in the theological sense was abolished; and there remained only the error which separates Man from Science, which is perfection of life and happiness.

2. *His Limitations.* We should, however, recognize Quimby's limitations. Although he discovered important verities, the world has not accepted them as the whole truth. He was mistaken in his belief that the primary mission of Jesus consisted in healing the sick. With Swedenborg, whose encyclopedic mind embraced virtually all knowledge, the problem of physical health played an even smaller, although a significant, role. In assuming, as Quimby did, that health encompasses all success and happiness, he was certainly in error; for a multitude of other factors are involved in the complex business of a successful life. Finally, when he declared that all sickness and disease exist only because they are previously created by an error of the mind, either in the victim or in the doctor or in the community as a whole, his diagnosis was certainly incorrect. Had he followed Mesmer by stating that only those burdened by emotional maladjustments could be treated successfully under his therapy, he might now be recognized as a great creative genius; but then he would not have inspired the founder of Christian Science to scale the heights of incredible achievement.

3. *Quimby's Patients.* His success was due, in large part, to the

failure of others; for there is little doubt that the patients who came to him did so only as a last resort.[244] This meant that only those who had undergone the standard medical treatments without benefit, but who had still managed to survive, were likely to become his clients; and these were precisely the ones he could help. For had these victims suffered from organic or physical illness, they would either, in most cases, have died or recovered; but the hypochondriacs, those trapped by strange neuroses, or sick to distraction from religious fears or psychotic disturbances were (1) beyond the aid of conventional medicine; (2) in little danger of imminent death, no matter how crippled, miserable, or laden with the symptoms of physical illness; and (3) highly susceptible to mental suggestion and physical improvement when peace of mind had been restored or an emotional catharsis achieved. It was as simple as that.

There were, a hundred years ago, and there are today, countless sufferers who cannot be healed or cured by drugs or surgery and who, without help, face a lifetime of infinite misery; and to many of these, Quimby was an angel of hope and mercy.

4. *Saving the Terrified.* New England teemed with the victims of Calvinist terror: actually, the old wild religious revivals had served a profound therapeutic purpose for thousands who otherwise might have gone quite mad. Quimby parted company with Lucius Burkmar at the very moment when the last great revival (the Millerite) was in its climax; such relief was therefore no longer available to the distressed victims of phantasmagoric fear. Quimby offered such people—and to the lame, the halt, the speechless, the broken, the hopeless, the frustrated, and the bedridden, and to those awaiting death in quivering terror—a new hope, the assurance that God is beneficent, that disease exists only as an error of the mind. He proclaimed that the ministers who had threatened them with eternal hell-fire were liars, charlatans, and imposters; that the doctors, who had taken their precious money while accentuating the maladies, were the original creators of the diseases which cursed them. To all these, whose suffering actually originated in their minds or emotions, Quimby's gospel was one of joy and deliverance.

If Quimby had discarded his religious terminology, if he had recognized the fact that his patients almost exclusively suffered from emotional rather than physical ailments, and had he understood that his treatment constituted a therapy specifically aimed at the solution of their psychic maladies, it is possible that he, instead of Freud or Adler, would now be regarded as the founder of modern psychiatry.

5. *The Architect of New Thought.* Innocent of formal learning, without medical or anatomical training, without any broad grasp of human problems as a whole, Quimby nevertheless looms large on the horizon; he made an original and significant contribution, religious, psychological, and therapeutic. It is possible that even without him there might have been a New Thought movement, but it assuredly would not have taken the course it did, nor could it have become what it is today; and it is incontrovertible that no Warren Felt Evans, Julius Dresser, or Mary Baker Eddy could have followed.

Quimby was a principal creator on American soil of what we may call the religion of health, success, prosperity, and happiness.

Chapter IV

WARREN FELT EVANS

I. THE MAN HIMSELF

1. *His Unique Position*. Warren Felt Evans (1817-1889), although less original than Quimby, was a widely read scholar, a tireless investigator, and a gifted writer who made all forms of psychotherapy his province, which he practiced throughout his mature life. He was the first who reduced this system of healing into an intellectual discipline, preached it to the world, and described it in a series of books—which sold widely—expounding his wide-ranging principles. He also sought to prepare others to practice his therapies.

2. *Cure in Portland*. He was ordained a Methodist minister about 1838; shortly thereafter, however, he fell under the fascination of Swedenborg, whose lifelong devotee he became. An important factor in his life was a mysterious malady because of which he sought help from Quimby in 1863; along with Mary Baker Patterson, Annetta

Seabury, and her soon-to-be husband, Julius A. Dresser, Evans experienced personal relief, and when he witnessed the recovery of others without benefit of material medication, he discovered the basis for a new career of his own.

3. *Writings.* Even before meeting with Quimby, however, Evans was already a psychotherapist; but thereafter he became a pioneer and prophet. Years before Mary Baker Eddy was able to present her ideas to students, Warren F. Evans was lecturing, writing, and healing at his own clinic. In 1869, only three years after the death of Quimby and six years before *Science and Health* appeared, Evans published *The Mental-Cure, Illustrating the Influence of the Mind upon the Body.* His second mature work, *Mental Medicine: A Theoretical and Practical Treatise on Medical Psychology*, was printed in 1872; his third, *Soul and Body: Or the Spiritual Science of Health and Disease*, in 1876; his fourth, *The Divine Law of Cure*, in 1881; his fifth, *The Primitive Mind-Cure, the Nature and Power of Faith*, in 1884; and his last, *Esoteric Christianity and Mental Therapeutics*, in 1886.

4. *The Swedenborgian.* As Julius Dresser declares, Evans had already found in Swedenborg the principles "which directly lead to the practical method for which Dr. Quimby stood"; and it was only necessary for him "to find a man who was actually proving what he had theoretically anticipated in order to accept the entire therapeutic doctrine."[1]

The Swedenborgianism absorbed by Evans before 1863 was already his dominating influence. It is possible that he could have entered upon what became his life-ministry without Quimby; but it is more likely that the meeting with the Portland doctor was the catalyst which enabled him to formulate his own philosophy and make the decision to become a therapeutic healer. Had he not become ill, had he not met or been helped by Quimby, it is likely that he would have remained a minister in the Church of the New Jerusalem, engaging, meanwhile, in part-time therapy, as before; instead, he blazed a new trail for the religion of science, health, success, happiness, and prosperity.

Evans, however, seems to have considered Quimby of minor importance in his own development; for, although he often echoes or reproduces the very ideas proclaimed by Quimby, he refers to him only once in all his books, and then, not as an authority, but simply as one of many successful mental healers who had flourished from time to time.* In 1864, the year following his encounter with Quimby, Evans published *The New Age and Its Messenger*—who, of course, was Swedenborg.

Previous to his meeting with Quimby, Evans had already published two books summarizing and popularizing the teachings of his master.[2] We know that he had already practiced mental healing, because he wrote in 1884 that he had at that time been engaged in this pursuit for twenty-five years.[3] "The writings of Swedenborg," says Evans in 1864, "have taken a deep hold upon my mind, and affected my inner life." And he continues: "A new Jerusalem, then, can mean nothing but a new church, for a new and a better dispensation."[4] And he added, "Emanuel Swedenborg, servant of the Lord Jesus Christ, was the instrument of Providence for ushering in a new and a better age...."[5]

Although Evans cites a vast number of other authors, Swedenborg continued from first to last as the overriding influence. In his six mature works, he names the Swedish seer as his source and authority no less than 160 times; and definitely Swedenborgian concepts appear in more than 250 other passages. In 1876, he calls his master "the pioneer and John the Baptist of the new age...."[6] and declares that his own "doctrine of health and disease will be readily accepted by the disciples of Emanuel Swedenborg, and all those who are acquainted with his doctrine of correspondence between soul and body...."[7]

In 1881, Evans wrote: "In Emanuel Swedenborg, we see a man in whom science and religion were so wedded as to render even a temporary divorce an impossibility. His intellect was always and everywhere religious, and his religion was at all times intellectual.... The system of spiritual science which is unfolded in his voluminous writings, and exemplified in his remarkable experiences, is having a silent but powerful influence in molding and modifying the religious beliefs and changing the thoughts of men, throughout Christendom...."[8]

Evans remained always a devout Swedenborgian; in his last work, he declares: "He who carefully studies that development of Christian-

---

* Evans wrote in 1872: "The late Dr. Quimby, of Portland, one of the most successful healers of this or any age, embraced this view of the nature of disease, and by a long succession of most remarkable cures, effected by psychopathic remedies, at the same time proved the truth of the theory and the efficiency of that mode of treatment.... He seemed to reproduce the wonders of the Gospel history." (*Mental Medicine*, p. 210.) Of course none of Quimby's writings were available at that time.

ity which we have in the writings of Swedenborg will find there all the truth that exists in the various schools of mental cure."⁹

5. *Popularity*. We do not know how many copies of Evans' works were sold between 1864 and 1900; but at a time when *Science and Health* was yet in the future or had made little impact upon the general public, the works of Evans were in wide demand. For example, *Mental Medicine* (1872) had sold 15,000 copies by 1885,[10] and was in its fifteenth edition in 1897; other even more popular titles were reprinted in quantity again and again, distributed all over the country, sold without an organization to promote them, and exercised direct and indirect influence upon all New Thought writers and organizations.

II. EVANS' PHILOSOPHICAL SYSTEM

1. *The Developing Technique.* A complex of philosophical and theological concepts, drawn substantially from Swedenborg, continued unaltered in all of Evans' writings; and even though his therapeutic technique evolved over the years in the direction of a purely psychological method, the influence of Swedenborg continued undiminished. Since, therefore, we have a philosophical superstructure in addition to a technical therapy, it is necessary that we treat them separately.

2. *Theology*. At the center of Evans' system stands precisely the same theological concept that we find in Swedenborg: God is an impersonal, universal power, by which all nature and every living creature lives, moves, and has its being. God is the central Sun, the Primal Force, the source of light, heat, and vitality, without which the cosmos would be totally dark and devoid of life. This concept, which runs like a red thread through all his works, is the very essence of his religion and of New Thought. "God," he says, "is the First and the Last.... Everything, from the insect to the angel, exists by virtue of a life proceeding from him. We live because he lives, our life being the stream of which he is the fountain, or it is a ray of which he is the central sun.... It is the inmost essence of all created things."[11] "The Central Sun of our system" he explains, "is what Jesus calls the Father, because from Him everything springs."[12] God is "the ever-present, ever-acting, and indivisible life of the world."[13] He "emanates from this

living center, and is communicated to all, constituting the ground of all finite existence."[14] This Central Life "is the life of God in nature which perpetually creates and unerringly governs the world and all it contains."[15] God is the "universal life-principle," the "primal matter and cosmic substance...."[16] And, finally: "This only saving, healing principle in the universe is identical with the *sun* of the spiritual world as described by Swedenborg, and which he defines as the proximate emanation from the 'invisible God.' "[17]

From all this stems the metaphysical thesis which constitutes the core of New Thought therapy. Since God is "the verimost essential in the universe," and because all souls find "their *immediate* principle, beginning, or ground of existence in" Him, they "are *consubstantial* with Him and also with one another."[18] All of us are therefore sons of God, bound indivisibly by a divine unity which Swedenborg describes as the "deific point, where God and man meet within the soul..."[19] and where man is brought into "conjunction with the Central Life."[20] "Each immortal spirit," says Evans, "is...a direct emanation of the universal spirit...and is possessed of all the attributes of its parent source...."[21] Evans rejects the three-headed god of the creeds with scorn and contempt in favor of a unitary Mother-Father Deity.[22]

3. *Christology.* The Holy Spirit, or the "Christ within," declares Evans, is "the immortal and incorruptible self, which is forever exempt from disease and death."[23] In Jesus, "God was *manifested* in the flesh...." He was "the God-Man and the Man-God. In his personality there was a humanization of the Divine and a deification of the human."[24] The Christ or the Christ-Power is a phenomenon which has appeared "many times and in various parts of the world...."[25] and sometimes, as in Jesus, with such intensity as to transform the recipients into prophets or revelators. All men and women partake of this illumination to a greater or lesser degree in a "grand unity of spirit... just as a drop of the ocean possesses all the qualities...of the great deep...."[26]

Evans, like Swedenborg, repudiates totally all the dogmas of orthodox Christianity. He condemns the doctrine "of the infinite God begetting *Himself*" through the medium of a woman as a monstrous, even a blasphemous absurdity.[27] He declares that "the incredible dogma of a literal resurrection" refers only "to a state of emancipation from material and corporeal thralldom...."[28] He denounces the doctrine of "vicarious atonement"[29] and the orthodox concept of redemption as a "total inversion of the divine order...." and he assures us that the fall of man did not occur as "the result of...eating some forbidden fruit...." It was, in contrast, a gradual and individual process by which the natural man gains dominion over the spiritual. "By redemption," he continues, "we mean a deliverance from the controlling influence of the body...and it is only because" men have fallen "under the dominion of the...animal senses" that they need salvation at all.[30] Furthermore to believe that the sacramental bread and wine "represent the presence of God" is sheer nonsense or ignorance, or the evidence of a feeble mind.[31] "Our redemption or liberation from corporeal bondage is not effected by the passion of the cross, nor by anything external, but always comes from *within*. It is a development of the inmost and real Self." Redemption through Christ Jesus is possible because, by making "his life and his righteousness our own," we can live as he lived and so rise into a similar state of perfection.[32]

The life of Jesus exhibits the triumph of faith "over disease, misery, and death. It was in him a living power that united him to God, the Central Life."[33] When it is said that Jesus gave his life "a ransom for many," we are to understand that by the "impartation of sanative virtue and vital force, he delivered multitudes from diseased states of mind and body. Thus men were saved by him, not by his death ...."[34] Jesus, or Joshua, means "savior, or health-giver, and he was sent into the world" to redeem humanity from "the spiritual seeds of disease."[35]

Thus, with a few bold strokes, Evans, like Swedenborg, abolished the creeds of Christendom. Just what, then, *was* Jesus and why is he called the *Christ*? Here Evans, like his master and the Shakers, embraces the Adoptionist doctrine taught in the third century by Paul of Samosata: "Jesus, the son of Mary and 'the son of man,' became the Christ...by his receptivity of the Logos, or the Word...."[36] Jesus was a human being, "the son of Joseph and Mary." The Christ, however, "is Jesus...with the immense addition of an open communication with the Divine Intellect and Life."[37] He "was not born the Christ any more than Abraham Lincoln was born President of the United States."[38]

It was through his "unexampled spiritual evolution" that the man Jesus "became merged and blended into a unity with...the Universal Christ."[39] This marvelous development or unfoldment made of this "*man* Christ Jesus more of a Savior, Restorer, and Redeemer than all the church creeds have ever done.... If this is a heresy, may it rapidly spread over the entire globe...."[40] Ours, he continues, is not "the Christ of the popular theology, where the idea shrinks and dwindles down to an isolated personality...." He is, instead, "a larger, fuller, diviner ...eternal...all-pervading, all-containing, and universal Christ. This is the universal spirit, first emanation from the Father, whom no man knoweth, and who is beyond the reach of thought."[41]

Evans, like a Shaker namesake, was certain that Jesus as well as Luke had been members of the Essene order which had transmitted the esoteric wisdom of their brotherhoods to the first Christian community.[42]

The true objective of Jesus was otherwise than is taught in the "orthodox" churches. It is true, Evans states, that the Christ-Power was manifested for the purpose of redeeming mankind, but we must understand that the sin he came to eradicate is simply "the cause of disease" resulting from "an error, a wrong way of thinking, feeling, and acting."[43] The overwhelming and omnipresent sin under which mankind, in its manifold misery, now staggers toward its untimely grave is the persuasion that disease exists in the body, or that it is anything other than an erroneous opinion. And the true function of the Christian ministry is to achieve redemption for others by healing them after the manner of Jesus—by casting out these demons of false belief. The paramount "error of the world" is the fact that men do not yet understand that "sin and disease are no part of the immortal and real man...."[44]

May there soon, says Evans hopefully, be raised up "thousands of such followers of Jesus the Christ" that they may "in a world of sickness and sorrow, pain and death be qualified by the perception of his spirit to perform this sublime and sacred function" of healing as he healed.[45] "To follow Christ," we read, "is to reproduce his life and experience," which was made by him "the essential condition of discipleship."[46] In his "spiritual philosophy...religion and health" are always identical. The power to obtain or confer these is latent in every human being; for we are all part and parcel of the universal Christ, and draw our powers from the same source which gave him dominion over the devils of madness and disease.

4. *The Doctrine of Influx.* The concept of Influx is descibed or discussed more than a hundred times in Evans' mature works. "The

word influx," we read, "signifies" what "constitutes our essential life" and "is momentarily received from its central source...."[47] Simply by *"breathing we are connected with the Universal-Life-Principle."*[48] "All life is continual influx from the Deity, the only fountain of being...the Central Life."[49] "Creation has gone forth from this, and the life that thrills in the universe owes its origin to this primal source...it goes out in endless and perpetual undulations, and all live by virtue of life transmitted from him."[50]

"If we open our hearts to receive the influx of the divine and heavenly life," we become "finite receptables of the divine good and truth."[51] "This primary and exhaustless source of life and spiritual energy we have in the sun of the spiritual world, as described by Swedenborg...."[52] From Swedenborg we also know that this "spiritual something that answers to an umbilical attachment and forever binds us to God, the Primal and Central Life, has never been severed."[53]

Influx from this source enables the recipient (who may thus become a Christ-Healer) not only to enjoy life abundantly himself, but also to impart this beneficence to others, so that they too may be placed "in contact with the Universal Life, where they may buy for themselves, and thus become divinely self-reliant."[54]

5. *The Spiritual World.* Angels, says Evans, are only "the spirits of men who have graduated to the inner world, and passed into the heavens."[55] "The world of spirit," he continues, "is as real in itself, and to the sensations of its inhabitants, as this outside range of created things."[56] Our relationship with the "universal and ever-present spiritual world is a vital one, as Swedenborg taught"; and, as the inhabitants of that other realm come into greater communication with us, they "bring down to mankind a higher and happier physical and mental existence...."[57] In fact, "the truly spiritual man" has already "found the ever-present kingdom of the heavens. He dwells on the borderland between the two worlds...." To him, therefore, death is but "an empty name...." for such as he already "live and move in the antechamber of the celestial habitations."[58]

6. *Matter and Spirit.* Evans' beliefs concerning the nature of men are, in general, an expression of historic idealism, but based specifically on Swedenborgian sources. Here again we have a fundamental metaphysical element without which his therapeutic principles would not have been possible. The natural man, the body, the outward and

visible apparition, indeed exists: but it is only a projection into space of the spirit, the real and essential man. Whatever is present in the soul is reflected in its integument; and the latter appears or vanishes as it is created or abolished by the eternal reality of which the body is the shadow. All material manifestations, in fact, are simply outward forms assumed by the underlying spiritual *esse*. "For it is an established law of the divine order that a man must inevitably become outwardly what he is inwardly, and in this life physically what he is mentally."[59] "The relation between the body and soul is that of correspondence..." in which each adjusts itself into harmony with the other,[60] a fact which is of the greatest importance in psychotherapy. When the inner man sheds "its fleshly envelope, there remains the same consciousness of a body as before."[61] As Swedenborg reveals, "the body is perpetually derived from the soul"; it is only "the *form* or external boundary" by "which the soul enters into time and space."[62]

Evans means that what we call matter is only phenomenal manifestation: "*there is not*," he elaborates, "*one single quality, attribute, or property of the body of which we can form any conception that is not in the mind....* The soul, the mind, the spirit...is the only *substance*. Without it, nothing material could exist...the soul perpetually creates its body out of itself, just as God creates the universe, not from nothing, but from Himself.... This destroys the dualistic conception of man as being made up of soul *and* body, and reduces the two departments of nature to an indivisible and inseparable unity."[63]

7. *The Curse of Orthodox Religion*. Echoing Quimby closely, Evans describes the "unhappy patient" who "imagines that the theological scarecrows, hung up by the pulpit, are, in his case at least, living realities, that he is the most wicked of men, has blasphemed the Holy Ghost, committed the sin unto death...and is guilty of all manner of imaginary evil. Such persons suffer untold misery...overwhelmed by a sense of guilt...."[64]

Those who attend the established churches ask "for bread and get a stone"; when they seek the truth, they "are turned off with a scorpion." "They go through their round of outward ceremonies" and "rehearse an unintelligible creed...."[65] As used in these communions, prayer is little less than blasphemy, since it is devoted to selfish and even hurtful ends; unless its purpose is to obtain a larger portion of sanative influx, it is a "solemn mockery...."[66] The "unhappy soul would be brought nearer to heaven by a judicious application of soap and water...."[67]

Jesus came to cast out demons and heal the sick—that is, to "save the world from error and disease."[68] Nine-tenths of his public life was spent in curing diseases of the mind and body. To truly follow Christ is to do the same.[69] Evans cites the mandate of Mark 16:17-18, that if the Church cannot now cast out demons and cause the sick to recover, it has become dead or moribund.[70]

Evans declares that "the apostles and primitive believers" knew nothing of "the incomprehensible...jargon of the Athanasian Creed...."[71] The leaders of the Church, he stated, "took away the keys of the kingdom of heaven and neither entered themselves nor suffered those who would, to enter in. The dark and bloody history of the Church has been the result...an inhuman religion, a relentless and persecuting bigotry."[72]

8. *The Realm of Psychoanalysis.* Basing his theories on Swedenborg, Evans developed psychoanalytical formulations leading directly to Freud. According to a book published in 1872, he declared that there are "two distinct departments of the mind," in the first of which "the intellectual predominates, in the other the affectional or emotional."[73] He adds that our rational thought is under "the control of our volitions, but the feelings and emotions are not so."[74] There is, therefore, a twofold psychic life "which manifests itself in the two forms of conscious and unconscious mental action."[75] However, each of these spheres exists "in three degrees or planes of mental life...imaged in the cerebral system." These consist, first, of "the *cerebrum*, the large brain...; then we have the *cerebellum*, or little brain, about one-eighth of the former in size.... Next we have the primitive brain, or *medulla oblongata*...which would weigh but little more than the Koinoor...the celebrated diamond of Queen Victoria, much smaller than the *cerebellum*, but a myriad times more sensitive and vital. These three distinct brains are correspondences and organs of the three degrees of mind.... In our normal state and our waking hours, we use the cerebrum as the instrument of our thought and volitions. This, in sleep, becomes quiescent.... Its vital force has retreated downward and backward to the *cerebellum*. On the dividing line between sleeping and waking, the mysterious dreamland, the mental powers become greatly

exalted and quickened, so that the experiences and perceptions of hours, and even weeks and months, are crowded into moments. Thus the mind breaks loose from its material limitations of time, place, and sense, and asserts its innate freedom. It sees without the external eye, and to distances almost unlimited. It perceives distant objects, persons, and things...."[76]

By 1876, Evans, having developed his formulations further, wrote that of the three levels of human consciousness the "outermost, which lies next to the body and the external world, is what we call sensation; the interior is intelligence; and the inmost is love" (a term denoting passion and emotion). He adds that "there is a spiritual principle of sensation, one of intellect or intelligence, and one of love, manifesting itself, or coming to consciousness, in affections, desires, and emotions."[77] Although the terms and applications diverge somewhat, it is clear that Evans is here describing the three planes of psychic activity which Freud was one day to call the *Id*, the *Ego*, and the *Superego*.

In his latest works, published in 1884 and 1886, Evans delineates the human psyche in a pattern which makes its lowest level identical to the Freudian *Id*: "The lowest degree of our immortal nature is called the animal soul...the basement story of our immaterial intellectual nature. It is the region in us of the evil and the false, of sin and disease....

"The next degree or region of the mind is where it rises above the darkness and fallacies of the senses, and thinks and acts on the plane of pure intellect.... It has been called also the rational soul...as reason belongs to the psychical man.... In it also is found conscience, of which animals are destitute....

"The *pneuma* or spirit is the supreme degree of the mind or thinking principle—the dome of the temple of God in man...denominated by Pythagoras, the *Nous*, pure intelligence.... It is the Christ-principle within; [in] its divine and immortal nature, it is never diseased or unhappy."[78]

Evans prepared a diagram which may well have been used by the Freudian analysts. Here we find depicted the triune man, consisting of four circles of diminishing size. In the highest aspect, he is *Nous*, Pure Intelligence, the Inward Voice or Conscience, Intuition, the Indwelling Christ, or the Real Self. In the next lower level, Man's psyche embraces Justice, Ideas, Reality, the Intellectual or Human Mind. In the lowest or Animal Soul, we have Instinct, External Sense, Opinion, Appetites,

Passion, Evil, Sin, Disease. At the extreme bottom, is Matter, Maia, Shadow, Body, Soma, the Unreal Man.[79]

9. *The Spiritual Sense of the Word.* Another teaching, without which New Thought could not have based itself on the Christian Scriptures, was the conviction that these contain arcane mysteries, wholly obscured by the external sense. "That the deepest mysteries lie concealed in the internal sense of the word," writes Evans, is manifest as "Swedenborg plainly teaches."[80] Swedenborg's profound ability to interpret the Scriptures spiritually enabled him to proclaim a reconstituted form of Christianity. Evans declares that "this living light" remains today the highest achievement of Christianity[81]; and he utilizes this method throughout his mature writings. It also has become standard procedure in New Thought, and is found particularly in such works as Charles Fillmore's *Metaphysical Dictionary*.

10. *The Anatomist.* Like Swedenborg, Evans was deeply fascinated by anatomy. In a passage written in 1869, he discusses the marvelous composition of the skin, with its millions of pores[82]; and in another, the heart and lungs, with their "six million blood cells," the complicated intestinal tract, and the stomach, with all its varied functions.[83] In 1867, we find him describing the functions of the liver, the bile, the lungs, the gall-bladder, and the epigastrium.[84] By 1872, he had embarked upon research in the nature of the brain, the nervous system, and the spinal column,[85] which led to his extraordinary formulations concerning the triune nature of the human psyche.

III. THE THEORY OF HEALING

1. *The Instructor.* Evans declares that a study of the book *Mental Medicine* would qualify "every person of ordinary intelligence to be his own family physician."[86] *Primitive Mind-Cure*, says the author, was written "in the interest of self-healing, and contains the essential features of the instruction...given to numerous persons during the last twenty years."[87] However, Evans sought also to prepare others to practice the phrenopathic method, and his works are intended as texts "which should elevate the subject to the dignity of a science."[88] He declares in *Mental Medicine* (1872) that at that date, long before the appearance of *Science and Health*, many were already "successfully

practicing this apostolic mode of healing the sick without fee or reward...."[89] And in his final work he states that it had been his "aim to educate men and women up to that degree of spiritual development" which would enable them to become "successful practitioners."[90]

2.   *The Healing Sun.* Basic in Evans' therapeutic system is the Swedenborgian doctrine that when we open the sluice-gates of our egos for the reception of the divine influx, we place ourselves in direct communication with the healing power of the Central Sun. "Any remedial agency that places the sick in body or mind in vital communication with the Central Life is a holy sacrament and means of grace."[91]

3.   *Whence Comes Disease?* What we call disease is an apparent disorder in the body, which reflects an error existing in the mind; since this stems from spiritual sources, it can be eliminated by eradicating from the soul, which is the Real Man, the causes of the affliction.

4.   *The Power of Suggestion.* Disease and healing are, therefore, alike psychosomatic: there was, for example, the case of food poisoned by the grief occasioned by a funeral.[92] It has been found that "bread pills, water drops, and homeopathic pellets have been attended with marked beneficial results." Such relief or cure stems from "the influence of a physician's psychic force over the medicine he prescribes and prepares, and his power of suggestion...."[93]

5.   *The Ministers of Health.* "To save a man from bodily disease without an effort of the soul, is to act like the fireman who should rush into a burning building to rescue a sleeping inmate, and should seize only his clothes...."[94] Those "who would cure disease of mind and body by psychic and spiritual force, must have faith," which unites them "with the Central Life" and which "augments the power of every faculty of the human mind," since it places "the soul in vital conjunction with the divine omnipotence."[95] Unless the psychic practitioner "himself be in sympathy with the fountain of life and light...."[96] he can never heal as Jesus healed. "In the cure of disease by the psychopathic treatment," declares Evans, "we should have a boundless confidence in spiritual aid, and an undoubting faith in the power of mind over matter."[97] Did Jesus, demands Evans, "deal in pills and potions?"[98] Many maladies will yield to the Christ-Healer, whose function it is to reunite his patient in a harmonious relationship "with the...living universe...."[99]

In sharp contrast to the impotent parrots of a moribund creed, the new healer "comes into conjunction with the Central Life and Power of the Universe...." As a result, "a divine energy will burst forth from him, and exhibit itself in works of healing the souls and bodies of men."[100] The professions of ministry and medicine should never have been divided; for "the priest, as in the older civilizations, should" still continue to be "the physician of both soul and body."[101] The power of healing will be revived one day when Christianity is restored as a religion of abundant life and well-being.[102]

6. *Scientific Psychotherapy.* The cures effected by Jesus were in no sense "miraculous"; they were entirely scientific, since they were in accord with universal law,[103] through which the power of God may be intensified by the minister who expels madness and disease. Evans declared that "the teaching of Jesus the Christ is Christian Science, and *scientifically religious*—the only true metaphysics."[104] The authority under which Evans operated was a "Gnosis, or absolute interior knowledge and certitude of the truth...."[105] The "umbilical attachment" which forever "binds us to God, the Primal and Central Life, has never been severed."[106] Anyone who masters these teachings and principles "has won the key that unlocks the spiritual mystery of health and disease...."[107]

As practitioners of the psychopathic art, says Evans, "we should so consecrate ourselves...that we may become organs of communication between the Universal Divine Life and the diseased and unhappy one to whom we are called to minister."[108] Successful mental healers must be of "high mental and moral character...."[109] When the healer opens his own soul to receive the inexhaustible store from the spiritual realm, he can convey the sanative force to his patient.[110] If we expel the morbid idea "from its throne...convalescence will commence."[111] Although we do not "deny the *fact* of the disease, as a state of consciousness," continues Evans, we declare "that the immortal Ego, the spiritual entity and real man, is neither diseased nor unhappy."[112]

7. *the Microcosm and the Macrocosm.* "After we have thoroughly mastered the doctrine of the triune nature of man, it ought not be difficult to form a true idea of a patient."[113] "The man that I am in Christ...is the God of the microcosmic man, as the Universal Christ is the God of the macrocosm.... When the spirit penetrates and pervades" even our "corporeal organism, this is the divine ideal becoming the actual.... This is full salvation, and perfect health."[114]

8. *Limitations.* It is certainly to Evans' credit that he did not claim absolute jurisdiction for psychotherapy. He maintains, however, that

mental diseases were in his day heavily on the increase[115]; and he had no doubt that all "nervous disorders," which are often reflected in the physical organism, "are wholly mental."[116] He was also certain that psychopathic cures could be achieved in many cases after the best medical science had pronounced the sentence of death.[117] Yet Evans never denounced the regular medical fraternity in such sweeping terms as we find in Quimby. Even Jesus, we read, could cure only "the receptive few, and left the unreceptive many as they were."[118] "I do not affirm, or believe," says Evans, "that this system of medical psychology will cure every form of disease...."[119] He never denied that poisons can kill, regardless of belief; and he stated frankly in 1884 that if anyone should ask him "to swallow stricnia or Prussic acid," he would tell his tempter, " 'Get thee behind me, Satan....' "[120] Elsewhere he admits that medical science has real value[121]; and in his last book, he pays a glowing tribute "to the modern science of surgery, which is accomplishing such marvels in saving life."[122] He never maintained that a bone could be set or the flow of blood from an open wound stanched by psychotherapy. But he emphasized again and again that his system of phrenopathy was identical to that of Jesus and, in its field, infinitely superior to all others.[123]

IV. THE EVOLUTION OF EVANS' THERAPEUTIC TECHNIQUE

1. *The First Phase.* In *Mental Cure* (1869) Evans, although still a Mesmeric healer, based his metaphysical system largely on Swedenborgian premises. At that time, however, he was still using the "magnetic treatment," which he then considered most successful.[124] He was, in fact, a follower of Mesmer himself, rather than of his disciples, except that he was hypnotizing his patients by conscious design.

"In the trance," he declared, "both the cerebrum and the cerebellum are quiescent...and their vital force has passed into the primitive brain, the *medulla oblongata*.... Usually, but not *necessarily*, there is a loss of consciousness...and the soul is transported...to the perception" of the spiritual world.[125]

As control over the patient's psyche is surrendered, says Evans, first by the cerebrum and then by the cerebellum, the real or celestial man places the subject in direct communication with the Central force and enables him to receive the divine and redemptive influx. A conviction of his spirituality thus established, the subject understands that sin, error, and disease are manifestations of his inner nature; health and well-being are the result. Futhermore, the practitioner is able to speak directly to the celestial aspect of his subject and compel the departure of the disease.[126]

2. *The Second Phase.* In *Mental Medicine* (1872) Evans is still the Mesmeric healer, using the techniques of various hypnotists who are cited over and over.[127] However, he has rejected the principal technique of the Mesmerizers; he never used a medium, and he declares that "it is only necessary that the patient be thrown into the *impressible conscious state.*"[128] which can be done by the operator.[129] He stated that he had established "by hundreds of successful experiments" that in this condition it is possible to "increase or diminish the action of the heart...affect, in any desirable way...the vital action of any organ of the body, render any part insensible to pain, and calm the excited nerves, and, in a word, produce the specific effects of any medicine that was ever administered...." When this impressible state is fully established, "*the silent suggestion of the operator, or his simple will, without any vocal expression, will act with equal force....*"[130]

Evans explains that although he usually placed his patients in the impressible or hypnotized condition by manipulating the head, he could achieve the same results without touching, even at a distance.[131] By this method, spiritual cures are accomplished by placing the subject in direct communication with the Central Power of the universe,[132] from which we naturally imbibe the living soul of all things. The subject is restored "to harmony and sympathy with external nature..." so that all his "organic movements shall keep pace with the grand symphony of the universe."[133]

3. *The Third Phase.* By 1876, when the slender volume *Soul and Body* was published, Evans had undergone a profound development: Mesmerism, the magnetic treatment, the transferral of vital force from practitioner to subject, the efficacy of manipulation, and the necessity of inducing the somnambulic state had all been abandoned. Here, health and happiness are achieved by the patient in proportion as he understands his own nature and his relationship to the Central Sun, and as his mind, soul, or spirit establishes complete control over the body, which has now passed from operator or physician to patient.

4. *The Fourth Phase. The Divine Law and Cure* (1881) was Evans' most successful and influential work; in this, the last vestige of Mesmerism has vanished, and he had become an even more voracious scholar and investigator than ever. His research now attempts to encompass the historic background of all human thought; and thus he made a profound impact on later New Thought writers, many of whom proclaim that the movement's foundations are to be found in countless thinkers and prophets. In this book he states that the real curative power resides within the patient himself or is absorbed by him directly through influx from the Central Sun; *it does not come from or through the physician*, who has now become simply an instructor or way-shower, who points the way by which the sick may heal themselves. Thus, Evans had at last virtually ceased being a practicing physician; instead, he had become seer and prophet, the instructor pointing the way of health and happiness.

5. *The Fifth Phase.* In *Primitive Mind-Cure* (1884) we find that Evans had progressed still further. His transcendental theory had now at last resolved into a single grand objective: that of teaching all mankind exactly how to accomplish its own spiritualization. A "change of thought," he declares, "adjusts the form of the intellectual soul into its representative image, and this latter molds" the spiritual body "into its expression, and through this it passes outward to the physical organism." And so by the "law of correspondence...the outward body" is transfigured into an expression of the mind "on a material plane."[134]

6. *The Sixth Phase.* When Evans wrote *Esoteric Christianity* in 1886, his system had already been completed; and the value of this work consists in the lucidity with which he restates his mature principles. The very title indicates its mystical premises; yet Swedenborg, whose name and doctrines are cited some fifty times, continues to the end as the overriding authority. In a much-reduced field of other sources, Plato and the Kabala alone are prominent.

He now declares that "the magnetic sleep is not necessary or even desirable...." and only so much of the magnetic force is to be used as is necessary to place the patient in complete rapport with his physician.[135]

V. SUMMARY AND CONCLUSIONS

1. *Prophet and Formulator.* We would say, then, (1) that Warren Felt Evans drew almost all of his basic religious, metaphysical, and therapeutic concepts from Emanuel Swedenborg; (2) that he made Swedenborgianism the living force in a world-wide religious movement now embracing millions of communicants or sympathizers; (3) that he was the most important New Thought theorist who had yet appeared; (4) that in spelling out the ideology of the movement, he placed it upon a firm philosophical foundation; (5) that by gathering a great number of various authorities together, he gave the movement a much broader historical base than it could otherwise have had; and (6) that almost every thought, practice, or technique found in New Thought was fully set forth in his writings.

2. *Basic Concepts and Teachings.* Among the central ideas enunciated by Evans, we may list the following:

(1) that God is the impersonal, Central Sun or Creative Force, the vital power of the universe, the source of life, health, and existence;

(2) that from this Central Point a stream of vitality or beneficent influx flows constantly throughout the cosmos, and may be received by every human being, in whom it naturally creates health and well-being;

(3) that the Christ-Power, which is an aspect of deity, is the active, energizing, life-giving, and redemptive force in the universe, of which all men may share, but which possessed Jesus so completely that he was able to perform the task of human redemption through an adoptionist process, during which this Christ-Power assumed entire control of his psyche;

(4) that every practitioner of the same healing art is actually another Christ, carrying on the work of the Master;

(5) that the orthodox doctrines concerning the Trinity, the Virgin Birth, the divinity and the resurrection of Jesus, the vicarious Atonement, the orthodox teaching concerning the Fall of Man, the metaphysical corruption of human nature, the necessity of such sacraments as baptism and the eucharist—and, in fact, the entire complex of both Catholic and Protestant dogma—are totally false and should be rejected summarily;

(6) that matter, being only the shadow of mind or soul, has no real—that is, essential or eternal—existence;

(7) that man is an immortal and celestial spirit, which is his permanent reality;

(8) that at death nothing happens except that the body, the shadow, the integument, is laid aside, while the Real Man goes on as before;

(9) that, since the human body is only the temporary shadow without real existence and since nothing appears in this shadow except what already exists in the mind, therefore disease can be eradicated by spiritual action, or influence;

(10) that sin and error are synonymous and may be eradicated by replacing them with spiritual truth;

(11) that a world of spirits does exist, in which we are to spend eternity and of which we are already actually a part;

(12) that the human psyche operates upon three distinct levels, which may be called the super-conscious, the conscious, and the sub-conscious and called by some spirit, mind, and soul—an early deliniation of the Freudian super-ego, ego, and id;

(13) that the Christian Scriptures possess an interior or spiritual meaning, which is their most important aspect;

(14) that the search for health and happiness is the highest and most laudable objective taught in the religion of Jesus the Christ;

(15) that this doctrine and therapy are as demonstrable as a mathematical theorem or as an experiment in a laboratory; that this is, therefore, a scientific Christianity, a Christian Science.

3. *An Appraisal.* We must understand that the founder of a cult has no room for compromise; true believers in mystical psychotherapy will not embrace a limited gospel. Had Evans declared that his science was effective only for certain maladies, he might have made a substantial contribution to modern psychoanalysis, but he would not have helped to create the basis for a great religious movement.

It is easy to say that he went too far and claimed too much, that he was wrong in saying that every disease which appears in the body is first created in the mind, or that its annihilation will follow the denial of its existence. Nevertheless, even conservative medical science today candidly admits the reality of psychosomatic maladies and that body and mind interact in many strange and potent ways. Had Evans simply admitted that colds are caused by a virus, that cancer kills irrespective of belief, and that contagious diseases infect their victims with or without mental influence, he might now be recognized as one of the pioneers in scientific psychical research. As it is, he was certainly one of the most important forerunners of present-day psychoanalysis, and did, without question, give ultimate formulations to the principles of New Thought. And we will find that later spokesmen for the movement, while no longer embracing the extreme positions of this scholar, still base their teachings concerning religion, health, and happiness upon the general principles laid down by Warren Felt Evans.

Furthermore, we believe that if people would observe a few simple rules relating to diet, rest, and exercise; if they would cease poisoning themselves with nicotine, alcohol, and narcotics; if they would avoid sweets and fattening foods; if they would live so as to avoid the economic worries and personal conflicts which now plague them almost day and night; if they could enjoy intellectual pleasures during maturity by developing their minds during the earlier years; if they would develop their knowledge and understanding so that they would not fall victims to economic, religious, and other kinds of criminals and charlatans; if they would protect themselves against the hazards of heat, cold, loss of sleep, self-abuse, over-exertion, etc.; and if they would cease worrying about every little physical disturbance, which soon passes away of itself—we believe that those seeking relief from the medical profession could be reduced by more than seventy-five percent.

Few will now deny that physical diseases and maladies *do* exist in the body, that many of these can be cured or alleviated by the medical profession, and that, in spite of the healthiest mind, they often kill. However, it is no less certain that the mind does influence the body in manifold ways. Men have been struck blind on a battlefield and have recovered their sight when the danger was over; a shock of black hair has turned snow white in a few hours because of terror. Entire bodies have been covered with rash because of sudden panic. Similar instances without number have been officially recorded.

I have known several persons—mostly women—who were ill for years or decades; most of them developed their maladies because of some deep-seated neuroses, to which the illness offered a species of emotional relief. I have known them to complain of diseases which were confirmed by expert diagnosticians but which disappeared when the sufferers had no further emotional need for them. Such victims may be bedridden for years, without organic affliction; and I have known at least one who, like Mary Baker Eddy, arose from her sick-bed and became a dynamo of achievement and energy when she discovered an activity which satisfied her neurotic needs.

It seems that there were thousands of such cases in Evans' day; now that religious terror is less prevalent, the proportion of persons so afflicted may be less, but other causes continually operate to augment the number of emotional invalids.

If the therapy of Warren F. Evans served to alleviate the tortures of one such victim, it was not in vain; it seems, however, that it has aided thousands, and that millions could profit from something similar.

Evans recognized the extraordinary capacity of nature for self-healing. "In consequence of this indwelling God," he declares, "which is the common life of the Universe, in us, recuperation is natural to the human body and to all living things. There is a Divine energy inherent in the system that immediately and with omniscient skill reacts against every disorder of mind or body and exhibits itself in a psychical and physiological effort to restore harmony."[136] If left alone and simply ignored, "at least four-fifths" of all diseases "come to an end by their own accord by the principle of self-limitation."[137]

I have known a number of people of both sexes who have become parents, raised families, and continued in sound mental and physical health and activity until the age of seventy or more without ever, even once, calling for any ministration by a physician, except in the case of a broken bone or some similar exigency. If the Shakers could enjoy far greater health and longevity than the rest of the American community, continue to work well into their eighties, and outlive their neighbors by fifty percent while outlawing the medical profession in their communes, why cannot we do better than we do? Are millions of us doomed to the use of drugs, tranquilizers, and barbiturates? Are the medical expenses of our people to become so onerous as to make us the slaves of the medical profession and our multitudinous maladies?

I consider it an incontrovertible fact that, even though Evans is no longer in popular vogue, New Thought owes him an enormous debt, which is too often forgotten, but which should now be fully acknowledged. Emanuel Swedenborg was the foundation and Warren Felt Evans perhaps the most important early expositor of New Thought in

America: a movement which seeks health, happiness, success, and prosperity as its *summon bonum*, its highest goal, both temporal and eternal.

And so, like other creative individuals, Warren Felt Evans remains the prophet who built for the human spirit a temple not made with hands; following him, others, many others, lesser mortals, constructing less-enduring monuments, built churches and cathedrals of steel, glass, and granite.

Chapter V
CHRISTIAN SCIENCE

PART I: MARY BAKER EDDY AND HER CHURCH

I. THE SCIENTISTS

1. *Members and Services.* Christian Scientists are usually substantial individuals with high ethical standards who tend toward conservatism. They avoid debate concerning their tenets; but no other group is more determined that no one shall denigrate its faith or cast aspersions upon its Church or its founder. Neither the members themselves nor the organization have any contacts with other groups.

As the attacks upon Mrs. Eddy became more virulent late in her life, she established the Committee on Publication, which was followed by the Committee on Business. The former, centered in Boston, has full-time representatives in every state and in various foreign countries. According to Sec. 2, Art. XXXIII of the *Church Manual*, its purpose is "to correct in a Christian manner imposition on the public in regard to Christian Science...." which may appear in the public press. As a result of pressure upon editors, publishers, and booksellers, anything the Mother Church considers inimical to itself rarely appears in print.

Each Sunday morning, every Christian Science church conducts an identical service prepared by the Boston headquarters. There are two readers, a man and a woman. There are three congregational songs from the Christian Science hymnal, of which one is always a composition by Mary Baker Eddy. There is also an aria, sung by a male or female soloist. There is no interpretation, and not a word is spoken except what is authorized and prepared by the Mother Church. Preceding the "Lesson," there is a responsive reading of the Lord's Prayer, in which the congregation repeats the words from Matthew 6:9-13 and the readers, in unison, respond with Mrs. Eddy's spiritual interpretation of each portion as follows:

Our Father which art in heaven,

Our Father-Mother God, All-harmonious,

Hallowed be Thy name.

Adorable One.

Thy kingdom come.

Thy kingdom is come; Thou art ever present.

Thy will be done on earth, as it is in heaven.

Enable us to know—as in heaven, so on earth—God is omnipotent, supreme.

Give us this day our daily bread;

Give us grace for today; feed the famished affections;

And forgive us our debts, as we forgive our debtors.

And Love is reflected in love;

And lead us not into temptation, but deliver us from evil;

And God leadeth us not into temptation, but delivereth us from sin, disease, and death.

For thine is the kingdom, and the power, and the glory, forever.

For God is infinite, all power, all life, Truth, Love, over all, and All.

The principal portion of the service consists in the rendition of Bible texts by the female reader and of "correlative" passages from *Science and Health* by the male reader. The ritual then closes with a recitation by the male reader of Mrs. Eddy's Scientific Statement of Being: "There is no life, truth, intelligence, nor substance in matter. All is infinite mind and its infinite manifestation, for God is All-in-All. Spirit is immortal truth; matter is mortal error. Spirit is the real and eternal; matter is unreal and temporal. Spirit is God, and Man is His image and likeness. Therefore man is not material; he is spiritual."

One who has not winged his way from Sense to Soul may regard all this as trite, stilted, and even ridiculous. But for the True Believer, it can be an experience that transcends anything else that life can offer. As he or she gazes with spiritual eyes, a vision appears that never was on sea or land; and high above rises a majestic figure in resplendent robes, crowned with twelve stars; she gleams as a presence holy and divine. This is Mary Baker Eddy herself.

2. *An Incredible Personage.* Mark Twain called her "easily the most interesting person on the planet, and, in several ways, as easily the most extraordinary ever born upon it."[1] Then he added that, according to her detractors, she was "grasping, sordid, penurious, famishing for everything she sees—money, power, glory—vain, untruthful, jealous, despotic, arrogant, insolent, pitiless...illiterate, shallow, incapable of reasoning outside commercial lines, immeasurably selfish...." But, according to her followers, she was "patient, gentle, loving, compassionate, noble-hearted, unselfish, sinless, widely cultured, splendidly equipped mentally, a profound thinker, an able writer, a divine personage, an inspired messenger whose acts are dictated from the Throne, and whose every utterance is the Voice of God."[2]

She was indeed a strange complex. Even if her early writings were crude and sometimes ungrammatical, they burned with an insistent message. Even if many of her ideas were absorbed from others, we must recognize that no other woman in the history of religion has equaled her accomplishments. Repeatedly, key assistants rebelled; but she rose triumphant over every obstacle. Her proud spirit, which o'er-informed her fragile tenement of clay, never accepted defeat. Most of those who turned against her sank into obscurity; she had the vision and determination leading to ultimate victory. She conquered because she saw herself as the great hierophant; and, in due course, she found an audience which accepted her at her own valuation. As she clothed herself with the aura of Holy Writ, she used her servants to advance her gospel; and, rich or poor, rejected or invested with power, she was always a personage of regal mien and bearing.

II. CHRISTIAN SCIENCE LITERATURE

1. *Various Categories.* Several types of literature must be studied to obtain a comprehensive understanding of Christian Science: (1)

works offered by its Publishing Society which consist largely of Mrs. Eddy's works and her authorized biographies; (2) studies by objective scholars, such as Georgine Milmine, Edwin Franden Dakin, and Charles S. Braden; (3) critiques or denunciations which may be described as exposés, such as Mark Twain's book, Peabody's *Religio-Medical Masquerade*, and Powell's first biography called *Christian Science—The Faith and Its Founder*; (4) books by Scientists who remained loyal to Mrs. Eddy but parted company with the Mother Church, such as Augusta Stetson, Herbert Eustace, Alice Orgain, and Studdert-Kennedy; (5) treatises by ex-Scientists who rose in fury against the church and its founder also, such as Josephine Woodbury, Annie Bill, and John V. Dittemore; (6) expositions by mental healers who embraced the general principles of Mrs. Eddy's gospel, but rejected certain of its elements: among these are Ursula Gestefeld, Emma Curtis Hopkins, Margaret Laird, Frances Lord, Julius Dresser, George Quimby, Horatio W. Dresser, and many others, all of whom are regarded by Christian Scientists as adulterers of the divine Word; and (7) certain writings produced by the most reverential protagonists of the Church, but which it prefers to suppress: these include the early editions of *Science and Health*; early files of the *Journal of Christian Science*; Calvin Frye's *Diaries*; Samuel Putnam Bancroft's *Mrs. Eddy, As I Knew Her in 1870*; and, most of all, the *Memoirs of Mary Baker Eddy*, by Adam H. Dickey.

2. *Science and Health.* The first edition of this work was published in 1875, the second in 1878, and the third in 1881; copies of these became unavailable until reissued by the Rare Book Company. The fourth and fifth were reprints of the third; but the sixth through the fifteenth contained a number of significant changes. The sixteenth through the forty-ninth editions (1886-1891) reflect the skillful handiwork of the Reverend James Henry Wiggin. In 1906, the book attained its final form.

The Christian Science Publishing Society also distributes Mrs. Eddy's *Prose Works*, a compilation consisting of more than 1,300 pages; this ranks in importance and authority just below the Church *Manual* and *Science and Health* itself.

3. *Mark Twain.* Although his book is a biting satire, he gives Mrs. Eddy extravagant credit for accomplishments. He said that by 1930, there would be nearly 40 million Scientists in the United States and Great Britain alone[3]; that the cult would assume political control of

this country by 1940; that before long the Mother Church would be collecting vast revenues from 300 million members[4]; and that it would conquer one-half of Christendom within a century,[5] for the simple reason that more than four-fifths of all human ailments have no physical reality.

4. *A Monumental Work.* Georgine Milmine's *Life of Mary Baker Eddy and the History of Christian Science* is a vast mine of source material. About 1905, *McClure's Magazine* commissioned the author to write a series of articles; with a team of co-workers, she followed the trail of Mrs. Eddy from her earliest childhood, obtained affidavits from a great many persons who had known her personally, and transcribed a mass of documents and records, which throw a sharp light on Mrs. Eddy's activities over a period of more than 70 years.

5. *A Book for the Faithful.* Following the series in *McClure's*, the obscure periodical *Human Life* began the publication of very different material, intended as an antidote for the Milmine revelations. This *Life Story of Mary Baker Eddy* by Sibyl Wilbur, published in 1907, has been awarded canonical status by the Church. It was the first of several such books, highly regarded, and distributed by the Publishing Society.

6. *The Rector Who About-Faced.* Lyman P. Powell, an Episcopal clergyman, published *Christian Science, the Faith and Its Founder* in 1908, in which he described Milmine's investigations as of "singular accuracy."[6] In 1930, however, as a commission from the Church, he published *Mary Baker Eddy, a Life-Size Portrait*, in which she emerges as an incomparably unselfish, gentle, angelic, generous, beneficent, and self-sacrificing saint, who had merely overrated Quimby.[7]

7. *The Devastating Disciple.* Adam H. Dickey was Mrs. Eddy's closest confidant and advisor during the last three years of her life. Her last official act made him a director of the Mother Church; and in due course, he became Chairman of the Board. His naive and sincere *Memoirs of Mary Baker Eddy*, written as her last request and published in 1927 by his widow, two years after *his* death, was highly embarrassing to the Church Directors; and rare copies of the book have commanded fabulous prices.

8. *A Battle over a Book.* The publication by Scribners in 1930 of *Mary Baker Eddy: The Biography of a Virginal Mind*, by Edwin Franden Dakin, was, like the work of Milmine, supported by massive

documentation. Many newspapers refused paid advertising for it. However, it has passed through several printings and sold thousands of copies.

9. *The Time Bomb.* In 1932, Alfred Knopf published *Mary Baker Eddy, the Truth and the Tradition*, by John Valentine Dittemore and Ernest Sutherland Bates, who collaborated in giving the world another treasure-trove of source-material which the Church would like to suppress.

10. *A Kindly Critic and Scholar.* In 1958, Charles S. Braden published his well-documented *Christian Science Today: Power, Policy, and Practice*, which is now generally accepted outside the Christian Science denomination as a definitive work.

III. MARY BAKER EDDY HERSELF

1. *Forbears and Relatives.* Mary Morse Baker-Glover-Patterson-Eddy was born July 16, 1821, in Bow Township, near Concord, New Hampshire. Her father, the dominating Mark Baker, was a strict Congregationalist. She had three brothers and two sisters, all of whom became respected and conventional citizens.[8]

2. *The Dominating Child.* Even as a young girl, Mary induced the other members of her family to do her will. Opposition brought on hysterical, even catatonic, seizures[9]; and she became addicted to morphine, a curse which dogged her to the grave.[10]

3. *The Wedded Child and Her Infant.* And so Mary became a full-grown child, whose illiteracy is reflected in various letters published by Dittemore.[11] However, when it pleased her, she could exhibit a charming personality; and so it was that George Glover, a bluff young contractor, became so enamored that he married her on December 12, 1843, when she was twenty-two. She accompanied him to the South, where he died a few months later of yellow fever. Mary returned to her father's house, where her child, George, was born the following September.

4. *The Spiritualist.* Shortly before this time, the Shakers had practiced Spiritualism and it had achieved popular vogue as a result of the Fox sisters of Rochester, New York. It should, therefore, not be surprising that the volatile Mary Glover "developed the habit of falling into trances. Often, in the course of a social call, she would close her

eyes and sink into a state of apparent unconsciousness, during which she would describe scenes and events. The curious and superstitious began to seek her advice...." Frequent seances were held in Mark Baker's house.[12]

5.   *Little George and a Second Marriage.* When her mother died in 1849, Mary was nearly thirty. When her father remarried, George was about seven years old; two years later,[13] when Mahala Sanborn married Russell Cheney, the boy became a permanent member of their household.[14] At the age of thirteen, in 1857, George accompanied his foster parents to the West.[15] After Mary married Dr. Patterson, she faced the normal duties of housekeeper but if he dreamed that she, who was destined to dwell among the stars, would scrub floors or wash dishes, he was much mistaken. She required her husband "to keep the wooden bridge over the creek covered with sawdust to deaden the sound of footsteps or vehicles, and...he spent many evenings killing the discordant frogs, whose noise disturbed her."[16]

6.   *From Pillar to Post.* In March 1860, Dr. Patterson failed to meet the mortgage payment on the house[17] and eviction followed. Residing at a boarding house, and propped up amidst her pillows, Mary declared that she was suffering from a spinal affliction.[18] The harried dentist then escaped to the arena of the Civil War, where he hoped to gain federal employment; however, captured by the Confederates in 1862, he was confined in a prison-camp.[19] Penniless, Mary fell back on her long-suffering sister, Abigail, who was living in Tilton, New Hampshire.

7.   *Resurrection in Portland.* In the meantime, the fame of Phineas Parkhurst Quimby had been growing. On October 14, 1861, Dr. Patterson had written him that his wife had "been an invalid for a number of years, and is able to sit up but a little." On May 29, 1862, Mary wrote to Quimby herself[20] saying that she must die unless he could save her; and added that her sister was anxious that he should attend her. When she arrived at Quimby's office in October, she was assisted up the stairway and introduced to him by Julius Dresser.[21]

And now the supreme experience of Mary's life began: for it was achievement, rather than health, that she was seeking so compulsively. It seems that Quimby developed a distinct interest in this "devilish bright woman..."[22] Not only was she cured of her ailments: visions of new fields opened up before her, more attractive than Spiritualism. On

November 8, 1862, she published a long article in the Portland *Courier* in which she compared the healings of her benefactor to those of Christ: "the belief of my recovery had died...." she declared. "With this mental and physical depression I first visited P.P. Quimby; and in less that one week from that time I ascended by a stairway of one hundred and eighty-two steps to the dome of the City Hall, and am improving *ad infinitum*."[23] She explained that Quimby used neither Spiritualism nor animal magnetism, and: "now I can see dimly at first, and only as trees walking, the great principle which underlies Dr. Quimby's faith and works.... This truth which he opposes to the error of giving intelligence to matter...changes the currents of the system to their normal action; and the mechanism of the body goes on undisturbed. That this is a science capable of demonstrating becomes clear...."[24]

When the rival *Advertiser* ridiculed Quimby and his fervent disciple, she was moved to an even more explicit declaration: "P.P. Quimby stands upon the plane of wisdom with his truth...." He "heals...as never man healed since Christ...is not this the Christ which is in him...?" And she continued: "P.P. Quimby rolls away the stone from the sepulchre of error, and health is the resurrection."[25] Shortly thereafter the *Courier* printed a sonnet which Mary offered as a tribute to Quimby:

> "Mid light of science sits the sage profound
> Awing the classics with his starry lore,
> Climbing to Venus, chasing Saturn round,
> Turning his mystic pages o'er and o'er...."[26]

8. *A Prophetess Is Come!* Mrs. Patterson returned to Sanbornton Bridge in November 1862. Since her husband had escaped from the Confederate prison, sister Abigail fed and housed them both. But Mary was no longer the whining invalid; instead, she was filled with a burning mission to convert the world to Quimbyism. If the hypochondriac had been a nuisance, the flaming evangelist was even more intolerable to her sister. Anyone who doubts Mrs. Patterson's attitude toward Quimby during this period should read her letters—all fourteen of which are printed in the first edition of the *Quimby Manuscripts*, which, as a result of legal action by the Christian Science Church, may no longer be reproduced.[27]

Early in 1864, Mary returned to Portland, where she spent ten or twelve weeks studying Quimby's methods with avidity.

9.   *A Husband Escapes.* In June 1864, Mary returned to her husband in Lynn, Massachusetts, where, it seems, he had at last come to the end of his matrimonial journey. He agreed to pay his estranged wife $200 annually—which he did for a number of years.[28]

From August 1864 to the fall of 1865, Mary lived again with her sister; but now there could be no peace unless everyone accepted her new gospel of health and happiness as expounded by Dr. P.P. Quimby. After a violent scene, Abigail slammed the door in Mary's face and left orders that she must never again be admitted to the house.[29]

10.   *The Death of the Teacher.* Dr. Quimby died January 16, 1866; and Mary published a poem in the Lynn newspaper which concluded:

> "Rest should reward him who hath made us whole,
> Seeking, though tremblers, where his footsteps trod."[30]

11.   *The Great Fall.* Two weeks later, an event occurred which then had little significance, but which in time was to be invested with epochal importance. On February 1, Mrs. Patterson fell on the ice, was taken to a nearby house, treated by Dr. Cushing, and removed the next day to her own rooms. According to the official version, her case was beyond the reach of medical science,[31] but she suddenly recovered completely on the third day while reading Matt. 9:2-7: "in that hour," we are told, she "received a revelation for which she had been preparing her heart in every event of her life."[32] Rising from her bed, says Beasley,[33] she astonished the people of the household, who had already sent for a minister to console her in her final hour. Years later, the attending physician, who still retained his clinical notes, signed an affidavit declaring that the accident was not serious.[34]

12.   *Refuge at Last!* In June 1866 began a period of tragic wandering.[35] However, Mary found a home with a seamstress, Mrs. Sarah Bagley, whom she instructed in the Quimby science.[36] Wherever she went, she assumed her place as the guest of honor.[37] In the fall of 1868, she moved to Stoughton, where she taught her science to Mrs. Sally Wentworth for a fee of $300; the teaching was based on a document, copied by the pupil and almost identical to the chapter in the *Quimby Manuscripts* called "Questions and Answers." However, before very long, she was forced to seek shelter elsewhere.[38]

IV. THE GENESIS OF THE CHRISTIAN SCIENCE MOVEMENT

1. *Science Established.* Mrs. Patterson then returned to Mrs. Sarah Bagley in Amesbury,[39] where she met a bright and interesting young man, Richard Kennedy, then eighteen. He showed such a lively understanding of the new science that he became a potential partner. In 1870, these two rented quarters from a Miss Magoun in Lynn, where Kennedy became the first Christian Science practitioner and the science of mental healing emerged as a going concern.[40] He received patients in his office, while Mrs. Patterson met her classes and worked on her manuscript on the second floor. He agreed to give her half of his gross income and pay *all* expenses from his share.[41] He channeled many applicants into her three-week course: each paid $100 for twelve lessons, and agreed to pay her ten per cent of all professional earnings *for life.*

Mary then raised her fee to $300. In two years, her bank account swelled from almost nothing to $6,000.[42] As students flowered into practitioners, they went forth to spread the gospel of Health and Happiness, and Mary Patterson became a personage, having already accomplished something that neither Quimby nor Evans ever achieved. However, one student, Wallace Wright, publicly challenged her to demonstrate that she could raise the dead, walk on water in her bare feet, heal broken bones without artificial means, live twenty-four hours without air, and abstain from food for twenty-four days without ill effects.[43]

2. *Exit Kennedy.* Friction had gradually developed in the Patterson-Kennedy operation because of their inequitable contract. On Thanksgiving Day in 1871, he threw his contract into the fire; Mary begged and threatened, but from that moment he was through with her; and he set up his own practice, in which he was quite successful.[44]

3. *Battling Upward Again.* Since recruits to Mrs. Patterson's classes no longer were available from Kennedy's labors, she was forced to give up the accommodations at Miss Magoun's. Nevertheless, she gradually made new contacts; and on March 31, 1875, she bought the house, now a Christian Science shrine, at 8 Broad Street in Lynn for $5,650, assuming a mortgage of $2,800. She rented out the first floor, conducted classes on the second, and used a small cubicle on the third

as a study; here she read proofs for the first edition of *Science and Health* and prepared the second and third.[45]

At last the great opus was ready for publication; only money was lacking. She therefore induced two of her students, George W. Barry and Elizabeth Newhall, to advance $1,500 for this purpose.[46] As Mary tasted the first fruits of success, Quimby gradually faded from her consciousness; her book contains only a single, patronizing reference to him.[47] At that time, she made no claims to revelation or divine authority; nevertheless, her sentences reverberate with the echoes of a prophet of Yahweh.

Mary's brainchild, published in 1875, was stillborn; it was not her book, but her students and practitioners who made Christian Science successful. A man named Spofford, who had helped in the preparation of the book, finally achieved some success by spending $500 of his own money for publicity and forsaking his own lucrative business[48] to give full time to this effort without personal compensation.

4.   *A Church!* On July 4, 1876, her students organized as the Association of Christian Scientists; and on May 16, 1878, these disciples arranged that Mary Baker Patterson would preach to them.[49] Eight of these pledged various sums for one year, ranging from fifty cents to two dollars weekly and totalling ten dollars for the support of their instructor. The first meeting was attended by about sixty people.[50]

On August 6, 1879, the Church of Christ (Scientist) applied for a charter, which was granted on August 23. During the first sixteen months, Sunday services, sometimes attended by only four or five persons, were held at the homes of members. Meanwhile Clara Choate conducted meetings in Boston and Christian Science had become a going concern.

V. WARFARE, REBELLION, AND M.A.M.

1.   *Enter Eros.* And now a strange development occurred. Mrs. Patterson wished to marry Spofford or at least wanted him free from his marital bonds: he therefore brought suit to divorce his wife, which was denied.[51] Thereupon Mary, quite suddenly, informed one of her students, Asa Gilbert Eddy, whom Spofford had introduced to her,

that she would marry him, and this obedient, unassuming individual became her husband on January 1, 1877.[52]

2. *Failure*. When the abortive second edition, consisting of 500 copies with 167 pages, was completed in 1878, Mrs. Eddy was unable to obtain the money to pay for it from her students; and since she refused to use her own, the printer simply destroyed the stock rather than let her have it without the payment. In the meantime, Spofford refused to supply any more money or free work and was expelled.

As complete failure stared her in the face, Mrs. Eddy became convinced that her enemies were projecting into the atmosphere streams of evil which ruined her students and caused general devastation. This she called Malicious Animal Magnetism, or M.A.M.

3. *Sedition in Lynn*. In 1881, the third edition of *Science and Health* saw the light; the publisher was listed as Asa G. Eddy. It consisted of two volumes and 484 pages; it bristled with demonology, the name given Chapter VI, in which Kennedy and Spofford were bitterly excoriated. By this time, a man named Arens, another ex-student, had also become anathema because he accused Mrs. Eddy of taking her ideas from Quimby.

However, after eleven years, Mrs. Eddy's M.A.M. and other notoriety had created such disillusionment among her students that eight of the most prominent, including Dorcas Brown and Miranda Rice, resigned on October 22, 1881.[53] This was a crushing defeat.

4. *In the Hub*. Before this debacle, however, Mrs. Eddy's practitioners had struck root in New York, Cincinnati, Philadelphia, and especially in Boston, where Mrs. Clara Choate had established a steadily paying clientele. The Massachusetts Metaphysical College, empowered to grant medical degrees, was chartered on January 31, 1881, while the Eddys were still in Lynn. In April 1882 they removed to Boston, and leased for $1,000 a year a building at 569 Columbus Avenue, which housed the College until its dissolution.[54]

5. *The Death of Mr. Eddy*. As Mr. Eddy declined in health, his wife was persuaded that Arens had exercised "Mesmeric influence" upon him, which she called "arsenical poison, mentally administered."[55] However, she soon found a replacement for her docile husband in the person of Calvin Frye, who served her in various capacities with a certain proud but loyal servility until her death nearly thirty years later.

VI. THE CONSOLIDATION OF CHRISTIAN SCIENCE

1. *A Feminist Success.* Christian Science became a success when it was able to reach isolated individuals scattered across the country, as it could with a publication and a central headquarters. Settling in Boston was, therefore, the great turning point in Mrs. Eddy's career; as faithful practitioners sent her students who graduated from her College, the cult began to spread rapidly. In addition to Mrs. Choate, other leaders of ability emerged, including Arthur Buswell, Julia Bartlett, Hanover P. Smith, Emma Curtis Hopkins, Josephine Woodbury, and Augusta Stetson.

Whatever else Christian Science may have been, it was definitely a part of the feminist movement then sweeping the nation. The Shakers and Dr. Quimby had proclaimed the superiority of women; and Christian Science proclaimed their rights and priority in the most emphatic terms.

Every city, town, and hamlet had its quota of frustrated spinsters, many of whom were hypochondriacs with little income or property, who ate the bitter bread of charity, or who were infested with countless pains and mysterious maladies. Exploiting this bonanza, Christian Science grew by leaps and bounds. Over the years, statistics show that the great majority of Christian Science members and practitioners have been women.

2. *The Great College.* The Massachusetts Metaphysical College began its operations in 1882. Mrs. Eddy declared that she taught more than 4,000 students there. In 1932, however, Dittemore published the complete roster[56]; a total of 532 had taken the primary course, of whom 370 were women. The number of students increased from 29 in three classes in 1882 to 68 in a single class in 1889, which was also the last. Of the 162 men, more than half received free tuition, including Edward A. Kimball, Ira O. Knapp, Joseph Armstrong, Erastus N. Bates, Alfred Farlow, William Nixon, and James Henry Wiggin, all of whom testified to the magnetic personality of their teacher. Even allowing for the free tuitions, the total income was probably about $200,000 in seven years, which, after all, undoubtedly made Mrs. Eddy the best-paid teacher who, at that time, had ever lived on this planet.

The College, chartered under an act of 1874, was soon in danger of losing its license. Fear of legal restriction, however, was not the only reason for closing this highly lucrative undertaking. Mrs. Eddy had an uncanny sense of timing; her strength was waning; and it was becoming necessary to conceal her physical ailments from her disciples and the public. She must also have sensed that her power was greatest over those with whom she did not long continue in personal contact: since she now had two or three hundred successful practitioners—many conducting their own classes or institutes—an ample number of new healers were being prepared; and she knew that the time had come for her to become a mysterious, almost inaccessible divinity. Finally, the golden stream, now accruing from her publications and other commerce, reduced to insignificance the money she could obtain by giving seven lectures in a few days. Thus it was that, after 1889, she ruled her empire *by remote control.*

3. *The Instructor Turns Editor.* After establishing her College, Mrs. Eddy's second stroke of genius consisted in the creation of her bi-monthly eight page *Journal of Christian Science,* the first issue of which was dated April 14, 1883. It carried the names of her practitioners and included testimonials of remarkable healings. At first the circulation was very small; but soon "copies found their way to remote villages...where people had much time for reflection, little excitement, and a great need to believe in miracles.... Mrs. Eddy and Christian Science began to be talked of far away.... Lonely and discouraged people brooded over these editorials which promised happiness to sorrow and success to failure. The desperately ill had no quarrel with the artificial rhetoric of these testimonials in which people declared that they had been snatched from the brink of the grave."[57]

4. *Another Defector.* On December 27, 1883, Emma Curtis Hopkins had enrolled in Mrs. Eddy's primary course. Residing among the elite at 569 Columbus Avenue, she became editor of the *Journal* in June 1884. Under her direction, it was greatly enlarged, vastly improved, made into a monthly, and, in April 1885, renamed the *Christian Science Journal.* After two years, however, she turned her back on Mrs. Eddy and became a part of that wider and freer movement known as New Thought.

5. *A Faithful but Cynical Servant.* Since Mrs. Eddy's vocabulary, grammar, diction, repetitiousness, and artificial style were the butt of widespread ridicule, her acumen was again demonstrated when she engaged the services of a sybaritic dramatic critic in 1885, the Reverend James H. Wiggin, a Unitarian minister-turned-literary-entrepreneur, whose belief was a species of agnostic skepticism which,

among much else, denied the historicity of Jesus. He laughed inwardly at Mrs. Eddy's cryptic prose, but he had a profound respect for her financial astuteness; and he performed faithfully the literary task for which she paid him a reported $40,000. She insisted that, in rewriting her prose, he leave the thought intact, which he did.

Beginning in 1886, with its Wigginite polish, *Science and Health* became a best seller. Before that date, some 15,000 copies had been printed; but by 1895, the total was 95,000; and by 1901, 211,000; by 1904, 300,000; and by 1906, "over four hundred thousand...."[58] Practitioners and loyal scientists were urged to purchase copies of every new edition, each of which consisted of 1,000 copies.

5.   *The Boston Church.* As early as 1878, Mrs. Eddy appeared in Boston, where she addressed small audiences on Sunday afternoon in the Baptist Tabernacle on Shawmut Avenue. In 1879, the services were moved to the Parker Fraternity Building on Appleton Street.[59] In December 1880, the congregation moved to Hawthorne Hall on Park Street. By June 1884, there were sixty-one members in addition to a periphery of interested people.[60] In order to meet future needs, a site was purchased on Falmouth Street in the Back Bay area in 1885; a cash payment of $2,000 left a mortgage of $8,763.50, which, by December 1888, had been reduced to $4,963.50.[61] The financial transactions by which Mrs. Eddy obtained personal title to this property reflect her canny foresight.[62]

VII. REVOLT, HERESY, AND AUTOCRACY

1.   *Rebellion in Boston.* However, Mrs. Eddy's rigid rule, her claims to divinity, and her reputation for greed and self-glorification became intolerable to some of her followers. "Worse than all else was the everlasting M.A.M., which exerted its pervasive and sinister influence...."[63]

On June 6, 1888, there was a stormy congregational meeting in which Mrs. Eddy was denounced. But, since she was attending the National Association Convention in Chicago, she could not deal with the sedition until her return. Most of the insurgents wished only to part with her forever. But, since the by-laws provided that anyone who withdrew broke his oath and was guilty of immorality, this was not easy. By a stratagem, however, thirty-five of the dissenters obtained possession of the Church records, which were returned only when the defectors received honorable letters of dismissal. When the loyal Boston following was thus reduced from 200 to 14, Mrs. Eddy made elaborate plans to prevent the recurrence of such a disaster.[64]

2. *The War on Heresy.* At this time, Mrs. Eddy began her attack against deviationist literature emanating from a group of extremely capable healers and writers who had developed around the Quimby-Evans-Dresser school and who included several of Mrs. Eddy's most gifted former students, such as Kennedy, Ursula Gestefeld, Frances Lord, and Emma C. Hopkins whose *Scientific Christian Mental Practice* is still a New Thought classic. All of these were teaching, healing, and publishing pamphlets, books, and periodicals precisely as if Mrs. Eddy did not exist. All repudiated autocracy, rejected M.A.M., and denied all claim to unique revelation or divine authority. Frances Lord's *Christian Science Healing* may still be found in second-hand bookstores. Mrs. Gestefeld had been a student in the class of 1884; in 1888, she published *A Statement of Christian Science*, a lucid presentation of Mrs. Eddy's basic theories; but, since it deleted M.A.M. and omitted all reference to her as the Second Christ, Mrs. Gestefeld was expelled from the Chicago church as a Mesmerist. When she countered with her *Jesuitism in Christian Science*, she became, not only another diabolist, but also another influential worker in New Thought.[65]

Mrs. Eddy lived in constant terror that her followers might draw inspiration from sources other than herself; she therefore decreed in the twenty-second *Manual* that her students must not "buy, sell, nor circulate Christian Science literature which is not thoroughly correct..." (now Section 11, Art. VIII). Christian Scientists are forbidden to read works antagonistic to their faith.[66] They need no publications except the Bible and those offered by the Publishing Society; the *Monitor* even eliminates the need for a local daily newspaper.

3. *The Affluent Autocrat.* In 1889, Mrs. Eddy moved to Concord, where she purchased and renovated an estate called Pleasant View, and there she concentrated on the consolidation of her organization. She also established "Seven Fixed Rules" by which she made herself virtually inaccessible.[67]

4. *The Mother Church.* On September 23, 1892, the First Church of Christ, Scientist, reorganized with twelve First Members and Mary Baker Eddy as Pastor Emeritus; by-laws were also adopted which made her the supreme and perpetual ruler.[68]

Thus the Mother Church, the First Church of Christ, Scientist, was founded. It was to be owned and ruled by four (after 1902, five) Directors, who, in turn, were to be ruled by Mrs. Eddy throughout her lifetime, and thereafter by her *Manual*. A few years later, Mrs. Eddy purchased the Christian Science Publishing Society for $1.00, and, by another deed of trust dated January 25, 1898, gave it to a corporation ruled by three trustees under provisions similar to those which gave her control of the Mother Church.

VIII. THE WAR AGAINST CHRISTIAN SCIENCE

1.   *The Ironic Wit.* Between 1899 and 1902-03, Mark Twain published a series of articles in the *Cosmopolitan* and another in the *North American Review*. These were combined in *Christian Science*, published in 1907. The author's trenchant wit ridiculed Mrs. Eddy's claims to divine revelation. Thereupon, she renounced the title of Mother in the twenty-ninth edition of the *Manual*; and wrote in the New York *Herald*: "I believe in one Christ, teach one only Christ, know of but one Christ. I believe in but one incarnation, one Mother Mary. I know I am not that one and I have never claimed to be...."[69]

2.   *The Heavy Artillery.* By 1907, the attacks upon Christian Science and Mrs. Eddy were coming thick and fast. Peabody followed his pamphlet *The Complete Exposure of Christian Science* with his pitiless book, *The Religio-Medical Masquerade*; and the old-line ministers as well as the medical establishment took up the cudgels.

In the midst of these diatribes, *McClure's Magazine* commissioned Georgine Milmine and a team of investigators to prepare an objective study, which was published in a series of articles in 1907-08 and released in book form by Doubleday in 1909.

IX. THE HIEROPHANT OF CHESTNUT HILL

1.   *Removal to Boston.* Believing that her house at Pleasant View was infested with M.A.M., Mrs. Eddy ordered her trustees to find her a more suitable retreat. They found a mansion in the Boston suburb of Chestnut Hill, which was purchased for $100,000, and on which a similar sum was spent for improvements.[70]

2.   *The Monitor.* On August 8, 1908, Mrs. Eddy ordered her pub-

lishing society to establish the *Christian Science Monitor*, which would not carry news dealing with crime, corruption, or scandals, but would meet the secular needs of scientists and appeal to the world at large.

After only twenty-seven months as the occupant of the great mansion on Chestnut Hill, she surrendered her restless spirit on December 3, 1910. Her body found its final resting place in a grave on the shores of Halcyon Lake.[71]

4. *The Revenge of Calvin Frye*. During his many years of faithful service, Frye kept a diary in shorthand, which, upon his death, came into the possession of a disillusioned ex-scientist named John V. Dittemore[72] and which contained information highly embarrassing to the Church, including the fact that Mary had been receiving both medical and dental service regularly; that she had been subject to epileptic seizures; and had, for many years, been a narcotics addict.[73] Mrs. Eddy herself admitted that she had used morphine since childhood.[74]

5. *The Incredible Adam H. Dickey*. Mrs. Eddy's last official act was to make Adam H. Dickey a director of the Mother Church. With naive devotion, he had served as a member of her household and had become her closest confidant. When he died in 1925, he was Chairman of the Board. In 1908, he had promised that he would publish a history concerning her death.[75] He wrote and his widow published the small volume called *The Memoirs of Mary Baker Eddy*, which the Church has attempted to suppress.

X. QUIMBY AND MARY BAKER EDDY

1. *The Genesis of New Thought*. Those who defected in 1888 all believed with Mrs. Eddy in certain metaphysical principles; but they rejected her M.A.M. and her claims to revelation. They joined forces in the general New Thought movement; all were individualists who traced their techniques rather to Quimby and Warren Felt Evans.

2. *The Divided Stream*. Christian Science and New Thought, therefore, even before 1900, had split into two streams, both of which believed in the supremacy of mind over matter. However, the defectors denied that matter is without objective reality or existence; or that sin, disease, and death are simply mythical errors of mortal mind.

3. *The Great Fall*. In the first edition of *Science and Health*, the

accidental fall in Lynn is simply cited as one of the hundreds of cures beyond the reach of *materia medica*, but accomplished by divine science.[76] However, in 1881, Mrs. Eddy declared that the accident would have been fatal except for a miraculous cure.[77] In the edition of *Science and Health* in 1886, we find a new version; as a result of the healing, she arose from her bed and by this means discovered metaphysical healing and called it Christian Science. Thus 1866 became the Year of the Great Discovery.[78]

4.   *The Great Controversy.* After Arens charged Mrs. Eddy with plagiarizing her ideas from Quimby, her attitude toward her once-revered mentor became one of hostile condescension; she admitted that the "old gentleman" had some advanced views about healing, but was neither religious nor scholarly. She said that she had left some of her own writings with him; and that the only work of his that she ever saw was one of perhaps twelve pages, most of which she had herself composed. Since he used manipulation, his method was physical and not mental.[79]

Beginning in 1883, a great controversy began between Mrs. Eddy and Julius Dresser and his wife Annetta. On February 6, 1887, he delivered a lecture entitled *The True History of Mental Science*, in which he quoted several of Mrs. Patterson's effusive declarations concerning Quimby, including some of her letters to him.[80] When she turned to Wiggin, asking what she should do, and when she admitted writing this material, he remarked tersely that there was nothing more to be said.[81]

5.   *The First Important Quimby Publication.* In 1895 Annetta, now the widow of Julius Dresser, published the 114-page *Philosophy of P.P. Quimby*, which reproduced extensive selections from his essays.

6.   *The Official Position.* The official version concerning Mrs. Patterson's tributes to Quimby was, in the words of Lyman P. Powell in his second biography of Mrs. Eddy, that she overrated "in a grateful woman's way what she owed to Quimby...."[82]

XI. THE EVOLUTION AND STRENGTH OF CHRISTIAN SCIENCE

The *Manual* (Sec. 28, Art. VIII) decrees that no report for publication shall be made of the number of Church members. However, such statistics were supplied to the Federal Government for 1906, 1916, 1926, and 1936 to be used in the Census of Religious Bodies. Other statistics in the following tables are taken from the *Christian Science Journal.*

EARLY CHRISTIAN SCIENCE
MEMBERSHIP AND ORGANIZATION

Year	1893	1899	1901	1902	1906	1908
Members, MotherChurch	1,545	16,000	21,631	24,278	40,011	43,000
Number, Branch Churches				682		
Number, Societies				267		
Members of 614 Churches				41,944		
Estimated Total Members				50,000		

We have also the *Christian Science Journal*, which lists churches, societies, teachers, and practitioners. In 1926, there were 1,206 sanctuaries; in 1936, there were 1,600.

CHRISTIAN SCIENCE MEMBERSHIP
IN THE UNITED STATES

1906	Mother Church Members (counted twice)	85,717
	Total of different members (census estimate)	65,717
	The probably correct estimate	50,000
1926		202,298
1936		268,915

PRACTITIONERS, TEACHERS, CHURCHES, AND SOCIETIES

Year	Pract. & Teachers in World	In World		Churches and Societies In United States			Abroad		
	World	Total	Chs.	Socs.	Total	Chs.	Socs.	Total	Chs.	Socs.
1906						638				
1906		949	682	267						
1916	5,660	1,505	845	720	1,388	759	629	177	86	91
1927	9,293	1,944	2,372	572	1,665	1,210	459	279	162	117
1936					2,112					
1936	11,165	2,740	1,687	1,053	2,164	1,383	781	576	304	272
1946	11,123	2,744	1,804	940	2,148	1,473	675	596	334	265
1956	9,769	3,112	2,114	998	2,366	1,706	660	746	408	338
1966	7,919	3,136	2,233	903	2,366	1,809	587	770	424	346
1976	6,200	2,991	2,441	750	2,252	1,787	465	739	454	285
1980	5,592	2,876	2,164	713	2,145	1,708	437	731	451	275
1982	4,664	2,745	2,042	703	2,077	1,627	450	668	415	253
1986	4,476	2,723	2,036	687	1,945	1,544	412	767	492	275

The Peak is Passed. It is obvious that, had Christian Science continued to expand at its early rate, it would today have become a major religious denomination. Between 1906 and 1936, its churches and societies quadrupled; had this continued until the present time, there would now be about 20,000 congregations with perhaps 4 or 5 million members. Instead, they have actually declined in number since 1936 in the United States, while the population has doubled.

Lest anyone conclude however, that the Mother Church has suffered any serious diminution of wealth, we suggest that he visit the magnificent complex in Boston which comprises the national headquarters and which has been enhanced by the addition of a splendid high-rise office building, completed a few years ago, at a cost of $82 million.

According to the statistics in the previous tables, the average Christian Science congregation in 1906 had 53 members; in 1925-27, 110; in 1936, 125.

Since it is a cult of healing, the number of active practitioners is the most reliable index to growth or decline. The total of these grew proportionately with congregations from 3,280 in 1911 to 11,166 in 1936, but dropped to 9,769 in 1956, in 6,200 in 1975, and 4,476 in 1986. The number of churches in the U.S. declined from 1,809 in 1966 to 1,544 in 1986.

We believe that the rigid control of the Mother Church is a serious deterrent to growth. We believe also that another factor is very important: namely the extraordinary growth and expansion of other New Thought organizations. The religion of health and happiness has not diminished; on the contrary, it has increased rapidly. But the growth has occurred entirely among the freer communions, led by people who hearken back to Swedenborg, Evans, Quimby, Dresser, and others, and may now embrace fully a half million adherents, in addition to millions of others who have been influenced directly or indirectly.

XII. THE SUCCESSIVE EDITIONS OF *SCIENCE AND HEALTH*

1. *The Eddy Cycle*. Probably no other work in religious history has undergone such a long and constant evolution under the control of a single individual as *Science and Health*. The first edition is certainly

closer to Quimby than its immediate successors; yet it embodies the ultimate Christology, therapeutics, and metaphysical concepts of mature Christian Science. There were a number of revisions in the third edition.

2. *The Wiggin Handiwork*. Beginning with the sixteenth edition, in 1886, we have a basic development: here, God becomes the Mother-Father deity; the entire work is a revelation; and Mrs. Eddy, at least by implication, is the Woman of the Apocalypse. Furthermore, the name Christian Science is found on almost every page, which indicates that, as Quimby receded in time, much of his influence actually became more prevalent.

This edition is deeply tinged with the handiwork of the skillful agnostic, James Henry Wiggin, who was true to his trust: he did not alter ideas—he merely clothed them in a more felicitous garb. When Mrs. Eddy engaged him she wanted a crash program for her revision; but he found it necessary "to begin absolutely at the first page and rewrite the whole thing!" Which, as he concluded later, "was the very thing she had intended that I should do in the first place."[83]

To realize what Dr. Wiggin did, it is only necessary to compare almost any passage in the fifteenth and sixteenth editions:

Fifteenth Edition, II, 1, 1885	Sixteenth Edition, 234, 1886
Phenomena not understood surround us, every day is a mystery, while we are pecking our shells to learn somewhat of our surroundings and to enter the laboratory of the real.	Mortal life is an enigma. Every day is a mystery. The testimony of the senses cannot inform us what is reality and what is delusion; but the revelations of Science unlock the treasures of truth.

In the sixteenth edition, the word *Wayshower* appears for the first time as a name for Jesus.[84] Thereafter, it became one of Mrs. Eddy's favorite appellations for him. It is found several times in the final version of *Science and Health*[85]; it occurs twelve times in her *Prose Works*; and one of her most popular hymns is called "Shepherd, Show Me How to Go."

Wiggin began his revision in 1886 and continued to revise until the virtually definitive edition appeared in 1891 as the fiftieth. Here we find that an all-pervasive internal transformation has occurred. It is no longer possible to follow the text by juxtaposing it with previous editions: for not only has almost every sentence and paragraph been again rewritten, the material itself has been completely rearranged.

In 1891, Mrs. Eddy parted company with Mr. Wiggin, charging him with the "most shocking flippancy."[86] However, we can be sure that his services were terminated because his work had been completed. The final version of *Science and Health* was a reality.

Part II: DOCTRINE AND PRACTICE

I. THEOLOGICAL DOCTRINES

While most of Mrs. Eddy's doctrines remained substantially unchanged, portions of her system underwent a basic evolution. Her Christology, and her theories concerning sickness, health, therapy, sex, eschatology, and soteriology belong in the first category; but her persuasions concerning deity, revelation, personal apotheosis, and demonic obsessions belong to the latter.

In Christian Science, as in New Thought in general, God is not a person, but a Principle. All theories of a personal God must now yield to science.[87] God is infinite, the only life, substance, Spirit, or Soul, the only Intelligence in the universe, including man. In place of the tripersonal God, Christian Science offers a triune Principle called Life, Truth, and Love.[88] Thus "God...is a trinity in unity, not three persons in one, but three statements of one principle."[89]

This impersonal power constitutes the law, intelligence, vitality, and the spiritual substance of the cosmos. Prayers cannot influence him;[90] they cannot cancel sin.[91] If prayer should seem to overcome disease, this is only one false belief casting out another.[92]

About the year 1885, Mrs. Eddy absorbed the ancient Gnostic and modern Shaker-Evans concept of the Father-Mother God. According to this, the "true man and true woman, the all-harmonious 'male and female'" are of "spiritual origin, God's reflection," and the "children of one common parent"[93] who is "all-wise, all-knowing, all-loving...."[94] In Mrs. Eddy's system, as "applied to Deity, Father and Mother are synonymous terms; they signify one god. Father, Son, and Holy Ghost mean God, man and divine Science"[95] and constitute "our Father-Mother God."[96]

Mrs. Eddy's Christology is similar to an ancient Gnostic one which held that Jesus was born in the ordinary manner but was endowed with the Christ-Spirit at his baptism. The Great Exemplar, Teacher, or Instructor were appellations commonly used. "Jesus was the son of Mary," declared Mrs. Eddy, "but the Christ-Jesus represented...a spiritual, divine emanation...."[97]

In healing the sick by divine science, Jesus accomplished his first great demonstration; rising from the grave with the same body as before was his second[98]; and his ascent into the celestial realms and sending the Comforter, which has now appeared as divine Science, constitutes his third and supreme demonstration.[99] Jesus, we read, "was the most scientific man on record" or that ever trod the globe[100]; he was therefore able to achieve in his own life what will be possible for all humanity after the complete victory of Christian Science.

Like Quimby, Swedenborg, Evans, and some others, Christian Science repudiates the central dogmas of orthodox Christianity, namely, that by his death Christ-Jesus accomplished a sacrificial and vicarious atonement for humanity, otherwise damned in original sin. Worthy only of contempt are those who believe they can reach perfection and immortality through the sacrifice and suffering of another.[101] For God to vent his wrath on his only son, is neither humane nor logical and only a man-made belief.[102] Jesus never ransomed man by paying the debt which sin incurs, for whosoever sins must suffer.[103] No one may be pardoned from sin by a substitute.[104] Every dereliction must meet its own retribution, and restitution must precede forgiveness.[105]

"It was not to appease the wrath of God, but to show the allness of Love and the nothingness of hate, sin, and death that Jesus suffered.... The at-one-ment with Christ has appeared—not through vicarious suffering, whereby the unjust obtain pardon from the just—but through the eternal law of justice; wherein sinners suffer for their own sins, repent, forsake sin, love God, and keep his commandments, thence to receive the reward of righteousness: salvation from sin, not through the *death* of a man, but through a divine *Life*, which is our Redeemer."[106]

II. MATTER, SUBSTANCE, AND REALITY

1. *A Study in Semantics.* Mrs. Eddy, who seems never fully to have understood the philosophy of Quimby and Swedenborg concern-

ing matter, concluded that it and even the cosmos have no actual existence. In her early writings, she declared categorically "that all is mind and there is no matter."[107] Substance, she said, "is eternal, and incapable of discord or decay. Truth, Life, and Love are substance.... Spirit is substance, Soul is substance, and man is shadow. God is substance, and the universe is shadow."[108] Furthermore, "If God is Spirit, and God is all, surely there can be no matter; for the divine All must be Spirit."[109]

Beginning with the fiftieth edition of *Science and Health*, however, perhaps under the influence of Wiggin, similar declarations are less absolute; nevertheless, the original implications remain. We are told that if matter is substance, then spirit is not the only creator[110] and that Christian Scientists regard substance as Spirit, while opponents believe that it is matter.[111]

2. *The Spiritualization of Man.* Since God is All and Spirit, sin, disease, and death are only a suppositional absence of life[112]; and growth into spiritual immortality "will be rapid, if you love good supremely, and understand and obey the Wayshower, who, going before you, has scaled the steep ascent of Christian Science, stands upon the mount of holiness...and bathes in the baptismal font of eternal love."[113]

3. *Physical Impressions.* Since spirit is the only reality and matter has no objective existence, it follows that impressions gained through the material media are erroneous. "Sickness, or sensation in matter...is an illusion..." in which "the sick are like the insane...."[114] Since the evils of existence come from the physical senses, neither pain nor pleasure can exist in matter.[115] And since sensations come through the mind, they belong to the soul. The five senses are only beliefs, the source of error and discord.[116]

Since health is a condition of mind and not of matter, the senses cannot be trusted.[117] And since matter can neither suffer nor enjoy, it has no relationship with pain or pleasure.[118] It therefore follows that the nerves cannot feel, the brain think or the stomach make a man cross; neither can limbs cripple him nor matter kill.[119] That the body can suffer from heat, cold, or fatigue is only a false belief.[120] To transform each of these into its opposite, it is only necessary for anyone to change his opinion concerning them.[121] The arm of the blacksmith grows strong only because he believes that exercise will make it so.[122]

Thus man requires meat and bread only because of his delusions[123]; when first created, man's life was self-sustaining.[124] Food neither helps nor harms[125]; there is only false evidence that it is necessary to sustain life.[126] Eating never made a man live nor has abstention from it ever caused death.[127]

Since mind is everything, so-called matter is nothing. The human being and (mortal) mind are only myths. Since the body does not really exist, it never lives or dies[128]; and since man is immortal, he can never undergo death.[129] It necessarily follows, therefore, that mind controls the physical body. One man died of cholera because he imagined himself infected with it.[130] A cold apple can burn the hand if it is believed to be hot[131]; a Mesmerist can cause a blister to rise and then to disappear.[132] A woman who became insane at twenty-one never aged thereafter during half a century because she thought she was still young.[133]

We should note, however, that very few Scientists today actually believe all this.

In Christian Science, as in New Thought generally, heaven is not a locality[134]; it is, instead, a state or condition, "the reign of divine Science...a mental state."[135] Man does not die when the body becomes lifeless, because life was never in the body.[136] "Waking from the dream of death proves to him who thought he had died that it was a dream and that he did not die...."[137] After the change or transition, man does not lose his identity; his mind remains "still in a conscious state of existence...."[138]

According to Mrs. Eddy, there is no final judgment.[139] The ultimate fate of each and every man will be determined by his or her progress here and in the evolution that will follow; either each will rise from sense to soul or degenerate into nothingness. Once the change has occurred, "the departed...progress according to their fitness to partake of...heaven."[140] Those who have advanced on earth, "awake from a sense of death to a sense of Life in Christ...because their lives have grown so far...that they are ready for a spiritual transfiguration...."[141]

III. SEX, MARRIAGE, AND GENERATION

"Man and woman," declares Mrs. Eddy in her early writings, "were created by God and not by a union of the sexes...."[142] Such false beliefs are strongest among those who have the most material natures.[143] Bees and butterflies propagate without a male element[144]; various animals multiply without sexual conditions.[145] Many organisms reproduce by means of eggs, buds, and self-division. In the beginning, crops grew without seed.[146]

There can be little doubt that Christian Science in its attitude toward sex is basically ascetic. Marriage, we are told, is *not* better than celibacy[147]; in fact, it is "synonymous with legalized lust...."[148] If "the wife esteems not" the privilege of becoming a mother, she may, "by mutual consent," gain more "exalted and increased affection...."[149] The words of Matthew, she wrote tersely, which say that it is good not to marry, have a "special application for Christian Scientists...."[150] Nevertheless, and again bowing to expediency, she declared: "Until time matures human growth, marriage and progeny will continue unprohibited in Christian Science."[151]

"We look to future generations," she declared, "for ability to comply with absolute Science, when marriage shall be found to be man's oneness with God...."[152] And the day will come when masculine Wisdom and feminine Love will generate the race without the necessity of sexual union.[153]

The chapter on Marriage in the first edition of *Science and Health* closes with the Scriptural passage from Luke (20:35) upon which the ancient Gnostics and the modern Shakers based their mandatory celibacy.

IV. MORTAL MIND AND MALICIOUS ANIMAL MAGNETISM

1.   *Mortal Mind.* Quite exclusive with Mrs. Eddy were the term and concept of *Mortal Mind*, which scarcely occurs in the first edition of *Science and Health*, but is found 238 times in the 211th edition and 144 times in the *Prose Works*. Whatever this may be, it pervades Christian Science and constitutes the basis for a novel dualism. Since "God is just," we must "admit the total depravity of mortals, *alias* mortal mind...."[154] Human beings are, then, totally corrupt, for they are identical with mortal mind, which, like the Pauline Original Sin,[155] is the source of human motivation and leads to every disorder in the body.

However, we are told elsewhere that "mortal mind is a myth...."[156] and has no actual existence.[157] Yet it is the worst foe of the body.[158] Nevertheless, the two are one and the same; neither can exist without the other, and both can be destroyed by Immortal Mind, which creates the superstructure of which the material body is the grosser portion.[159] However, we read also that mortal or carnal mind is not mind at all; and that sin finds a residence there only because an illusion of mind in matter still lingers with us.[160]

What, then, is Mortal Mind? How can it accomplish such devastation if it does not exist? If God is the only mind in the universe, is not man, who is also immortal, his divine derivative? If man is thus spiritual and immortal, why is he so burdened with the depravity of mortal mind? If all mind and all creation come from God, and he can produce nothing unlike himself, [161] how can man or mortal mind be so depraved? How indeed!

2. *The Great Malevolence.* In the early editions of *Science and Health*, the doctrine of demonology, known also as Mesmerism, mental malpractice, or simply M.A.M., was pervasive. This was Mrs. Eddy's distinctive concept of diabolism which she used to account for the existence of evil. As Georgine Milmine points out, it added "certain abnormalities" to Quimby's system, "which, if universally believed and practiced, would make of Christian Science the revolt of the species against its own physical structure...."[162]

However, all reference to diabolists and M.A.M. were meticulously expunged from the editions of *Science and Health* following Wiggin's revision: and ever since the turn of the century, the Church has been careful to ignore this phase of its earlier teachings.

V. THE SPIRITUAL MEANINGS OF SCRIPTURE

Like Quimby, Evans, and Swedenborg, Mrs. Eddy rejected Biblical literalism. The profound truths of Scripture, she declared, have been overlaid with a vast accretion of fable, inconsistencies, and outright error.[163] The New Testament can scarcely be an accurate rendition of the Gospel as taught by Jesus, since this existed only as an oral tradition for 300 years.[164] Since many passages are opposed to Love and Wisdom, we can accept them only as the opinions of pagans who transcribed the inspired texts.[165]

The Scriptures have a spiritual import which teaches the science of life.[166] Should this be removed, they can no more help humanity than moonbeams can melt a frozen river.[167] They "cannot properly be interpreted in a literal way.... There is a dual meaning to every Biblical passage...and to get at the highest, or metaphysical, it is necessary rightly to read what the inspired writers left for our spiritual instruction. The literal rendering...often is the foundation of unbelief and hopelessness."[168]

The Glossary,[169] composed in the Swedenborgian tradition, gives the spiritual meaning of Biblical words. Like those of Quimby and Swedenborg, Mrs. Eddy's works are studded with such interpretations. For example, Christ crucified signifies truth and the cross that attends it.[170] When Jesus declared that his followers could handle serpents without injury, he meant that they should put "down all subtle falsities and illusions...."[171] The commandment "Thou shalt have no other gods before me" signifies that we must not believe that life is mortal. The evil spirits cast out by Jesus were simply false beliefs.[172] When he said that "he that believeth in me shall not see death," he meant that whoever understands the true idea of life no longer accepts a belief in death.[173]

VI. RELIGIOUS AND MEDICAL DECLARATIONS

On the front cover of *Science and Health*, we find the following inscription: "Heal the Sick, Raise the Dead, Cast out Demons, Cleanse the Lepers." This is the power which has been lost by Christianity for centuries, but which Science now restores to mankind.[174]

For Mrs. Eddy, as for Quimby and Evans, Christ-Jesus was the great healer who promised health, happiness, prosperity, well-being, and an abundant life. She considered the conventional churches and their hired expositors as hypocrites who had subverted the message of Christ. Even after she established her own congregation, Mrs. Eddy declared it unnecessary to "ordain pastors and to dedicate churches.... If our church is organized, it is only to meet the demand, 'Suffer it to be so now!' "[175] The time will come, she continues, "when the religious element, or Church of Christ, shall...need no organization...."[176] She stated that religion as now practiced draws us away from spiritual Truth.[177] Prayers ground out in lofty edifices are worth no more than those for which small coins are paid in the Orient.[178]

Again and again, Mrs. Eddy attacked credalized and dogmatic religion: material concepts of God have "overturned empires in demoniacal contests over religion." And "speculative theology" has "made monsters of men.... The eternal roasting amidst noxious vapors, the election of the minority to be saved and the majority to be eternally punished, the wrath of God to be appeased by the sacrifice and torture of His favorite Son—are some of the beliefs that have produced sin, sickness, and death...."[179]

In her early days, Mrs. Eddy bristled with virulence against both doctors and clerics. Even the definitive *Science and Health* is studded with passages which reflect her true feelings. It is recorded, she states, that professional medicine began with the idolatry of pagan priestcraft[180]; and it is certain that the armies of Aesculapius are filling the world with diseases.[181] Echoing Quimby and Evans, she continues that doctors frequently plant diseases in the thoughts of their patients,[182] to whom the doctor's diagnosis is like a sentence of death, which actually creates the diseases that kill.[183]

Since, in her system, the body is a myth, Mrs. Eddy had nothing but contempt for rules of hygiene and the laws of sanitation. Statistics prove, she declared, that laws dealing with health have neither reduced sickness nor lengthened life; since man-made theories replaced primitive Christianity, acute diseases have become fatal and death more sudden. Mrs. Eddy conceded, however, that it would not be in obedience to Wisdom for a man to rush into the flames of a burning building or remain in a storm until his body was frozen[184]; in fact, her practical sanity became evident whenever her theories threatened to involve her or Christian Science in any legal difficulty. She admitted, for example, that for a broken bone or dislocated joint, a surgeon should be called until further advances are made in mental science.[185] When seized with a violent pain, even a Christian Scientist may receive a hypodermic injection.[186] She also wrote that "rather than quarrel over vaccination, I recommend, if the law demand, that an individual submit to this...."[187]

VII. THEORY AND TECHNIQUE

1. *The Nature of Disease*. The fundamental principles of Christian Science therapy may thus be summarized: (1) since spirit is everything and matter nothing, sin, sickness, and death are only false beliefs or

errors or mortal mind; (2) this being true, it is only necessary for those afflicted with mental or physical disorders to arrive at a correct understanding of truth or Principle, in order to abolish sin and sickness; (3) when this enlightenment or resurrection occurs, it constitutes the cure, and all devils or evils harbored by mortal mind vanish and the patient becomes virtuous, healthy, and immortal; (4) the process of regeneration is accompanied by a chemicalization which renews mind and body, and restores both to pristine purity; and (5) this system of therapy is effective for every kind of disease, malady, or injury, whether it is called mental, functional, organic, or physical. In Science, cures result, not from faith, but from *knowledge*; the sick are healed because they *know* there is no sickness.[188]

2.   *Drugs and Man-Made Theories*. Faith in drugs and the rules of health simply beget disease.[189] Nevertheless, faith in them sometimes does bring a cure, because placebos are just as effective as drugs,[190] which belong in the same category as whiskey.[191]

Birds and wild creatures are never sick. Savages enjoyed perfect health until missionaries brought them a knowledge of disease.[192] Our own ancestors lived ruggedly and free from sickness[193]; their ignorance concerning medicine and laws of health kept them well.[194] Climate is unhealthy only when we believe it to be so.[195] Only the mind can determine whether or not a wound will cause the discoloration of the flesh.[196]

3.   *Christ, the Wayshower*. "In Science...you cannot eradicate disease if you admit that God sends it or sees it."[197] Healing the sick and reforming the sinner are one and the same[198]; it is "a divine largess" through which "the great Wayshower, invested with glory...illustrates "the way, the truth, and the life!"[199] Every patient is healed when his belief in sickness vanishes.[200]

VIII. THE DEIFICATION OF MARY BAKER EDDY

1.   *Science Becomes Holy*. In the early versions of *Science and Health*, although couched in the language of authority, there is no indication that the author had received a personal revelation or that she was endowed with an aura of holiness. Her system of therapy was then merely scientific. The revised *Science of Man*, however, published

in 1883, declares that "the Holy Ghost is Science, the only revelator of God—the principle of man and the universe—and was the Comforter to come that should lead into all truth."[201] Even this, however, was only a modest prelude to the proclamations which followed.

2. *The Swedenborgian Key.* In the sixteenth edition of *Science and Health* (1886) the Key to the Scriptures—a Swedenborgian innovation—first became a major division of the book. The Key consists of four chapters; Genesis, Prayer and Atonement, Revelation, and Glossary. The exegesis of the first and last books of the Bible consists of sixty-four pages; the method is precisely that of Swedenborg; after each Scriptural text, its spiritual import is explained. However, little more than the first chapters of Genesis and a few texts from the twelfth chapter of Revelation are analyzed.

In the fifteenth edition of 1891, the Key attains its final stature. The chapter on Prayer and Atonement is now placed under two headings in the main section; the exposition of Genesis is somewhat expanded; and the interpretation of the Apocalypse is increased to twenty pages, in which additional texts from Chapters 10 and 12 are presented as prophecies of Christian Science and its founder.

3. *The Role of Mrs. Eddy.* She declared that although "Jesus of Nazareth was a natural and divine Scientist..." the ultimate divine Science must be a new discovery and "Woman must give it birth...."[202] To Jesus, God revealed only the spirit, not the absolute letter of Christian Science. He, therefore, could teach only a general outline of divine Principle, and he never prepared any exact rule for its demonstration, now finally revealed in Christian Science.[203]

Since God had entrusted Mrs. Eddy with this ultimate revelation, she could not "choose but obey."[204] "No person," she declared, "can take the place of the author of Science and Health, the Discoverer and Founder of Christian Science.... The second appearing of Jesus is, unquestionably, the spiritual advent of the advancing idea of God, as in Christian Science."[205] Divine Science is the Comforter promised by John, and is certainly the true Logos.[206]

Mrs. Eddy, then, was the final interpreter of the Scriptures and the supreme revelator. And so, by successive escalation, she rose (1) from the humble discipleship of Quimby to an authority in mind-healing, and did so by her own efforts and a will of iron; (2) thence to the status of Revelator for an infallible Christ-Science; (3) then to divinity as the

Second Christ; (4) to recognition as the Woman of the Apocalypse whose Little Book should transform and rule mankind; and (5) finally to membership in the supreme godhead as the embodiment of the Mother Principle in deity. We believe that in all this she was influenced by Ann Lee, foundress of the Shaker cult, who declared Swedenborg to have been her John the Baptist, whose chief theoretician was Frederick William Evans—a dyed-in-the-wool Swedenborgian—who proclaimed that she embodied the Second Manifestation of Christ, now revealed in the Superior Female.

4. *Mrs. Eddy, Star-Crowned.* The advent of Mrs. Eddy as the sun-clothed woman of revelation was first set forth in 1886, in the sixteenth edition of *Science and Health*,[207] where we learn that the twelfth chapter of revelation refers to the nineteenth century and the establishment of Christian Science in the vision in which the Revelator foresaw "a great wonder in heaven—a woman clothed with the sun and the moon under her feet, and upon her head a crown of twelve stars."[208]

On the ceiling of the great Mother Church Extension in Boston, there is an immense painting of the Woman of the Apocalypse, illumined by the light of the sun, with the moon under her feet, and her head crowned with twelve stars.

In cryptic language, Mrs. Eddy thus elevates herself into the third aspect of the Servetian-Swedenborgian modalistic Trinity. Christian Science recognizes God as a triune principle: Life, which is the Father; Truth, which is the son or the Word; and Love, which is the Mother.[209] The faithful understand full well that their Leader constitutes in herself the highest attribute of deity.

5. *Divine Science Is the Little Book Open.* We find further that the "mighty angel" of Revelation 10:1-2, who "had in his hand a little book open," is a prefiguration of Divine Science,[210] and contains its revelation. Actually, it is *Science and Health with Key to the Scriptures*, to which the voice from heaven referred when it commanded: "Go and take the little book...." Mortals should obey this heavenly gospel and accept divine Science. Read, study, and absorb this book.[211]

6. *Hailed As a Divinity.* Augusta Stetson, the most successful Christian Science preacher and organizer, who built the magnificent New York Church, attributed to Mrs. Eddy even greater perquisites of divinity. And Alice Orgain, in two books discussing the progressive editions of the Church *Manual* and *Science and Health*, saw in every

word uttered or written and in every act performed by Mrs. Eddy portents of universal significance for the destiny of all mankind. The attitude of the faithful Julia Field-King, an educated and cultured woman, later excommunicated, was probably typical. In a letter to Mrs. Eddy, she declared: "I see that a greater than Jesus is here," who is "the divinely chosen of Divine Principle for a present Savior.... You," she added, "have been appointed as my Wayshower, and I will follow even to the hour of the Ascension...Science and Health...is the Absolute Word of God to me."[212]

7. *Tomlinson's Deification*. It remained, however, for Irving Tomlinson to write the definitive apotheosis which Christian Science has bestowed upon its founder—all denials to the contrary notwithstanding. In his *Revelation of St. John an Open Book*, he wrote 257 pages to expound precisely, verse by verse, how every facet of Christian Science was foretold and described in the Apocalypse.

IX. SUMMARY

The mature ideas of Mrs. Eddy concerning herself are, then, based upon those of her amazing forerunner, Ann Lee; but the format and the general coloring in which she represents them were modelled upon originals created by Swedenborg.

New Thought, including Christian Science, which is a far-reaching reconstruction and repudiation of historical Christianity, revolutionizes the entire New Testament Gospel, both in its Synoptic and Pauline-Johannine forms. It has as its objective the transformation of the conventional religion into a system of therapy, philosophy, and theology intended to confer health, success and happiness upon the human race and to make life in the here and now a triumphant experience. Of all this, Emanuel Swedenborg was the supreme hierophant; and Mary Baker Eddy was one of the most remarkable laborers who have ever toiled in this vineyard of renascent faith. She and she alone could and did advance deific claims for herself and pontificate them in language that thousands would accept. This it was that set her apart among the stars in a position which no one else has ever been able to share.

In this brief study, we have been able only to summarize some of the important elements of Christian Science. We have been forced to omit a great deal which we do not consider of permanent importance. We should point out, however, that the cult utilized to the full the techniques of every successful new religion: while it purported to accept the historical and canonical Scriptures and glorified its deified savior, it offered startlingly new interpretations of the former and an entirely novel concept of the latter. In addition, it offered new revelations, equal in authority to those long established; and thus created a bridge over which converts could march from their previous habitations into their new mansions. By so doing, they could embrace a profession which transformed the recipients into special vessels of enlightenment, perfection, and salvation.

By this process, Christian Science also forged its powerful hold upon converts and provided them with a faith that could withstand the shocks of defeat and laugh at every merely rational attempt to undermine or destroy it.

For such is the nature of FAITH, devout and all-consuming. As Edward Franden Dakin declared, the greatest miracle of all is the capacity of people *to believe*.

Chapter VI
THE GREAT POPULARIZERS

INTRODUCTORY

In this chapter, we present brief analyses of the teachings and philosophies of a number of important individuals who belong specifically in the cycle of New Thought and whose writings have exercised great influence on the religious and therapeutic persuasions and practices, not only of the American people, but also of those in the entire Western world. They did not attempt to establish churches or organizations, probably feeling that these would lead to formalism, creeds, and ecclesiastical polities; but they wrote a great many books, they lectured, and they conducted seminars and healing services, all of which contributed immensely to the development and expansion of the movement.

Although they differ in various details, they generally agree on a philosophic syndrome, which may be summarized as follows:

1. That God is a great, central, and impersonal force and energy

129

immanent in the universe as a whole and in every portion thereof; and is co-extensive with the universe and comprises all substance.

2. That the universe is governed by immutable law.

3. That, since this is true, prayer addressed to the deity is as meaningless as a plea directed to an electric dynamo; that prayer can be nothing more than an expression of personal need and yearning. Affirmative prayer, however, can be highly beneficial.

4. That a stream of influx flows into, or is available to, every human being from this source of energy, sometimes referred to as the Central Sun or Fire, which gives heat, light, and life to all that live.

5. That there is no such thing as inherited or original sin from which humanity need be redeemed.

6. That the orthodox doctrine of salvation or redemption through the sacrifice of Jesus on the Cross is an erroneous concept.

7. That Jesus is neither savior nor redeemer, but simply the Great Exemplar, uniquely and especially endowed with the Christ-Power, which enabled him to accomplish his great mission in the world.

8. That every person is responsible for his own actions; and that personal salvation is the result of right living among our fellow-men.

9. That Christ is not a person or an entity, but a universal power or illumination available to every man, woman, and child.

10. That, since Christ became manifest so that we might have life and have it more abundantly, the purpose of true religion is realized when we achieve the utmost in health, success, prosperity, happiness, and general well-being in every phase of life.

11. That death is merely a transition to another similar but more spiritualized plane; and that heaven and hell are not places, but simply conditions of the mind and emotions.

12. That physical and mental health is and should be one of the prime objectives of religion.

13. That the human psyche exists on three levels: the conscious, the subconscious, and the superconscious; and that these are closely intertwined with and interdependent upon the health of the physical body.

14. That physical health can be achieved, at least in many instances, by mental science, which consists in cleansing the mind or psyche of evil, corrosive, destructive, and negative beliefs, errors, or emotions.

15. That the Bible, properly interpreted, is a vast storehouse of

wisdom and revealed truth; nevertheless, much of it must never be taken literally, since its spiritual or true import differs from the literal meaning.

16. That true religion may draw heavily from various, including occult, sources, for verifications of Biblical revelation.

17. That heavy emphasis should be placed on mental therapy.

18. That, since institutionalized ecclesiasticism as found in the orthodox churches and in Christian Science leads to formalism and loss of freedom, no restrictions may be placed upon the search for truth.

19. That, therefore, the gospel of New Thought may be propagated through books, lectures, classes, and personal contact, as well as organized groups.

20. That even though churches and denominations may be established to minister to those seeking permanent fellowship, these should be devoid of creeds, rites, specific doctrines, or centralized authority.

There has been a host of influential New Thought proponents— lecturers, writers, teachers, theoreticians, philosophers. In the following pages, we attempt to delineate the principal teachings of some of its most popular proponents.

I. THE UNITARIAN SWEDENBORGIANS

Although the eminent English Unitarian and scientist Joseph Priestley came to the United States in 1794, where he soon established a congregation in Philadelphia, William Ellery Channing is considered the "father" of American Unitarianism. Having embraced an Arian Christology, he became the leader of a group in 1819. Once the wall of orthodoxy was thus breached, others soon went far beyond him in their ideology.

Among these, Ralph Waldo Emerson (1803-1882) was probably the most famous; he also holds a unique and honored position in American letters. Since he was an inveterate individualist, it would be inaccurate to place any particular label upon him; for his was an immense intellect which absorbed various elements from disparate sources. Yet the Swedenborgian influence doubtless transcended all others of a specifically religious nature. Although he rejected many of the elements of this faith, he discovered a great deal in the Swedish seer that he found to be not only unique, but also the truth he was seeking, impregnable to attack. He declared, therefore, that supreme honor was due this Representative Man.

Emerson's 1838 Divinity School Address at Harvard was a landmark in American religious development.[1] Paying homage to Swedenborg by name, its total thrust, from beginning to end, is based on the concept that the central sun is the divine power of the universe, the deific source which fills and animates all things, whether they be stars, trees, men, or grains of sand. God is the vital, omnipresent power without which there would be nothing but darkness and death. Emerson's religion deifies Nature and makes each man and woman a divine creature of the cosmos. His soteriology is Swedenborgian: "He who does a good deed is instantly ennobled. He who does a mean deed is by the action itself contracted. He who puts off impurity...so far is he God.... Thus of their own volition souls proceed into heaven, into hell."[2]

In his theological cosmology, "one mind is everywhere active, in each ray of the star, in each wavelet of the pool.... Good is positive. Evil is merely privative...like cold. All things proceed out of the same spirit.... The perception of this law of laws awakens in the mind a sentiment which we call religious.... By it is the universe made safe and habitable...."[3]

Emerson repudiates the superstructure of orthodox theology and erects in its place a faith based upon the Over-Soul and the Cosmic Natural God. "Yourself," he proclaims, "a new-born bard of the Holy Ghost, cast behind you all conformity, and acquaint men at first hand with Deity."[4] Addressing the seminarians directly, he declared: "All men with you are open to the influx of the all-knowing spirit, which annihilates before its broad noon the little shades and gradations of intelligence...."[5]

Among Emerson's Representative Men (as written in 1845-46), Swedenborg alone appears as seer and prophet. "This man," he declares, "who appeared to his contemporaries as a visionary...no doubt led the most real life of any man then in the world: and...he begins to spread himself into the minds of thousands."[6] "A colossal soul, he lies vast abroad on his times, uncomprehended by them, and requires a long focal distance to be seen...."[7] Emerson pours forth tribute after tribute: "The moral insight of Swedenborg, the correction of popular errors, the announcements of ethical laws take him out of comparison with any modern writer and entitles him to a place, vacant for some ages, among the lawgivers of mankind. That slow but commanding influence which he has acquired...will pass forth into the common stock of wise and just thinking. The world...attracts what is excellent in its children, and lets fall the infirmities and limitations of the grandest mind."[8]

And again: "His books have become a monument...in this immolation of genius and fame at the shrine of conscience, there is a merit sublime beyond praise. He...observed and published the laws of nature ...he was fired with piety at the harmonies he felt, and abandoned himself to his joy and worship.... If the glory was too bright for his eyes to bear, if he staggered under the trance of delight, the more excellent is the spectacle...of being which beams and blazes through him...."[9]

None of the other Representative Men—Plato, Montaigne, Shakespeare, Napoleon, and Goethe—were deemed worthy of such accolades.

After the Unitarians established Brook Farm as a communal experiment—which was soon abandoned—they embraced Fourierism for a short period; but this also was soon rejected, and, about 1845, they embarked upon an enterprise which has left its permanent marks upon American society. It became an intellectual center for the propagation of Swedenborgianism with a group of highly talented individuals as leaders. Among these were W.E. Channing, Margaret Fuller, George Ripley, Theodore Parker, Charles A. Dana, John S. Dwight, Parke Goodwin, Murat Pratt, and Elizabeth Peabody. Several periodicals emanating from Brook Farm, or under the control of its leaders, proclaimed to the world the sublime virtues and doctrines of the Swedish seer. In addition, a group of very capable men explained Swedenborgianism from their pulpits and in the classrooms of liberal seminaries. It was accepted by philosophers such as Henry James the Elder; through many channels, it began to permeate the whole culture and to become a definite element in the American heritage. Those who adopted Swedenborgianism as a total revelation were then and have ever remained few; but those who accepted certain elements expanded into millions until scarcely anyone remained totally immune or untouched.

One of the leading personalities in the development of American

Unitarianism was Theodore Parker (1810-60). If we are justified in calling Emerson a fifty-percent Swedenborgian, it would be accurate to classify Parker as seventy-five percent of this persuasion. As a leader among the Brook Farm radicals, he was openly identified with, and committed to, this theology. He also fought for women's suffrage and against slavery; denounced the war of 1846-48[10]; conspired with and aided John Brown; was condemned and ostracized by the members of his own church. Instead of proclaiming the Over-Soul of Emerson, his was a rationalist theology. He stated categorically that Jesus was not the Son of God[11]; that the Old Testament and most of the Bible stories were nothing but myths and fables[12]; that Nature is our only true religious book[13]; and that creeds and sacraments are worthless.[14] Like many ancient Gnostics and the modern Mormons and Christian Scientists, he postulated a Mother-Father God.[15] Love, he said, is the feminine savior of mankind.[16]

Swedenborgian concepts permeate Parker's thinking, in which God is the Central Sun of the Universe. Among his works, we find a series of so-called prayers, which are actual invocations, since it was inconceivable to him that God would intervene in the individual affairs of men. God is the "Central Fire, and Radiant Light of all," and the "Infinite Spirit who thyself art perpetual presentness, whom the heaven of heavens cannot contain, but who hast thy dwelling place in every little flower that blooms, and in every humble heart...."[17]

And again, re-echoing the modalist Trinity of Servetus and Swedenborg: "The stone I sit on is in communion with God; the pencil I write with; the gray field fly reposing in the sunshine at my foot. Let God withdraw from the space occupied by the stone, the pencil, the fly, they cease to be.... The mineral, the vegetable, and the animal represent three modes of existence; and hence so many modes and degrees of dependence on God and of communion with him...."[18] "Should God withdraw himself or any of his qualities from my mind, I could not think; from conscience, I should know nothing of the right; from the heart, there could be no love; from the soul, there could be no holiness, no faith in Him who made it."[19]

The doctrine of influx pervades Parker's thought: "Thus does the man, that will, hold commune with his Father, face to face, and get great income from the Soul of all.... Thus...human souls communicate with the great central Fire and Light of all the world, the lodestone of the Universe, and thus grow...blessed and strong."[20]

As Parker discarded the historic doctrines and practices of the old churches, he embraced the Swedenborgian concepts to an ever-increasing degree. "Our Father and our Mother," he cries, "we thank thee for that transcendent world near to the earth of matter and the soul of man, wherein thou dwellest, thou and the blessed spirits thou enclosest, as the sea her multitudinous and her fruitful waves."[21] And again: "We thank thee for the just ones made perfect who have gone from us, and those who in their imperfection have been translated, for we know that thou placest them in the line of advancement, and leadest them ever upwards, and still further on."[22]

Thus it is clear that the Unitarian movement during the middle of the nineteenth century developed largely on a Swedenborgian base and made significant contributions to what eventually came to be known as New Thought. It was therefore no accident that a considerable number of Unitarian—and sometimes Universalist—clergymen transferred to the New Thought movement when that established churches of its own.

II. HENRY JAMES, SR.

William James (1778-1832) was an Irish Presbyterian immigrant who arrived in this country in 1793, accumulated a considerable fortune, established himself as a leading, solid citizen of Albany, New York, and reared a large family there, of whom the most outstanding was Henry James, Sr. (1811-1882).

It is a never-ending cause for amazement to observe how some disciples of the Swede differ in their interpretations of their master. Henry James, Sr., who considered himself a Swedenborgian *par excellence*, ignores much that is central in his mentor. In several areas, he is actually in basic disagreement. The truth is that he, like so many others, by eclectic absorption, appropriated only those concepts that appealed to him. Or possibly he had read and studied only selected works.

In 1830, Henry graduated from Union College, to which his father had made large contributions; and in 1835, he matriculated at Princeton Theological Seminary, where, at the age of twenty-eight, he discovered his antipathy to the dogmas of Calvinism. He thus abandoned both the school and his father's religion at the same time.

In 1844, he visited England for the second time, where he was plunged into an emotional and physical depression so devastating that he lost all will to live: overcome by a sense of shame, guilt, and unworthiness, "he could find neither meaning nor objective in existence...this ghastly condition of mind continued...for two years...."[1]

The supreme experience of his life occurred when he met a Swedenborgian lady who explained that he was merely undergoing "vastation"—an experience that was the prerequisite for the New Birth, the secret of divine creation and providence. He was so impressed that he journeyed to London, where he obtained copies of *The Divine Love and Wisdom* and *The Divine Providence*. As their message flowed through his mind, he experienced his Great Illumination. "Imagine," he wrote years later, "a fever patient, sufficiently restored of his malady to be able to think of something beside himself, suddenly transported where the free airs of heaven blow upon him, and the sound of running waters refreshes his jaded sense, and you have a feeble imagine of my delight.... Or, better still imagine a subject...filled to the brim with sentiments of indestructible life, and you will have a true picture of my emancipated condition."

And he continued: "Swedenborg's writings...[bring] to the aching heart and to the void mind...infinite balm and contentment."[2] Elsewhere he declares: "The incomparable depth and splendor of Swedenborg's genius are shown in this, that he alone of men has even dared to bring creation within the bounds of consciousness—within the grasp of the soul...."[3]

Here and now, as C. Hartley Grattan observes, "Henry James had found his truth. Henceforth he never traveled without carrying Swedenborg's works with him."[4] He also became a close friend of John Garth Wilkinson, the English Swedenborgian who gave the world a beautiful translation of his master's works.

During the remainder of his life, James published a dozen books, all of which are Swedenborgian analyses of speculative metaphysics.

We believe that Swedenborg provided an infinite experience for James because in him he found the instrument with which to demolish not only the claims of the medieval authoritarian church, but also those of Calvinism, Protestantism in general, and even the current Arian Unitarianism proclaimed by William E. Channing. He even condemned the current Swedenborgian churches because they were too sectarian.

James explained repeatedly that democracy implies the disappearance of both the Catholic and Protestant churches and their gradual disintegration.[5] Instead, he envisions what he calls the Christian Church "because all but it are destitute of a philosophic basis; that is, [they] profess no doctrine of God in nature, but only in the private soul. The Christian Church is immortal because its fundamental dogma involves a doctrine of God so ample and clear as to satisfy every profoundest want of the heart and every most urgent demand of the head towards God forever."[6]

In his visions, James saw a church that would be co-extensive with society as a whole. It would "reveal the incessant operation of laws by which man's physical and social relations will be brought into the complete subjection of his inward or divine personality. It is the demonstration of a plenary unity between man and nature and man and man."[7]

Although various non-Swedenborgian elements are to be found in Henry James, in most aspects of his ideology Swedenborg's thought is accurately reproduced. Like many other proponents of New Thought, he embraced a Gnostic Christology, in which the second attribute of the Godhead becomes the Christ-Power, a deific emanation available to every member of the human race.[8] As Frederic H. Young notes, "James derived the basic structure and much of his philosophical terminology from the Swedish thinker," especially in regard to moral perfection, the spiritual creation, the trinity of operational manifestation, the nature of the Esse or Divine Substance, the Central Sun of the Universe as God, and the nature of the so-called Incarnation.[9] James adopted fully the Swedenborgian concept of influx, which flows into every man and woman from the central sun as well as from the spirits in the spirit-world, in the existence of which he had a childlike faith and where he was certain he would one day rejoin his adorable wife.[10]

The theology of James is certainly Swedenborgian. "God," we read, "is the sole substance or reality of everything embraced in the sensible universe, from its central sun to the planetary earths that encircle it, and from these again to the tiniest mineral, vegetable, and animal forms that enliven their surface."[11]

Since it is a fact that a great and ultimate influence is wielded by those whose thought permeates the great popularizers, there can be little doubt but that the philosophy of Henry James, Sr., has affected millions who are not aware of its source. Although his two famous sons (one a novelist and the other a philosopher) were neither Swedenborgians nor protagonists of New Thought *per se*, various elements of this nature filtered through them into the general stream of culture. The docetic Christology of James; his theology which postulated a deity who is also the central sun; and his concept of a Christology which would one day create the ideal and perfect society, all distinguish him as one of that galaxy of Americans who belong definitely in the New Thought tradition and who contributed to the establishment of a religion of health, happiness, and prosperity.

III. HENRY DRUMMOND

During his brief life, Henry Drummond (1851-1897) who began his education at the University of Edinburgh, not only became an evangelist in the spirit of Moody and Sankey, but also developed into an outstanding scientific exponent of Swedenborgianism, wherein he made a unique and creative contribution to New Thought. He wrote a number of immensely popular books and tracts, among which *The Greatest Thing in the World*—circulated in millions of copies—is the best known. In 1888, he published *Tropical Africa* and in 1894, *The Ascent of Man*, both of which evince deep sympathy for, and understanding of, animals. Since, like Swedenborg, he was deeply versed in scientific lore, it was no accident that his *Natural Law in the Spiritual World*, which, throughout, bears the imprint of Swedenborg, should be recognized as the foremost attempt of the nineteenth century to base revealed Christianity upon a scientific foundation. In 1877, he lectured on science at the Free College of Glasgow; and in 1884, he became a minister-professor in the Church of the New Jerusalem.

Drummond declares that since the "difficulty...which men of Science feel about religion is real and inevitable,"[1] it is necessary to show, not merely that there is no contradiction between them, but also that there is, on the contrary, a sublime and universal agreement. No one who "feels the universal need of a Religion, can stand idly by while the intellect of the age is slowly divorcing itself from" religion.[2] What must be done, therefore, is to establish "the naturalness of the super-natural..."[3] And even as Newton and other scientists have demon-strated the reign of law in the Natural World so must we "see the Reign of Law...in the spiritual Sphere."[4] If the reign of law were not univer-sal, the cosmos would quickly descend into a state of chaos.[5]

Throughout, the author seeks to equate the two realms: just as science demonstrates the Rule of Law in the natural world, so does revelation give concomitant evidence of Law in the Spiritual. And the first foundation on which this edifice is constructed is the Swedenbor-gian Law of Correspondences. "Is there not reason to believe," he demands, "that many of the Laws of the Spiritual World...are simply the Laws of the Natural World?"[6] And he continues: did the Creator "divide the world into two, a cosmos and a chaos...?" Since this is impossible, we are told that "the phenomena of the Spiritual World are in analogy with the phenomena of the Natural World...."[7] Drummond reproduces a Swedenborgian passage which states his own view: "In our doctrine of representations and correspondences, we shall treat of both" as if "the physical world was purely symbolical of the spiritual world."[8] Its laws are, therefore, not only "analogous to the Natural Laws, but...they *are the same Laws*."[9] According to Drummond's Law of Continuity, which is the Law of Laws, the lowest form of matter (the inorganic) proceeds upward through the vegetative, the animal, the human, and finally to the everlasting existence in the world of spirits.[10] This follows from the fact that the precedent spiritual world was the model after which the natural was formed.[11]

Since the reign of law is universal, it must exist also in the spiritual world[12]; otherwise religion and theology would be totally without foundation.[13] The latter have, in the past, depended upon authority; but now "a new basis" in universal law "must be sought and found" for them.[14] We must have a scientific theology; and we must proceed on the basis of "positive method of thought."[15] As for proof of life in the spiritual world, this will be discovered in the same manner as in the natural.[16] Thus it is that the latter becomes spiritual; for "Nature is not a mere image or emblem of the Spiritual. It is a working model...."[17]

Science has done much to purify religion[18]; but "with the inspiration of Nature to illuminate what... Revelation has left obscure, heresy in certain whole departments shall become impossible.... Theology must draw upon...the seen for the further revelation of the unseen."[19] Therefore, "the greatest among the theological Laws are the Laws of Nature in disguise."[20] The Creator would "simply project the higher Laws downward so that the Natural World would become an incarnation, a visible representation, a working model of the spiritual."[21]

In a series of chapters, the author elaborates his position partly by science, partly by revelation. The first of these, called Biogenesis, lays down the thesis that like can spring only from like; matter from pre-existing matter, vegetation from vegetation, etc.; and, finally, that Spiritual life can come only from the pre-existing and eternal Spiritual Life, which, in Drummond's Swedenborgian system, is God.[22] The proposition is presented in detail; it means, in short, that "the Spiritual Life is the gift of the Living Spirit."[23] And he declares: "with the elevation of Biogenesis to the rank of scientifc fact, all problems concerning the Origin of Life" are solved.[24] Since there is no life in inorganic matter,[25] and since there is "no passage from one Kingdom to another...the intervention of Life is a scientific necessity...."[26]

What, then, is the life that is given to man? It is the "Christ" which "is the source of Life in the Spiritual World"[27]; and "a remarkable harmony exists here between the Organic World as arranged by Science and the Spiritual World as arranged by Scripture."[28] And so "the inquiry into the Origin of Life is the fundamental question alike of Biology and Christianity."[29]

This leads directly to Drummond's Swedenborgian explication of soteriology. The difference between the Christian and the non-Christian is neither in intellect nor morality: it is the possession of something here called Life, and is similar to what differentiates the Organic from the Inorganic.[30] "He who lives the spiritual Life has a distinct kind of Life added to all other phases..." thereof[31]; and this determines "what he shall be."[32] There is life in plants, insects and animals[33]; but when a man has the Christ within him, he has "an endowment from the spiritual world...."[34] We are redeemed not through a vicarious atonement, but by living the Christ-Life, which we achieve by acting unselfishly for the benefit of mankind; and we do this not because it will eventuate in a final reward but because our given nature is so transformed *that we cannot do otherwise*.[35]

The chapter entitled "Degeneration"[36] notes that unless we work with our limbs, they lose their power, and atrophy; likewise, unless we exercise ourselves in virtue, the soul dies.[37] Unless we develop the capacity to escape from the world of sin and selfishness, we can never "escape to heaven"; for "where is the capacity for heaven to come from if it be not developed on earth?"[38] "Escape," says Drummond, "means nothing more than the gradual emergence of the higher from the lower...it means the gradual putting off of all that cannot enter into the higher state, or heaven, and...the putting on of Christ."[39] The good life "being a germ of the Christ-Life, it must unfold into *a Christ*."[40] "The regenerated soul is a new creature in...Christ-Jesus."[41]

This brings us to Drummond's concept of God, who or which is that force or power in the universe from which Life emerges and without whom or which the cosmos would be nothing more than inorganic matter. We may call our relation to this a correspondence or a communion, without which we would be spiritually dead.[42]

God, however, is something more than the force and power which exists in nature; he is rather "an everlasting and perfect Mind, supreme over the universe...." To believe in this "is to invest moral distinction with immensity and eternity...to the imperishable theatre of all being."[43] God is the "Spiritual Environment" without which "there is no thought, no energy, nothing...."[44] Although, in an embryonic state, all living creatures are virtually identical, God is the Life and the Artist which makes one embryo into a fish and another into a man.[45]

The chapter on "mortification" is an elaboration of Drummond's soteriology. In order to gain the Spiritual Life, we must not steal, embezzle, deceive, exploit, indulge in evil temper; for, in so doing, we die in sin.[46] "The love of money up to a certain point is necessary, and therefore good; beyond that it may become the worst of sins."[47]

In the chapter on "Eternal Life" we read that organisms enjoy longevity in ratio to their complexity. And since human beings live longer than lower forms of animals, they approach more nearly the spiritual level. When "a spiritual organism" is in "perfect correspondence with a spiritual Environment," the "conditions necessary to Eternal Life are satisfied."[48]

It is interesting to note that while the orthodox churches repudiated the theory of evolution, Drummond, the scientist, postulated his entire system upon it. The condition necessary for the further evolution of man "is that the spiritual be released from the natural. That is to say, tne condition of the further Evolution...is the indispensable factor of the higher life.... This is the last and the greatest contribution to mankind. Over the mouth of the grave, the perfect and the imperfect submit to their final separation. Each goes to his own—earth to earth, ashes to ashes, dust to dust, spirit to spirit."[49] In Drummond's system, there is no Hell—only annihilation for the non-spiritual.

The chapter on "Semi-Parasitism"[50] is a further development of Drummond's soteriology. The person who seeks salvation in the Roman Catholic or the Protestant churches is like the hermit crab, which moves into the shell abandoned by another crustacean and therefore loses the use of his limbs and becomes the host for parasites. The members of such churches depend upon an institution or on the atonement of Christ for redemption, rather than upon the exercise of their own capacities. The orthodox churches all preach a parasite-doctrine[51]; there can be no hope in or from a church which declares that "a blackguard from the streets" can, by agreeing to a "plausible formula," become an instantaneous convert. Between the Evangelical and Roman churches there is a deep affinity; and both are utterly false and immoral.[52] Salvation is possible only by achieving a "*likeness to Christ*."[53] Seeking "a mechanical security that we may cover inertia and find a whole salvation in which there is no personal sanctification—this is Parasitism."[54]

If the hermit crab lives a semi-parasitical life, then the organism which receives its food and security from another is a total parasite, examples of which are frequent in nature. In the same manner, that person who accepts his Truth "by imbibation from the Church" soon finds that his "faculties for receiving the truth...become distorted. He who abandons the personal search for truth...abandons truth."[55] This is the condition of all those who accept their beliefs on authority.

This Draconic edict, reminiscent of Milton, is indeed strong medicine; but Drummond demands nothing less, for this only can serve as a passport to the spiritual world. He condemns the great churches in truly Swedenborgian terminology: "The effect of a doctrinal theology is the effect of Infallibility...." And the result "is mere Credulity.... Those who framed the Thirty-Nine Articles or the Westminster Confession are responsible."[56] We must not accept the orthodox belief in the Trinity or the Atonement upon authority[57]; rather we must work, think, separate, dissolve, absorb, digest; and "this we must do for ourselves."[58] "Better a little faith dearly won...than perish on the splendid plenty of richest creeds."[59]

In the last chapter, "Classification," Drummond declares that Christianity is a religion based on biological science[60]; that the Christian is separated from the world in his "uncompromising allegiance to the Kingdom of God..."[61]; that the kingdom which progresses beyond the Organic is the Spiritual, which is the Kingdom of God[62]; and that this is the goal of man's ultimate evolution.[63]

Drummond concludes with a statement stemming from Swedenborgian nebular theory: "of the...first development of the earth from the nebular matrix of space, Science speaks with reserve. The second, the evolution of each individual from the simple protoplasmic cell to the formed adult, is proved. The still wider evolution...of all individuals ...is at least suspected.... But now, at last, we see the Kingdoms themselves evolving. And that supreme law...now begins again directly the evolution of these million-peopled worlds as if they were simple cells or organisms.... This is the final triumph of Continuity, the heart secret of creation, the unspoken prophecy of Christianity. To Science...this mighty process...is simply *Evolution*. To Christianity...it is *Redemption*."[64]

Such was the heart of Drummond's philosophy and his scientific analysis of religion.

IV. EMMA CURTIS HOPKINS

Emma Curtis Hopkins (1855-1925) was known as The Teacher of Teachers and the Grand Lady of New Thought. She taught classes in various cities which sometimes enrolled as many as 1,000 students, each of whom paid fifty dollars for a two-week course of twelve lessons. For years, she operated the Christian Science Theological Seminary established in Chicago in 1887. Charles Braden observes that a roster of those who received instruction from her "reads like a *Who's Who* among New Thought leaders. To name only a few, there were Frances Lord; Annie Rix Millitz and Harriet Rix; Malinda E. Cramer, co-founder of Divine Science; Mrs. Bingham, teacher of Nona L. Brooks; Helen Wilmans; Charles and Myrtle Fillmore, founders of the Unity School of Christianity; Charles A. and Josephine Barton, editor of *The Life*...Dr. Emilie Cady, writer of the Unity textbook, *Lessons in Truth*; Ella Wheeler Wilcox, New Thought poetess; Elizabeth Towne... and Ernest Holmes, founder of the Church of Religious Science."[1]

Thus we see that although Mrs. Hopkins did not establish a church of her own, she was instrumental in starting or shaping the careers of those who founded the most important New Thought organizations (not including the Christian Science Church) which exist today in the United States.

Mrs. Hopkins matriculated in Mrs. Eddy's Primary Class of December 1883. Her abilities must have been extraordinary for, instead of continuing with advanced studies or as private practitioner, she became the editor of the *Christian Science Journal* in September 1884, and so continued for more than a year. However, she found the restrictions imposed upon her quite intolerable, and was dismissed from the post in October 1885, the reason being, according to Bates and Dittemore, that she was absorbing metaphysical material from sources other than Mrs. Eddy.[2] This is undoubtedly true, since her writings are studded with references to, or citations from, Emerson, Swedenborg, Eckhardt, Plato, Plotinus, Zoroaster, *The Book of the Dead*, and the *Bhagavad Gita*.

As a practitioner in Chicago in 1886, Mrs. Hopkins was still intensely loyal to Mrs. Eddy; we believe, in fact, that she would have preferred so to continue. However, her capacious and inquisitive mind led her into pathways which made her excommunication inevitable. In 1887 and again in 1888, Mrs. Eddy condemned her and Julius Dresser by name in the *Journal* as "Mind-Quacks" who were "spreading abroad patchwork books, false compendiums of my system, crediting some ignoramus or infidel with teachings they have stolen from me. The unweaned suckling whines while spitting out the breast-milk which sustained him...."[3]

By 1890, therefore, Mrs. Hopkins was well launched on her own brilliant career, which spanned several decades. The profound influence she exercised is reflected in a statement, probably written by Charles Fillmore, which appeared in *Modern Thought*, announcing a class to be conducted by her in Kansas City, beginning January 6, 1890. "She is undoubtedly the most successful teacher in the world...in many instances those who enter her classes confirmed invalids come out at the end of the course perfectly well...her very presence heals and those who listen are filled with new life." He doubted that "ever before on this planet were such words of burning truth so eloquently spoken through woman."[4]

After the death of Mrs. Hopkins in 1925, her sister continued her work from headquarters established at Joy Farms (later High Watch Farm) in Connecticut. The operation was continued as the High Watch Fellowship at Cornwall Bridge. Excerpts from the writings of Mrs. Hopkins, entitled *Understanding the Scriptures*, were published in mimeographed form in 1940, as were the twelve lessons used in her classes and called *Scientific Christian Mental Practice*. The latter, published in a handsome printed volume in 1958, is available from the Rare Book Company in Freehold, N.J. This volume, as well as *Bible Interpretations, High Mysticism, Resumé*, and other works, may be obtained from the De Vorss Company in Marina del Rey, California.

The literature of New Thought (1) is characterized by certain general and well-defined metaphysical premises, but (2) is distinguished also by a great variety of individual differences among its exponents. Whereas Christian Science imposed a total uniformity and conformity, many proponents reacted against this authoritarianism by permitting, even encouraging, an infinitude of variation. Thus, while Christian Science enjoys the security of certainty, New Thought luxuriates in freedom—a libertarianism which has fostered many remarkable careers, but has made it difficult to establish powerful sectarian denominations.

These facts are well illustrated in the career and teachings of Emma Curtis Hopkins. Her following was enormous; but, since she did not claim a special revelation or emphasize an authoritarian approach, her direct, personal influence died with her. Had it not been that some of those whom she inspired established organizations with vested property and revenue, she would now be little more than a memory.

Since she began her career as the editor of the *Christian Science Journal* and called her school the Christian Science Theological Seminary, and was, moreover, an ardent admirer of Mary Baker Eddy, it is not surprising that her class instruction comes nearer to orthodox Christian Science than those of most of the other New Thought teachers. In her own writings, as in *Science and Health*, we find a virtual denial of material existence. Since God is All-Good, sin and sickness are false affirmations[5]; in the twelve lessons, her system is often referred to as Christian Science; one of the first things she impressed upon her students was her Statement of Being, which reminds us of Mrs. Eddy's and is the title of Lesson One. She repeats Mrs. Eddy's basic dictum that "there is no life, substance, or intelligence in matter"[6]; and declares categorically that there is no sin, sickness, or death[7] and that all illness results from false belief.[8] Doctors, we read, think the healing power acts through drugs, but the scientist knows that the cure comes from the belief in their efficacy.[9]

Mrs. Hopkins, however, not only deleted from her system several elements that are crucial in *Science and Health*, such as Malicious Animal Magnetism and the near-deification of Mary Baker Eddy; she also added others, or at least developed them on a new basis. She called the commonly held errors of mankind—who look upon sin, evil, sickness, poverty, and death as inevitable—race beliefs[10] or race inequities,[11] a concept found also in the ideology of Troward and Holmes. She declared over and over—in fact, it was the basis of her therapy—that sin, sickness, poverty, etc., do not exist at all; and the cure of those who have false beliefs consists simply in declaring them nonexistent.

Even St. Augustine sometimes interpreted Scriptures "spiritually"—a technique which Swedenborg and Quimby and New Thought in general elevated into a kind of science. However, nowhere have we found such interesting and radical examples of the method as in Mrs. Hopkins. For example, in the parable of the Lost Sheep, the ninety-and-nine symbolize our herd of thoughts, which must be so kept under control as not to think a false note; and the thought that must be recovered signifies the everlasting soul.[12] When God ordered the earth to bring forth cattle, these symbolize schools, homes, family, and governments; while the "creeping things" signify "affairs like business, daily tasks, eating, drinking, sleeping."[13]

The faith of Mrs. Hopkins was of the kind that can move mountains. For example, there can be no such thing as stealing; for "is not God the only living being? Can God steal?"[14] Elsewhere, she states that when we order coffee and tea not to make us nervous, they become harmless[15]; since God is everywhere, we have as much intelligence in our feet as in our brains[16]; and that a certain Negress made the kinky hair on her child straight by talking to it.[17]

In the Bible Lesson published in *Inter-Ocean*, April 2, 1893, Mrs.

Hopkins explained her metaphysical principles, which may have been derived directly from Swedenborg and which may have influenced both Troward and Holmes, since they are reproduced in them. "There is," she declares, "one indestructible substance pervading all things from the remotest star to the nearest dust particle.... It can only be cognized by the mind.... And only the understanding power of the mind can make it useful. He who by any manner...handles this substance and realizes that its nature is his nature soon finds himself experiencing vital renewals throughout body and mind." In the *Inter-Ocean* article we find also a restatement of the Doctrine of Influx, which is often made or implied in her writings. It was the power deriving from this universal emanation that constituted the impersonal Christ-power which enabled Jesus to perform his mighty works. "By a progress he made clear to His disciples, He made a draught upon the universal principle...and He healed every blindness by His radiation of the seeing mind with which He had stored Himself. He called it the Father sometimes. He called it God sometimes. He called it Lord Spirit."

"Jesus Christ by his coming forth unharmed from material injuries brought to light the immortality of all powers of mankind...." And she continued: "The life stuff of which his being inhaled to overflowing was the Christ. All who learn the way of life that he taught...are also Christ."

And further: "The glory of Jesus Christ was that, having all the virtues through drawing rightly upon all the life of the universe, he took each man's estate and explained unto him separately how, through all time, he should proceed to have more abundant life.... The man who molds the vital ethers of omnipotence by right thoughts about its bounty brings forth bountifully."

When the poor hear this gospel, it means resurrection for them: for "the life stuff pervading all things now may be manifested in all things as infinite life, infinite health, infinite strength of any faculty."

Mrs. Hopkins's technique of healing was adopted virtually intact by Ernest Holmes: treatment consisted primarily of positive affirmations. The first six lessons in *Scientific Christian Mental Practice* set forth the general metaphysical principles on which the system is based; the last six propose specific techniques for different patients; and each closes with a formal statement to be made orally or silently by the practitioner. Lesson Twelve, "The Crown of Glory," closes with the following affirmation or exhortation:

"You are a perfect creation of the Living God, spiritual, harmonious, fearless, free. You reflect all the universe of Good.

"From every direction, everywhere, come words of Truth, making you know that you are free, wise, and happy.

"You are satisfied with the world in which you live.

"You show forth to the world health, wisdom, peace.

"You show to me perfect health in every part of your being.

"You are fearless, free, strong, wise, and able to do everything that belongs to you to do each day. God works through you to will and to do that which ought to be done by you.

"You are a living demonstration of the power of Truth to set free into health and strength for living service to the world.

"You acknowledge to the world that you are every whit whole.

"You acknowledge to yourself, and to me, that you are well and strong and alive through and through.

"God is your life, health, strength, and support forever.

" In the name of the Father, and of the Son, and of the Holy Ghost, I pronounce you well and strong.

"As God saw the works of His hands Good, so I see you Good. All is Good. Amen."[18]

If this sounds like wholly impractical optimism, let it be recorded that thousands found comfort and healing in this therapy; and let it be noted also that the genius and spirit of Emma Curtis Hopkins has indeed left footsteps on the sands of time.

V. THOMAS TROWARD

1. *His Importance*. Judge Thomas Troward—who was for many years a Divisional Judge in Punjab, India—was well versed in Hindu lore and the art of painting. Shortly after returning to retire in England about 1900, he discovered the New Thought movement, in which he carved out a brilliant career for himself. In fact, he is now widely recognized throughout the world as one of its principal exponents and theoreticians. For this reason, we devote more space to him than to some of the other Great Popularizers.

In 1904, he gave *The Edinburgh Lectures on Mental Science* at Queens Hall; these have been published in countless editions comprising hundreds of thousands of copies. Even more famous, the *Doré Lectures*, given at the Doré Art Gallery in London in 1906, have gone through something like thirty printings.

To this day, Troward remains the most influential exponent of the new religion in Great Britain; and he has exercised a profound influence upon many American leaders, especially the Holmes Brothers, whose writings are studded with Trowardian words, phrases, ideas, and healing techniques.* We may say that this system is the most original, brilliant, and compelling elaboration and restatement of the Servetian-Swedenborgian theology and cosmology ever produced. Although his works consist of only a few slender volumes, their influence has reached to the ends of the earth.

In addition to the two volumes of lectures, Troward wrote three other important books: *The Creative Process in the Individual, The Law and the Word,* and *The Hidden Power.*

2. *A Religion Based on Science.* In *The Edinburgh* and *The Doré Lectures,* we find a religion based primarily on science. The author uses Scriptural quotations and references, sometimes, in substantial numbers; but these are offered as corroborative evidence, not authoritarian revelation. As Troward views world history, he finds glimpses of Truth revealed in various ages, among many peoples, and in different religions. There can be little doubt that he would have constructed the same ideological synthesis had there been no Christianity in the Western world. His intellectual debt is not to the Bible—which is regarded like any other book—but to Swedenborg and modern science. Following in the footsteps of Henry Drummond,[1] he offers an explanation of nature and the universe which derives from logic, experiment, metaphysics, and the Swedish seer. Citations from the Scriptures are used to confirm and reinforce his philosophic superstructure. "The Science of Spirit," he declares, "is not one whit less scientific than the Science of Matter...."[2] It is the business of the Mental Scientist "to regard even the most exalted spiritual phenomena

---

* Such terms as "livingness," "The Thing Itself," "The cosmic mind of consciousness," and the use of affirmation as a means of emplacing curative and creative powers in the subconscious of the patient.

from a purely scientific standpoint, which is...the working of a universal natural Law."[3]

3. *The Cosmic Spirit or Intelligence.* Since the *Doré* Lectures set forth the Trowardian theses with supreme clarity, we feel that a summary of them may be helpful.

In order that any object, from a leaf or an insect to the great universe itself, may possess life, it must be animated by what Troward calls Spirit; and since the cosmos is instinct with Life, there must always have existed an "originating Spirit of Life."[4] This Power is not only Life but Intelligence also, which expresses itself in a scheme of cosmic progression, seeking ever to proliferate into higher forms.[5]

This Creative Spirit is without individual personality; it "can only work cosmically by a *generic* Law...."[6] Working through untold ages with deathless energy, it seeks a perpetual advance to ever higher degrees of life.[7]

4. *The Relation of the Individual to the Universal.* "The whole problem of life consists in finding the true relation of the individual to the Universal Originating Spirit,"[8] which can act on the plane of the Particular and through expression in the individual.[9] "Man's place in the cosmic order is that of distributor of the Divine Power...."[10] The Divine Mind, the Central Creative Agency, is like a great dynamo, which transmits vitality to every portion of the universe.[11] Individual man is thus made into "the creative center of his own world."[12] The "All-Originating Power" works in and through him at all times, according to the law that governs the universe.

We have, therefore, a single Universal but an unlimited number of Individual Minds,[13] which "is the individualizing of the Universal Spirit,"[14] the "power which concentrates the primordial ether into forms, and endows these forms with various modes of motion, from the simply mechanical motion of the planets to the volitional motion in man."[15]

The supreme and universal intelligence flows from the Great Center into every existing phenomenon, and adapts all these to their specific purposes.[16] This "Divine operation is always for expansion and fuller expression, and this means the production of something beyond what has gone before...since the Divine cannot change its inherent nature, it must operate in the same manner in me; consequently, in my own special world, of which I am the centre, it will move forward to produce new conditions in advance of any that have gone before."[17]

This leads to what Troward calls the Law of Reciprocity: man receives the influx from the Creative Power; but he becomes himself a finite center, a microcosm, from which power also emanates in all directions.[18] It is thus that we become the differentiated and "differentiating centers of Divine Thought...."[19]

Since we are replicas of the Infinite Central Power, why are not all human beings great, noble, successful? The answer is simple enough: only a few have learned to cooperate with the Spirit—to live in harmony with its immutable laws.[20] The "Divine Ideal can only be externalized in our objective life in proportion as it is first formed in our thought; and it takes form in our thought only to the extent to which we apprehend its existence in the Divine Mind."[21] What people have not learned but must comprehend "is that the human mind forms a new point of departure for the work of the Creative Spirit...." It is only as we realize this truth that we find ourselves entering into the new order of life in which we become less and less subject to the old limitations.[22]

Every earthly "manifestation" is in essence the expression of the "Parent Mind,"[23] which presses forward "through the individual and particular"; and our lives will be great precisely in proportion as we utilize this universally available power and operate according to its laws.[24] Since we are the offspring of this Parent Mind and can always draw upon its power, there is no limit to our potential.[25] We are the "sons and daughters of the Almighty," the children of the All-Originating Divine Mind,[26] which operates in the individual[27] as the Christ-Idea—which is simply a universal principle capable of reproduction in every human personality.[28]

5. *The Primordial Creation.* At the base of Troward's cosmic system is the Swedenborgian nebular hypothesis. "The physical history of our planet," he states, "shows us first an incandescent nebula dispersed over vast infinitudes of space; later, this condenses into a central sun surrounded by a family of glowing planets, hardly yet consolidated from the plastic primordial matter...."[29] Animating all this, there is "Pure Spirit," which "is the Life-principle considered apart from the matrix in which it takes...a particular form. In this aspect, it is pure intelligence undifferentiated into individuality."[30] And, as such, it "is the Formless principle of Life...."[31] It may also be

called "Atomic intelligence"[32]; furthermore, "this primordial, all-generating living spirit must be commensurate with infinitude...."[33] It must also be a unity which "can be neither multiplied nor divided"[34]; and, since this "Originating Life Principle is infinite...the *whole* of it must be present"[35] in all its parts. Its substantive properties must be life and light, from which power proceeds.[36] For this all-originating spirit we must predicate an eternal existence.[37]

God (Troward rarely uses the word) is thus "the intelligence of undifferentiated spirit."[38] It is identical in all its specific modes.[39] It is, furthermore, wholly devoid of individual personality in its operation as the life-principle which gives rise to all the particular manifestations of nature; this power is a unity in essence which finds multiplicity in expression.[40] Those who attribute personality to the Universal Mind are guilty of the error which has sapped the foundations of religion in all ages.[41] This impersonal power is without specific intention; instead, it works by a law of averages for the advancement of the race as a whole, and is never concerned with the individual.[42]

This originating force is "the primordial substance"; but it is inseparable from spirit, for the latter contains the primary substance. There can be no duality, for then we should have to postulate another power in the universe.[43] There is a single intelligence subsisting throughout nature, everywhere inherent in its manifestations, which is the ultimate foundation for every material creation.[44]

Thus it is that we live "in the midst of an ocean of undifferentiated, yet intelligent, Life, above, below, all around, and permeating ourselves both mentally and corporeally...."[45] Underlying and directing this totality of things, there is a great Intelligence[46] which is seen throughout the cosmic scheme, where matter adheres because of the cosmic will.[47]

Immutable law is the governing principle of this infinitude; and from this there can never be any departure in any portion of the universe.[48] It applies as well in the invisible as in the material world.[49] The reign of law is the pillar on which the universe is founded.[50] It is also the foundation of all mental science.[51] There can be no exception to law, since the acts of God are never capricious, motivated by favoritism, or influenced by bribes or flattery.[52] If chance were to rule the universe, it would quickly be reduced to chaos.[53]

Although the Creative Force is impersonal, it is endowed with what

Troward calls "*personalness*," which implies a generalized divine consciousness. We must, however, never impute to it the concept of individuality.[54]

The "Originating Spirit," we read, holds "a boundless potential of Creativeness...."[55] This is a process "inherent in the Universal Mind,"[56] which not only confers life but, by its own imperative, seeks to create higher forms of evolutionary law.[57] Thus, "the higher the grade of life, the higher the intelligence," a truth "clearly demonstrated by the grand natural order of the universe."[58] Nor can we conceive of any limit to evolution.[59] In achieving higher levels, man simply fulfills the creative process.[60]

6. *The Law of Continuity in the Universe.* Troward recognizes several kingdoms, all endowed with differing degrees of intelligence or "livingness": minerals, plants, animals, and man, to which he adds a fifth[61]—man spiritualized after he was "passed over" or become, while still in this world, a "Son of God."[62] The organic world is superimposed upon the inorganic in this march toward higher forms; and the science of embryology foreshadows spiritual prototypes.[63] The creative process necessitates what Troward calls the Law of Progression, ever impelling life to seek higher forms[64]; and there is a universal Law of Continuity which develops ever more perfect individuals and impels life-forms upward from mineral to vegetative to animal to human and finally to spiritual.[65] And, since this creative evolution is inexorable, the Law of Continuity, as in Drummond, is unbreakable.[66] In this way, the cosmic intelligence becomes individualized in infinite diversity based upon a universal unity[67]; and we can, therefore, realize our "own identity of being with the Universal Mind, which is commensurate with the Universal Law."[68]

The universal life "forever unfolds itself in all the infinite evolutionary forces of the cosmic scheme and" and, in its onward march, evolves "into higher and higher conscious intelligence in the successive races of mankind...."[69] At the apex of this development, "every human soul is an individualization of that Universal Being, or All-Spirit, which we call God" and which "can never be shorn of its powers, but, like Fire, which is its symbol, must always be fully and perfectly itself...."[70]

This metaphysical substance leads to the Doctrine of Correspondences, which Troward interlocks with the concept of the microcosm and the macrocosm. "You are the world and the universe in miniature,"[71] he declares. "Our own consciousness of personality can only be accounted for by the existence...of a corresponding quality in the Originating Spirit."[72] The first step, he continues, in "the production of any external fact must be the creation of its spiritual prototype..." as "elaborated by...Swedenborg in his doctrine of correspondences...."[73]

Since all human minds are projections of the cosmic mind,[74] the same laws which govern the macrocosm apply equally to the microcosm[75]; and, since this is true, we can, by investigating ourselves, comprehend the corresponding principles which exist throughout the invisible universe.[76]

True religious worship, therefore, consists not in creeds, dogmas, rituals, or any purported written revelations, but in "the study of the Universal Life-Principle, 'the Father,' in its nature and its modes of action...."[77] But we are warned against attributing personality to the Father, since the term is purely symbolic.[78]

7. *The Theory of Healing.* The Trowardian theory of healing stems from the Swedenborgian doctrine of Influx, which postulates the "Good" as a "stream flowing from the exhaustless Infinite...."[79] The universal Life or Power is, as it were, the central dynamo from which we draw vitality. Nature in her "most arcane depths, is one vast storehouse of life and good, entirely devoted to our individual use." And we can draw streams of vital energy from her for the accomplishment of whatever we desire.[80] By opening up a channel in himself, "the individual lives directly from the Orginating Life...."[81] We can "find in the boundless ocean of central living Spirit the source from which we can go on taking *ad infinitum*...."[82] This "All-Originating Love and Beauty will thus flow out as peace of mind, health of body, discretion in the management of our affairs, and power in carrying out our undertakings...."[83]

The cosmic mind, which has no individuality, is implanted in every manifestation of life; and in human beings it appears as subjective mind, in contrast to the objective, or conscious.[84] The former reasons only deductively, while the latter can do so inductively as well [85] and therefore controls the former,[86] which, however, is endowed with various extraordinary powers, such as thought-transference, clairvoyance, etc.; and beyond all this, a unique capacity for building the body and creating health.[87]

This universal mind is the creative power in nature[88]; and since it is impersonal, the subjective human mind is the same.[89] Health can therefore be induced by suggestion from the objective mind[90]; the solid basis for Mental Science rests upon the fact that health can be externalized in the body by the action of the subjective mind, the creative power lodged within us.[91] The cure itself depends on belief.[92] In every healing process, therefore, the right belief is essential.[93] Wrong beliefs externalize as sickness, for they regard secondary causes as primary.[94] In this area, Troward approaches the doctrines of Quimby and Christian Science. "The only conception you can have of *yourself* in the absolute...is as *purely living spirit*...and therefore not subject to illness; and when this idea is firmly impressed upon the subconscious mind, it will externalize it" and banish disease.[95]

Healers must "understand our relation to the great impersonal power we are using" and operate as its instruments.[96] In thought, healer and patient must ignore the symptoms of disease and recognize only "the purely spiritual individuality...."[97] When the outer mind of the patient is receptive, [98] the healer can address the patient's subconscious as though it were his own, for both are identical.[99] The function of the healer is to employ the objective mind as a link between the universal and the patient's subjective mind.[100]

Again and again, Troward declares that thoughts are potent facts,[101] "one of the great forces in the Universe."[102] In fact, the "Universal Spirit, by Self-contemplation, evolves Universal Substance."[103] "Thoughts are things," he continues, and "therefore, as we *will* our thoughts to be, so" will outward things become.[104] Since mental creations are spiritual realities[105] and positive thought produces positive results,[106] the healer need only transfer the conceptions of the cosmic spirit to the level of the individualized particular in order to create the conditions which externalize in health.[107] The power of thought is without limit; the individual simply gives direction to a force infinitely greater than his own.[108] The Law of Correspondence guarantees a similar externalization. "And to this law there is no limit."[109]

There is indeed a universally creative and all-permeating intelligence; however, this cannot confer health through mental treatment unless the patient's mind is receptive.[110] When this response is present, "thought-power is able to produce results on the material plane...."[111]

In effecting a cure, "the Law will serve us exactly to the extent that we first observe the Law."[112] Nature will obey us precisely as we first obey her[113]; but every infraction carries a punitive consequence.[114] Except through knowledge, there is no escape from this law; but if we obey and cooperate with Nature, it becomes our unfailing friend and servant.[115] Thus we draw from the cosmic resources virtually unlimited psychic, mental, moral, and financial benefits. Since the universal creative power has no mind of its own, it can be placed under the direction of positive thought; and, since it never abrogates its function as creative power, it performs the work assigned to it. Thus it is that "mental action produces a corresponding reaction in the mind of the Spirit...."[116] Thought-power acts upon the cosmic element inherent in all things, from mineral to man; being impersonal, it has "no private purpose of its own with which to oppose the suggestion impressed upon it."[117] It is through the "cosmic element, inherent in all things from mineral to man, that Thought-Power acts...."[118]

As an indispensible condition for healing, the practitioner and patient alike must picture to themselves the fulfillment of their "desires as already accomplished on the spiritual plane...."[119] Through a union of the individual's subconscious with the all-creative spirit, "specialized effects can be produced in his body" which "transcend our past experiences...."[120] The power of the word, cosmic or individual, "whether spoken or only dwelt upon in Thought, impresses itself upon the impersonal element around us, whether in persons or things."[121] Since space does not exist for the cosmic mind, absent treatment is equally effective.[122] The word of the healer produces a "corresponding vibration in the soul of the subject"; and this communicates similar ones to its body.[123] The creative thought thus externalizes in health. When we realize that we are pure spirit, we can "send forth our thought to produce any effect we will."[124]

Since there is no duality in the universe and since the creative power is all-good, it can have no opposite except mental negation. If you admit that evil has reality, you create it, together with all its consequences of sorrow, sickness, and death. Since disease and death are negations of life, we know that spirit cannot embody disease or death.[125] By acting negatively, we oppose the spirit.[126] The constant influx of health, happiness, and prosperity from the universal spirit is available to the individual only when there is no inversion in his presentation of himself to the Originating Power.[127] The healer should use the cosmic mind to make suggestions to the subconscious of his patient[128] and thus create in him a nucleus which draws creative power to itself, which, in turn, will externalize in a corresponding form.[129] Our thought is like a magnet attracting to us those conditions which accurately correspond to itself. Since thoughts are things, if we *think* life, illumination, harmony, prosperity, and happiness, all these will be added unto us.[130]

Since the originating spirit operates only according to the law of Reciprocity,[131] and is altogether good,[132] we cannot establish rapport with the cosmic mind unless our own motives and intentions are pure.[133] And, as we come into a full understanding of Mental Science, we learn that we must guard against all negative or hostile thoughts and words.[134]

Healing is accomplished when the practitioner can "speak to the subconscious mind of the patient as though it were his own, for both being pure spirit, the *thought* of their identity *makes* them identical..."[135] By repeating "I am—therefore I can—therefore I will," we experience a "projection of our powers, whether interior or external, to the accomplishment of the desired object."[136]

Troward emphasizes the deleterious effects of what he calls negative Race-Thought or Consciousness, that is, inherited false beliefs, which are not easily banished[137] and which accept the inevitability of sickness and death.[138] The essence of the New Thought gospel consists in the creation of a new standard in which these will no longer be unavoidable because we will know that they have no existence in the eternal essence.[139]

8. *The Rejection of Orthodoxy.* As in New Thought generally, the old and orthodox dogmas are rejected in the Trowardian system. God is an impersonal power; nothing is said concerning the practice or the efficacy of prayer; sin consists in negations which prevent the beneficent influx[140]; and sin punishes itself.[141] The doctrine of atonement means simply "that in the Person of Christ every human being, past, present, and to come, was self-offered for the condemnation of his [own] sin...."[142] The Trowardian Christology expresses the same docetic concept found in Swedenborg and throughout New Thought. "Christ," we are told, "is the Son of God, that is, the Divine Principle of Humanity out of which we originated and subsisting in us all, however unconsciously to ourselves...."[143]

In addition to these abstract principles, there are intensely practical elements in Troward's system. It is not money but the love of it for its own sake that is the root of all evil; the *spirit* of opulence is precisely the thing which is furthest removed from this. If you *think* opulence, you will also realize the means of achieving it; for it "will flow to you from all quarters, whether as money or as a hundred other things not to be reckoned in cash."[144]

New Thought, declares Troward, promises "health to the body, peace of mind, earthly prosperity, prolongation of life, and, finally, even the conquest of death itself...."[145] Although God does not put cash in our pockets by some conjuring trick,[146] the "Law of Supply will...bring us into a new world where the useful employment of all our powers, whether mental or physical, will be...a perpetual source of health and happiness...."[147]

Such was the message of Thomas Troward.

VI. CHARLES BRODIE PATTERSON

1. *Biographical.* Charles B. Patterson (1854-1936), previously editor of *Mind*, became the supervising editor of *Arena* in 1900; since these were then probably the most influential publications in the New Thought movement, there can be no doubt that Patterson exercised great influence in shaping its course. He was president of the International Metaphysical League and secretary of the subsequent New Thought Federation. In addition to the various official positions he occupied and the many lectures he delivered, he wrote a number of books which were widely read, some of which may still be found in second-hand bookstores. Among these, we may mention *The Will to Be Well, The Measure of a Man, Dominion and Power, A New Heaven and a New Earth, Love's Song of Life*, and, finally, *What Is New Thought?*

A general characteristic among all New Thought leaders of note—and this is particularly true of Patterson—is their general intellectual dependence on Swedenborg,* although with individual variations.

---

* Patterson declared: "Yes, the dream of the alchemist, the vision of a St. John or a Swedenborg, shall become realized in our daily lives."[1]

Only a few, such as Quimby, Evans, Emerson, Drummond, and Troward, were sufficiently creative to make their contributions permanent elements in the movement; thereafter, lesser intellects, often far more successful as popularizers, gave manifold expression to the gospel of health, happiness, and success.

2. *Cosmic Theory*. Since cosmic theory is so important in New Thought, we must examine Patterson's metaphysical system. The "enlightened soul," he states, "perceives that God and His creation is all there is; that in spirit we are one with God; that in our bodies we are one with all forms; that the spirit within is God, and the body without His handiwork; that whatever we possess or whatever we are comes from the One giver of every good and perfect gift...."[2] And again: "God is the Father and Mother of all humanity;...all men and women are brothers and sisters...."[3] "We are so related to one another that there is among us in continual operation an alternative outflow and influx—and the latter inevitably partakes of the qualities of the former."[4]

This theology is repeated over and over. "The whole visible creation is the outer, the visible Word of God, and man, as Image and Likeness of God, must become the epitomized universe in physical form...."[5]

Patterson often emphasizes an idea which had permeated New Thought by 1900: "The soul is differentiated *spirit*; that is, each soul contains within itself a picture (or image) of the great, universal soul" which "is the all-comprehensive Soul. Everything that is in God enters into the human soul; thus does God seek expression through the life of man."[6] The human soul is "the differentiated...individual spirit, the microcosm, which contains within herself the complete picture of the universal God, the macrocosm...."[7] There is a constant influx of life, which flows through the grand organism, which is also the only life and intelligence.[8]

The cosmos is governed by immutable law. "Nothing ever happens ...there is no chance."[9] Again: "Everything in the universe is subject to the operation of the eternal and unchanging law of God, which regulates every part...."[10]

3. *Healing*. Since human beings share in the nature of God, they must also be immortal.[11] "Life is eternal; health is a natural condition; worries, difficulties, sorrows, cease" as we pass from death into life.[12] Although the planet Earth will one day reclaim the body which "it has loaned for a season"[13] in the transition known as death, we know that,

since "life is indestructible...the departing tenant lives" on and will "build a new temple,"[14] a celestial body. There can be no such thing as a soul without a body.

Although the mental and spiritual aspects of man take precedence over the physical, we must understand "that life is one, that there is really no separation between the physical, mental, and spiritual planes of being...."[15] "When we all come to the conviction that the causes of disease are mental, then in eliminating one cause we will at the same time have thus wiped out of existence perhaps half a dozen so-called diseases.... The Germ of disease is not physical; it is in the mind...."[16] In every sickness, the mind is the first to get well.[17] "It is much easier...to retain health...than it is to regain it...." "Forethought saves us from many mistakes...."[18] "Ignorance, sin, sorrow, pain, disease are nothing in and of themselves—only seeming conditions to be overcome by the light of truth...."[19] When we realize this profound fact, "evil loses its seeming power...and we can at any moment bring the light of the Central Life to dispel all the outer darkness which we call evil."[20] It is the diseased thought that begets the diseased body.[21] Once man realizes that he is one with Universal Life, sickness and diseases are under control.[22]

All this is the Master Key to Patterson's technique of healing. When it is fully understood that evil and destructive thoughts create disease, "no one will resort to any medicine or to any physician..." and "a diseased body will be literally unknown."[23] Whatever we strongly desire becomes "the greatest factor in causing the desire to be realized."[24] All thoughts and mental pictures "take from, and express themselves in, one's physical organism...."[25] Again: "Whatever we feel and whatever we think that we become...."[26] Every person "has also a magnet within his own life, that is attracting to him...whatever he is attuned to...."[27] By thinking good, unselfish thoughts, "we attract to ourselves everything necessary to our well-being—happiness, health, strength, friends."[28]

4. *Divergencies.* Despite all this, Patterson candidly admits the existence of sickness. He rejects "the false or so-called animal magnetism."[29] Disease, he declares, is very real,[30] and it would be absurd to deny the existence of sin, sickness, and death.[31] "If you say that there is no sin, sickness, or disease, you have simply succeeded in hypnotizing yourself into an erroneous belief."[32] "I do not believe," he states, that

"there is any good reason why anyone should be ill, but good health does not come to an individual without...effort...."[33] And he continues: "If we breathe and sleep properly, there is no reason why we may not, at the age of a hundred years, be enjoying the full use of every faculty...."[34] Nothing is more destructive than worry.[35] "Fear is at the root of all so-called Evil; all sin, sorrow, disease, and death have their origin in fear...."[36] "Fear and doubt not only paralyze mental activity, but dissipate physical vitality. These two false emotions, which mother a brood of kindred spirits, poison the mind and this in turn expresses itself as physical poison in the body...."[37]

5. *The Subconscious.* Concerning the psyche, Patterson declares: "All conscious mental action becomes later subconscious, establishing habits of thought and action...."[38] Everything that a man ever does "survives in his subconscious mind...a whole menagerie of wild animals lurk in the jungle of the subconscious only awaiting some conscious impulse of anger or hate to become fully awakened and to dominate life as it was ruled in the past."[39] "We are," he states, "writing the book of life daily...."[40] Thus it is that "man makes his own fate."[41] So we find that Patterson had developed a psychoanalytical approach at least equal to that of Freud.

"New Thought," he declares, "teaches neither future punishment nor reward other than that the individual rewards or punishes himself as he conforms to or opposes the Laws of Life...."[42]

Although Patterson does not deny the desirability of material things, he stresses the importance of "supply" or prosperity somewhat less than many of the New Thought proponents. The pursuit of personal, selfish pleasure breeds satiety[43]; and real "happiness is made up of a continual giving and receiving...."[44] Remember, he warns, "that success does not, of necessity, include material riches...."[45] for they are only a golden calf,[46] a shadow worship.[47] However, there is nothing "wrong in using mind and body for the acquisition of material wealth...."[48] Our physical needs should be properly evaluated, "for religion must be practical or nothing."[49]

6. *Spiritual Interpretation.* Patterson interprets Scripture in the best tradition of Quimby and Swedenborg. The tares and thistles, for example, that must be consumed in fire and the sheep that shall be divided from the goats are the unreal conditions of life to which humanity has been subjected.[50] Elsewhere, he declares that "the second

coming of Christ means the coming of the Universal Christ in the hearts of all people."[51] The shedding of Jesus' blood was the casting off of the old nature, no longer useful.[52]

7. *The Attack against Orthodoxy.* Patterson assailed traditional religious dogma very much as Quimby did. "The gentle Nazarene," we read, "whose greatest object in life was to bring peace and good-will to all men, is made to stand, as it were, sponsor for this so-called Christian civilization, which has in it the cruelty of the tiger and the rapacity of the hyena."[53] "Of what use," he demands, "is it to Christianize the people of the world unless you can inculcate the real Christian doctrine of Life?" As now practiced, "Christianity is...a religion of hypocrisy, cant, and deceit."[54] For centuries, "we have been trying to enforce on other people, at the point of the sword and the bayonet, Christian doctrines which we ourselves have not practised."[55]

"What the world needs today," he continues, "is practical, not theoretical Christianity."[56] The worldly nature of the Church is manifest in the outward trappings it displays.[57] This materialistic church is spiritually bankrupt. "Viewed from the dogmatic, theological standpoint, it is...a colossal" failure.[58] "The reign of this dogmatic, theological Christianity is passing away" for "it has had its day...."[59] And the time has come for "the Church...to make a new statement of the vital truths of the Christian religion; let it burn away the straw and the stubble of the past and build on a new foundation...."[60] "Religious creeds, forms, and symbols are all of man's own making."[61] "How long," he thunders, "shall the self-appointed priesthood or clergy seek to blind the eyes...of their followers in order that they may have temporal power?"[62]

In Patterson's system, the old theology and Christology are swept away. "Some," he says, "would have us fall down and worship the man [Jesus]; they would have us believe that it is through the shedding of his material blood that we are saved."[63] The evil was invented to account for the existence of sickness and death. "Then came the idea that something must be sacrificed to propitiate an angry deity, and perfect things without blemish were offered up by the priests...."[64]

8. *Strictures against the Medical Profession.* In the light of the preceding, we are not surprised at his condemnation of the medical profession. "Doctors make strenuous efforts to procure legislation prohibiting the practice of Mental and Christian Science," not because

they are concerned over the public welfare, but because of interference with their incomes.[65] "If the bodies of people could have been made well and whole through physical remedies, surely by this time the so-called science of medicine should have overcome all kinds of physical diseases; but the fact is that diseases multiply as fast as new remedies multiply, and the science of drug-medication today is really no further advanced than it was in the dark ages."[66]

9. *Social Justice.* Since New Thought had as one of its principal objectives the achievement of human happiness, Patterson was imbued with a strong bent for social justice. All people are entitled to equal rights, whether rich or poor, whether men or women.[67] He excoriates the practice of jailing men simply because they have no visible means of support.[68] Society will one day understand that it is far better to keep all its members usefully employed. Today, we have wealthy parasites who exert a far more pernicious influence than the poverty-stricken drones. In that better world which is dawning, we will have neither sluggards nor laggards, but all will rejoice in useful work.[69]

However, Patterson was a firm believer in self-reliance: "of late years," he laments, "a most pernicious doctrine has been instilled into the minds of many...: that they can get something for nothing."[70] "In a really civilized community, there should be no drones, no people living at the expense of other people...."[71] And, since all life is an infinite unity, it is an ethical imperative that our lives be spent in the service of mankind.[72] Greatness requires work, work, work.[73]

10. *Health and Affirmative Prayer.* Healing occurs by principles already emphasized by Judge Troward and Emma Curtis Hopkins. "New Thought teaches that health, happiness, and success in life constitute the legitimate birthright of every child of the All-loving Father-Mother God, and that through knowledge of, and conformity with, Divine Law, one enters into his real inheritance."[74] Again: "Physical health may be fully and freely realized when we take the one way that is open, and steadily follow in that way. Picture in your mind all that you wish...your body to become.... In this way, each ideal shall be realized...."[75]

Since the power of God is the force that creates health, "the healer then supplies the medium through which that power passes to reach the patient...."[76] The secret of healing lies in positive declaration:

"Error is to be overcome, not by the denial that error exists, but by affirming the existence and power of the eternal truths."[77] Every person should say: "It is right that I should be well and strong. God is the Source of my life; in him I live and move and have my being."[78]

To achieve and retain health, therefore, we must obey the laws of life and recite the New Thought Credo, which is simply an Affirmative Prayer: "I am one with all life. I am one with all Intelligence. I am one with all the Health and Wholeness of Universal Health and Universal Wholeness. I live, I move, and have my being in God. I now have the eternal life. I am rich because all things are mine. I am powerful because my will is one with Universal Will. Through heart and mind, I control and direct the full force of my own life. My rightful inheritance as a Child of God brings to me every good and every perfect gift.... The deep within me speaks to the Everlasting Deep, and I know that I am a Son of God, joint heir with Christ having dominion and power both in the age that now is and in the age that is to come."[79]

VII. ELLA WHEELER WILCOX

Ella Wheeler Wilcox (1850-1919) flashed across the firmament like a comet in the days of her halcyon splendor. For years, she wrote a daily poem for a syndicate of newspapers, and her name, like that of Edgar Guest in later years, became a household word. The *Cumulative Book Index* listed thirty-three of her titles in 1922, seventeen in 1928, but none in 1937. Today her books are rarely found even in good libraries or large second-hand bookstores. De Vorss carries no reprint of them; neither histories nor anthologies of American literature accord her much space; and yet her name has achieved a niche of its own in the lore of this nation.

As a student of Emma Curtis Hopkins in the mid-1880s, she embraced the New Thought gospel with an all-consuming passion that continued throughout her life and is stated most succinctly, perhaps, in a thin but handsome volume of prose entitled *The Heart of New Thought*, published by the Psychic Research Company of Chicago in 1902.

Although Mrs. Wilcox proclaims the general principles and attitudes of New Thought, she is distinguished by certain characteristics of her own. For example, she was sure that proper diet, cleanliness, deep breathing, and exercise are absolutely necessary to good health.[1] She gave ample attention to the practical and the physical. People who eat too much or take unhealthful foods are sure to become obese and have gastric disturbances. We should exercise great care in our diet and never overeat; two meals a day are enough for most people.[2] She declared emphatically that old clothes should be discarded, since they are relics of past days; but, at the same time, if given to charity, they should be bestowed only upon the deserving, for otherwise they would perpetuate idleness,[3] which is infinitely worse than poverty. Although child labor, pauperism, and wage-earning mothers are serious evils, unearned wealth is even worse.[4]

Mrs. Wilcox warned against the belief that difficulties or disabilities can be overcome quickly; indeed, in many cases, they are irremediable. Since these are in many instances not attributable to the sufferers, she embraced the Hindu-Buddhist doctrines of karma and reincarnation: for in no other way could they be reconciled with the concept of law and a God of justice. "The three-year-old child who toddles in front of a trolley car," we read, "cannot be blamed for wrong thinking.... Neither can the deaf mute or the child born blind or deformed. We must go farther back, to former lives, to find the first cause of such misfortunes."[5]

"Remember," she declares, "you are the maker and molder of your own destiny."[6] And again: "Every thought, word and deed is helping decide your next place in the Creator's magnificent universe. You will be beautiful or ugly, wise or ignorant, fortunate or unfortunate, according to what use you make of yourself here and now.... Even if you escape the immediate results" of your "course of action here, you must face the law of *cause and effect* in the next state. It is inevitable. God, the maker of all things, does not change His laws."[7] And further: "You can destroy the body, but the *You* who suffers in mind and spirit will suffer still, and live still. You will only change your location from one state to another. You did not make yourself and you cannot unmake yourself. You can merely put yourself among the spiritual tramps who hang about the earth's borders, because they have not prepared themselves for a better place...."[8] Such souls will be like the unburied Greeks and those in Dante's Limbo.

Like many other proponents of New Thought, Mrs. Wilcox proclaims the substantiality of *thoughts* and their decisive influence; and she does so in poetic accents of great power:

> "You never can tell what your thoughts will do
>   In bringing you hate and love,
> For thoughts are things, and their airy wings
>   Are swift as a carrier dove.
> They follow the law of the universe—
>   Each thing must create its kind,
> And they speed o'er the track to bring you back
>   Whatever went forth from your mind."[9]

And again:

> "Our thoughts are shaping unmade spheres,
>   And, like a blessing or a curse,
> They thunder down the formless years
>   And ring throughout the universe."[10]

Since thoughts are so potent, "if you think peace, hope, and happiness, you are sending a note of harmony and success."[11] Watch your temper—keep it even. "Clear your mind of every gloomy, selfish. angry, or revengeful thought. Allow no resentment or grudge toward man or fate to stay in your heart overnight."[12]

There are hundreds of thousands of people who believe themselves "sick, sorrowful, and poverty-stricken," but who "would be well, glad, and prosperous if they only thought themselves so."[13] Many people think only the worst: for example, the millionaire who complained that he had been robbed because he was not permitted to make his own fortune.[14]

Mrs. Wilcox attacked the old creeds and churches with sharp virility. The "orthodox" Christian who declares that all humanity is "vile—selfish—sinful"[15] carries "a moral malaria with him, which poisons the air...and...is projecting pernicious mind stuff into space, which is as dangerous to the peace of the community as dynamite bombs" and constitutes a "false, unholy, and blasphemous 'religion.' "[16] She was filled with pity and sorrow when she heard some "orthodox" woman repeat the old cliché that we are born to endure suffering and misery.

"Thank God," she exclaims, "that the wave of 'New Thought' is sweeping over the land, and washing away those old blasphemous errors of mistaken creeds."[17]

Man has the power to recreate himself. To this end, he must "think success, prosperity, usefulness."[18] "We are heirs of God's kingdom, and rightful inheritors of happiness, and health, and success."[19] Since "*man is what he thinks*," he can free himself "from any chains, whether of poverty, sin, ill health, or unhappiness."[20]

In contrast with Christian Daa Larson, however, Mrs. Wilcox warns against a mere philosophy of optimism. Although the world was full of New Thought literature, it was effective only for those who would undertake the task of remaking themselves from within. Those who have accepted the necessity of sin, ill health, poverty, or unhappiness, "must not expect to batter down the walls you have built during a lifetime in a week, or a month, or a year."[21] Victory may require a long time, but it will come. "All that our dearest hopes desire will come to us, if we believe in ourselves as rightful heirs to Divine Opulence, and work and think always on those lines."[22]

Failure or success is not measured by the wealth one accumulates or the fame or success one attains; on the contrary, it consists in the building of character that will confer peace and happiness in this life and guarantee a better destiny for the next.[23] Woe unto him "who cultivates his mental and spiritual powers only" to gain wealth or power![24] "Into the Great Scheme of Existence, as first conceived by the Creator, money did not enter.... There was no millionaire and no pauper soul created by God."[25]

Mrs. Wilcox was acutely aware that, since New Thought was a new idea, it attracted "hysterical women, unbalanced men: the erratic and the irresponsible."[26] She denounced the belief that health, wealth, youth, beauty, etc., were to be had in a miraculous way, or that practitioners could become great healers in a brief space of time.[27] None of these things can be attained by reading occult literature,[28] or through an instant illumination.[29]

In the final article in *The Heart of New Thought*, Mrs. Wilcox virtually labels the followers of Mary Baker Eddy as cranks or lunatics. "I once chanced to call on a lady who," she discovered, "considered her illness a mere 'claim' her 'mortal mind' had made...."[30] All such talk "is very ridiculous,"[31] as are the absurd notions that one day we will require neither food nor money.

And this, perhaps, marks the point of departure that separated some of Mrs. Hopkins's students from the fountainhead of the Christian Science Church.

VIII. RALPH WALDO TRINE

1. *Amazing Personality.* One of the most famous and effective popularizers of Swedenborgianism was Ralph Waldo Trine (1866-1958), named to bear the illustrious mantle of Emerson, to whom, in due course, he was to accord second place among the sages of mankind.[1] Neither a churchman nor a healer, nor yet an original thinker, he was an author and lecturer whose message influenced millions, especially through his most successful book, *In Tune with the Infinite*, which, completed at the age of thirty, went through more than fifty editions in a few years and sold more than one and a half million copies in the United States alone; it was translated into more than twenty languages, where it sold another million copies. It has now probably sold at least four million copies, and therefore ranks as the most popular New Thought book ever written. Henry Ford attributed his inspiration to succeed from it. Although Trine attained the age of ninety-two, his most productive period extended from 1895 to 1915, when he still had more than forty years of life remaining. *In Tune with the Infinite* is available from De Vorss in paperback.

2. *The Eclectic Amalgam. What All the World's A-Seeking*, published in 1896, reflects an admixture of influences drawn primarily from Emerson, W.F. Evans, and Greek and socialist sources. Here we find no direct Swedenborgian influence. Happiness and greatness, we read, are the by-products of a life spent in service to others; thoughts are things and exercise influence for good or evil[2]; we must get rid of creeds and dogmas[3]; surplus wealth is useless and destructive[4]; animals may have immortal souls[5]; and sin is the result of ignorance.[6] He then launched into a discussion of the class-struggle,[7] of working people and the churches from a definitely socialist point of view[8]; and he praises economic cooperation.[9] Christ, we read, is not a sacrificial

savior, but an exemplar. The body, we read, is good and beautiful in all its parts[10]; and asceticism should be outlawed. The world is a manifestation of God[11]; and Christ is the divinity existing within. Death is simply "that transition" in which "all material accumulations and possessions are left behind, and the soul takes with it only the unfoldment and growth of the real life" in the Spirit World.[12] The book closes with a denial of original sin and an Emersonian dithyramb to virtue and self-reliance.

3. *Swedenborg Discovered.* About 1896, Trine must have discovered the Swedish seer because his next and most famous book, *In Tune with the Infinite (1897)*, is a symphony vibrating with a new vision based on his revelations. Afire with his newfound gospel, Trine burst into jubilation; and, since it was simplistic and practical, the book reached the heart of all humanity. Swedenborg, declares Trine, is "the highly illumined seer...pointing out the great laws in connection with what he termed the divine influx, and how we may open ourselves more fully to its operations."[13] The whole book is a philosophic popularization of his new master. "The great central fact of the universe," we read, "is that Spirit of Infinite Life and Power that is back of all, that animates all, that manifests itself in and through all; that self-existent principle of life from which all has come and...is continually coming.... This Infinite Power is creating, working, ruling through an agency of great immutable laws and forces that run through the universe.... God, then, is this Infinite Spirit which fills all the universe with Himself alone, so that all is from Him and in Him and there is nothing that is outside."[14]

The doctrine of influx is stated or implied on almost every page; we "can open ourselves so fully to the incoming of the divine inflow, and so to the operation of those higher forces, inspirations and powers, that we can indeed and in truth become what we may well term God-men."[15] Again: "In the degree that we open ourselves to the inflowing of this immanent and transcendent life, do we make ourselves channels through which the Infinite Intelligence and Power can work."[16]

The idea is repeated again and again. "The man of power, Centered in the Infinite...has...connected himself with...the great powerhouse of the universe.... His strong, positive, and hence constructive thought is continually working success for him along all lines.... Silent, unseen forces are at work which will sooner or later be made manifest in the visible."[17]

Another recurring theme deals with health and disease, and is based on Swedenborgian hypotheses. "The moment a person realizes this oneness with the Infinite Spirit, he...no longer makes the mistake of regarding himself as body, subject to ills and diseases, but he realizes the fact that he is spirit, spirit now as much as he will or ever can be...."[18] "In the degree...that you come into...oneness with the Infinite Spirit of Life...you open yourself to the divine inflow" and "set into operation forces that will sooner or later bring even the physical body into a state of abounding health and strength. For...this Infinite Spirit of Life can from its very nature admit of no disease...."[19] "I then as spirit...can in my own real nature admit of no disease. I now open my body, in which disease has gotten a foothold...fully to the inflowing tide of this Infinite Life...and the healing process is going on."[20]

Evil emotions and bad mental attitudes (similar to the Swedenborgian infestation) are the causes of physical ailments. "Practically all disease, with its consequent suffering, has its origin in perverted mental and emotional states and conditions.... No disease can enter...our bodies unless it find therein something corresponding to itself...."[21]

The theme is reiterated. "The time will come when...the physician will not...attempt to heal the body, but to heal the mind, which in turn will heal the body...and...there will come a time when each will be his own physician.... As a rule, those who think least of their bodies enjoy the best health."[22]

Trine, however, never denies the reality of matter, the physical. "Give the body the nourishment, the exercise, the fresh air, the sunlight it requires, keep it clean, and then think of it as little as possible.... Don't talk of sickness and disease. By talking of these you do yourself harm and you do harm to those who listen to you."[23] Sleep is a great restorer[24]; and we should avoid "the heavier, grosser, less valuable kinds of food and drink, such as the flesh of animals, alcoholic drinks, and all things of the class that stimulate the body and passions rather than build the body and the brain into a strong, clean, well-nourished, enduring, and fibrous condition."[25] "When you allow your thoughts of anger, hatred, malice, jealousy, envy, criticism, or scorn to exercise sway, they have a corroding and poisoning effect upon the organism;

they pull it down, and if allowed to continue, will eventually tear it to pieces by externalizing themselves in...particular forms of disease...."[26]

Many millions who have long been invalids could be restored to health by a "vital realization of...oneness with the Infinite Power" and by opening themselves "completely to the divine inflow..."[27] Trine never tires of exposing the corrosive effects of destructive emotions. "Fear has become with millions a fixed habit.... To live in continual dread, continual cringing, continual fear of anything, be it loss of love, loss of money, loss of position or situation, is to take the readiest means to lose" everything we have.[28] The action "of fear, grief, worry, despondency...upon the various bodily organs and functions seems to be of a slow, corroding, lowering of activity, and slowly poisoning nature...a falling state of mind is always followed by a falling condition of the body."[29]

Like his mentors, Trine repudiated all orthodox dogma. In the spirit of Emerson, he finds one basic principle in all the religions of the world[30]; he even finds greatness in every kind of dissident: since "God...is the Infinite Spirit of Life and Power...there can be no infidels or atheists.... The earnest, sincere heretic is one of the greatest friends true religion can have. Heretics are among God's greatest servants.... Christ was one of the greatest heretics the world has ever known."[31]

Trine elaborates the Swedenborgian doctrine of correspondence. "Within and above every physical planet is a corresponding ethereal planet, or soul world, as within and above every physical organism is a corresponding ethereal organism or soul body, of which the physical is but the external counterpart and material expression."[32] The *ipsissima verba* of Scripture pose no difficulty, for they are always susceptible to spiritual interpretation. "Blessed are the pure in heart for they shall see God" means simply, "Blessed are they who in all the universe recognize only God, for by such God shall be seen."[33]

4. *Happiness and Opulence.* Trine equated the new Christianity not only with mental and physical well-being, but also with happiness and success. "This is the Spirit of Infinite Plenty...continually bringing all things into expression in material form. He who lives in the realization of his oneness with the Infinite Power becomes a magnet to attract to himself a continued supply of whatever he desires.... The old and... prevalent idea of godliness and poverty has absolutely no basis for its existence, and the sooner we get away from it the better...It had its

origin...in the minds of those who had a distorted, one-sided view of life."[34]

"Opulence," we read, "is the law of the universe, an abundant supply for every need...."[35] Furthermore, since "the supply is always equal to the demand...."[36] there is no excuse for want or poverty and no reason for it except our own deficiencies. "Suggest prosperity to yourself. See yourself in a prosperous condition. Affirm that before long you will be in a prosperous condition; affirm it calmly and quietly, but strongly and confidently. Believe it.... Accept it.... You thus make yourself a magnet to attract the things that you desire."[37] Do this, and you will have health, happiness, success, and prosperity!

Yet (and again following Swedenborg) Trine emphasizes over and over that wealth should not be sought for its own sake. "He who is enslaved with the sole desire for material possessions here will continue to be enslaved even after he no longer retains his body.... Perchance this torture may be increased by his seeing the accumulations he thought were his now being scattered and wasted by spendthrifts."[38] Wealth is good and useful as a trust in the service of humanity. "All about us are persons with lives now stunted and dwarfed who could make them rich and beautiful, filled with a perennial joy, if they would begin wisely to use that which they have spent the greater portion of their lives in accumulating."[39]

5.   *Health.* In *The Alignment of Life*, written in 1913, we find that Trine, although still a Swedenborgian, has absorbed various new elements; he has become deeply interested in the history of the Catholic Church, which he condemns as a mere paganized subversion of the original gospel. And here we find an even greater interest in physical health than in previous works. The spiritual, moral, and physical aspects of man, he declares, are inseparable. "If a man stops thinking wrongful, immoral, or sinful thoughts, then the wrongful, immoral, and sinful actions will not occur...."[40] Likewise, the number of those "whose bodies have been reduced to a low and sluggish tone...both mentally and physically...is simply enormous.... The number of stomach and digestive disorders" thus created "are simply legion.... This is also true of the vast company of those whose nervous breakdown...is primarily, if not entirely, due to this cause," as are "pulmonary troubles...which *always* bring about a lowering of the tone of the system.... The condition of the blood determines...the

condition of the entire physical organism... Mind and body are continually acting and reacting upon one another."[41]

Such was the gospel of Ralph Waldo Trine.

IX. JOEL GOLDSMITH

1. *General Characteristics.* Joel Goldsmith (1882-1964), who began his career as an independent healer at the age of forty-six and who devoted himself exclusively to therapy, is a unique personality in New Thought. Although his ideology is largely in accord with the general principles of the movement, it exudes an aura of its own. Without affiliation to any church or organization, his books attained wide and continuing popularity. In addition to eight pamphlets, De Vorss offers no less than thirty-three full-length books, most of which were produced after he was sixty years old. After 1949, he made his home in Hawaii; but he travelled and lectured all over the world. And he remains one of the most influential authors in the entire New Thought movement.

He delineated his teaching or philosophy in a series of widely distributed volumes called *The Infinite Way*, issued between 1954 and 1959. Other well-known titles are *The Art of Meditation, God the Substance of All Form, Conscious Union with God, Living the Infinite Way, Contemplative Meditation, The Art of Spiritual Healing, The Spiritual Interpretation of Scripture*, and *Attitude of Prayer*. In all of these, similar ideas are reiterated over and over. He also wrote pamphlets with such names as *Business and Salesmanship*.

Since he had been for sixteen years a Christian Science practitioner before he struck out on his own, we need not be surprised that he uses many terms characteristic of this Church. When he abandoned institutionalized religion in 1928, he widened his message so that it might appeal, not only to the followers of Unity, Divine Science, and Science of Mind, etc., but also to many of those still in the conventional churches.[1] He made no attempt to establish a new organization, or to align himself with one already existing.[2] Instead, he sought and found his audience through lectures and books throughout the field of New Thought.

2. *Oriental Influence.* He must have studied Eastern religions, for

we find a strong admixture of orientalism, particularly the lore of India, in Goldsmith.[3] Like Fox and others, he believed in Karma, pre-existence, and reincarnation[4]; but since in the Western world no large religious following was possible except on the basis of the Christian Scriptures, he made these his principal authority, which, of course, he interpreted "spiritually."[5]

Goldsmith relied heavily on a number of Biblical passages, among which the following appear frequently:

> "Of myself I can do nothing."
> "I and the Father are one."
> "Before Abraham was, I am."
> "My grace is sufficient for thee."[6]
> "The Kingdom of God is within me."
> "I am come that you might have life and have it more abundantly."
> "Except the Lord build the house, they labor in vain that build it."
> "I will never leave nor forsake thee."

3. *Technique.* Goldsmith's healing differs from that of most metaphysicians, especially those of the Hopkins-Troward-Holmes school. We read again and again that affirmations are useless.[7] It is totally wrong, he declares, to tell Jane Smith that, since she is a child of God, she cannot be sick or sinful.[8] Repetition and "mental work" are likewise rejected[9] in favor of spiritual healing. We should never pray for anything specific, such as healing or wealth.[10] The practitioner should never give what is known as a "treatment."[11] Thought, as such, is not a power or a thing, but only an avenue of awareness[12]; and disease is never caused by thinking or "mortal mind."[13]

4. *Differences.* There seems to be a basic contradiction in his system; for, on the one hand, he admits that the medical profession does cure or alleviate many diseases; at the same time, however, he makes the most extreme claims for the Infinite Way—his individual contribution to New Thought theory and therapy. We should understand, therefore, that when he speaks of those healed by *materia medica*, he refers to those who have not achieved God-Consciousness through his gospel; the seemingly miraculous cures he proclaims, on the other hand, are achieved only on the higher plane of existence which he postulates as a possibility available to those who will attain The Infinite Way.

5.   *The Infinite Way*. Goldsmith says that this reveals the nature of God as a single infinite power, intelligence, and love; the nature of every individual is one with God in quality and character, but expressed in a multiplicity of forms; and the nature of discord is a misconception of God's manifestation in the universe.[14] It is a God-Experience, a realization of the Christ within.[15] This definition and description is elaborated in numerous passages,[16] and constitutes the core of Goldsmith's philosophy.

As in New Thought generally, the Swedenborgian concept of God is central here also, and is the foundation for the Infinite Way of Life and Healing. The Father-Mother God[17] is inscrutable, unknowable, indefinable: no one can name him, know what he is, or describe him.[18] At best, we can only comprehend some of his attributes: he is Immutable and Infinite Law[19]; the substance of all form[20]; the spiritual, creative principle of the universe[21]; the source of all being[22]; the One Life and Universal Consciousness.[23] He is Light and Life[24]; that which is manifest in creation[25]; the Central Office of the solar system[26]; the infinite ocean in which we all exist.[27] "God is a state of Being, a state of infinite Intelligence, and ever-present love."[28] He is the Infinite Invisible,[29] the Creative Principle,[30] the universal soul,[31] the power which is poured into every natural form.[32] He is the divine essence or presence.[33] Above all, God is One, and all dualist concepts can only create suffering wherever they are accepted.[34] God is the omnipresent and Infinite Father.[35] He is goodness and health[36]; he is All-Action[37]; he is the universal Intelligence, equally distributed among all members of the human race.[38] He is the spirit of Christ within you.[39]

Since God is in every individual form and is the source of all existence, we can understand that I and the Father are one. We are individualizations of everything that God is[40]; we are not merely human, but spiritual, beings[41]—everything that God is.[42] Christ is not a person or an historical entity,[43] but the universal mind manifested in Jesus[44] and a divine activity operative in all of us.[45] Christ is simply the human *self*,[46] that *I* which is something quite different from the body.[47] The coming of the Christ in the world signifies only the acceptance of the Christ-spirit among humanity.[48] The mission of Jesus was to introduce to mankind the divine ideas of spiritual freedom.[49] The *I*, the self, being eternal, has no beginning and can have no end.[50] Death is a transition,[51] a momentary lapse of consciousness,[52] which will quickly be restored on the next plane and continue as before.[53] Dying is no greater adventure than travelling to California or Europe.[54] Where the right belief exists, the body may undergo a degree of spiritualization even in the present life.[55]

In his discussion of sin, sickness, and error, Goldsmith declares on the one hand that they are akin to a mirage or a dream[56]; people are victimized by them because they are subject to the hypnosis or Mesmerism of false belief.[57] Aging is such an illusion; and there is no reason why we cannot be as vital at ninety as at nineteen.[58] Disease is man-created[59]; evil, sickness, and deformity are the result of suggestion.[60] No one dies except by his own consent.[61] Error is never a reality.[62] There are cripples in the world because people are subject to inherited race belief.[63] No person is actually sick, sinful, or impaired.[64] Since belief in cancer[65] or arthritis are inherited superstitions, they may be cured.[66] Every disease is merely a misinterpretation of some activity of God,[67] and may, therefore, be overcome.[68] Goldsmith declares that he cured many patients in a single hour[69]; he described cases of terminal cancer who became completely well[70]; and of tuberculosis which he had healed.[71]

6.   *Matter, Disease, and Medicine.* There are, however, passages in which Goldsmith seems conventional enough. Some people, he declares, are good, some bad, others intolerable.[72] The world has made all men mutual enemies.[73] Material things are the gods of this world,[74] and men worship fame, fortune, and position.[75] Matter, he declares, not only exists, but is indestructable.[76] Sin and disease are certainly indisputable facts of life.[77] He respects doctors [78] and admits that they have been so successful finding remedies for diseases that these may disappear within the next half century[79]; but this is because God now operates more effectively through this method than was once the case.[80] The body can be improved through exercise at a gymnasium.[81] If patients desire medical aid, they should be encouraged to seek it[82]; and no attempt should ever be made to administer spiritual healing to those who disbelieve in its efficacy.[83]

7.   *Healing.* Health is achieved through contact with God[84]; God's understanding heals us, when we become receptive; spiritual wisdom is health.[85] "Health is the realization of God as the source of all activity and the substance of all form...."[86] "The healing agency is the con-

sciousness that is developed through" rapport or attunement with "the Christ-consciousness of the practitioner...."[87] A perfect spiritualization results when the inner consciousness flows out to form the completely healthy body.[88] Health, happiness, prosperity, all flow into the outer life from within.[89] But if we cut ourselves off from the source of life, we soon wither away.[90]

"Health is of God," we read, and the universal recognition of this fact would make it available to everyone.[91] It can be realized by anyone who understands that "whatever is necessary in the government of the body is performed as an activity of God."[92] Healing takes place when we arrive "at a state of consciousness in which sin, disease, and death have no reality" for us and we no longer need rid ourselves of these forms of discord.[93] The secret of healing consists in understanding that God *is* and that he is good, that his nature is Love and Wisdom.[94] The patient must close his eyes and fill himself with God.[95] Health is achieved by the process of spiritualization[96] which is attained through the reading of spiritual literature, the hearing of spiritual wisdom and the association with those already on the spiritual path.[97]

Health, we read, is an eternal state of spiritual being,[98] attained or attainable when the individual realizes a true God-consciousness, [99] and depends on a personal realization of the divine presence.[100] When the consciousness is filled with the spirit of truth, one need say nothing, for the healing Christ then becomes operative.[101] It is not the body which is, or needs to be, healed[102]; rather, it is the real I, the eternal I AM, which is the individualized deity, thus transforming the body into the image of itself.

Goldsmith's principal thesis is that since God is infinite, nothing else and no other supply can exist. As soon as we realize the infinity of God and that he is closer than breathing, the result is infinite abundance.[103]

Healing follows the spiritualizing influx, of which we read again and again.[104] It is not something that one person does for another,[105] but rather something which everyone can and must do for himself.[106] It is achieved through meditation, an exercise reminiscent of the Hindu swami, whose methods are described in detail.[107] A consciousness of truth is thus established.[108] Goldsmith declares that he pursued this technique nine or ten hours daily,[109] handled as many as 135 calls a day, and worked seven days a week.[110] "This is the way—constant meditation, a constant turning within so that this inner impulse is kept fresh."[111] "Spiritual healing is accomplished through divine silence...."[112] It is the highway to the Kingdom of God.[113]

Healing is accomplished by mutual meditation on the part of healer and patient, which leads to spiritualization, or the realization of God-consciousness. "Our object," says the author, "is to attain a measure of that mind which was in Christ Jesus, and then let It do with us what It will."[114]

Goldsmith rejects the orthodox doctrine of the Atonement as a matter of course[115]; and, as we have seen, his Christ is not a person but a universal power.

8.   *Health and Success*. According to Goldsmith, "supply" and success do not consist of money or fame.[116] And we are admonished to relinquish material things.[117] Money and property, he declares, do not constitute "supply."[118] We should never work to make a living merely, but for the joy of the work itself,[119] and then let the livelihood be the by-product of the activity. We should never think of personal gain[120]; we should never pray for "things."[121] Health and wealth are not added to our lives, but are included in them as part of God-realization.[122] Sin, sickness, and poverty are simply the penalty for trying to live entirely on the material plane.[123] We should never attempt to heal or enrich *per se*[124]; we do not demonstrate health or wealth—only the God-Presence, of which all other good is a by-product.[125] We should never worry over "supply"[126]; for, once spiritualized, we will receive everything we need. We do not need dollars, nor need we be concerned over them: they should be regarded like streetcar transfers.[127] As we overcome the world, we no longer sweat and stew: for we understand that we do not live by bread alone. As for the body, keep it clean and then have no further concern over it; as for all outward necessities, take no thought of them either, for we are all in God's eternal keeping.[128]

Such was the message and the teaching of Joel Goldsmith.

X. EMMET FOX

1.   *Biographical*. Emmet Fox (1886-1951) was a layman who became a great exponent of New Thought. And, like Drummond, Troward, and others, he was an Englishman who had already made his

mark in another field—electrical engineering. Soon after entering the movement, he lectured to growing audiences at Higher Thought Centers in England; his real career, however, began when he arrived in the United States in 1930.

Dr. W. John Murray had founded the Church of the Healing Christ in New York in 1906, and had spoken to large crowds in the ballroom of the Hotel Waldorf-Astoria; when he died, his place was assumed for a while by Dr. A.C. Grier, who shortly resigned. Emmet Fox, already launched on an independent career, was called to the ministry of this church, and occupied its pulpit for nearly twenty years. After he was ordained to the ministry by Nona Brooks, the Church was renamed The First Church of Divine Science of New York.

2. *Success.* The success of this church was simply fantastic. The congregation grew into the thousands. As an exponent of New Thought, Fox remains almost without peer in America or the world. At first, meetings were held in the Hippodrome; when this was demolished, services were held in the Manhattan Opera House; and finally in Carnegie Hall, where overflow audiences filled auxiliary rooms twice a week.

For more than forty years, books and pamphlets by Fox have been bestsellers; only Trine and Norman Vincent Peale have been more popular through the written word. De Vorss offers ten full-length books and many booklets by Fox. Such titles as *Alter Your Life* (1931), *Power through Constructive Thinking* (1932), *The Sermon on the Mount* (1934), and *Sparks of Truth* (1937) have sold in the hundreds of thousands; they are found on the book tables of most New Thought churches; are dispensed in hundreds of religious bookstores; and are used by ministers of many denominations. What is even more extraordinary is the fact that their luster has not faded with the years—a fate which has overtaken so many others.

Having read seven of his books, I am amazed at the power of Emmet Fox. There is nothing even remotely original in his thought; his appeal, I believe, lies in its simplicity and forthrightness. He said he would never use a three-syllable word if one of two would express his idea; and he declared that he would write nothing beyond the understanding of a ten-year-old. While the esoteric creator may find a small audience, only the popularizer can reach the masses. Charles Braden says[1] that when he attended a service in Carnegie Hall in 1947, Dr. Fox impressed him as one who spoke with authority, not one who theorized; not as one who merely believed, but as one who *knew*.

Furthermore, Fox was limited in his range of thought. His themes were few, but direct and filled with conviction. His sermon, says Dr. Braden, lasted only twenty minutes; he spoke without oratorical flourish or elaboration. But the audience was intent, almost spellbound. And when the service was over, hundreds clustered around the literature tables, where four people were kept extremely busy selling the books and pamphlets authored by the speaker.

Most of his volumes consist of essays or sermons previously composed. *Power through Constructive Thinking* and *The Sermon on the Mount* seem to be his only complete and original works. Pamphlets and booklets are reprints of chapters or sections taken from works already published. Such volumes as *Sparks of Truth* and *Make Your Life Worth While* (1942) consist of short compositions, many taken from earlier books. *Around the Year with Emmet Fox*, published in 1952, contains 365 short pieces, never more than a page, to be read as devotional exercises on each day of the year. The fact that such a book remains popular after more than thirty years indicates that Fox has become, for countless devotees, a source of profound inspiration.

3.   *Message and Method.* Fox was a master of New Thought ideology. God, he declares, is Infinite Mind.[2] He is the Great Source, Substance Itself.[3] The universe is instinct with this imperial deity, who has Seven Main Aspects: Life, Truth, Love, Intelligence, Soul, Spirit, and Principle.[4] Fox often uses the Swedenborgian methods of exegesis to interpret the Scriptures: the Lord's Prayer[5] and the story of Daniel in the Lion's Den[6] are given extensive expositions in this manner, as are The Four Horsemen of the Apocalypse—where we learn that more than ninety percent of all humanity are riding the Pale Horse.[7] Genesis and the Seven Days of Creation[8] as well as Adam and Eve[9] are treated in a similar manner. In fact, what is perhaps the author's principal work, *The Sermon on the Mount*, is simply a scriptural interpretation of chapters five, six, and seven of the Gospel of Matthew.

Without the spiritual interpretation of scripture, we do not see how New Thought—at least as a religion founded primarily on Christian documents—could have been established. Fox tells us again and again that the letter killeth and the spirit giveth life and light.[10] "The Bible is not like any other book," he observes. "It is a spiritual vortex through which spiritual power pours from heaven to earth, and the reason why most people derive comparatively little profit from its study is that they lack the spiritual key."[11]

As he employs Swedenborgian methods, every expression becomes a wonderful revelation of supreme and living truth. Such terms as Lebanon, Carmel, and Sharon signify "certain spiritual faculties" which gradually develop as man awakens spiritually.[12] When we read of the heathen, the wicked, or the enemies within our own households, the reference is always to our own evil thoughts.[13] Jerusalem means the awakened spiritual consciousness.[14] *Heart* in the Bible means the subconscious mind.[15] Since Daniel is Everyman, being assailed with trouble is being thrown into the lion's den.[16] When we are told to turn the other cheek, this means only that we should change our thoughts when faced with error.[17] The Four Horsemen of the Apocalypse symbolize the four elements found in human nature.[18] The fish, fowl, and beasts of Genesis represent the qualities which belong to the spiritual man.[19] Adam symbolizes body and Eve soul.[20] Eating of the forbidden fruit means belief in limitation.[21]

As a whole, Fox is an orthodox exponent of New Thought. Again and again, he proclaims the potency of spiritual influx[22]; that the universe is governed by Cosmic Law[23]; and that there is no such thing as luck or chance.[24] God works through us by means of scientific prayer[25]; and sickness is treated successfully by positive affirmation.[26] Belief in the reality of evil is the cause of sickness.[27] Old age and senility are only beliefs.[28] Worry creates our hell[29]; and evil emotions, especially fear, are the cause of evil.[30] We attract and gravitate toward whatever is similar to ourselves.[31]

There is no fiery hell hereafter; nor is there any fate except that which we create for ourselves. There will be no idleness or harp-playing in the next dispensation.[32]

Organized religion is always in danger of becoming an industry to provide a good living for numerous officials.[33] And first and most of all, each and every one of us should understand that health, prosperity, and happiness constitute God's will and plan for all mankind.[34]

4. *Eschatology.* Although the concept of a spiritual body and the painless transition at death to the spiritual plane or realm is found throughout New Thought, it is nowhere proclaimed with greater simplicity or detail than in Emmet Fox. The Swedish seer presented this as

a revelation based on personal knowledge: he declared that he had visited the spirit-world and conversed with many of the departed. Fox, however, never tells us how he knows about this; he merely states it as if it were common and accepted knowledge.

He delineates what happens at death[35]—where the spirit goes and what it does—what kind of body it possesses; a celestial one, which slips from the physical but continues as the seat of all feeling or sensation.[36] Even in normal life, this etheric entity (as with Swedenborg) can slip away at will, but remains attached to the physical like a kite soaring away on a Silver Cord, the severing of which is known as death. Following this transition, we wake up very much as one rising from sleep; and with this, the new life begins.[37] On the spiritual plane, we will all be young again, and communicate through extrasensory perception.[38]

Such is the core of the simple, direct, popular, and highly effective message of Emmet Fox.

XI. CHRISTIAN DAA LARSON

1. *Rise and Decline.* Christian Daa Larson (1874-1945) is unique in the history of American letters and especially in New Thought. He and his philosophy of optimism flourished for more than twenty years following 1907; he conducted correspondence courses in which great numbers, including Ernest Holmes, were enrolled; his books, published by Thomas Y. Crowell, sold in the hundreds of thousands. But his meteoric career waned under the Great Depression of the Thirties. The *Cumulative Book Index* for 1912 lists twelve of his titles; that for 1928 twenty-seven; but in 1933, only three were still in print; and thereafter none at all. The Library of Congress lists forty-two of his books in its master catalog. But now his name is rarely found in biographical dictionaries; and only one or two of his titles are available from De Vorss.

Neither his popularity nor his decline is too difficult to understand: he was a product and the spokesman of the current Zeitgeist. There is little original in his writings; but his pages are packed with information and they abound with echoes from Troward, whom he must have studied assiduously, as well as concepts originating with Swedenborg.

His writings are filled with joy and unlimited hope and optimism; they are, however, in the main simplistic. We believe that his personal magnetism must have been the secret of his unparalleled popularity and success; and it is certainly true that he had a very powerful message, not only for his own generation, but for all time.

He wrote books with such titles as *Brains, and How to Get Them*; *The Pathway of Roses*; *Business Psychology*; *How to Stay Young*; *Perfect Health: What Is Truth?*; *The Ideal Made Real*; *How Great Men Succeed*; *Mind Cure*; *Nothing Succeeds Like Success*; *Your Forces and How to Use Them*; and *Poise and Power*. These inspirational messages were extremely popular in the business community, where his gospel of health, happiness, and prosperity was received enthusiastically, especially during the halcyon years following World War I.

2.   *Literary Style*. Passages in *The Pathway of Roses*, which are paralleled in Troward, illustrate his style. "There is only one will in the universe just as there is only one mind. The one mind is the mind of God, the one will is the will of God. The mind of individual man is an individual or differentiated expression of the Infinite Mind, and the largeness of this human mind depends upon how much of the one mind man may decide to appropriate. Man has the freedom to incorporate in his own individual consciousness as much of the Infinite Mind as he may desire; and as the mind of the Infinite is limitless, the mind of man may continue to become larger and larger without any end."

And again: "The path of the divine will is upward and onward forever, and its power is employed exclusively in building more lofty mansions for the soul. Therefore, the will of God does not produce sickness, adversity, or death; on the contrary, the will of God eternally wills to produce wholeness, harmony, and life."[1]

3.   *Philosophy*. The concept of Influx is often implied and the Laws of Correspondence are stated repeatedly.[2] The universe is necessarily good. Evil is simply emptiness, resulting "from lack of life."[3] It is an inherited race-belief[4]; it is created when we go away from God[5]; and when we express a material belief, we create disease.[6] The cosmos is governed by immutable law[7]; and if we observe it, all ills must disappear.[8] Caring properly for the body, which is the temple of the living spirit,[9] constitutes simply obedience to the cosmic law.[10] "Whoever

discerns clearly the spiritual essence or divine substance, which is the basis or soul of all reality, will manifest...not only purity, but absolute immunity from all disease...."[11]

We read a great deal about "cosmic consciousness"[12]; this is the supreme good which flows into our minds and bodies when we open up the channel to receive it.[13] "Open the heart to the Influx of Infinite Love, and all that God can give will come with His love."[14]

Larson is a firm exponent of Trowardian Affirmation, which plays so large a role in the healing techniques of Ernest Holmes also. "Give positive expression, in thought, word, action and life, to that which we know to be real.... Make your life a living affirmation of the great things that are before...."[15]

The world which God desires for us "is not a future state of existence, but an eternal state...; it is therefore at hand, here and now. To enter the 'Pearly Gates' is to enter that better world—God's own true world, where all is well."[16] In this immediately attainable heaven, we are to think nothing but opulence, whether this be in the form of "life, health, power, wisdom, spirituality, or greater abundance in external things...."[17] Christ came that we might have life and have it more abundantly.[18] This being true, the very idea of self-sacrifice must be eliminated. Being filled with the Christ-Spirit means that we are able to enjoy all that is good in this life, spiritual, emotional, material.[19]

The author emphasizes the Trowardian theory of evolution. "To enter into the cosmic world, therefore, is to enter into freedom, health, harmony, and wholeness...everything that promotes the highest good for body, mind, and soul. The cosmic life is the apex of all ascending life...the realization of everything that is ideal...the attainment of the one supreme goal in the living of divine life."[20] And thus, we become the "Sons of God."[21]

Although an impersonal God is postulated, this concept is reconciled with the idea of personalities in the Trowardian tradition.[22] Through the individualization of the human soul, the cosmic power assumes personality. All souls are therefore one. "God is not a personality, but he is personal to every personality in existence."[23] He is the "limitless sea of divinity in which we live and move and have our being."[24] And when this Christ-power enters and takes possession of us, we are filled with the same essence which was in Christ-Jesus to the degree that made him unique in the history of mankind.[25]

4. *Redemption*. This occurs on entering "the cosmic state," where "the world is clothed with the sun; the waters of the deep reflect the radiant glory of celestial kingdoms, and the mountains proclaim the majesty and the power of the life that is lived on the heights. Nature sings the everlasting praises of Him who is closer than breathing, nearer than hands and feet, and every human countenance beams with the beautiful smile of God. The flowers declare the thoughts of the Infinite; the forest chants the silent prelude to worship, while the birds inspire the soul to ascend to the vast empyrean blue. We are speechless with ecstasy...."[26]

As the preceding illustrates the lofty style of the writer, so the following reflects his spiritual theory. "The righteous man is never weak, never sick, and is never in a state of discord or disorder.... Sickness, weakness, discord and all other adverse conditions come from the violation of law somewhere in human life, but the righteous man violates no law."[27] Again: "No person could become sick that is always filled and protected with the power of right thought."[28]

There are passages, however, in which the author seems somewhat more realistic. "Worry," he declares, "has crippled thousands of fine minds and brought millions to an early grave. We simply cannot afford to worry and must never do so under any condition whatever."[29] We must not be critical or hostile toward others, for to be so is self-destructive[30]; if we would have peace of mind, we must show love and kindness and practice justice.[31]

5. *Health, Happiness, and Prosperity*. This is the message of Christian Daa Larson; and it is emphasized particularly in a chapter entitled "Talk Health, Happiness, and Prosperity."[32] We are to think and affirm these benefits at all times, on all occasions, to all people, and in all places. "Talk happiness. When things look dark, talk happiness. When things look bright, talk more happiness. When others are sad, insist on being glad."[33]

Again: "Talk health. It is the best medicine. When people stop talking sickness, they will stop getting sick. Talk health and stay well. Talk health to the person who is sick and you will cause him to think health. He who thinks health will live health, and he who lives health will produce health."[34]

Finally: "Talk prosperity. When times are not good, man himself must make them better, and he can make them better by doing his best and having faith in that power that produces prosperity. When men have faith in prosperity, they will think prosperity...and you can give men faith in prosperity by constantly talking prosperity and then men will live prosperity and thus do that which produces prosperity. They may not listen at first, but perserverance always wins. Prosperity is extremely attractive.... Think prosperity, talk prosperity, and live prosperity.... You can remove fear by talking prosperity."[35]

6. *The Psyche*. The only Larson title recently in print is *Your Forces and How to Use Them*, first published in 1912. In this, the author reflects the New Psychology of Evans and Freud as a solution for human problems; here we find detailed discussions of the conscious, the subconscious and the superconscious levels of the human psyche.[36] His approach is secular, and reflects a profound understanding of the subject. We find virtually no reference to Christian or religious sources: the Christ is mentioned only in a single paragraph,[37] and the only allusion to God is found in a sentence where we are told never to kneel before him.[38]

Larson is chiefly interested in the conscious and the subconscious aspects of the mind. His thesis is that the latter constitutes a vast reservoir of potential power and accomplishment, into which we can channel positive and constructive thought; by so doing, we develop the capacity to achieve whatever goal we may desire. "The subconscious," he says, "may be defined as a vast mental field permeating the entire objective personality...or as a great mental sea of life, energy, and power, the force and capacity of which has never been measured."[39] The human system is a living, creative dynamo,[40] which can produce surplus energy,[41] but which, unless utilized, simply lies dormant and useless.[42]

7. *Success*. The "I AM," or the Ego, is the center of each individual life. It is the Supreme You.[43] It is the Great Within, and when it comes into contact with the source of all things, we reach the borderland of cosmic consciousness.[44]

The *sine qua non* of success and greatness is to be an individual[45] and to make every desire, feeling, and thought positive.[46] To succeed in life, a man must be thinking "all the time of what he wishes to obtain and achieve."[47] Since the majority of people do not know what they really want, they accomplish little, and usually fail.[48] They do not continue long enough or concentrate sufficiently[49] on a single objective, and thus they scatter their energies.[50]

To achieve success and greatness, we must avoid all the evil and destructive passions, such as anger, hatred, malice, envy, jealousy, revenge, worry, and fear.[51] If, on the other hand, you think constructively, you "accumulate volume, capacity, and power in your mental world, until you finally become a mental giant."[52]

We become whatever we channel into the subconscious mind. We can train our bodies "to possess the same virile youth at one hundred as the healthiest man or woman of twenty may possess." The only reason we grow old is "the result of what the subconscious mind has been directed to do during past generations."[53] Present "possibilities indicate that improvement along any line, whether it be in working capacity, ability, health, happiness, or character, can be secured without fail if the subconscious is properly directed."[54] "It is when we combine mental action in the conscious, subconscious, and superconscious that we get the results we desire."[55] You can do whatever you are determined to do[56]; you can realize any ambition.[57] If you think success, you will achieve it. [58] Men become mental giants because they have great thoughts.[59]

The Law of Success is this: "Know what you want, and then want it with all the power that is in you."[60] As you channel this energy into your subconscious, it becomes a source of unlimited power.

Larson had no illusions concerning humanity as a whole. Most people are only driftwood[61]; although Nature gives everyone the power to achieve greatness, few do so because they fail to utilize their latent forces.[62] Success comes to those only who have the character and stamina to press on to higher attainment and greater achievement, year after year.[63] Greatness is a lifelong undertaking and superior men and women are the result of constant endeavor. To date, humanity has achieved greatness only among a few individuals; but what they have done, all can do—and if they were to do so, we would have a race of supermen.[64]

Such was the message of Christian Daa Larson.

XII. HORATIO W. DRESSER

1. *History*. Few names in New Thought are more illustrious than that of Horatio W. Dresser (1866-1954). And surely no one could have been more amply endowed for his destined work: his parents, Julius and Annetta Gertrude Dresser, had, as we have seen, been patients and devotees of Phineas Quimby. Born in the year Quimby died, Horatio continued throughout a long career to be one of the most prolific and popular New Thought writers. Although neither an organizer nor an original scholar or thinker, he was the herald of a new religious psychotherapy which recognized that its true field lay in ministering to the mentally disturbed. In volume after volume, he proclaimed this gospel: Charles S. Braden lists thirty-two books credited to him,[1] all of which present various facets of developing New Thought. In addition to other activities, he became editor of *Arena* in 1898; and from this position of authority, exercised great direct influence upon the movement. However, his books have not attained the popularity of some others; De Vorss now offers only his *Quimby MSS*.

2. *Studies*. Dresser never identified himself with any group, but remained for several decades the outstanding spokesman for the movement in general. His first book, *The Power of Silence*, published in 1895, had gone through fifteen editions by 1903[2]; and it was during the years immediately preceding and following 1903 that he wrote most of his popular expositions of Quimby-Swedenborgianism. In 1905, he undertook advanced studies at Harvard under the tutelage of William James and Josiah Royce, where he was awarded a Ph.D. in 1907—at the age of forty-one. We may well believe that these men interacted intellectually, and that the Swedenborgian echoes in *The Varieties of Religious Experience* stem as much from contacts with Dresser as from the influence of the Elder James.

For a time, Dresser served as a lecturer at the Theological Seminary of the New Church in Cambridge, and in 1919 he was ordained a Swedenborgian minister. In 1925, however, he retired from clerical life; his books, written between 1923 and 1930, deal with ethics, psychology, history, and comparative religion. His last work, *Knowing and Helping People* (1933), was written from the Unitarian rather than the specifically New Thought or Swedenborgian point of view.

3. *Evaluation: The Psychic Scientist*. With unflagging interest the

present writer has perused eight of Dresser's books, all preceding 1920. They are precise, intellectual, and carefully worded. Although they lack the fire and intensity of R.W. Trine, each is a milestone in the development of New Thought. In his second book, *In Search of a Soul* (1897), we find a pre-Freudian exposition of the three-level construction of the human psyche, which the author must have absorbed from Evans and Swedenborg. "First we have," he declares, "the plane of acute consciousness, of passing sensations, of thoughts about them, of all sorts of moods, selves, ideas, emotions, fears, hopes, and desires. Then we have the plane of subconscious action, governed by the suggestions given it by the conscious self; and, finally, the higher or reflective self, the self of illumination or superconsciousness, of guidance, reason."[3]

The Higher Self of Dresser is similar to the Freudian conscience, and the Lower Self to the Freudian Id. However, we find that this is a moral division rather than one depending on inherited characteristics and social indoctrination. "The term 'higher self' I...use to denote the revelation of God in the finite soul...."[4] "The first evidence, then, that there really is a higher self is its contrast with the lower—the self of doubts, distrusts, temptations, and selfish motives...looking upward with longing to the higher."[5] "The lower self urges one to follow its dictates, holding out inducements and rewards. The conscience simply presents its 'ought' for one's consideration: ours is the choice to turn aside or to obey."[6] "One knows that there is a higher self because one is thrown into discord with the lower. And one knows there is a lower self, because one would at all times be like the higher, and cannot; for the lower asserts its sway...."[7]

4. *Theology*. The Higher Self is God immanent, or "Mind," which, when acting "according to the laws...better understood, will be our salvation from error, sin, and disease."[8] We have, therefore, within us, for our use or misuse, *"the greatest power in the universe."*[9] This is true because the Swedenborgian deity is omnipresent. "There is only one ultimate force, of which heat, light, electricity, etc., are manifestations.... All events, as well as all particular manifestations of the one force, therefore belong together."[10] "Physical man seems to be the only creature who is open to all these interpenetrating forces...your body or mine may at the same time be open to all the physical forces resident in the ether...spiritually open to the soul-life which more intimately

connects us with the mind and heart of God."[11] This leads to Dresser's persuasion of immortality. "The individual soul is really never separate or apart from the divine self-hood...you and I are instruments...of the divine nature, embodiments of its life, wisdom and power...not limited by time, without beginning and without ending..."[12]

The doctrine of influx is often reiterated. "Again and again one turns to the fountainhead of life's stream, to become recreated and strengthened.... The incarnation of the Spirit in the forms of worlds, rocks, plants, men—this is the miracle of the universe."[13] "Starting with the coarser grades of manifestations—the rocks, the vegetable world, and the lower forms of animal life—we find them less highly organized, and consequently revealing less of what we term the higher nature, or soul of the universe.... The higher we ascend, the more closely we approach the very heart and beauty of life...."[14]

5. *Theory of Healing*. Dresser's next treatise, *Methods and Problems of Spiritual Healing*, was published in 1899. In the preface, he declares that he is not in the business of mental healing nor does he "give advice concerning specific application of mental cure...." He is "not a follower of any sect and does not subscribe to the full creed of those who advocate mental remedies in the cure of disease." He is "simply a truth-seeker...."[15] He declares that not only pain, but physical disease also, is real. "Moreover," he continues, "one has good reason to doubt if the 'cures' " of Christian Science "really are cures; for actual facts are almost never procurable from a Christian Scientist."[16] It should be noted that they "have permitted people to die rather than call a regular physician" and have thus "harmed the cause of mental healing more than they have helped it by their fanatical zeal."[17] And therefore "the time must come when every Christian Scientist shall...be 'brought low'; and, if some fall so far from the throne of abstract grace as to require the help of a regular physician, out of this severe lesson they will probably learn more wisdom than is contained in their entire philosophy of idealistic abstraction."[18]

The secret of health and mental healing is inseparable from a true theology and the reality of divine influx. When the higher self is in control and when the mind-body entity of man is in full communication with deity, then the physical is far less likely to be contaminated by disease. "You may make the changed state...permanent by opening the mind and receiving new life and power directly from the fountainhead.... If you have entered the silence and communed with God, you will know what I mean."[19]

In one of the more elaborate passages, Dresser declares: "There is no need for an external creator, only the existence of a resident, progressive Power, moving within us, and carrying onward to remoter ends that which already exists.... It is perpetual flux, except so far as law and the sum total of force are concerned. It is universal, owning matter and consciousness, things and ideas alike. It is the great becoming, achieving life of the universe, the progressive revelation of God.

"Thus broadly understood, there is not an atom, not a star, not an accident, nor a purpose, that lies outside of its sphere. It is the greatest revelation the human mind has ever made; and, from the time of the general discovery and proclamation of the law, every branch of knowledge has gradually been falling into line.... It is incontestably the only hypothesis which in any way accounts for the development of life...."[20]

One of Dresser's most important theoretical works is *Health and the Inner Life* (1906). Chapter I describes the methods and contributions of Quimby; Chapter II is a personal testimony written by his mother, Annetta Dresser, in tribute to her healer. Among the First Teachers, priority is given to Warren Felt Evans, whose "acquaintance with the writings of Swedenborg...enabled him so readily to grasp and develop the ideas he gained from Mr. Quimby.... But in books like...*The Divine Love and Wisdom*, there are teachings which lead very directly to the practical method for which Mr. Quimby stood. Dr. Evans only needed to find a man who was actually proving what he had theoretically anticipated in order to accept the entire therapeutic doctrine."[21] In another passage, we read: "Mr. Quimby and his followers point out, agreeing with Swedenborg, that man has no life and power of his own, no good quality apart from God: for God alone is the source of life."[22]

6. *Psychotherapy*. The idea of Influx is here, as throughout New Thought, repeated again and again. "This First Cause, or God, or Father, is, therefore, the great generative source of all that exists...this first Cause...is literally the omnipresent life and mover of every living thing...."[23] Now "this wisdom, being omnipresent, is not limited to any one person. All can have it whether they now possess it or not."[24] As "Healer and patient advance together...they are filled with the divine influx."[25]

Here we find Dresser deeply concerned over the physical effects of morbid fears. He recalls the young Calvinist whom Quimby told that his religion was killing him.[26] He "found that the fears, emotions, and beliefs which were factors in producing the patient's disease were intimately connected with religious creeds and experiences."[27] And now we find Dresser emphasizing that New Thought is the key, not only to health, but also to "happiness and success" in every aspect of life.[28]

In *A Physician to the Soul* (1908), Dresser had advanced significantly in the direction of religious psychoanalytic therapy. Throughout, he implies not only the actuality of matter, but also of physical diseases which are beyond the reach of mental cure. He praises the work of the "Emmanuel Church, Boston," which has "spread to other churches. Wisely conservative, the founders of this movement first won the cooperation of the medical profession, then limited the practice of psychotherapy to the cases of functional and nervous diseases which were pronounced eligible by competent physicians."[29]

Thus a specific, yet grandiose, vista for mind-cure beckons the mental practitioner. Since the psychosomatic ailments of mankind may outnumber the purely physical, and since the body is unquestionably and profoundly influenced by psychic states, mental healers should candidly admit the reality of matter and physical diseases and leave the treatment of such maladies to the regular physicians. The mental healers can still pre-empt a rich harvest from their own beneficent activity. Although Quimby had not fully realized this great truth, he was actually a precursor of the psychoanalysts; his patients were beyond the reach of ordinary medicine for the simple reason that their maladies were not of physical, but of mental, origin.

Perhaps the most distinctive contribution of Dresser consists in the fact that he may have been the first who fully realized, well before Freudian psychology was known in America, the relationship between ill-health and neurosis. "There are people of a neurotic type," he wrote, "who wear upon us, not merely because of their nervous 'atmosphere'; but because of the underlying mental attitude, usually one of self-centeredness.... Then there are vampires, neurological parasites, who cling like vines and send out psycho-physical tentacles much more tenacious than a vine. There are imperious, dominating personalities of power sufficient to rule an entire household...."[30]

Dresser understood that the mentally ill "need patient analysis, together with gentle advice...."[31] The healer "should know (1) the actual state of the patients, mentally, physically, socially; (2) the chief causes of the most central of these states, in the light of his inner history; and (3) the underlying moral or religious attitude." When this is changed, "moral regeneration will begin; there will be an altered mental tone and accompanying physical responses."[32]

To many people, observes Dresser, "it is still an entirely new idea that mental states bear any relation to bodily health...little is known about mental influences in general...." However, "it is well known that religious emotions produce powerful effects, and nearly everybody knows something about the power of imagination; but here acquaintance with the subject usually ceases."[33] "To know how and why mental influences affect the body for good and evil, we must understand these disturbing influences and learn the ways in which mental life may be shaped anew."[34]

Dresser cites many cases of neurasthenic disease and cure. For example, there was the ex-Christian Scientist who literally believed that there is no matter. She dwelt in an artificial world, and, attempting to break with her "scientist" teacher, induced a profoundly traumatic experience. Only through gradual and sympathetic analysis was this woman enabled to escape her prison into a world of freedom and reality where she could finally accept the actual existence of trees and flowers.[35]

He describes "the daughter whose mother is out of sympathy with her, whose sisters despise her, while a whimsical father rules over all and defeats every plan for a change in home life. Or, it is a wife in distress who has grown morbid because she pines for the attention her husband might give her...."[36] Again: "Here is a young woman...bound to a selfish mother, less intelligent than herself, whom she vainly tries to please. The more she does for her mother, the more is expected and the less her efforts are appreciated. Opportunities to change her occupation or to travel have come to her which she has been obliged to decline because her mother refused to change her abode. She has repeatedly overworked, become nervously prostrated, and been compelled to go to a sanitarium or hospital. Health partially regained, she has" gone "through the same round again, not a whit wiser, mystified by her repeated illnesses, unable to get light from specialists in nervous diseases."[37]

The world is filled with similar tragedies; and very often the mental-moral dislocation assumes a purely physical appearance. To help such people, then, becomes the role of the counsellor, the mental healer, the ministers of New Thought.

7. *A Literary Colossus.* One of Dresser's most ambitious works is *Th Philosophy of the Spirit* (1908), which includes his Ph.D. thesis, *The Element of Irrationality in the Hegelian Dialectic*, which may be considered the author's most extensive exposition of Swedenborgianism; its central message is its theology, which envisions God "as the central reality, the eternal basis of all that lives and thinks...the abiding essence within and behind both the inner world of states and the world of things."[38]

In 1917, Dresser published *The Spirit of the New Thought*, consisting of twenty-two essays by himself and other leaders in the movement written between 1887 and 1916.

In 1919, Dresser published *A History of the New Thought Movement*, which remained the classic work on the subject until Charles S. Braden's *Spirits in Rebellion* appeared in 1963. In 1921, however, as we have noted, Dresser gave the world his crowning literary labor, *The Quimby Manuscripts*, carefully edited by him; thus, once and for all was settled the precise contribution of that extraordinary innovator who ministered to the victims of psychosomatic ailments.

The collected works of Horatio W. Dresser constitute a small library.

We would say that perhaps his greatest contribution to New Thought and its therapy consists in the fact that he frankly recognized the existence of physical diseases which require the ministrations of the regular medical fraternity; and in showing that, nevertheless, there is a horde of terrible psychosomatic ailments which are beyond the reach of drugs or medicine, but which often appear as purely physical maladies. To the relief and cure of these, he dedicated himself, his efforts, and the Movement. His place in the development of New Thought is therefore not merely unique, but extremely important.

Chapter VII

THE CHURCH OF DIVINE SCIENCE

I. HISTORY

The early history of the Church of Divine Science is related in the volume *Divine Science: Its Principles and Practice*, "as told by Nona Brooks, Co-founder" (1861-1945). She states that in 1886 she was living with her sister in Pueblo, Colorado, and was a close friend of Mrs. Frank Bingham, who had been seriously ill for months. Since local physicians were unable to do anything for her, Mrs. Bingham sought the aid of specialists in Chicago, who informed her that her case was extremely critical; that they could not promise a cure; and that she would have to remain there for a year under special treatment.

A friend then suggested that she seek the aid of Emma Curtis Hopkins; three weeks with her brought a marvellous restoration of radiant health. Mrs. Bingham returned to Pueblo filled with the new gospel; and she soon began holding classes of her own, to reveal her discovery and impart her knowledge to others.

Nona Brooks had herself been in very poor physical condition for several months, able to eat only soft food. Although she at first placed little faith in Mrs. Bingham's teaching, she nevertheless attended her classes, during the fourth of which she was healed, "flooded," she says, "with a great light.... It filled me! It surrounded me! I discovered that I had been instantly and completely healed.... I love to tell of the blessed change in outlook that came to me; the remarkable healing; of the quick improvement in the financial situation" of her family. "In fact, our entire lives were transformed."

However, Nona Brooks and her sister, Fannie B. James, rejected the concept of a nonexisting universe, since it was visible; instead they decided that form was the product of God's creative activity and that the visible world was something not to be denied, but to be interpreted correctly and understood. They concluded early that they must emphasize God and his action in human life and focus attention on his presence rather than on the false concepts entertained in the community.

They had no thought at this time (1887) of establishing a church or a movement. However, they soon formulated a metaphysical system in which creation is the expression of God and partakes of the same substance. This is the concept most frequently expressed in Divine Science literature and is called Omnipresence.

Now the three sisters, including Alethea, began working together "earnestly studying our basis, the Omnipresence of God, in order to discover ever deeper meanings to this fundamental truth of our philosophy and to learn to apply it more definitely to the welfare of ourselves and others...."

It so happened that for several years before these women began their work in Colorado, another lady, Malinda E. Cramer, had come to almost identical conclusions. "She burned," we read, "with the desire to show others that...they could be freed from disease, poverty, and inharmonies of all kinds." She held meetings and taught classes in her home in San Francisco. She also did effective healing. She had incorporated a Home College of Divine Science in 1887; and two years later, came to Denver, where she met Nona and her two married sisters. When they came face to face, they knew at once that they belonged together, and there was the closest feeling of unity. "Mrs. Cramer's healings," says Nona, "were the most remarkable I have ever seen." When Mrs. Cramer died in 1907, Denver became the headquarters for Divine Science, as it has been ever since.

Soon more and more people began asking for help, and classes were started. In 1896, Nona resigned as a school teacher to devote her entire efforts to healing and teaching. As the work expanded, headquarters were established in a downtown building, in which an office and a classroom were located.

At the Divine Science College, incorporated in 1898, teachers were trained, churches were organized, and ministers and practitioners were developed. In 1899, the First Divine Science Church was established, in which Nona served as minister for thirty years. Sister Fannie was president of the College for fifteen years.

Charles Braden supplies additional historical data (*Spirits in Rebellion*, pp. 264-284). As a denomination, the Church developed slowly. In 1916, there were still only three congregations; in 1925, fifteen; in 1986 there are still only thirty-three. The Denver Church—costing $90,000—was dedicated in 1922, and its debt was liquidated three years later. This, along with its Educational Center, is located on East 14th Street.

In 1922, Nona Brooks took her movement into INTA, which now lists sixteen of its thirty-three congregations, placing it fourth in the number of churches to be found in any New Thought denomination in America.

In 1902, Nona began the publication of a small monthly called *Fulfillment*, which was superseded in 1906 by the *Divine Science Quarterly*; this, in turn, gave way to *Power Magazine* in 1912, which continued until 1915, when the publication *Daily Studies in Divine Science* began; this was incorporated with the *Divine Science Monthly* in 1930, which became *Aspire* in 1951, and which has now been renamed *Spirit*.

The Divine Science Federation was established in 1957; this is located in the Denver Educational Center and is responsible for the publication and distribution of all Divine Science literature.

II. DIVINE SCIENCE THEOLOGY AND CHRISTOLOGY

The omnipresence of God is the basic principle of Divine Science[1]; and we find that this oft-stated concept is all-pervasive. "God," we read, is "everywhere. We know the Universe as the One Substance in action. A universal God must be present in his creation...."[2] And further: "God is His universe...."[3] "God is Creator and Creation..."[4] and God is "substance in manifestation...."[5] "He is the life, intelligence, love, and power of all that is" throughout the entire universe.[6] "He is the substance of all that is created...."[7] We learn, furthermore, that since God is all and everywhere, Man also must be divine and partake of His nature. "As we know that which is true of God's nature is also true of our own—for we are the image and likeness of God—we enter into a state of mind which accepts the truth that God has provided for us all that we can possibly need. This is the first step in meditation. It is called *Recognition of Omnipresence*."[8]

The concept of Jesus and of the Christ in Divine Science is basically the same as in all New Thought. As manifested in the flesh, Jesus "became the personification of Christ. By his resurrection, he revealed that life is greater than death...."[9] "The same Christ-principle which evolved in Jesus is in each of us and is wholly capable of guiding our unfoldment to its destined goal...."[10] "Jesus attained the highest concept of sonship.... He was a *conscious* Son of God. He accepted the Christ; He lived as the Christ...."[11] "Jesus is our Wayshower because his clear realization of the Fatherhood of God and the Sonship of man demonstrated how the Christ manifests in the flesh...until the man, *the effect*, becomes the true embodiment of the Christ, *the indwelling cause*...."[12] Thus "Jesus attained his Christhood by recognizing...the divine nature of the Christ...the impersonal idea of Man in and of the infinite Mind before any individual existence, and is the substance of all individual existence."[13]

There is, therefore, a Universal Christ-Spirit which permeates and vivifies all creation and from which we can draw for our own unfoldment and fulfillment without limitation. Jesus was simply *conscious* of this fact and was therefore able to absorb so much of it that he could perform his divine mission.

III. STATEMENTS OF FAITH

If Divine Science can be said to have a creed, it is contained in its Statement of Being and Belief:

STATEMENT OF BEING[14]

God is All, both invisible and visible.
One Presence, One Mind, One Power is all.
This One that is all is perfect life, perfect love, and perfect substance.
Man is the individualized expression of God and is ever one with this
  perfect life, perfect love, and perfect substance.

STATEMENT OF BELIEF[15]

God is Life.
What God is comes forth in Divine activity.
We live, move, and have our Being in God-Life.
By Divine Power we are alive now.
I know that Life is perfect, for God is All.
Man is Living Soul, brought forth perfect in nature.
Man is divine, because he is one with God.
Man has the power to realize the truth of Being, and to accomplish the
  best in every relation and activity.
Consciousness of God is the light of the world.

WHAT DIVINE SCIENCE TEACHES[16]

The Fatherhood of God and the brotherhood of man.
The incarnation of the Spirit of God in mankind.
The spiritual source of all substance.
The unity of life in all its phases.
The immortality of the individual soul.
The transcendence and immanence of God.
God, the Uncreate and the Create, the Invisible and the Visible, the
  Absolute and the Relative, the Universal and the Individual.
The power of right thinking to release into expression man's divine
  inheritance.

IV. RELIGION AS SCIENCE

As we know, the word *science* is used constantly in New Thought;
Quimby practiced *science*; and most New Thought churches feature
the term. This is reminiscent of the ancient Gnostics, who declared that
their teaching was a *gnosis*, or certain knowledge. It is therefore

perhaps no mere coincidence that these early Christians held that the Christ was simply a divine emanation or Spirit, which endowed Jesus with unique powers which enabled him to be the Great Exemplar.

Divine Science constantly stresses the close relationship between science and the Christ-religion. It is a divine science because it is based on the omnipresence of God and proves by the law of expression that innately man can be only what God really is.[17] Since we know that the universe is a unity and is governed by unchangeable law, and since God is the substance thereof in manifestation, there can be no doubt that whatever applies to God applies likewise to the human race. Since all this is true, the system is one of *gnosis*; it depends, not on faith or speculation, but on demonstrable fact.

Thus, there is no possible conflict between the discoveries of the great scientists and the basis of true religion; actually, they complement and reinforce each other in a unity or dichotomy which creates a single whole.

V. THE CONCEPT OF EVIL

Evil in Divine Science is and must of necessity be unreal; for, since God is all and He is All-Good, there is no room for duality,[18] and only a conceptual—not an actual—existence can be postulated for evil. There is no such thing as Mortal Mind as set forth in Christian Science teaching.[19] "There is, " we read, "no evil to the one who lives with the vision of God before him. Evil is the result of a mental condition caused by fear, ignorance, doubt, unbelief. As fear is the cause of suffering, so is it the cause of evil...."[20] Again and again the power of thought is emphasized: evil and suffering are usually the result of wrong thinking.[21] "Gradually," we learn, "during the progress of man's slow growth through the ages, individuals have discovered that thought is of great importance; that it is a determining factor in making man's outer world; that it is a ready tool for improving his affairs...."[22] Illness, to a considerable degree, is the result of race-mind or consciousness, which weighs heavily upon the masses; since people have believed that sickness is a reality, most people accept this error and are therefore "susceptible to race experiences..."[23] in life. Thus, since God is omnipresent and "infinite, there is no evil."[24]

If it is difficult for an outsider to grasp, or agree with, this, we must understand that it is basic in Divine Science. Ignorance alone is the cause of evil in the form of ill-health in man.[25] Since Man and God are identical[26] in their essence, "we are alive in God. Can God," asks Nona Brooks, "suffer and be sick? Since the good is eternal, what about evil? Has it any place in the plan of existence? Could it really exist? Like suffering, evil is in the thought-realm...."[27] Thus, "evil is a temporary condition of the mentality, which can be banished when we choose to live aright.... Evil is being overcome by the setting of a higher thought standard for the race."[28]

VI. INTERPRETATION OF ORTHODOX DOCTRINES

Divine Science, like New Thought in general, denies that Jesus died as a sacrifice to atone for human sin; instead, there is an At-one-ment by which "the Christ consciousness within is the redeemer of world thought, and is 'the way, and the truth' that brings each into *conscious* at-one-ment, or agreement, with his Source, and this way Jesus is revealed."[29]

By the Immaculate Conception, we are simply to understand the truth of all births as revealed in Jesus which makes us all the children of God. "It is the realization that man's source is in the Perfect...God...."[30]

There is no such thing as original or inherited sin; for every individual is born in purity as a son of God.

Baptism, instead of being in water, is "the immersion of every thought in divine consciousness (the Holy Spirit), in Love that seeketh not its own, in parity of purpose, of thought, and of deed. 'Fire' is the light of understanding which consumes darkness and ignorance."[31]

Since Divine Science is in complete accord with modern scientific discovery, "evolution is" simply "man's coming to know. 'Evolution...is the outshining of divinity in man....' "[32] Evolution in Divine Science means the attainment of completeness and perfection by following the light of the Holy Ghost.[33]

Divine Science rejects the ritual of communion in which the bread and blood of Jesus are ingested, either sacramentally or symbolically. We drink his blood as we receive a true consciousness of life and we eat his flesh when we realize that our own bodies are divine portions of the Omnipresence. "In a Divine Science communion service, we come together to learn how to commune every moment."[34]

Millions of individuals have awaited and still expect a literal return of Jesus at the head of a great host of angels to establish the Kingdom of Heaven. However, the Second Coming is simply the "redemption" which "comes by revelation of what always is.... The second appearing or coming is seeing omnipresent life, love, intelligence, and substance.... When man discovers that he is the Truth, God manifest in flesh, he knows he is the Christ, and Christ has come the second time."[35]

"Resurrection," we read, "is the culmination of life process in the one who lives in the resurrection consciousness: it is the end of one process and the beginning of another."[36]

Divine Science has definite teachings concerning death. In one respect, it is what happens to an individual when he becomes the victim of sin or ignorance, which is the opposite of freedom. "He who frees himself from these limitations—sin, sickness, and fear—shall not taste of death...."[37] In another respect, however, it is simply a transition of the immortal entity from this plane of existence to another and higher one.[38] "Why, then, should we dread journeying from one plane of activity to another" when "we are promoted to the next higher; so it is when we have learned the lessons in one stage of development in the process of education...."[39] And further: "Do you believe in God? If you do, you must see that death is only a name for an event in Life Eternal."[40]

Interesting also is the teaching in regard to True Prayer, which, we read, "is acknowledging, approving, and acting according to the true nature of Being. Prayer is a state of receptivity in which Truth is accepted. It is communion with God and realization of the Divine Presence."[41]

We enter into prayer during meditation in which "we make our definite affirmative statement of the truth we wish to dwell upon in order to attain a deeper realization of it as an actuality in our own experience. We repeat this affirmation several times until we feel its truth and think of nothing else. As we dwell upon it with all our attention, feel it in the core of our hearts, we lift our consciousness into a state of true prayer. This is the second step in meditation and is called *affirmation*.[42]

And again: "To pray and depend upon God as the source of life and strength is to worship in Spirit and in Truth.... This is consciousness of life Eternal."[43]

Prayer consists basically in addressing the subconscious self in order to impress upon it the highest aspirations of the conscious intellect. It does not consist of requests to any external power or entity for gifts, help, or favors; quite the reverse—it consists in the statement of truth which will enable the individual to advance into higher planes of living, enable him to achieve success in all endeavors, and accomplish the best possible aims and objectives. It is, in short, the means of spiritual realization—of attaining identity with the Creative force of the Universe.

Six steps are prescribed for the art of meditation[44] during which Affirmative Prayer creates the inner consciousness which leads to victory over all conceptions of evil. "Meditation and practice are the two phases of strong living...."[45] "Regular, persistent practice of affirmative Prayer will bring us eventually to the place where we will establish a strong, unwavering belief in the Christ Mind, which is the eternal Self of each one."[46]

VII. THE THEORY OF HEALING AND WELL-BEING

In Divine Science, we have not only ordained ministers, but also practitioners, or healers, whose role may be even more significant. There is no feeling of antipathy or resentment toward the regular medical profession; one with a broken bone is told to seek help there; if one has an aching or abscessed tooth, he should go to a dentist. However, Divine Science declares that even illnesses which present all the symptoms of organic disease can often be healed—such as arthritis or carcinoma. However, not everyone is healed. And this is indeed a mysterious field which perhaps no one fully understands.

There is no doubt that millions suffer from psychosomatic illness of various kinds. For example, I knew a woman who developed an elaborate hypochondria at an early age; she could and did project into her body various acute symptoms diagnosed by medical experts as a serious heart condition or some other ailment; when one ailment no longer met her subconscious needs, it disappeared and she promptly developed another. The point is that she *wanted* these ailments; had she desired to be free of them, there is no doubt that a wise practitioner could have guided her to success.

The Divine Scientist does not tell his "student" what to do or not to do; but, instead, conveys his own spirit of wholeness or health, which completely changes the attitude and thinking of the one who is suffering. Thus, one who is addicted to alcohol, tobacco, or drugs is not told to abstain; his thought processes are so altered that he no longer needs or desires them. This is the cure.

The same is true of that vast horde of corrosive emotions which fill the minds of countless victims as they swell up from the subconscious and create destructive desires and often culminate in fears, deceit, violence, or a guilt-complex. When all levels of the psyche are cleansed, there is healing—a resurrection into a new and better life.

Nona Brooks declares that health is the natural condition of man.[47] "Mental healing does not differ much from the old conception of healing the body by external means, for the mental power of one person [the practitioner] is supposed to restore another to health. Spiritual healing is realization; it does not bring about anything, but realizes what is already there...."[48] Thus "healing is not a physical process, but a spiritual realization; and...health is not a condition of physical well-being only, but the realization of a state of wholeness in the individual."[49]

"Healing," we read, "goes much deeper than the getting rid of a particular illness or complaint. It is a process of whole-making, a process which is always at work within us if we will but recognize it and cooperate with it...."[50] Again: "Healing consists of getting back into the righteousness of Life, the original creative order...."[51] "The Infinite created us out of its own health; healing is the awareness of that health as our own nature...."[52] Thus, you must "*think and speak health only, if you wish to realize it.*"[53]

"A practitioner is one who is skilled in ignoring appearances and seeing only the perfection of real Being. Consequently, he is able to assist a student in knowing the truth more clearly.... A practitioner understands that unfoldment into knowledge precedes the desired unfoldment into a health consciousness...he trains us to come to a realization of our unity with the Infinite, and when this is accepted, we recognize our consequent wholeness and permanent healing results."[54]

Significant are the teachings in regard to aging—the later years of life. Old age is simply a belief about the body.[55] There is no need to go downhill simply because of advancing years. Not to live fully is the only real death.[56] Aging is largely a mental, not a physical, condition of man.[57] "There is neither youth nor age to the one who knows God as his life; there is increasingly powerful living. The use of our faculties should not be affected by the addition of years. What are years in themselves? How shall we keep young? How shall we overcome the belief in years? It is all worked within. The mentality must be kept active and powerful by identifying it with the one Mind which knows neither youth nor age. Let us keep alert; inertia is a sign that we are forgetting to keep close to God."[58]

Thus, the Divine Scientist exclaims with Browning:

> Grow old along with me! The best is yet to be,
> The last of life, for which the first was made.

VIII. THE DIVINE SCIENCE OPERATION

Dr. Donald Perry, Executive-Secretary of the Divine Science Federation International for twenty-five years, explained that the Church has three closely-related corporations, all organized under the laws of Colorado; in addition to the Federation, there is the First Divine Science Church of Denver and the Divine Science Educational Center, all of which are situated in a complex of fine buildings located at the corner of 1819 East 14th Avenue and Williams Street. The Church itself is an impressive structure with a triple-arch entrance, rows of Ionic columns, and a seating capacity of about 800. The Educational Center and Federation have offices in wings which extend on both sides of the sanctuary. Some 25 or 30 persons work in the headquarters.

The Federation, which was established in 1957, produces and distributes all Divine Science literature, including a number of books and the monthly periodical, *Spirit*. It also ordains ministers and licenses Practitioners and Teachers. It also serves as the center for all Divine Science churches.

All local churches are completely autonomous and financed by their own membership. However, in order to use the name Divine Science, or be a member of the Federation International, they must have a minister prepared by the Educational Center and ordained by the Federation. Qualified Practitioners and Teachers must be licensed by the Federation and their certificates must be renewed annually. The property of local churches is wholly under the control of their own boards of trustees; and should the congregation dissolve or terminate its activity, the disposal of its assets is subject only to federal law.

Considerable latitude may exist among ministers, teachers, and practitioners; however, since they must give evidence of substantial adherence to the teachings of the Church, especially as set forth in the textbook, *Divine Science: Its Principles and Practice*, and since teachers and practitioners must renew their certificates every year, it is not likely that any of these will deviate very far from the basic teachings of the Church. Should any minister, church, or congregation go off on an extreme tangent—which, it seems, has never happened—its affiliation could and would be terminated and it would not be permitted to use the name. This provision in the by-laws of every local congregation is a prerequisite for membership in the Federation International.

The Federation is an integral part of INTA; however, the membership of individual churches is left entirely to their own decision. As we have noted, of the thirty-three Divine Science churches, sixteen maintain membership in INTA.

Before ordination by the Church, a minister is required to serve at least two years in the pulpit of a local Divine Science congregation.

IX. THE WRITINGS AND TEACHINGS OF JOSEPH MURPHY

1. *His Most Popular Book*. Joseph Murphy, a Jesuit in early life—who was for many years the minister of the Divine Science Church in Los Angeles—is perhaps the most popular writer in New Thought. The Autumn 1982 issue of the magazine of that name carries a full-page ad featuring forty-one of his publications and fifty-four of his cassettes. De Vorss offers thirty-four of his books and pamphlets. At the time of his death in 1980, he had "retired" to accept the ministry of the Divine Science Church of El Toro, California, near Leisure World. During his career, he lectured and conducted classes not only in many parts of the United States, but also abroad.

First, we will briefly summarize some of the ideas expressed in his most popular book, *The Power of the Subconscious Mind*, published in 1963, which had sold more than a million copies by 1985.

It seems that the author was attracted to New Thought shortly after 1920, when he was healed of a cancerous growth called a sarcoma "by using the power of the subconscious mind, which created me and still governs all my vital functions." Since he found himself in close agreement with Divine Science, he devoted the remainder of his long life to its ministry.

Although he does not mention Nona Brooks or her church in this book, his philosophical and theological foundations are the same as theirs, or an extension and elaboration of their teachings. In his long discussions concerning the efficacy of Affirmative Prayer, which is addressed by the conscious to the mysterious and all-powerful Subconscious Mind, he declares that health is the normal and sickness the abnormal condition of humanity; right. thinking, transmitted by the conscious to the subconscious, creates health in mind and body; this process can, and frequently does, accomplish miraculous healings, as evidenced at Lourdes and elsewhere; he cites instances where lung cancer and tuberculosis have been healed by this method; poverty, he says, is simply an unnecessary condition of mind; material riches are highly desirable and within the reach of everyone by the technique of Affirmative and Positive Prayer.

However, there is much of a practical nature acceptable to vast numbers of afflicted individuals. He declares, for example, that for a student to succeed in a chosen profession, he must work hard and long; and this effort must arise from a profound love for the work itself. In order to get along with others, we must regard them with respect and empathy; for marriage to bestow happiness, the pair must love and cherish each other and never try to make each other over in their own images. Fear, he declares, is perhaps man's greatest enemy; and he prescribes steps by which it can be overcome. *Success* should be the lot of everyone; and for its attainment, it is only necessary that the Subconscious Mind be imbued with the correct desires and convictions; for in its operation, this aspect of the human psyche is supreme in potential achievement.

Although Dr. Murphy does claim healing of organic diseases by the power of the Subconscious, the principal thrust of his work deals with the passions, which lurk in the depths of the human Id, which he calls the subconscious mind; thus, his work is directed toward problems which belong specifically in the field of psychoanalysis—no doubt of primary importance throughout New Thought. He explains how we can become well-liked among colleagues and fellow-workers; how to attract the best marriage partner; how to overcome the desire for tobacco, alcohol, and drugs, as well as other addictive substances; how to free oneself from a guilt-complex; how to make advancing years the best and most fruitful of life. "Age," he says, "is not the flight of years, but the dawn of wisdom."

Since Murphy's books are written in a simple and direct idiom, we are not surprised that they have sold in the millions and continue among the best sellers of all time, not only specifically in New Thought, but in the general religious and devotional literature of the modern world, and even outside the churches or their followings themselves. All in all, we would say that his impact on the movement may have exceeded that of any other minister or author, at least since the death of Ernest Holmes.

There are many other very popular writers in the New Thought movement, but Murphy's books are featured so widely and given such prominence that we feel this special attention should be accorded him. The following summary and analysis is drawn from, and based upon, eight or ten of his other books.

2. *The Author's Claims*. Murphy states that thousands who had followed the techniques he advocated had declared to him that they had achieved "miraculous results" in their lives, and that they had found healing from so-called incurable diseases; complete freedom from guilt; success and prosperity in business; the way to become and stay well all the time; how to obtain good fortune; how to enjoy peace of mind, fulfillment of desire, and marital happiness; and how to create harmony at home or places of work, where previously there had been nothing but discord and suffering.[59]

The key to all this was the great discovery that their destiny was in their own hands and that they could obtain finer, happier, and richer lives—or, as he calls it, Triumphant Living—by placing the right input into their subconscious and bringing this in tune with the Infinite.[60]

3. *The Basic Thesis*. The means by which all this is to be accomplished is expressed in many passages, and particularly in *The Amazing Laws of Cosmic Mind Power*, wherein he declared[61] that when you see clearly that what you think, feel, believe and to which you give mental consent, either consciously or subconsciously, will determine all happenings, events, and circumstances of your life, you will be able to banish fear, resentments, or condemnation of yourself and others. Since individuals can influence the subconscious mind either positively or negatively and since the latter is amoral and impersonal, everyone, through his freedom of choice, can create the kind of inner psychic life in which he will enjoy health, happiness, and prosperity.[62]

By purifying your inner emotions, you can transform yourself completely[63] simply by impregnating your subconscious mind with high and pure thoughts and ideals.[64]

4. *The Concept of God.* God, declares Murphy, is the Universal Presence and Power which is available to everyone, whether atheist, agnostic, or holy man.[65] God is the Cosmic Energizer; the Living Spirit which animates all things[66]; the Life Principle expressed in all human beings[67]; the mighty psychic power which exists within them.[68] He is *not* anthropomorphic in any sense.[69] The greatest secret and discovery of the age is that God is indivisible, the only Presence and Power, Cause and Substance in the Universe.[70] He is the Power which exists in all men[71]; the Omnipresent Spirit[72]; the Infinite and Creative Intelligence.[73] He is the One Mind, the One Life, the One Law, the One Life in the Universe, Our Father.[74] He is the Higher Self in Man, which makes him a child of God.[75] He is the only Presence and Power which exists—he is Life and this is the Life of Man.[76] All things are One—the Substance of God.[77] He is everywhere—omnipresent.[78] He is the Power of Life flowing into Man's subconscious mind, [79] the sense of oneness with God, with all there is, with Life, the Universe, and all men.[80]

5. *God and Man.* Perhaps no concept in Murphy is more pervasive than that which expresses the unity of man with God. You and all men are the children of God, or the Sons of God.[81] Since God is all there is, I am one with God, who is my Father.[82] Since all there is is a revelation of Spirit or God, I am a perfect reflection of God.[83] I am the temple of the Living God—God is the entire life within me.[84] God prospers me in mind, body, and affairs.[85] His Spirit makes me whole, radiant, healthy, and more youthful.[86]

Since God is personified in all human beings, I am divine and fearless.[87] God is my inner voice, my identity with an infinite source of supply.[88] I am a channel for the divinity which is the God in everything—the river of peace which flows through me.[89] Since we are all the children of God, we are also brethren.[90]

6. *The Concept of Jesus and the Christ.* When Jesus, who was illumined conscious mind, put on the vision of the subconscious, he became Jesus Christ—the ideal man.[91] He is called the Wayshower.[92] The same Christ-Power which was in him exists in all of us.[93] He was born like all others, but he attained great heights through discipline, meditation, prayer, and communion with God. Since God is infinite

and since all men share the same power,[94] you represent the illumined reason and the Christ-Power in your subjective or subconscious self.[95]

7.   *Spiritual Interpretation of Scripture*. In this regard, we find that Murphy follows the examples of Swedenborg, Quimby, Mary Baker Eddy, Charles Fillmore, and many others, who could not accept all of the Bible as statements of literal fact. We must not, he warns, use this sacred volume in the traditional way.[96] His book *Peace within Yourself* consists of a line-by-line symbolic interpretation of the Fourth Gospel. The same method of interpreting Scripture is found throughout Murphy's writings. For example, *born again* means to think in a new way.[97] When Jesus went up on the Mount of Olives he was simply ascending spiritual understanding.[98] The New Heaven is our new state of consciousness.[99]

8.   *Money and Success*. Again and again, Murphy emphasizes the goodness and desirability of money, wealth, and supply. Poverty, he declares, is a mental disease[100]; it is certainly no virtue, for God wants us all to have abundance.[101] There is no good in asceticism.[102] We are all born to succeed.[103] Money is simply the symbol of God's opulence.[104]

However, this does not mean that we may injure others in obtaining a sufficiency for ourselves. We can be wealthy and prosperous without doing harm to anyone. If we cheat others, we are robbing ourselves.[105] Getting, as such, should never be our goal.[106] It is the excessive desire for money for its own sake which is evil.[107] We should practice the Golden Rule by claiming for ourselves only what we claim for all others.[108] Finally, the willingness to contribute to the good of mankind will make you wealthy—for riches are primarily a state of mind.[109] To be happy and prosperous it is only necessary that we *feel* happy and prosperous.[110]

9.   *Rejection of Orthodox Dogmas and Concepts*. Like other proponents of New Thought, Murphy completely denies the conventional religious concepts. In one passage, he specifically rejects the doctrines of the Immaculate Conception, the fall of man, the judgment day, the blood of the Lamb, salvation, hell, and damnation—all of which, he declares, must be regarded as old myths exemplifying inner psychological and spiritual truths.[111] There is no devil, or even evil[112]; difficulties and problems are our devils[113]; nor is there any such thing as original sin.[114] God condemns no one[115]; and by at-one-ment is

simply meant the union of two souls seeking their way back to the heart of reality.[116]

However unorthodox Murphy's concept of the hereafter might be, he never doubted the continuation of the human entity; there is no actual death, he declares, for you will always be alive somewhere[117]; the so-called dead are only people who have gone to another dimension[118]; they have departed onward and upward to a higher form of existence.[119]

10. *The Power of Thought and Faith.* Like Charles Fillmore, Ernest Holmes, and other leaders in New Thought, Murphy constantly stresses the crucial importance of conscious thought and its power in shaping and transforming life by a proper input into the subconscious. The entire volume *Quiet Moments with God* consists of affirmative prayers in which the former implants into the latter the concepts which will reshape the individual's life and create a firm foundation for a realizing faith, which confers the power to attain whatever goal or objective the person may desire. Man has this power to change and transform his subconscious.[120] This is accomplished by a spiritual treatment which can remake all the cells in the body and thus create a health that will reject disease[121]; and, in addition, confer wealth and prosperity.[122] This thought is creative, for you have dominion; your subconscious mind obeys you.[123] Man is whatever he constantly thinks.[124]

It must be understood, however, that for the subconscious mind to become effective, it must believe that it can and will achieve what it desires; when this is accomplished, the Amazing Laws of Cosmic Mind Power come into play; and for this, Mark 11:23 serves as the Biblical authority, since it states:

> For verily I say unto you, That whosoever shall say unto this mountain [your problem, difficulty], Be thou removed [that is, eradicated, dissolved], and be thou cast into the sea [that means the "sea" or your subconscious, where the healing, or solution, takes place and problems disappear]; and shall not doubt in his heart [the heart means your subconscious mind, i.e., your conscious thought and your subjective feeling must agree], but shall believe that these things which he saith shall come to pass; he shall have whatsoever he saith.[125]

Thus, whenever our conscious thought has implanted in the subconscious a total belief or faith that whatever is desired will come to pass, then it is certain that success will follow. When such faith and belief is expressed in affirmative prayer, it will not fail to achieve the envisioned results.[126]

The power of thought, therefore, can accomplish miracles in every aspect of life; can create a heaven within; can transform us into images of perfection; and, at the least, can confer such blessings as health, happiness, and prosperity.

However, evil or negative thoughts are like gangsters, thieves, and assassins that maim and kill.[127] And a sense of guilt is a common mental disease.[128]

In *Telepsychics*, the author goes into great detail concerning this operation. When the right mental image is created in the subconscious,[129] this becomes the Law.[130] It can produce a hell or a heaven in the state of our consciousness, depending on the kind of thought we have placed therein.[131]

11.   *The Power to Heal*. The union of the subconscious mind with the Universal Power which is God confers upon the former a remarkable capacity for healing and well-being. Sometimes this is called the Cosmic Energizer, Telepsychics, the Power within You, the Cosmic Mind Power, or the Dynamics of Mind; but all mean essentially the same: the unique influence of the human subconscious, working with the Universal Mind, to create the kind of life the individual desires for himself.[132]

Although most of the many cases cited by Murphy deal with psychosomatic ailments and problems, there are various others in which organic diseases are said to have been healed. Most of them, whatever their nature, are caused by disturbances which accompany the emotions of fear, hatred, hostility, jealousy, guilt or inferiority complexes, or the condemnation of self or others.[133] Millions are literally sick from worry.[134] And alcoholism—as well as other destructive habits—have psychosomatic causes which can be overcome by spiritual healing.[135] When the mind is cleansed of these evils, discords, or devils, marvellous healings can result.

Murphy describes case after case in which evil emotions caused physical ailments. One woman developed colitis because her dominating mother prevented her from marrying; but when she freed herself, this inflammation disappeared.[136] An educated, wealthy, and virtuous woman possessing all the luxuries of life developed a corrosive guilt-complex because years before she had been a call-girl. When she was relieved of this guilt, she became well and happy, at peace with herself.[137] One woman became overweight because she hated her husband; but when she forgave him and herself, her problem was solved.[138] One man, now happily married, had a fearful guilt-complex because many years before he had deserted a pregnant wife; he had a habit of finding fault with everyone in the office, and became very unpopular. When he sent his ex-wife $30,000, he forgave himself, was promoted at his place of work, and established rapport with his twenty-year-old daughter by the previous marriage.[139] One woman had suffered an illness for years because of suppressed hatred for her mother-in-law; but when she forgave herself for doing so and ceased harboring negative and destructive thoughts about her, and, instead, blessed her in affirmative prayer, she was completely healed.[140] One young woman who had already gone through four divorces discovered that her troubles were caused by resentment and jealousy—emotions which debilitated her entire organism. When she blessed her former husbands and overcame her negations, she achieved perfect happiness and peace of mind.[141] One woman who had ulcers and was totally miserable was filled with resentment toward others; when she discovered this, her troubles disappeared.[142] One man who blamed his blindness on the malefic stars found that the real cause of his trouble was his jealousy of a business associate and his resentment toward his mother-in-law. When he blessed his associate and persuaded his mother-in-law to move, he regained his vision.[143] In another case, a woman developed arthritis because of a festering hatred for an ex-husband and mother-in-law. When she overcame this hostility, the malady disappeared.[144]

Murphy declares that he had personally observed psychosomatic healings of this kind thousands of times. He declared that, in some cases, corrosive emotions had caused cancer and arthritis. Marvellous results can be attained through the power of the subconscious mind. He tells, for example, the story of the young man who believed that he was denied the opportunity to obtain an education because of his race and religion and that because of this he could never go to medical school; but when he imagined that he saw a doctor's diploma with his name inscribed thereon and hanging on the wall in front of him, doors opened for him and in due course he became a physician.[145] By similar techniques, a shy girl, who never had any dates, obtained an engagement ring and a wonderful husband.[146] An actress who had been unable to obtain any parts because she was filled with fear and a low estimate of herself became a great performer.[147] The reason for these achievements was that consciousness of anything produces it, and thought is the road to success and opulence.[148]

Murphy found, however, various instances in which desires were not fulfilled, even though the people involved believed they had used the correct technique for achievement. The Law of Life, he declares, is the Law of Belief; we demonstrate what we believe; and whatever we sow into our subconscious, that shall we also reap. There are not incurable diseases—only incurable people. Thus, those who pray for health, happiness, and prosperity, but do not believe they are truly worthy of them or have doubts that they will eventuate, will have no success.[149] One man declared that, while his wife's prayers were always answered, his were not; but the reason for this was that, while *she* really believed, he did *not*.[150]

There are differing degrees of belief and faith; and consequently only comparable success in achievement. To each will be given according to his faith. The subconscious can heal an ulcer in one individual; but another with a greater degree of belief will overcome cancer or tuberculosis; for this is as easily done by God as it is for the body to heal a cut on a finger.[151]

The road to success in healing consists in quiet meditation, during which the individual addresses his subconscious with affirmative prayer. The mind removes all tension from the body by talking to it—as Myrtle Fillmore did—telling it to relax, and then it must obey. In that quiet, receptive, peaceful condition, attention is focused on whatever is desired; and the results can be amazing success and triumph.[152]

In the practice of spiritual or mind-healing, we should follow these four steps:

(1) turn away from the ugly picture and acknowledge the Infinite Healing Power;

(2) contemplate God and declare that Divine Love and Harmony fill your entire being;

(3) decree that the Infinite Healing Presence is silently permeating your entire being and producing wholeness, beauty, and perfection there; and

(4) continue to give thanks for the action of the Healing Presence; and then wonders can happen to you.[153]

Chapter VIII

THE UNITY SCHOOL OF CHRISTIANITY

I. HISTORY

1. *Sources.* The Unity School of Christianity was founded by Charles and Myrtle Fillmore in 1889; their story and that of their organization is told by James Dillet Freeman in *The Household of Faith*, published in 1951, and more fully in the same work expanded as *The Story of Unity* (1978). Additional sources are Hugh D'Andrade's *Charles Fillmore*, published in 1974; Thomas E. Witherspoon's *Myrtle Fillmore: Mother of Unity* (1977); and *The Unity Way*, by Marcus Back (1982).

2. *Early Background.* Charles Fillmore (1854-1948) and Myrtle Page (1845-1931), who became his wife in 1881, first met in Dennison, Texas, when he was a clerk in a railroad office and she was a school teacher. She was reared in a Methodist-Episcopal family with nine children; and it seems that from girlhood she had been taught, or had developed the tendency, to think of herself as an invalid or subject to physical incapacities or diseases. Charles had a very different child-

215

hood; born in what were then the wilds of Minnesota, he lived in a log cabin in a climate so cold that often the thermometer hovered around forty below zero. At the age of ten, he had a serious accident when skating, in which his leg was severely injured; as Freeman notes in *The Story of Unity*,[1] this was probably the determining incident of his life. Although his dislocated leg and the terrible infections which followed were treated by a series of physicians, he grew steadily worse. Charles later declared that he "was bled, leached, cupped, seasoned, lanced, blistered, and raveled. Six running sores were artificially produced on my leg to drain out the diseased condition that was presumed to be within...."[2] He hobbled around on crutches, and sometimes it seemed that he would be unable to survive. When the infection finally healed after two years, it left a withered leg. For years, he wore a metal brace and walked only with the aid of a cane.

After the meeting in Texas, Myrtle returned to Clinton, Missouri, while Charles went to Colorado, where he entered the real-estate business. In the meantime, they carried on a lively correspondence, through which their attraction ripened into love. They were married on March 29, 1881, in her home town. They left at once for Colorado, where he again undertook the real-estate business, this time in Pueblo. There he prospered and there their son Lowell was born in 1882, followed by Rickert in 1884. However, they soon left for Kansas City, Missouri, which was then in the midst of a tremendous boom, in which property prices were reaching unprecedented levels. Again, he entered the real-estate business and was soon earning substantial income. However, since Myrtle's health was failing, they made a brief trip to Colorado, but soon returned to Kansas City, where Myrtle was struck with tuberculosis. Her health deteriorated to a point at which the future seemed almost hopeless. According to an unverified legend, she had, at that time, considerable faith in medicine and drugs; and had a cabinet full of bottles containing pills and medications of various kinds. For a time, they toyed with the idea of going again to the clear, mountain air of the West, but decided against it. So the couple, with their growing boys—later joined by a third, Royal, born in 1889— remained in Kansas City. As a result, the Great Illumination of their lives was soon to occur there.

3.   *Rebirth and Healing.* By 1886, Myrtle had become so ill and discouraged that she was ready to try almost anything, no matter how

absurd or irrational it might seem. Everything had been tried and had failed; she was now almost ready to die. And so it was that when Emma Curtis Hopkins sent one of her representatives from her Metaphysical College of Chicago, Dr. E.B. Weeks, to lecture in Kansas City, Myrtle decided to attend. Charles accompanied her.

Although the lecture did not impress *him* very much, to *her* it was a revelation of infinite magnitude. She was totally transformed. She obtained a new and different conviction which blazed in her mind. One statement made by the speaker was, she believed, directed especially to her; and she felt a great wave of healing power surge through and engulf her in ecstasy. "I am a child of God and therefore I do not inherit sickness," she repeated over and over; and, as she did so, her malady began to subside. In two years she could exult in the possession of a vibrant, permanent, and infectious condition of perfect health. Thus, at the age of forty-one, she experienced, as it were, a resurrection into a new and glorious life. She stated in a letter published in *Unity* that, as she talked to the various parts of her body, they were gradually cleansed of all impurities, and became completely sound and well.

The Fillmores later revisited Emma Curtis Hopkins in Chicago; and in future years she was often a speaker at Unity headquarters in Kansas City. They also studied at the Metaphysical College.

With Charles, things proceeded in a different tempo. As he observed his beloved wife rise from deathly illness into glorious health and happiness, he could not deny the evidence of his senses. He therefore began an extensive study of metaphysics; gradually, he was convinced and, in due course, became not only a convert to the new faith, but one of the most important and effective apostles of New Thought. This development resulted not so much from his wife's seemingly miraculous cure as from the fact that, as his own convictions solidified, a marvellous healing occurred for him; his hip healed completely and, in time, he discarded the steel extension on his leg and walked without a cane, an experience which he described in detail in his *Atom Smashing Power of Mind*.[3]

I can testify to my own healing of tuberculosis of the hip. When a boy of ten, I was taken with what was at first diagnosed as rheumatism but developed into a very serious case of hip disease. I was in bed over a year, and from that time an invalid in constant pain for twenty-five years, or until I began the application of the divine law. Two very large tubercular abscesses developed at the head of the hip bone, which the doctor said would finally drain away my life. But I managed to get about on crutches and with a four-inch cork-and-steel extension on the right leg. The hip bone was out of the socket and stiff. The leg shriveled and ceased to grow. The whole right side became involved; my right ear was deaf and my right eye weak. From hip to knee, the flesh was a glassy adhesion with but little sensation.

When I began applying the spiritual treatment, there was for a long time slight response in the leg, but I felt better, and I found that I began to hear with the right ear. Then gradually I noticed that I had more feeling in the leg. Then, as the years went by, the ossified joint began to get limber, and the shrunken flesh filled out until the right leg was almost equal to the other. Then I discarded the cork-and-steel extension and wore an ordinary shoe with a double heel about an inch in height. Now the leg is almost as large as the other; the muscles are restored, and although the hipbone is not yet in the socket, I am certain that it soon will be and that I shall be made perfectly whole.

4.   *The Beginning of Unity.* As the fame of these healings spread, more and more people came to the Fillmores for help and counsel. For a time, Charles continued in real estate, giving part of his time to spreading the new faith. In order to reach a growing audience, he brought out the first issue of *Modern Thought* in April 1889, devoted, as it said, to the Spiritualization of Humanity from an independent standpoint. At first, it had no distinctive orientation or point of view; it was not long, however, before Charles began the formulation of his convictions in his own mind. Thus, in a few months, he wrote an editorial divorcing himself from all forms of occultism, hypnotism, spiritualism, palmistry, astrology, and other popular forms of metaphysics; and dedicated his efforts to pure Mind Healing as demonstrated by Jesus Christ.[4] However, he made it clear that his ideas were not exactly those espoused by Christian Science.[5] In April 1890, the name of the magazine was changed to *Christian Science Thought*; in June 1891, it appeared in a format of eight pages with its permanent name of *Unity*.

In 1889, there were only a few subscribers; however, the next year, three rooms were rented in the Deardorff Building in downtown Kansas City, where the organization carried on the work with the help of one hired printer. For a few years, *Thought* and *Unity* were both published; however, in 1895, they were consolidated as *Unity*, which soon became a forty-page monthly. In 1893, *Wee Wisdom*, another monthly, was established, a magazine for children, under the editorship and direction of Myrtle Fillmore. The *Daily Word* began publication in 1924. In 1984, *Unity* had a circulation of about 430,000; *Wee Wisdom*, 100,000; and, of *Daily Word*, some 2,500,000 copies were printed every month.

5. *Unity under Way*. As soon as Unity had publications of its own, it became a going concern. Although it had not yet amassed any wealth or developed a substantial labor force, it so happened that H. Emilie Cady, a homeopathic physican in New York City, had so impressed the Fillmores with her book *Finding the Christ in Ourselves* that they induced her to write a series of articles outlining and explaining the Principles of Practical Christianity. In September 1894, the first of twelve articles appeared in *Unity*. When these were completed, they were published in book form under the title *Lessons in Truth*. This little volume of less than 200 pages has been of remarkable influence, not only in Unity, but in the entire New Thought movement. By 1983, almost two million copies had been printed; it probably constitutes the most complete and rounded statement of Unity principles and techniques available in a brief exposition. Although Dr. Cady never visited the Unity complex in Missouri, she soon began to devote her entire time and efforts to the movement, and her words have reached into the hearts and minds of people to the ends of the earth.

6. *Silent Unity*. Almost from the beginning Unity embarked on additional and unusual services. Of these, one of the first was The Society of Silent Help. In the April 1893 issue of *Thought*, Myrtle wrote, "All over the land are persons yearning for Truth, yet so dominated by the surrounding error that they find it almost impossible, without a helping hand, to come into harmony with the divine Spirit."[6] Unity, therefore, set out to supply aid, comfort, courage, and healing to anyone, anywhere, who asked for it. A group at headquarters met every evening at ten o'clock at night for at least fifteen minutes in silent thought, prayer, and meditation to repeat the following words:

God is all goodness and everywhere present. He is the loving Father, and I am His child and have all His attributes of life, love, Truth, and intelligence. In Him is all health, strength, wisdom, and harmony; and as His child, all these become mine by a recognition of the truth that God is all.[7]

All those who asked for help were told to commune with God at the same time and with the same words, wherever they might be. In time, great numbers were conducting this ritual of spiritual unity over wide areas. Letters asking for help soon streamed into headquarters in ever-increasing numbers from people who were sick, confused, or unhappy. As the circle of participants widened, it was found that it would be better to change the hour to nine; and the name was changed to Silent Unity.

At the beginning, all requests came in the form of letters; then, in due course, a twenty-four-hour, seven-days-a-week telephone service was instituted. Those grieved in mind, body, or spirit could call at any time and pour out their souls to a deeply sympathetic counselor. There is a toll-free line intended for those in urgent need or who cannot afford a long-distance call.

The extent to which Silent Unity has grown is one of the marvels among modern religious phenomena. In 1903, it had 10,000 correspondents; in 1978, there were more than a million. In 1900, half a dozen workers manned the project; in 1984, it required more than 200. There are more than 2,000 telephone calls and 5,000 letters every day, each and every one of which receives individual attention, even though no compensation is demanded or, in many cases, given. In 1982, Silent Unity received more than 2,500,000 letters from people seeking help.

Most of the healings are probably entirely psychosomatic; but countless beneficiaries have declared that they have been healed of such physical ailments as cancer, tuberculosis, blindness, deafness, and arthritis. And this does not include the hosts who were relieved of mental stress and various neuroses or psychoses, bordering sometimes on insanity. No wonder that the number of Unity churches and classes and their membership have proliferated.

7. *Expansion.* In 1890, the Fillmores moved their organization from the Deardorff to the Hall Building; in that year, they visited Chicago, as we have noted, and established a close working relationship with Emma Curtis Hopkins. They also attended the Columbian Exposition in 1893; in 1896, they were hosts to the International

Divine Science Association in Kansas City. Although Unity joined INTA when it was organized, Charles was disappointed with its heterogeneity and Unity withdrew. It rejoined in 1919, but remained only until 1922. Today many of its churches belong to the Alliance and one of its ministers is its president; but the organization as a whole is not a member.

The Unity Society of Practical Christianity was incorporated in 1903, not as a church, but "for scientific and educational purposes, viz.: the study and demonstration of universal law."[8] In this, it has never changed.

In 1898, the Fillmores obtained a house which had rooms large enough to serve for offices and headquarters and also for their meetings. By 1900, however, these accommodations were too small, and a hall was rented in which to conduct the Sunday services. Here and to the house came the lame, the halt, the blind, the sick, and the neurotic, who sometimes demanded and were given the floor to tell their stories and air their grievances.

Charles now determined that Unity must have a permanent headquarters of its own; he therefore initiated a Building Fund, which however, even by 1905, contained only $601. The future did not seem very promising. Since publications were mailed out at less than cost and since no fees were placed upon the services of Silent Unity, funds during the early years were scarce indeed. However, as healings occurred, grateful people began giving voluntarily, and the $601 increased rapidly. But had it not been for a businessman who mortgaged all his properties in order to lend $40,000 to the organization, the new headquarters at 913 Tracy could not have been completed at an early date. Here the cornerstone for a three-story building, forty by seventy feet, was laid in 1906. This included a chapel seating 200 and a library, reception rooms, and offices; it also had accommodations for Silent Unity, a printing shop, and the distribution of the Unity publications.

In due course, other buildings were erected on or near the same site; thus, after seventeen years, the organization had a substantial and commodious home and center of its own, and it remained at this location until 1948. At the end of thirty-four years, when it had 400 staff workers, the operation was moved to Unity Village at Lees

Summit, Missouri, where it now has 1,650 acres of land and a complex of buildings and facilities possibly worth at least $50,000,000.

8. *Further Growth and Development*. Financing in Unity differed sharply from that in most religious organizations. Since it never pressed people for donations or conducted high-pressure fund-raising campaigns, many doubted that sufficient money would ever be available. However, as the outreach of Silent Unity became more widespread, and as Unity literature penetrated further and more deeply, people, who had been raised from despair or had been healed of maladies responded with gifts, sometimes generous or even munificent. Thus it was that a gradual but vast expansion became possible; and, in due course, a beautiful and debt-free headquarters in peaceful surroundings was completed—a phenomenon elsewhere without parallel in the Free New Thought movement.

In 1918, Unity brought a large lot on the Country Club Plaza in Kansas City, where the magnificent Unity Temple now stands. Begun in 1940, it was completed in 1948 at a cost of more than a million dollars.

The Fillmores had concluded that their future home should be away from the dirt, noise, and bustle of a great and growing metropolis. Thus it was that in 1920 Unity purchased fifty-eight acres about fifteen miles southwest of the city. This was the beginning of Unity Village, which has been expanded to its present size. The first buildings were constructed in the English Cotswold style and included a home for the Fillmores called the Arches, completed in 1925. At last, Myrtle had her dream house.[9] There were, of course, various others, including a 165-foot tower, which dominates the landscape, completed in 1929.

However, when the Great Depression struck in the fall of 1929, all work at Unity Village ceased and could not be resumed until the close of the Great War. In 1947, the development had proceeded to a point where the printing plant could be moved to the new location. In 1949, the whole complex was sufficiently advanced to house all departments. Facilities of all kinds have now for years been in place at Unity Village, including a motel, cafeteria, housing for students, etc. When the change occurred, the 400 workers moved from 913 Tracy Street in Kansas City to their new home.

Charles Braden states that in 1962 the replacement value of the plant was estimated at $5,000,000. Since then many new buildings and other facilities have been added; and the program still continues as the work of Unity goes on expanding. In 1983, there were some 500 permanent staff members there, including the 200 who man Silent Unity.

Tens of thousands of people visit Unity Village every year; it has a building completed in 1975 which includes a chapel seating 1,100, a cafeteria with dining space for 300, and several additional banquet rooms and other rooms for workshops.

From this center issue letters, pamphlets, periodicals, and other publications every year totaling tens of millions of pieces of mail; its outreach encompasses the globe.

Myrtle Fillmore died in 1931 at the age of eighty-six; Charles died in 1948 at the age of ninety-four. Lowell died in 1975 at the age of ninety-three.

The three sons carried on the work of Unity. The youngest, Royal, died in 1923; but Lowell and Rickert took up the mantle and continued in the footsteps of their parents. Rickert, who died in 1965, was the architect who superintended the early construction at Unity Village. Lowell undertook major responsibility for the organization, especially after the death of his father. Thus, even though many others have become deeply involved, Unity has been and remains essentially a Fillmore project. Charles Rickert Fillmore is now (in 1986) the president.

9. *Other Activities.* Unity publishes, in addition to scores of small pamphlets, the three monthly periodicals we have mentioned. The *Daily Word* appears in fourteen languages. Silent-70 sends its literature free to 8,000 public institutions in the United States and abroad.

In the early twenties, Unity purchased radio station WOQ in Kansas City, on which it broadcast regular programs until 1934. Then it was sold, because better results could be obtained by supplying commercial outlets with prepared materials. In the 1950s, Unity began a somewhat similar service for TV outlets, some of which carry the programs as a public service.

As James Dillet Freeman remarks,[10] the influence of Unity extends beyond the parameters of its own churches or memberships—a statement applicable to New Thought organizations in general. Their teachings have ameliorated the doctrines of the old-line denominations to a point where, compared to their predecessors, they are scarcely recognizable. Thousands of people, distressed in body, mind, or emotions and finding neither solace nor healing in the old churches, have found homes in Unity or other New Thought organizations.

10. *The Present Scope of Unity.* There is no doubt that, among those who have pioneered in and contributed to the growth and influence of New Thought, the Fillmores rank among the foremost. During the early years, *Unity* magazine did not even mention churches or ministers—only places where its literature could be obtained. Even in 1940, it listed only 160 conference members, of whom 72 were Licensed Teachers. In 1960, there were 203 Ministers and Teachers; the April 1970 issue of the publication lists 264 churches and study classes, without indicating how many there were of each. The 1985 *Directory* listed 479 churches and 140 study classes, of which 60 churches and 62 classes were in foreign lands.

If the expansion of Unity continues at the present rate, it is not unreasonable to expect that within a few years, its churches and classes will increase to well over a thousand.

II. A VISIT TO UNITY VILLAGE

1. *The Complex.* As the visitor approaches the Village, he passes between two large pillars and soon faces the 165-foot Tower, which dominates the scene and in which 100,000 gallons of water are stored. Just behind this stands the spacious two-story building, completed in 1929, which houses Silent Unity. Beyond and behind this, looms the immense and magnificent Administration Building, completed in 1950, with its red-tile roof, which combines beauty with massive utility. This stands as a permanent monument to the architectural genius of Rickert Fillmore. It is 765 feet long, has three floors, and includes a six-story tower-like structure. It is about 80 feet wide overall, but has large wings extending in both directions. About half of the first floor is underground, where the tremendous task of preparing and mailing some 85,000,000 pieces of literature is accomplished annually. On the second and third floors are great numbers of offices; one wing of the third floor houses rooms containing archives of Unity and New Thought literature and a library with 46,000 volumes, including 6,000 by New Thought authors. The Visitor's Center and Book Store are at the east end; just to the right is the new Activities Center,

with its splendid chapel seating 1,100; and to *its* right we find the Inn and Cafeteria. These two buildings, completed in 1975, cost between $3 and $3.5 million.

The power plant is located south of the Administration Building.

In addition to the motel and student cottages, we find many single homes scattered about the spacious premises; there is also a nine-hole golf course; there are tennis courts and other recreational facilities.

Mr. Otto Arni, long-time trustee, stated in an interview that the land may be worth about $10,000 an acre—or $16,500,000. He was very reluctant in making an estimate of the possible replacement value of the property—which is debt-free—but he agreed that $50,000,000 has been mentioned as a conservative amount.

He explained that the Unity School of Christianity is incorporated as a church-school facility under Missouri law; that it is governed by an eight-member, self-perpetuating Board of Trustees, who serve for life. He added that at one time the lay employees were not enrolled in Social Security, but that now they are. Since he stated that the average wage or salary of all Unity employees would probably approximate $10,000 a year, I concluded that the payroll, the Social Security contributions, the cost of paper, printing (press work is now performed by commercial contractors in the City), postage, heating, repairs, etc., could not have been less than $12 or $14 million a year—all of which was derived from subscriptions for periodicals, the sale of books, and, probably most of all, from contributions or "love offerings." Unity has never pressed anyone for money; has never conducted a money-raising campaign; and it depends heavily on gifts, bequests, donations, etc., which flow annually into headquarters in a multi-million-dollar stream.

To survey the beautiful, well-kept grounds and talk to the friendly people at Unity—as I did in December 1982—is indeed an inspirational experience.

2. *The Editor of* Unity *Magazine.* Mr. Thomas Witherspoon, editor of *Unity* magazine, perched high in his office in the Administration Building, proved a rich source of information. He said he received from thirty to fifty letters every day, all of which were carefully considered. Before him lay one from a woman who had sent in eight subscriptions, but no money. All the subscriptions would be filled in the hope that some of the subscribers might become Unity supporters.

One correspondent wanted extra copies to give to friends—the request would be honored. Another ordered the magazine, saying she would pay later when she could afford to do so. One woman wrote a long letter and sent one dollar; another enclosed forty-two dollars with a short note of appreciation. And so on and on.

Mr. Witherspoon said that of Emilie Cady's *Lessons in Truth*, 1,800,000 copies had been printed; that all the books written by Charles Fillmore had surpassed the million mark. Unity publishes scores of small pamphlets dealing with a great variety of subjects—many of which are given away free.

He stated that *Daily Word* is printed in two formats of differing size; and that it appears in fourteen languages. Its subscription price was two dollars a year, but many copies were given away or sent for one dollar. The subscription price of *Unity* magazine was four dollars a year; and of *Wee Wisdom*, five dollars.

He said that the Church Ministry is a secondary element in total Unity activity. For example, on a given Sunday, there might, he said, be 50,000 people in attendance; but Silent Unity alone handles no less than several million emergency letters and telephone calls annually from people of every description who ask for counsel or prayer. The churches, he said, came into existence almost as an accident, and have undergone considerable development.

He stated that Unity, as an organization, has not joined INTA because it refuses to include in its declaration of belief or principles a statement concerning Jesus Christ. However, individual churches and ministers are free to join the Alliance, and many have done so. He added that Unity has no relationship at all with Christian Science and only an indirect one with other New Thought organizations, which often ask for help or advice. Unity differs from these in that it has no practitioners as such, but emphasizes the work of Silent Unity and Silent-70, of which there are no comparable counterparts in any other organization.

Mr. Witherspoon noted that Unity has an enormous outreach among people of every religious persuasion, or none at all. Its literature is read by Jews, Catholics, rationalists, and adherents to every shade of Protestant opinion or belief. Unity never asks anyone what his religion or opinions may be: it merely seeks to help those in need of spiritual assurance, personal confidence, or help in some emotional problem. Most of those who receive Unity literature are unchurched or belong to some other church.

Unity literature reaches millions of people who have no affiliation or contact with its own churches. It had, for example, a Book Club of 60,000 members and a Cassette Club with 40,000, all of whom order the material emanating from Unity and help distribute it among their friends and acquaintances.

For the most part, Unity promotes only its own publications; but it handles some by other authors, such as Emmet Fox, whose writings are very popular in Unity circles.

3. *Silent-70*. In 1910, a project called Silent-70 was launched by the Fillmores, the purpose of which was to provide free literature to people who asked for it or who could not afford to pay for it. Publications such as *Lessons in Truth*, *Daily Word*, and *Unity* are sent to thousands of hospitals, convalescent homes, children's nurseries, public libraries, etc. Subscriptions are entered free for individuals in all branches of the Armed Services, as well as for chaplains, military hospitals, libraries, reading rooms, service centers, or clubs on military bases in the United States and abroad. Any member of the Armed Services who requests it receives free literature.

One special project of Silent-70 is the distribution of Unity literature to inmates in prisons and other penal institutions, where it is said to have transformed the lives of thousands. Any response from a prisoner or an ex-convict is given priority attention and he will receive a special packet of free literature.

Such material is also sent world-wide, especially to the peoples of emerging nations. Foreign institutions which care for orphans will be sent copies of *Wee Wisdom*; and displaced persons receive free Unity literature on six continents.

Nor are the needs of needy individuals forgotten or ignored, especially those who are visually or otherwise handicapped. Literature in Braille and in the form of cassettes is sent to countless thousands throughout the world, particularly the *Daily Word*, which, as we have noted, is printed in fourteen languages.

Thousands too poor to renew their subscriptions ask for and receive *Unity* and other literature without charge.

We do not know precisely how many pieces of literature are sent annually by Silent-70; however, we understand that millions belong in this category—with a total that continues to increase every year.

Like all Unity projects, Silent-70 is financed by "love offerings" received from those able and willing to contribute to this cause.

We know of no other church or organization that operates or offers a similar service to the public: it is therefore unique.

4. *Silent Unity*. The interview with James Dillet Freeman, then Director of Silent Unity, was one of the highlights in my visit to Unity Village. He is the author of many books, including *The Story of Unity*, which we have quoted. I met him in the office of the Silent Unity Building where Charles Fillmore once spent most of his working hours.

As I walked across the spacious first and second floors, I observed many of the 200 people who man this project. Theirs is indeed a tremendous task, handling an enormous number of letters and the telephone calls that come in every day, hour after hour, around the clock, without ceasing. throughout the year. As I passed the building the previous evening, I noted that the light in the fifth window from the left in the second story, where twelve neon bars—symbolizing the twelve powers of man—radiate from a central fixture and can be seen during all hours of darkness.

Mr. Freeman stated that the millions who write letters annually include nuns, priests, executives, workers, businessmen, rich and poor, people with or without religions of their own, all seeking help for some illness, for emotional turmoil, or for a friend or relative in need. Every letter is answered without delay and includes an affirmative prayer.

In 1969, there were 63,000 telephone calls; in 1982, 750,000, of which 13,000 came on the 800 toll-free line from people in a state of severe crisis who either could not pay for the call or were in a state of emergency. If, for example, someone calls who says he is on the verge of committing suicide, an effort is made to obtain his telephone number, which will be called in perhaps ten minutes to discover what has happened to the individual and whether he can be saved or helped. If his address is known, an attempt is made to reach some local agency which may intercede in his or her behalf.

Of the 200 employees of Silent Unity, about three-fourths answer letters and the others man the telephones. They try to keep calls to not more than five, or at most ten minutes, for there are always others waiting. There are fourteen lines in full operation between 7 A.M. and

11 P.M.—and five or six during the deep hours of the night. A new headquarters is under construction in 1986 to house its expanding needs.

No fees are charged or solicited for this service. There is no income except the "love offerings" from those who appreciate the work of Silent Unity. Since the payroll alone must have been at least $2 million a year even in 1982—in addition to the cost of mailing millions of letters and operating this immense telephone service, etc.—we believe that the voluntary contributions must have totaled at least $4 or $5 million.

Mr. Freeman stated that Silent Unity has never during its ninety year history put on a campaign to raise money. Once he put a short article in the *Daily Word* explaining the needs and the cost of service; the response was extremely generous.

Mr. Witherspoon declared—and Mr. Freeman agreed—that hundreds, perhaps thousands, have written that they have been healed of organic diseases of every description. Although there is no way to verify most of these statements, it is hard to doubt the actual authenticity of some of them. And then there are the grateful multitudes who, with the help of Unity, have overcome addiction to alcohol, tobacco, and other destructive habits, most of whom, even though they do not join Unity churches or become integral in the movement, take its literature and show their appreciation by making gifts, large or small, which, altogether, total millions of dollars every year.

At this point, we should point out that Unity has no quarrel with the medical profession; no one is told to abstain from medical help or the use of prescriptive medicines. Unity seeks simply to supplement the aid given by other means, especially when all of these have failed: for example, it will give a person who has suffered broken bones and terrible bodily injury in an accident the courage and hope without which recovery might be impossible. Unity would never think of telling such a victim to rely on Affirmative Prayer alone; but rather urges him to seek and use this to obtain the strength necessary to emerge victorious from the ordeal.

We should add that Unity looks upon the beneficent ministrations of the good physician as simply another illustration of the Law of God or Good, always operative in the Universe and in Man.

5. *The Unity School of Religious Studies.* We learned in an inter-

view with Connie Fillmore Strickland—great-granddaughter of Charles Fillmore—who is head of the Unity School of Religious Studies, that this is an integral part of Unity itself; and that it operates two principal programs—one only for lay students and the other for the preparation and ordination of ministers. There are usually from sixty to seventy students enrolled in the School at any one time; it is manned by a staff of eight or nine "professors." Plans for expansion were underway; and the requirements leading to ordination were quite elaborate and comparable to those found in the best seminaries.

The program for lay students has two divisions: one for individuals who wish merely to learn more about Unity teachings and practices—these come to Unity Village for two-week courses or seminars, and repeat the process for several years. When a person has accumulated 130 hours, he or she is given a Certificate of Recognition, which serves simply as a milestone of progress in Unity study, realization, and understanding. The other division offers courses leading to the status of Licensed Teacher, which require at least two years of residence study at Unity Village.

When asked concerning the range of freedom and variation to be found among Unity ministers, Miss Strickland stated that they must accept and teach the basic principles of Unity; however, a considerable degree of latitude is to be found in what she called "fine tuning," such as opinions in regard to reincarnation and whether God is a Mother-Father deity.

6.   *The Association of Unity Churches (AUC)*. Mr. Charles Neal, Director of Ministry Services in AUC in 1982, explained that this organization had replaced the former Field Department in 1966, which had monitored the Licensed Teachers and directed the ministers, with the issuance of Bulletin IV, which, in effect, relinquished central control over them and conferred substantially complete autonomy upon AUC, an independent corporation organized under the laws of the State of Georgia. It rents office space in the Administration Building, and is controlled by a twenty-one-member Board of Trustees, of whom seven are elected by the churches in seven areas, seven at the Annual Conference; and the remainder by the other fourteen. Presidents are elected for one-year terms.

AUC issues a newsletter called *Contact* ten times a year; this discusses various matters of interest to ministers and local churches.

Like other Unity activites, AUC operates almost entirely on the basis of "love offerings"; some churches give substantially, others perhaps little or nothing. The November 1982 issue states that the income for the five months ending August 31 was $255,956.93, and the expense $260,517.43—a shortfall of $4,450.40.

In order to use the Unity name and be a Unity Church, a local congregation—organized under the laws of its own state and completely independent and self-reliant financially—must include a provision in its articles of incorporation and bylaws that, should it dissolve and terminate its existence, its assets will revert to the AUC, which will then use them to establish a new Unity church in the same area.

Mr. Neal agreed with Connie Strickland and Mr. Witherspoon that considerable freedom and variation are to be found among individual ministries; however, if a Unity church is to go by that name it must conform substantially to Unity teachings as promulgated by the Unity School of Religious Studies and is found in the writings of Charles Fillmore. Mr. Neal stated, for example, that a minister could accept or reject a belief in reincarnation; but that he could not imagine a Unity minister who doubted the continuation of the soul in some form.

He stated that, although the financing is done on the local level, AUC now has an Expansion Program under which some form of assistance may be provided for beginners—such as those in a Study Class—attempting to become a regular church.

He stated that the AUC had 396 churches in 1982, 421 active and 150 inactive or retired ministers; and that there were about 140 Study Classes and 150 Licensed Teachers. He added that there are no formal requirements for the establishment of a Study Class. It can meet in a home and can consist of any number of persons. Sometimes it may be organized and led by a lay person who has received a Certificate of Recognition, sometimes by a Licensed Teacher, sometimes by no one in particular. But every now and then these embryonic originals become flourishing congregations.

Mr. Neal stated that he estimated the active church membership at about 75,000; that there are individual sanctuaries, such as the Temple in Kansas City, which could not be replaced for less than several million dollars; that he himself had been for years the minister of a Detroit congregation which had more than 2,000 attendees each Sunday; and that another, in Grosse Pointe nearby, was even larger.

Finally, I asked him where Unity ministers, for the most part, come from. And he declared, without hesitation, that they *all* come from other faiths—as he himself had emerged from the English High Episcopal Church, because they, like him, find the old creeds lacking in power to supply vital human needs and see that Unity meets this yearning for union with something greater than ourselves emanating from the Divine Reality of All-Embracing Existence.

III. STATEMENTS BY UNITY

Although Charles Fillmore is said to have stated that an explicit Statement of Faith would be inappropriate because Unity might change its opinion or belief at any time, we have found such declarations in Cady's *Lessons in Truth* and inside the front covers of the *Daily Word*. The former contains the following Affirmations or Declarations:[11]

> First: God is life, love, intelligence, substance, omnipotence, omniscience, omnipresence.
> Second: I am a child or manifestation of God, and every moment His life, love, wisdom, power, flow into and through me. I am one with God, and am governed by His laws.
> Third: I am Spirit, perfect, holy, harmonious. Nothing can hurt me or make me sick or afraid, for Spirit is God, and cannot be hurt or made sick or afraid. I manifest my real self through the body now.
> Fourth: God works in me to will and to do whatever He wishes me to do, and He cannot fail.

In the *Daily Word*, we find similar affirmations, which are usually continued unchanged in a series of issues. The following was printed in February 1967, but it was almost identical to the statements of previous years.

> PEACE: Let liberty, justice, peace, love and understanding be established in me and throughout the world, in the name of Jesus Christ.
> WORLD LEADERS: Through the Christ-Mind, you are unified in thought, purpose, and understanding, and inspired to right action for the security and freedom of all mankind.

ILLUMINATION: The love of Christ fills my heart, and shines through me, making me a radiant center of light.

PROSPERITY: The love of Christ fills my heart, and prepares the way for success and prosperity.

HEALING: The love of Christ fills my heart, and quickens the life forces within me. I am healed and restored.

Unity also publishes a small pamphlet called *Unity's Statement of Faith*, which contains some elements not accepted by many of its ministers, but which follows closely the teachings of Charles Fillmore. A statement called General Information reads as follows:

> Unity School of Christianity is a nondenominational religious organization of worldwide scope.... It has no strict creed or dogma and attempts to lead all people, regardless of organizational barriers or theological differences, to a new personal experience of spiritual unity with God and with one another. Unity emphasizes that God is in each individual, and through prayer and meditation each person can find God for himself.
>
> In the words...of Charles Fillmore, "Unity is a link in the great educational movement inaugurated by Jesus Christ...the Truth we teach is not new, neither do we claim special revelations or discovery of new religious principles.... Our purpose is to help and teach mankind to use and prove the eternal Truths...."
>
> Today, under the direction of Charles R. Fillmore, president (and grandson of the founders), Unity School offers a wide variety of services to aid individuals in their spiritual quests. Through its prayer ministry, worship services, and educational classes, as well as literature, cassette tapes, and radio and television programs, the Unity movement has attracted people of many ages, creeds, races, and nationalities....
>
> Unity School has retreat facilities for persons seeking inspiration and spiritual growth. Each year, the retreat staff plans a number of week-long retreats attended by persons of various faiths from many parts of the world. Retreats feature meditations, lectures, workshops, and Bible study, as well as times for relaxation, recreation, and music.
>
> Unity School operates one of the largest religious publishing houses in the Midwest.... Unity literature is printed in twelve languages and in Grade 2 Braille....
>
> Unity Village Chapel offers a wide variety of services, classes, and lectures for individuals who are seeking spiritual growth and greater

self-understanding. Each event is designed to present spiritual principles in a way that encourages individual application....

Free guided tours of Unity School are offered daily.... Formal gardens, fountains, fields, woodlands, and lakes accent the serene setting and provide an appropriate atmosphere for Unity's prayer, education, and publishing activities.

IV. THE SYSTEM OF EMILIE CADY

Since Emilie Cady's *Lessons in Truth* is the most popular and widely-used textbook in Unity, we believe it desirable that we summarize its teachings; though it was first published in 1894, our page references are to the 1936 edition.

"God," declares the author, "is Spirit, or the creative energy which is the cause of all things." He is not a "stern, angry judge only awaiting an opportunity somewhere to punish bad people who have failed to live a perfect life here" (page 6). Nor is he a person having life, intelligence, love, power. He is, instead, the total of good, manifested or unexpressed (page 7). He is "the substance" of each "rock, tree, animal, everything visible...differing only in degree of manifestation..." (page 8). God is the Father-Mother deity, an impersonal principle (page 11). The "real substance within everything we see is God..." (page 13). He is the Great Reservoir, of which every human being is a radiation (page 23). All joy and power are of God; all good that becomes visible is God (page 34).

Again: "God is the substance of all things"—the invisible out of which all visible things are formed (pages 56-57), and which is unlimited in supply (page 57). He is infinite substance as well as tender Father (page 113); the unifying substance of all things (page 134); as Mother-Father, he is an ever-present help in trouble.

The concept of Christ is likewise Servetian and in consonance with New Thought in general; "the Christ at the center of your being and your consciousness" is a hidden "place into which no outside person can either induct you or enter himself" (page 89). There is "a definite inner revealing of the reality of our indwelling Christ through whom and by whom come life, peace, power, all things—aye, who is all things..." (page 90). This Christ is the means by which the Father reveals himself (page 92); this is the Son of God—the Christ who lives in you (page 90).

Thus it is that we may have the mind of Christ in all things (page 97). In truth, Christ is the life, the quickening force, within us (page 104); he is the master of spiritual knowledge (page 111). Desired results will accrue to us when our thoughts turn to spiritual things "embodying the indwelling Christ in our entire being" (page 122). "It is through the indwelling Christ that we are to receive all that God has and is, as much or as little as we can or dare to claim" (page 142). Christ—the Spirit of God—speaking in Jesus, the Nazarene, its human embodiment, declared " 'I am the way, the truth, and the life' " (page 149).

Christ, then, is a universal power, an aspect or manifestation of God, and is available to everyone in whatever measure he can or desires to receive or partake of it.

Dr. Cady's concept of evil or Mortal Mind is simply "the consciousness of error" (page 10). Since man has free will, it is possible for Mortal Mind—the opposite of the divine or indwelling Christ—to control our thinking and our actions. Since God is universal spirit and substance, the only form of what we call evil consists in false beliefs, errors of thought. Thus "the mortal mind may make false reports" (page 18). "Our minds," we read, "have been turned toward the external of our being, and nearly all our information has been gotten through our five senses." Thus "we have thought wrong, because misinformed by these senses, and our troubles and sorrows are the result..." (page 20).

We know that grief can turn the hair white in a few hours; fear makes the heart beat wildly. Thoughts can turn the blood to acid; and the belief that we are miserable sinners can paralyze both mind and body. All this is error, wrong thinking; and these maladies are simply psychosomatic, as are a large portion of all human ailments.

The Real Self within us is never sick or afraid, or selfish (page 30); we need only deny the existence of such conditions in order to render them harmless (page 31). The road to health and happiness consists in the denial of mistaken beliefs (page 33).

Since God is the Universal All, including man (page 34), there can be no duality. Evil has no actual existence; it is only the absence of Good or God, even as darkness is nothing but the absence of light, as cold is the absence of warmth; and both vanish when the sun appears (page 35).

There is, therefore, no evil (or devil) (page 36).

There is no reality or life or intelligence apart from Spirit (page 36).

Pain, sickness, poverty, old age, and death are not real, and they have no power over me (page 36).

There is nothing in all the universe for me to fear (page 36).

Since evils are mere appearances, they need not, must not, disturb you (page 44).

All suffering results from a bondage to the flesh (page 138), which is the failure to recognize our spiritual nature and the fact that we are part and parcel of the Universal God.

These were the Affirmations of Dr. Emilie Cady.

In her system, it is our right and even our *duty* to enjoy life. No religious concept can be more erroneous than the belief that we must suffer want or pain here in order to be eligible for a joyous existence hereafter in another realm (page 27). We need not go or do without the good things of life here and now; did not Jesus say that he came that we might have life, and have it more abundantly? Did he not promise that if we ask, we shall receive? Did he not say that all things would be added unto us (page 29)? It is a false belief that sickness and poverty here are means of serving God (page 32). To believe that we serve God by renunciation is a totally false concept (page 145). We are to make our heaven in the here and now and enjoy life to the fullest degree.

Dr. Cady's doctrine of health and Influx are definitely Swedenborgian. Again and again, she speaks of the inflow of power and energy from the divine source, which is God, who continues to pour into us unlimited wisdom, life, power, all good, because to give is the law of His being (page 24). Again: "All your happiness, all your health and power come from God. They flow in an unbroken stream from the fountainhead into the very center of your being and radiate from center to circumference, or to the senses. When you acknowledge this constantly and deny that outside things can hinder your happiness or health or power, it helps the sense-nature to realize health and power and happiness" (pages 38, 48).

When we talk to God in Affirmative Prayer, "new life, new inspiration, new supplies from the Fountainhead may flow in"; and we achieve peace and harmony within ourselves and with all our surroundings (page 146).

All this leads directly to the author's doctrine and teaching concerning healing, mental and physical. "When first the Truth was taught," she declares, "that divine presence ever lives in man as perfect life, and can be drawn on by our recognition and faith to come forth into full and abundant life and abounding health, it attracted widespread attention, and justly so" (page 115). Teachers and students devoted their entire efforts to these ends. However, the time has now arrived when we should seek and achieve more than mere healing of body or emotional distress; for God wants to give us a great deal more than this, desirable and beautiful as it is.

In addition, therefore, to simple healing, the grand objective of New Thought should be to achieve the better and fuller life which comes with the consciousness of the Indwelling Christ in our entire beings (page 122). Thus, we will achieve a life in union with God and the Christ-Spirit who came and who constantly comes into the world that we might have life and have it more abundantly in all its forms and aspects.

V. THE SYSTEM AND TEACHINGS OF CHARLES FILLMORE

The following analysis is based upon his most popular books.

1. *Theology.* At the base of Fillmore's thought lies, of course, his concept of God or deity; and this resembles closely the Servetian Modal Trinity. It is not likely that anyone in American New Thought had studied Servetus, but we know that his concepts had been adopted by many who knew nothing of him *per se*. Since Swedenborg had a similar concept, he may have been the proximate source. At all events, it is certain that the theology of Unity is basically one of aspect or manifestation, although expressed under a variety of symbols.

The Father, we read, is Mind and Living Principle[12]; he is the source of all existence[13]; he is the unlimited reservoir of power[14]; he is the Primal Cause[15] and the living formless Substance[16]; he is the only Reality[17]; he is the Creative Mind[18]; he is the Universal Substance[19]; he is the Omnipresence which pervades all things and all space.[20]

In such a universal power or substance, there can be no such entity as a personal God.[21] God, instead, the Living Power, is omnipotent in the universe[22]; the only real existence[23] and the source of life and health[24] as well as the stream of energy which flows throughout the universe.[25] This deity is the all-nurturing Mother-Father God,[26] the All-in-All, which makes duality in creation impossible.[27]

This Servetian concept is expressed or implied in many passages. "When we say that there is one being with three attitudes of mind, we have stated in plain terms all that is involved in the intricate theological doctrine of the Trinity. The priesthood has always found it profitable to make complex that which is simple."[28] "The Father is Principle, the Son is Principle revealed in the creative plan. The Holy Spirit is the executive power of both the Father and the Son, carrying out the creative plan."[29]

God is thus unity manifested in three forms: "God and Holy Spirit ...are one fundamental Mind in its three creative aspects."[30] "This is a metaphysical statement of the divine Trinity, Father, Son and Holy Spirit."[31]

God, we read, is the universal, visible substance of the Universe, the only " 'substantial' substance." Second in the Godhead is "the Work of God...the revelation to man...of his own being...the Word is the working power of God." The "Holy Spirit, third in the Trinity," is an outpouring of spiritual quickening, which "speaks, searches, selects, reveals, reproves, testifies, leads, comforts, distributes, to every man...the 'deep things of God.' "[32]

This Servetian Trinity, then, consists of the Father who is the substance of the universe; the Son or Word, who is its energizing force or power; and the Holy Spirit, which is the quickening illumination that ministers to all men.

2. *Jesus and the Christ*. With Fillmore, as generally in New Thought, Jesus and the Christ are entirely different entities. The former was a human being, basically similar to all others; but the Christ with which he was so richly endowed pre-existed[33] and was that aspect of the Trinity known as the Word, the energizing force and power which pervades all existence, a divine emanation available to all men, which can be appropriated in whatever degree their capacities or receptiveness enable them to do so.

What, then, was Jesus? Again and again he is called the Wayshower, the Great Exemplar, the Teacher of Truth.[34] It was his consciousness of the indwelling Christ which gave him the power to accomplish his divine mission[35] and enabled him to purify his body so that it could become immortal.[36] By restoring the broken life-current between God and man, he became the "savior" for those who follow him.[37]

What, then, was the Christ? He was and is the light of God in the world,[38] the great and eternal I AM[39]; the perfect God-Idea[40]; the God-Mind imaged in everyone, [41] and the power that spoke through Jesus.[42]

The churches have taught entirely false doctrines concerning Christ and Jesus. For one thing, the Christ has appeared in many incarnations over the ages[43] and will be manifest again. No error could be greater than to believe that Jesus will return to earth in physical form.[44] By the first coming of Christ is meant simply receiving the Truth into the conscious mind; and the second is the awakening and regeneration of the subconscious mind through the superconscious or Christ-Mind in the human psyche.[45]

The church-doctrine that Jesus died as an atoning sacrifice for the sins of humanity is a total perversion of truth. All men were born as Sons of God and have no contamination except their own errors and misconceptions; they need only be taught the true and proper pathway to salvation. When men cease to believe in the personality of God and Christ, they may, in their consciousness, achieve unity with the God-Mind. "This is the at-one-ment with the Father" which "dissolves forever that inner monitor called accusing conscience."[46] "Atonement," we read, "means the reconciliation between God and man through Christ. Jesus became the way by which all who accept Him may 'pass over' to the higher consciousness."[47]

Again: "We have been taught by the Church that Jesus died for us—as an atonement for our sins. By human sense, this belief has been materialized into a flesh-and-blood process in which the death of the body on the cross played an important part. Herein has the sense of consciousness led the Church astray."[48] The at-one-ment consisted in uniting our state of consciousness with the more interior one of the Father. What died upon the cross was the consciousness of all mortal beliefs that hold us in bondage—such as sin, evil, sickness, fleshly lusts, and death—which he overcame.[49]

3. *The Spiritual Interpretation of Scripture.* Like other proponents of New Thought, Fillmore could accept only portions of Scripture in its literal sense. The Bible, he says, is absolute truth, but veiled

in symbols.[50] These have an inner and an outer meaning,[51] which must be understood. In fact, the entire Bible is an allegory.[52] Its every passage has a spiritual, as well as a literal, meaning.[53] In reading it, "we should go back of the letter and see the spiritual sense of the parables and symbols used to teach the truth...."[54]

Three of Fillmore's books are devoted to the spiritual interpretation of Scripture. The *Mysteries of John* quotes every verse of the Fourth Gospel and then gives its spiritual interpretation; the *Mysteries of Genesis* accomplishes a similar purpose. The *Metaphysical Dictionary* is an immense work which, in alphabetical sequence, interprets several thousand Biblical terms, with their commonly accepted and hidden meanings. For example, we learn that Gethsemane was, according to popular understanding, merely a garden near Jerusalem; but spiritually, it is "the struggle that takes place within the consciousness when Truth is realized as the one reality.... This is often the agony—the suffering—that the soul undergoes in giving up its cherished idols or in letting go of human consciousness." We are also told that the "devil" we are to overcome is the adverse will, which makes you believe you are a son of the flesh. There is no basis for a belief in hell or eternal punishment[55]; and hell is only a figure of speech, a state of mind in human beings.[56] The Holy City, the New Jerusalem, symbolizes the resurrected body,[57] as well as the heaven to be consummated in new conditions on earth to come.[58] The twelve sons of Jacob respresent twelve foundation faculties in man[59] and woman; and the twelve disciples of Jesus indicate a higher expression of these faculties.[60] The crucifixion means the giving up of the whole personality.[61]

The conventional concept concerning the sacrament assumes an entirely different meaning in Unity. "When we appropriate words of truth, 'eat them,' so to speak, we partake of the substance and life of Spirit and build the Christ body. This is partaking of the body and blood of Jesus Christ, the true sacrament that vitalizes the body by renewing the mind. Every student of Truth builds the Christ body as he constantly abides in the Christ Mind through daily meditation upon the words of Truth."[62]

The heaven of which people dream is only something that can exist within us all.[63] The serpent of the Old Testament is merely sense consciousness[64]; and Satan is merely sensation.[65] There is no such thing as evil (devil) unless your thought permits it to enter[66]; and to do so, it must be invited.[67]

4. *The Power of Thought.* Fillmore was certainly a pioneer and amazingly perceptive in the field of psychic philosophy; and, with him, it became the basis of his religion—as well as his healing technique in Practical Christianity. He recognized and understood the three-level operation of the human psyche. "Volumes," he declared "might be written about faith in relation to the conscious, subconscious, and superconscious departments of mind; or about its centers of action in the body."[68] Sometimes he calls them "spirit, soul, and body," by which "we come into the perfect expression of Godlikeness—one man, one Christ, one God...."[69]

Again and again he refers to these; briefly, the conscious mind is the reason or understanding by which we live in the world of sense; the subconscious is deeply buried in the psyche, but constitutes the driving and emotional force which shapes our lives; the superconscious is that higher faculty which some call conscience, [70] and that which is also the human aspect by which we live during sleep.[71]

"The subconscious mind is the vast, silent realm that lies back of the conscious mind and between it and the superconscious."[72] Though the average thinker knows nothing about the subconscious mind and very little about the superconscious, this book presupposes a knowledge of both.[73] We should note that this analysis was independent of Freud.

It is of the utmost importance, declares Fillmore, that we understand the relationship between the conscious and the subconscious, which "is the realm that contains all past thoughts. First, we think consciously and this thought becomes subconscious, carrying on the work of building up or tearing down, according to character. The subconscious mind cannot take the initiative, but depends on the conscious mind for direction. When one is quickened of Spirit, one's true thoughts are set to work and the subconscious states of error are broken up and dissolved."[74]

Thus, the conscious mind or reason thinks thoughts good or bad, and relays them into the subconscious, where they become operative in directing the human organism—physical, mental, emotional, and spiritual—into the conditions which will result. Since this process also controls the cells of the body, it will determine whether it will be healthy or diseased.

This analysis leads directly to the nature and crucial importance of THOUGHT.[75] The body is simply the instrument thereof.[76] The moving powers in life are men's thoughts and words.[77] Every organ of the body is affected by the action of the will.[78] The body obeys the mind, which is the secret of metaphysical healing.[79] Thus, the power of thought can produce health.[80] Man has the power to dissolve all discord and diseases by the power of words.[81] We develop diseases and we create perfection by imagining either of them.[82]

The effects of thought are all-pervasive, which is the reason that placebos can heal.[83] If we think evil exists, we make it an active force.[84] To achieve health, we must will it.[85] We can change the body by changing our attitude toward it.[86] Right desire will achieve its wish[87]; but negative thought brings destruction.[88] We must not carry a grudge against anyone.[89] Worry is a thief and a robber.[90] Therefore, we must cleanse our minds[91] and entertain only worthy thoughts.[92]

Thought can create old age[93] and the belief in death is killing thousands[94]; but a disbelief in sickness can drive it away.[95]

This power of thought becomes effective by Affirmative Prayer, in which the conscious mind fills the subconscious with truth and health.[96] Affirmation will create and establish peace, prosperity, and health.[97]

In prayer, we should never ask for gifts or special favors. We should, instead, ask that the will of God enter into us and become a moving factor in our lives.[98] Thus, prayer draws true ideas from the Universal Mind and man accumulates spiritual substance, life, and intelligence[99]; prayer should never be a supplication, but a jubilant thanksgiving,[100] an affirmation of what is awaiting us from the Father.[101] By this exercise of spiritual power, all things are possible.[102]

Because most people are influenced by Race Mind—that is, beliefs and opinions which have come down to us from our ancestors—man today has a diseased and dying body[103] which can be reformed and healed only by developing right thought through the affirmation of truth.

5. *Sin and Sickness vs. Health.* In the Unity system, sin, hell, sickness, the devil, and ignorance are largely equated with one

another; they are caused by, or consist of, hate, fear, and other negative or corrosive thoughts and emotions.[104] "A short definition of sin," we read, "is ignorance"[105]; but this has no power or reality of its own.[106] We are to be saved, not from hell, but from the delusions of sense.[107] Health is the normal condition[108] and the divine heritage of everyone.[109] The body is the temple of God and healing is a divine process.[110] Sickness, therefore, cannot be of God[111]; and we can make our own heaven (health) or hell (sickness) within ourselves.[112]

The relationship of man to God is the basis of healing and happiness. Our life in the Universal Divine Mind is unlimited[113]; we can heal ourselves from evil by confronting it.[114] We can pick up the universal life-current and thereby vitalize our bodies. These mental impulses start currents of energy that form and also stimulate molecules and cells already formed, producing life, strength, and animation where lethargy and impotence existed before.[115]

Fillmore declared that marvellous healings had occurred.[116] Many considered incurable by the medical profession had experienced incredible cures.[117] Even the dying had been raised from their beds.[118] The fact is, he says, that every organ in the body can thus be renewed.[119] By talking to the various parts of your body as if to a patient,[120] you can create new cells therein[121]; and by this treatment, you simply affirm their health and soundness.[122] You affirm the perfection of your body and deny the existence of sickness.[123] The power of your thought and your subconscious mind accomplish the cure.

6. *Distinctive Positions of Unity.* Fillmore had studied extensively and was himself a student of history, a thinker, and a scholar who clothed his New Thought in a distinctive garb. He declared that the Christianity of Jesus was killed less than 300 years after the crucifixion and that its true adherents were stoned, quartered, and burned by an aristocracy which ruled through a union of church and state.[124] The Church developed a tyrannical priesthood; creeds were established by a privileged clergy that paganized its teachings to a point where they became almost unrecognizable.[125] The Protestant Reformation accepted most of these doctrines and turned the literal meaning of the Scriptures into another idol. Creeds and dogmas, which subvert the religion of Christ-Jesus, elevated the clergy into a highly privileged class[126] which has kept the masses in ignorance for centuries.[127]

Thus, the churches have prevented the progress of the human

mind;[128] and a new and necessary reformation is now dawning upon mankind.[129]

The Swedenborgian doctrine of Influx appears often in Fillmore's writings, and is called by that name. However, in order to receive this divine emanation, we must open our minds to it and thus draw this spiritual substance into ourselves.[130] It is a universal stream of spiritual healing.[131] It is the expression of God's love.[132] It is the river of life flowing from its divine source.[133] When you affirm that "divine substance flows in all its fullness through me," you will be healed and you will enjoy prosperity also.[134]

Like the ancient Gnostics—and for similar reasons—Fillmore declared that Christianity is based on certain knowledge. "Christianity," like mathematics, "is a science because it is governed by scientific principles of mind action."[135] "The only real science," he declared, "is the science of the Spirit. It never changes.... So let it be understood that we are teaching the science of Spirit.... Understanding of the laws governing the realm of Spirit will make it possible to attain this consciousness and to receive the inspiration whenever requirements are met."[136]

7. *Practical Advice.* In addition to his metaphysics, Fillmore offered many practical suggestions for the attainment of successful living. For example, don't buy on the easy-payment plan[137]; don't live beyond your means[138]; conserve your energy[139]; in all your endeavors, you must help yourself if you are to succeed.[140] Prosperity is the reward of constant effort.[141]

For a full and satisfying life, you must focus on something more than, and beyond, the mere making of money.[142] However, the evil here lies not in the money itself—which is a necessary means of exchange—but in the danger of becoming a slave to it.[143]

Again and again, he emphasizes the evils and dangers of sex-abuse.[144] Evil sex habits now dominate a great many people[145]; and the sexual relations must be submitted to the rule of right reason. To indulge in bodily sensation for its own sake is sin[146]; and the passions should always be kept under strict control.

However, asceticism has no place in Fillmore's plan.[147] A simple life neither should nor need be ascetic.[148] To condemn or repress our natural needs and instincts is completely contrary to God's commands.[149]

Every person should seek, and has a right to own, property—a sufficiency of goods and supply; but this means something more than piling up possessions.[150] We should not accumulate riches for their own sake. There is, however, no virtue in poverty[151]; every home should be prosperous[152]; and it is God's will that it should be so.[153] Jesus never taught that poverty is a virtue in itself[154]; the universe contains plenty of Substance for everyone.[155] We certainly need not be poor to be righteous.[156]

One of the most successful methods of achieving true prosperity is by giving to the Lord[157]; by so doing, the soul becomes godlike[158]; we should put God first in our finances.[159] "True riches and real prosperity are in the understanding that there is an omnipotent substance from which all things come and that by the action of our mind we can supply ourselves with that substance...."[160]

We get more and more of God's gifts by the affirmation of prosperity; and, as an illustration of this, Fillmore revised the 23rd Psalm as follows[161]:

The Lord is my banker; my credit is good.
He maketh me to lie down in the consciousness of omnipresent
  abundance;
He giveth me the key to His strongbox.
He restoreth my faith in His riches;
He guideth me in the paths of prosperity for His name's sake.
Yes, though I walk in the very shadow of debt,
I shall fear no evil, for Thou art with me;
Thy silver and Thy gold, they secure me.
Thou preparest a way for me in the presence of the collector;
Thou fillest my wallet with plenty; my measure runneth over.
Surely goodness and plenty will follow me all the days of my life;
And I shall do business in the name of the Lord forever.

8. *Specific Teachings.* Since man is a free agent, he has the power to choose between good and evil; God never forces anyone to do anything; all things are within man's grasp.[162]

As we rise by affirmation, this results in regeneration: "a permanent transmutation of physical vitality into higher consciousness."[163] This "New Birth is simply the realization by man of his spiritual identity with the fullness of power and glory that follows."[164] This may also be called the Second Birth, "a process of mental adjustment and body transmutation that takes place here on earth."[165]

Fillmore declared that the body of man is by nature immortal[166]; and he believed that reincarnation occurs in a continuous cycle of life and death. After what is called death, those who have lived honestly and purely find peace and happiness for a time; and, in due course, reappear on earth in human form.[167] He declared this to be a logical process.[168]

This, in brief, is the religious and metaphysical system of Charles Fillmore.

VI. THE CURRENT PUBLICATIONS

Although the textbooks written by Emilie Cady and Charles Fillmore constitute the basic structure of Unity theology and metaphysics, it is necessary, in order to discover what the day-to-day teachings of the Church are, to attend a number of Sunday services and listen to their "lessons" or "messages"; and even more to examine the literature which streams so profusely from the headquarters at Unity Village. In this section, we will attempt a brief examination of the three magazines: *Wee Wisdom*, *Daily Word*, and *Unity*.

A. *Wee Wisdom*

This periodical, begun by Myrtle Fillmore in 1893 as an eight page magazine, is the oldest religious publication for children in the world. It is issued ten times a year and has forty eight pages, 5½ x 8½ inches in size; it is printed in large, bold-face type and includes pictures, drawings, and illustrations. As an example of its usual content, for November 1982 it had a dozen short poems written by children in the third to the seventh grades in their schools. The text is gauged for children from nine to twelve or thirteen years of age.

Of course, the publication is written from the Unity point of view, but not obtrusively. It could be, and probably is, received by many who belong to other faiths or to no particular creed. Everything is intended to entertain, give pleasure, and inculcate happiness and a high standard of moral conduct.

One story, called "The Hopi Way," is probably indicative of a general approach. A boy named Mark was constantly making himself obnoxious to the other children in his school. After he had broken the Kachina doll belonging to one of the girls, she went out of her way to show him kindness and consideration; and when she discovered that his parents were dead and that his grandparents, with whom he lived, had no interest in his school work, she offered him transportation to an evening party. This made such a deep impression upon him that he responded by making a belt for the doll—which had been mended— and from then on, he showed an entirely different and happier attitude toward everyone.

In the "Action Corner with Pete and Polly," the publishers take an opportunity to convey some Unity teaching and religious ideology. Here children are told that they become heroes if they return kindness for abuse; doing so constitutes greatness and makes one a hero. And we read: "Grandma says that a truly great hero, Jesus Christ, came to Earth to teach us about this greatness, this power within. It is our own Christ power. It is the Best Self in each of us that we can call upon at any time. It is our own special *braveness* that shows us how to be heroes in our own heart."

However, since this book is not written for children, we believe that we should give more attention to the two very important adult magazines, *Daily Word* and *Unity*.

B. *Daily Word*

More than 2,500,000 copies of this, begun in 1924, are printed every month with forty-eight pages. Basically, it is a project of Silent Unity. It appears in two formats: one, in heavy type, is 5½ by 8½ inches; the other, printed in much greater numbers, is 4 by 5½ inches and can be carried in a purse or in a vest pocket. On the back, we may find a short poem by James Dillet Freeman, who is now retired and seems to have become the laureate of Unity. Each issue includes, in addition to the Affirmation of Faith, one or two poems by other authors and two or three inspirational articles with such titles as "Four Solid Rules to Bring Happiness," "The God in You Is Coming Through," "Trust: Our Weapon against Worry," "The Dynamics of Prayer," and "Wonderful Words of Life."

However, the principal portion of the magazine consists of as many one-page devotionals as there are days in the month—each one being a day's Daily Word. There is an almost infinite variety of subjects; and at the bottom of each page, we find an appropriate verse from Scripture. In the November 1982 issue, we find such subjects as these: Healing, Forgiveness, Prosperity, Home, Science, Order, Rest, Love, Light, Comfort, Strength, Thanksgiving, Truth, and Courage. Each day the Unity disciple reads the given passage in silent communion, hoping for health, peace, happiness, and prosperity, subjects which seem to occur more often than any others. Success is another favorite topic; and for July 13, 1982 we find the following:

I AM A SUCCESS-ORIENTED, SPIRITUAL BEING

Success and achievement are much-desired goals, whether it be in business matters or career, or in our own soul growth and emotional unfoldment. We yearn to feel that we are progressing in life and making an important contribution to the world.

We are spiritual beings, on the pathway of progress and fulfillment, possessing the keys that open doors to outer success. Prayer helps us to recognize our true nature and also activates the inner urge to use more of our talents and abilities and to give expression to the God-potential within us. Prayer benefits us in another important way: it gives us peace of mind which enables us to enjoy the small successes of every day as we work toward the larger achievements.

Whatever our dreams and goals, we can know that we are success-oriented, achievement-oriented spiritual beings.

"Then you shall make your way prosperous, and then you shall have good success." (Josh. 1:8.)

Since nearly 25,000 of such texts have been printed, they are, of course, of almost infinite variety; and yet a few themes predominate. We are spiritual beings; we draw our strength from the universe, which is God; we can and should establish our own inner peace of mind by forgiveness, affirmative prayer, and a healthy outlook on life; health, happiness, and prosperity are principal objectives for everyone.

The August 1984 issue lists the following subjects for affirmative prayer during that month (similar suggestions are carried in other issues):

PEACE: God's harmonizing love fills my heart and overflows to establish peace in the world.

ILLUMINATION: God's light illumines me. I know this Truth, and I am assured of right decisions.

HEALING: I am created in God's image. I hold to this Truth and I am whole, well, and strong.

PROSPERITY: God provides for my every need. I hold to this Truth and I am prospered.

The devotional for August 13, 1984 reads as follows:

I AM IN TUNE WITH THE INFINITE AND EVERYTHING IS IN DIVINE ORDER

In tune with the Infinite! Isn't this a beautiful thought! To be in tune with the Infinite is to be in tune with God and His marvellous creation. It is to feel our oneness with God and with all that God is.

To be in tune with the Infinite is to be in tune with life, with power, with all that is good and perfect and true.

In tune with the Infinite. I am in tune with the creative force that makes all things possible. I am carried along on currents of faith and joy and thankfulness of spirit.

In tune with the Infinite. I experience divine order in all phases of my life and being—mind, body, and affairs. Divine order in my body sustains health and wholeness in every part. Divine order in my mind casts out confusion or doubt. Divine order in my affairs brings me success and happiness in all that I undertake.

"We know that in everything God works for good with those who love him." (Rom. 8:23.)

The text for August 15, 1984, reads as follows:

"WITH GOD ALL THINGS ARE POSSIBLE"

Does some situation before me seem impossible? I can meet and overcome it, for the invincible power of God is with me, and "with God all things are possible."

Have I been told that some condition is incurable? Hopeless? I do not accept this prognosis. I do not give up on God. The life of God is present in every cell of my body, and this life flows through me in a continuous, healing stream. The truth is that with God healing is always possible.

Have I thought of some door as closed to me? Have I resigned myself to some limitation simply because "that's the way it is"? I need not give in to any belief that keeps my good from me. I remind myself that with God all things are possible, and that the happiness and fulfillment I seek are right now seeking me. I am free to open the door to new life.

"With God all things are possible." (Matt. 19:26.)

The Daily Word for June 18, 1985 was as follows:

I RELAX AND FEEL AT ONE WITH THE FLOW OF DIVINE ORDER

Divine order has been termed the first law of the universe. I now relax and feel at one with this law. I do not think of divine order as something in the outer that I must strive to attain. Divine order is continually at work in and through me and in and through all creation.

As I tune in to the law of divine order, I am at peace in the midst of the activities of this day. I go forth to do what is before me knowing that I walk, talk, and work in the flow of divine order. I know when to speak and when to be quiet. I know when to be active and when to rest. My life and my world are in divine order.

I begin my day and end it by relaxing in the flow of divine order. I consciously choose to remain in the flow of divine order every moment. My life reflects the truth of God's law.

"His delight is in the law of the Lord, and on his law he meditates day and night." (Psalms 1:2.)

On the back of the June 1985 issue of *Daily Word*, we find this typical poem by James Dillet Freeman:

When the mountain meets the ocean,
Do they talk of heights or deeps?
Can a mountain think of motion
Or an ocean think of steeps?
In myself what ocean thunders
And what endless waters roll
While I wander and I wonder
Of what silent peaks of soul,
And on heights too high for going
I touch deeps too deep to know,
And from deeps too deep for knowing
Reach toward heights too high to go—
O matchless mystery of me
This is the mountain and the sea!

C. *Unity* Magazine

Although the monthly circulation of *Unity* (430,000) is much less than that of *Daily Word*, it is, in other respects, the most important publication emanating from Lee's Summit. Each issue has a beautiful nature scene on the cover and consists of sixty-four pages, most of them in two columns; each issue contains about twenty pieces of various length. To go into detail here describing the contents of various issues would require far too much space; we can only call attention to some of its principal features and summarize a few of its messages.

For many years, Marcus Bach, author of *The Unity Way*, has had a section called "Questions on the Quest," in which he discusses matters such as the following: Is being a Unitarian the same as being a member of Unity? How do we separate love from sex? What is Psychiana? What do you think or believe concerning the virgin birth of Christ? How shall I stop eating sweets which increase my weight? Is it true that a woman's place should be in the home only? Do you think Unity should establish parochial schools? What is your honest feeling about the second coming of Christ? If God is universal and all-in-all, how can evil exist in the world? If God loves us all and wants us to be prosperous, how can wars and famines exist in the world?

Mr. Bach answers them in the best Unity tradition.

During recent years, there has been a page called "Monthly Thoughts," which, in all cases, consist of different discussions or explanations of the words *Illumination*, *Healing*, and *Prosperity*. For example, in the issue of January 1980, we find the following:

ILLUMINATION: Happy, joyous thoughts open the way for the ever present Father-Mind to pour into our mind; we are enlightened and inspired. "...every perfect gift is from above, coming down from the Father of lights."

God is light. He directs my path and I am filled with guidance, inspiration, and vision.

HEALING. Jesus taught that God in His divine perfection is intimately associated with us in each of life's problems. We need only to ask and affirm in His name. If our need is health, this brings new life into our body and begins the healing, harmonizing action.

God is life. His perfection is manifested in my mind and body and I am healed.

PROSPERITY. God's ideas are the source of all that appears. We are realizing there has been prepared for us from the beginning an interpenetrating substance that, like a tenuous bread of heaven, showers us with its abundance.

God is good. He supplies unlimited abundance for my every need and I am prospered.

Every issue includes letters from people who have been helped or healed of ailments through Silent Unity. Some of these, which deal with organic maladies, seem almost miraculous.

There is also in every issue "A Message from Silent Unity" by James Dillet Freeman, who finally retired in 1984 as its director. He continues, after more than fifty-five years of service to Unity, to supply poems and other material for its publications.

Beginning in the October 1984 issue, there appeared a scholarly series of articles by Thomas Shepherd, who is an ordained minister in the Unitarian-Universalist as well as the Congregational Christian Church. However, in these articles, he writes primarily from the Unity point of view with frequent quotations from, and references to, the writings of Emilie Cady and Charles Fillmore.

Interestingly enough, he does not mention Servetus or Swedenborg, both of whom seem to have been outside the scope of his research. His principal thrust throughout is to discover and reveal ideas and insights in his subjects which foreshadow the teachings of the New Thought movement in general and Unity in particular.

The first article deals with Philo Judaeus, the first-century writer who flourished in Egypt. Shepherd sees him as a forerunner of New Thought for various reasons, but especially because he treated the Scriptures to a large extent as allegory.

The second article is about Origen, the great early Christian theologian and ascetic who died in 250 A.D. and whose Christology and theology were finally declared heretical by the Church. Because he held that the Father is eternally generating the Son or Word, and because he believed in reincarnation and universalism, he is considered a precursor of New Thought.

The third in the series deals with the fierce fifth-century dispute between St. Augustine and Pelagius over predestination and free will. Shepherd saw in the latter much that presaged the ideology of modern New Thought.

The fourth deals with a man who called himself Dionysius the Areopagite, which was simply the name assumed by an inspired writer who lived about the year 500. Later articles deal with John Scotus Erigenus (815-880), Duns Scotus (1265-1308), Meister Johannes Eckehart (1260-1327), the Quaker George Fox (1624-1691), and Georg Wilhelm Friedrich Hegel (1770-1831). As in all other cases, these men presented thought and concepts which have crept into New Thought. We should note, however, that these stalwarts were, as Charles Braden might have called them, predominantly Spirits in Rebellion against the religious powers and the orthodoxies of their day.

The ninth in the series appeared in June 1985, and is a glorification of Ralph Waldo Emerson and Theodore Parker, both considered important in the history of Unitarianism and whom Shepherd declares to have created the foundations for American New Thought. The tenth installment deals with Mary Baker Eddy, Emma Curtis Hopkins, and

Nona Brooks. The two final articles covered Dr. Paul Tillich and Father Pierre Teilhard de Chardin, prominent theologians.

Each issue includes a two- or three-page article excerpted from the writings of Charles Fillmore. In the issue of May 1985, we find the following citation: "Thoughts are things." It is an axiomatic truth of metaphysics "that the mind marshalls its faculties and literally makes into living entities the ideas that it entertains...our minds mold from an omnipresent element whatever takes form, shape, or intelligence, and becomes part of our thought-world."

Other articles in successive issues include David Schumacher's "View from the Mountain Top," Norman Olsson's "Way to Spiritual Fulfillment," Marion Brown's "Putting Life Back Together," and Andrew B. Carlson's "Release Your Inner Power."

Every issue also includes several poems, some of which reach a high level of artistry. Often the beauties of nature are depicted, together with the pleasure to be derived therefrom. Of some 250 pieces published each year, many deal with personal problems—financial, physical, emotional, or psychosomatic—and especially the paramount influence of the mind over its physical integument. For example, in the September 1984 issue there is an article called "Consider the Periwinkles," which tells how to reach our goals by slow, progressive steps, based on determined persistence. The April 1984 issue had an article by Glorie Malott on the importance of *Inspiration* and *positive thinking*, coupled with *action*. The August 1983 number has a box on page 53 in which Happiness is defined as "that genuinely good feeling we experience when we know and express what is right, true, good, and beautiful...when we *express* the principle of love, we are happy, and we will maintain happiness even if we are rejected by the world."

The February 1985 issue has an article by Marilyn Morgan Helleburg on how to "Free Yourself from Worry," and another by Donald Curtis on "The Uncluttered Mind." The issue for April 1985 has a very interesting treatise on "The Miraculous Power of Forgiveness" by Karen O'Connor. An article by Jim Rosemergy in January 1980 illustrates the manner in which Scripture is to be interpreted spiritually.

For years, Eric Butterworth, minister of the New York Unity church, contributed lead articles. In the October 1976 issue, he had a long treatise called "A Journey of Jubilation," in which he describes how a human life can be transformed into a joyous experience. In that of September 1984 he has another entitled "The Miracle Trap," the point and focus of which are that what seem like miracles are actually only events which occur according to the divine plan. "The great ideal of spiritual seeking," he declares, "is to be in tune with the Infinite.... There are no miracles in an orderly universe. All things [however] are possible."

VII. FINALE

A visit to Unity Village with its high water tower, spacious grounds, magnificent Administration Building, beautiful chapel, Silent Unity center, and various other installations, is indeed an exhilarating experience; and the general warmth and friendliness of the people who operate the complex will be long remembered. We know of nothing else quite comparable in the United States or, for that matter, in the world.

Charles Fillmore once stated that he did not wish to declare his beliefs in the form of a creed since he might change his mind at any time; and we must understand that the teachings of Unity are, to a certain degree, flexible and may undergo definite change and development; we have noted that many Unity ministers do not accept the doctrine of reincarnation or that of the Mother-Father God, or believe that the human body may become immortal.

In a letter to this writer, Mr. Thomas E. Witherspoon, author of *Myrtle Fillmore: Mother of Unity* and editor of *Unity* magazine until 1984, stated that the organization now is not what it was in the beginning. "We are not discarding the foundation he [Charles Fillmore] built, but we are constantly changing. The one constant is that *one, good God* idea.... You would get a better idea of what Unity is now by studying our current magazines and books—than by delving into what Mr. Fillmore wrote in 1910.... Some of those ideas are given short shrift today in Unity." (That is one reason why we have given so much space to the present-day publications. However, all the works of the founder are still featured and sold in great numbers and the ideas expressed there are, as we have noted, repeated in Unity's *Statement of Faith*.)

We should note that the organization now publishes, in addition to its three magazines, a great many books which are usually priced at $4.95; in addition there is a great number of booklets, pamphlets, cassettes, and other materials.

A visitor in the Administration Building may be surprised to find that at 11 A.M., all work ceases for a few moments while a sonorous voice intones the Lord's Prayer over the intercom system and the entire staff and all personnel assume a prayerful attitude.

The following Affirmation is on display in the lobby of the Administration Building; it was a favorite of Charles Fillmore:

The joy of the Lord is your strength.
God in me is infinite wisdom. He shows me what to do.
In all thy ways acknowledge him; and he will direct thy path.
I can do all things through Christ, which strengtheneth me.
Naught can disturb me, for Christ is my peace and my poise.
All things work together for good.
In quietness and in confidence shall be your strength.
Faith is the strength of the soul inside, and lost is the man without it.
The greatest teaching ever given us is—Christ in you, the hope and the glory.
God is my help in every need.

This short Prayer for Protection is on display at the Visitor's Center, and is often used as a benediction at the Unity church services:

The Light of God surrounds me;
The love of God enfolds me;
The power of God protects me;
The presence of God watches over me;
Wherever I am, God is!

Chapter IX
ERNEST HOLMES AND RELIGIOUS SCIENCE

I. EARLY HISTORY

1. *Final Split into Two Churches*. Since 1954, there have been two distinct denominations (now called the United Church of Religious Science and the Religious Science International Church) which base their teachings and theology upon the works of Ernest Shurtleff Holmes (1887-1960) and, to a lesser extent, upon those of his brother, Fenwicke; and they use *The Science of Mind* as their principal textbook. However, they have no interrelationship except as might be found in respect to any other New Thought group. Many individual churches belong to the International New Thought Alliance and both divisions are officially members thereof.

2. *Early Life and Education*. Ernest Holmes was born January 31, 1887 in Lincoln, Maine, a rural town, the youngest of nine children. He entered the public school at Grafton Notch at the age of five. In 1894, the family moved to Bethel, where, at the age of seventeen, he enrolled at Gould's Academy, which he left shortly thereafter. This seems to

have terminated his formal education. However, he was an avid reader; and, together with his parents, absorbed the contents of the Bible, a book called *The Story of the Bible*, and *The Natural Law in the Spiritual World*, by Henry Drummond.

Ernest had an extremely active and inquisitive mind. From earliest boyhood, he was constantly seeking answers to the profound questions and problems of life. He absorbed the writings of challenging authors, one after another: among the first of these, after Drummond and the Bible, which was to exercise a deep formative influence on his thinking, was Ralph Waldo Emerson, whom he "discovered" in 1907; then came Thomas Troward (the author of the Doré and Edinburgh Lectures); and shortly after, Walt Whitman and Robert Browning. Holmes often quotes Emerson: and there is little doubt that Troward influenced him profoundly and that Holmes did a great deal to bring the works of this English thinker to the attention of the New Thought movement in America.

In 1908, he enrolled in the Leland Powers School of Expression in Boston, where he also attended Christian Science services. In 1908, he began an intensive study of the writings of Christian Daa Larson, with whom, in later years, he established a close working relationship.

We believe, however, that the single most decisive catalyst in the development of Holmes's mature thought was Emma Curtis Hopkins, who, though well advanced in years, was still active when he studied under her in 1924. It was probably she who introduced to him the concept of cosmic consciousness, an idea which permeates much of his thought.

Fenwicke graduated from the Hartford Theological Seminary and became a very successful Congregational minister in Venice, California, in 1912, where he continued in this capacity for six years.

At twenty-five, Ernest visited his brother and decided to remain in California where he obtained employment as a playground director at a public school. In 1915, he attempted to fuse metaphysics, psychology, and philosophy.

Thus, we find that Ernest's intellectual and religious development proceeded on the basis of his own personal investigation and convictions; and his knowledge was derived from individual and eclectic sources—a fact common among the great creative and religious thinkers and innovators of all ages.

3.   *The First Activity and Publications.* The brothers published

their first magazine, *Uplift*, in 1916, and secured their first practitioner. In 1917, Fenwicke resigned from his pulpit, and joined Ernest in full-time endeavor. Their first action was to open a sanitarium in Los Angeles. In 1918, Ernest began a successful series of lectures at the Strand Theater. In 1919, they published their first books: Ernest's was *Creative Mind* and Fenwicke's *The Law of the Mind in Action*, which we will summarize briefly, and which is still widely used in Religious Science study classes and churches. Beginning in 1920, the brothers teamed up in lecture tours in various cities, especially in the East where they held free meetings in large theaters, filled to capacity; these were followed by classes, often attended by a thousand students, who paid twenty-five dollars each for a series of lessons.

In 1923, Ernest began lecturing in the Philharmonic Theater in Los Angeles to steadily growing audiences. He also conducted study classes, which were extremely popular. However, in 1925, the brothers decided to go separate ways; Fenwicke went East, where he was very successful as a lecturer. Ernest remained in the West, where he continued to study, attain a greater depth of understanding, and influence an ever-increasing circle of students and followers.

4. *The Textbook,* Science of Mind, *is Published.* In 1926, Ernest began holding Sunday services in the Ambassador Hotel Theater, and he brought out the first edition of his classic, *Science of Mind.* The Introduction to this 667-page opus consists of 35 pages, which, in brief, contain and set forth the underlying principles of Religious Science.

5. *No Desire for Religious Organization.* Like other leaders and writers in New Thought, Ernest Holmes—at least for many years— really had no desire to establish churches or a religious organization; he wanted simply to lecture, teach, train practitioners, and publish his materials. Had nothing more than this ever been done, in due course he would probably have taken his place as another historic figure, along with Quimby, Dresser, Troward, Larson, Fox, and others. As in the case of Unity, churches developed, largely as an accident and outside the personal volition or encouragement of the Founder.

6. *A Magazine and an Institute!* In 1927, two important events took place. The Institute of Religious Science and School of Philosophy was founded and chartered under the laws of the state of California, and the Ebell Club was rented, where lectures and classes were conducted. The purpose of this was to train an ever-increasing number of practitioners who would minister to those troubled in mind

or body with spiritual mind-healing and affirmative prayer. The second great step was the publication of the magazine *The Religious Science Monthly*, the name of which was changed to *Science of Mind* in 1929. It has been the principal current literary organ of the movement ever since. Its purpose, it declared, was to

> promote the universal consciousness of life which binds together all in one great whole and to show that there is such a thing as Truth, and that it may be known in a degree sufficient to enable the one knowing it to live a happy, useful life, wholesome, healthful, and constructive...

In accordance with Holmes's objectives, the Institute did not sponsor any churches or subdivisions for years. The sixty-four page issue of *Science of Mind* for December 1930 lists twenty-two practitioners, all in California; one of its principal portions, comparable to the *Daily Word* of Unity, had a Meditation for each day of the month, a feature which has been continued ever since. The name of this section was changed in 1950 to Inspiration for Today; and in 1955, to Daily Guide for Richer Living, which has been its heading ever since.

In 1935, the eighty-page magazine included a picture of the building at 3251 West Sixth Street which had just been purchased and which still serves as the headquarters of the corporation, the name of which was changed to The Institute of Religious Science and Philosophy in the same year. That issue of the magazine listed thirty-six practitioners, all in California, as well as sixty-one locations in various parts of the country where Religious Science literature could be obtained. In 1940, a ninety-six-page issue names seventy-nine practitioners, of whom forty operated out of the headquarters; and it lists seventy-three locations where literature was sold. It also names various places in California where meetings were being held currently, in addition to those at headquarters.

The eighty-page issue of December 1945 has a list of Chartered Religious Science Activities. In addition to meetings at headquarters, there were seventeen other locations in California, three in other states, and one in Canada—a total of twenty-two. It also listed 140 practitioners, of whom 128 were in California. Interestingly enough, Christian Daa Larson is among these.

7. *The Developing Organization.* After 1930, one important event followed another. In 1932, Robert H. Bitzer, whom Holmes had

invited to come from Boston to California, proposed that his congregation be incorporated as the Hollywood Institute of Religious Science. However, this was not done until 1940. In 1934, the auditorium at the Biltmore had become too small to accommodate the growing attendance at Holmes's Sunday lectures; as a result, the Wiltern Theater was leased. He continued to lecture there, and later at the Beverly, until 1956.

In March 1938, daily radio broadcasts were begun; and in September, the policy was initiated of establishing chapters of the Institute wherever groups with at least a hundred members applied for such status; the same month one was established in Glendale, and in October in Huntington Park.

In November, the Institute adopted definite rules for the ordination ritual of ministers; in February 1939, a chapter was established in Ventura, and in May, another in West Los Angeles. At the same time charter organization plans and bylaws were adopted; and in July, requirements for ministerial ordination were established. In 1941, a qualification policy for practitioners was adopted. In December 1942, Science of Mind Study Groups were authorized under the direction of qualified practitioners. In 1944, the Department of Education, operating under a full-time dean, replaced the Committee on Education.

8. *A Church Organization At Last!* Thus it was becoming obvious that a church-movement was underway, perhaps spontaneously, whether Ernest Holmes wanted it or not. A number of his students had established centers of worship and teaching where his ideas were emphasized and whose following continued to increase. Robert Bitzer, for example, conducted services for a large congregation at 7677 Sunset Boulevard in Hollywood. Other outstanding leaders were Carmelita Trowbridge in Alhambra, Charlotte Garrick-Cook in San Francisco, and Raymond C. Barker in New York. The June 1946 *Science of Mind* listed a Directory of Chartered Religious Science Activities, which included twenty branches or chapters of the Institute in California, eight in other states, and one in Montreal, Canada—a total of twenty-nine. These were not, we should note, called churches, and their ministers were called leaders; actually, they were teachers who gave lessons which is what the sermons in all Religious Science churches are usually called, every Sunday morning. However, in all but the name, these branches of the Institute of Religious Science and

Philosophy had by this time become a denomination or association of churches. This development had taken nearly twenty years, and, as we have noted, was really spontaneous if not accidental.

After 1945, the growth was rapid. The December 1946 issue of *Science of Mind* lists forty-five branches, of which sixteen were outside California; it also lists 249 practitioners, of whom 192 were in California, 53 in other states, and 4 in foreign countries. Obviously, *Science of Mind* was spreading far and wide. The 1949 issue also lists nineteen Study Groups, of which fourteen were in California and one in South Africa; it also lists twenty-four branches with leaders in California and eleven in other states, in addition to the Founders Institute at 3251 West Sixth Street in Los Angeles.

However, the pressure had been increasing for the creation of an official denomination or association of churches with all the financial and other advantages available to such an organization. Thus it was that in June 1949 the International Association of Religious Science Churches was established, and its Articles of Incorporation and By-laws approved, for the purpose of transforming the chapters or branches of the Institute of Religious Science and Philosophy into a regular church, incorporated under the laws of California. Chapter status was abolished; the branches became members of the IARSC. Holmes became a charter member and the honorary president of its Board of Trustees.

The new association was authorized to grant memberships to local groups: but any minister would have to be trained and ordained by the Institute, which continued as a separate entity; and the IARSC had no control over its policies or requirements. The Institute was governed by a self-perpetuating Board of Trustees, and on this the individual churches had no representation. This created some friction among the members. A slight compromise was effected when they were allowed to name two representatives to the Board of the Institute; however, the control remained in the hands of the self-perpetuating Board.

In 1953, the Institute proposed a new form of organization under which the IARSC would be replaced by the Church of Religious Science; the old by-laws were repealed and new ones adopted. However, substantial control, the educational work, and the preparation and ordination of ministers would still remain with the Institute.

9.   *Rejection and Withdrawal.* Since the IARSC was by this time a

functioning organization with its own by-laws and elected officials this program met with refusal from some of the churches, which perhaps regarded this arrangement as one similar to that existing in the Christian Science Church, with its central and authoritarian control.

Thus it was that nineteen members of the IARSC simply withdrew and severed all ties with the Institute; but, according to their historian, simply remained intact as an organization with complete autonomy and no integral relation with the headquarters on West Sixth Street in Los Angeles.[1]

Of the sixty-six churches listed in *Science of Mind* just preceding the rupture, forty-seven accepted the proposal and remained with the Founders' church and the Institute.

10. *An Identical Statement of Faith.* However, since both divisions looked upon Ernest Holmes as their Teacher and source of Truth and inspiration and both continued to use *Science of Mind* as their principal textbook, both to this day proclaim an identical Statement of Faith, which was formulated by Ernest Holmes and reads as follows:

> We believe in God, the Living Spirit Almighty; one, indestructible, perfect, absolute, and self-existent Cause. This One manifests itself in and through all creation but is not absorbed by its creation. The manifest universe is the body of God; it is the logical and necessary outcome of the infinite all-knowingness of God....
>
> We believe in the incarnation of the Spirit in man and that all men are incarnations of the One Spirit....
>
> We believe in the eternity, the immortality, and the continuity of the individual soul, forever, and ever expanding.
>
> We believe that the Kingdom of Heaven is within man and that we experience this Kingdom to the degree that we become conscious of it....
>
> We believe the ultimate goal of life to be a complete emancipation from all discord of every nature, and that this goal is sure to be attained by all....
>
> We believe in the unity of all life, and that the highest God and the innermost God is one God....
>
> We believe that God is personal to all those who feel this indwelling Presence....
>
> We believe in the direct revelation of Truth through the intuitive and spiritual nature of man, and that any man may become a revealer of Truth who lives in close contact with the indwelling God....

We believe that the Universal Spirit, which is God, operates through a Universal Mind, which is the Law of God; and that we are surrounded by this Creative Mind which receives the direct impress of our thought and acts upon it....

We believe in the healing of the sick through the power of the Mind....

We believe in the control of conditions through the power of this Mind....

We believe in the eternal Goodness, the eternal Loving-Kindness and the eternal Givingness of Life to all....

We believe in our own soul, our own spirit, and our own destiny; for we understand that the life of man is God.

In one statement, which is a favorite in the churches he founded, Ernest Holmes said: "Religious Science is a correlation of the laws of science, the opinions of philosophy, and the revelations of religion, applied to human needs and the aspirations of man."

Could anything be more direct, succinct, and all-encompassing? The following are some favorite citations from Holmes:

We all look forward to the day when science and religion shall walk hand in hand through the visible to the invisible.

Science knows nothing of opinion, but recognizes a government of law whose principles are universal.

Revelation must keep faith with reason and religion with law—while intuition is ever spreading its wings, for greater flights—and science must justify faith in the invisible.

In each of us there exists the Divine Image of ultimate perfection, for God indwells everything which He creates.

God is Power—the only Power. Center yourself in this God-Power, and you have every right to expect all the good which you desire.

Through an inherent law of Mind, we increase whatever we praise. Praise yourself from weakness into strength, from ignorance into intelligence, from poverty into abundance.

The Law of Reciprocity—of giving of your time, talent, and material possessions—should precede the asking and receiving of abundance.

The perfect body is the fulfillment of the Divine Ideal and is the real man which all of us hope to manifest.

I let God's wisdom inspire and direct me. I let God's spirit take over in me.

God wished to create a being who could respond to and understand Him. He could do this only by imparting His own nature to this being whom He called man. He must make him in His own image and likeness.

II. THE SYSTEM OF FENWICKE AND ERNEST HOLMES

1. *The Teachings of Fenwicke.* As we have noted, Fenwicke and Ernest Holmes worked closely together for a number of years. In addition to *The Science of Mind*, Ernest wrote a small library of literature, some of which we will examine in due course. First, however, let us make a brief analysis of the most important works of Fenwicke, who not only outlived his younger brother, but also wrote his biography.[2]

We find his teachings and system fully explained in two books: *The Law of the Mind in Action* and *The Faith That Heals* (1921). The theology herein set forth is based on the concept that God is the Central Sun or the Universal Power which exists in the universe and which is omnipotent and omnipresent. God, we read, is the "Creative Spirit, everywhere present, eternally here. In Him is all life.... He is unlimited."[3] God constitutes the substance of all that exists. He is the original stuff of the cosmos, the source of light, heat, vitality. He is the impersonal source of power, the infinite law and principle which governs the universe and every manifestation that exists; the stars, the planets, the earth, the animals, and all vegetation. Most of all, "man, child of God, is divine spirit," and, as such, "shares His resources, lives, moves, and has his being in God as an infinite sea."[4] He declares that "the same substance is in the flaming sunrise, the flying bird and the flowering bush. The one substance composes your body, your environment, and your wealth."[5] God is "all of Life, Love, and Wisdom, and not as a person...."[6] "To conceive of God *as a person* is to recognize *two* powers in the universe," which would reduce the cosmos to chaos and zero.[7] God is Life, Love, and Wisdom.[8]

This living, pulsating, creative, and ever-active force or power which Fenwicke Holmes usually calls Cosmic Consciousness, constantly and universally streams forth as a life-giving influx which sustains and heals every sentient thing and conscious creature. It is the impartial, impersonal spirit with universal powers and limitless resources from which man may draw substance and energy *"at his own will."*[9] It is *"the thinker that conceives things, the substance of which things are composed, and the power that sustains them."*[10]

Nothing in the universe or in human life is static, for the "Cosmic Consciousness is continuously creative."[11] This is, of course, a simple restatement of the Swedenborgian Doctrine of Influx, which Holmes emphasizes again and again. We must place ourselves in alliance with the Unseen, the supernal forces which will then possess us.[12] When a man enters the secret places of the Most High, he draws from the springs of life, peace, and plenty, and there the Lord will renew his strength because his mind and soul are receptive and his body will be healed.[13]

This influx is always available, but the "Creative Spirit enters only the door that is open," and benefits only that person who is receptive.[14] When this is the case, "the pure, clear stream of love divine" flows through his body and carries away all impure and selfish thoughts, and cleanses mind and body of all sin.[15] There are "certain brain-centers and nerve-systems especially adapted to the influx of pure ideas from the universal" creative force.[16] As the "Creative Mind becomes to us what we become to It," there is no limit except our own capacities to receive the beneficence available.[17] We are like electric bulbs which, according to their capacity, draw light from the central power system.[18]

The Swedenborgian Law of Correspondences lies at the base of Fenwicke's theory concerning disease and its cure. Since God is the Universal All, there can be no duality, or evil, in the universe. In his finite scope, Man is microcosm filled with macrocosmic deity; and since there is no sin, evil, or disease in God, these can have no reality in Man. For every material existence, there is a spiritual prototype or correspondence. The universal law of the cosmos must be obeyed if we are to "create our own heaven" and avoid "our own hell."[19] The universal mind, which is God, corresponds exactly to that of a human individual.[20] Under "the Law of Correspondences, you manifest or externalize...just what you think within."[21]

Since God is universal and Man is the microcosm, and since there is no evil force in the universe, neither organic nor functional disease can be endowed with reality.[22] However, since thoughts are potent things, wrong thinking attracts disease and right thinking casts it out.[23] We are all subject to, or influenced by, the contagious thought-atmosphere which surrounds us.[24] Whenever we permit a negative thought to rule, we become the victims of its suggestion; and we can be cured only by positive thinking.[25]

Since God is the Positive All-Good, negations are nonentities: "as darkness is legislated out of existence by...light, so evil is reduced to zero by the presence of a contrary thought."[26] Sin is not willful sickness, only ignorance, which never calls for moral judgment or condemnation.[27] To cast out evil, therefore, one need only declare: I am spirit, life, and Divine Mind. No evil can befall the spiritual mind.[28] To achieve the happy life, we need only "Bring up the Aggregate of Our Thinking for Health, Wealth, and Love So That It Shall Outbalance Any Possible Amount of Negative Thinking."[29]

This, according to Fenwicke L. Holmes, is the foundation for the religion of health, happiness, and prosperity.

2. *A General Outline of the System of Ernest Holmes.* The first four chapters of *Science of Mind* are called an Introduction and may be considered a summation of his general ideology under four headings: (1) The Thing Itself; (2) The Way It Works; (3) What It Does; and (4) How to Use It (pp. 25-60).

In *Science of Mind*, the Thing Itself may be defined as the First Cause, Spirit, Mind, or Essence, the ultimate source from which everything emanates. This is the one, basic Reality, the causative Mind, a limitless power which man has at his command and can utilize if he uses the proper methods.

How does this work? It is the Universal Mind, Intelligence, Spirit, or God, which finds expression in every human being to whatever extent he is able to absorb it. It works through us, as individualizations, or microcosms of the macrocosm, which is the universe. However, in order to make it work for us, we must recognize and accept it; in short, our belief sets the limits to the demonstration of this universal power.

What, then, does or can this power do in and through us? We must understand that it works only through Law. The mind must first conceive before the desired result can ensue, and we can capture only as much as we are able to embody. This is the Universal Law of Mind and it has no respect of persons, but is creative in each of us to the extent of our belief in and acceptance of it.

How, then, can we use this power? Only by our conscious thought will the universal Law of Mind operate in and through us to accomplish our hearts' desires. It is always creative and willing to operate on our behalf. We did not create nor can we change it, but it can work through us at our behest by spiritual treatment which brings to us the divine energy of the invisible world. It is an actual force, which must be consciously directed in order to produce specific results.

   3.   *The Basic Metaphysics of Ernest Holmes.* As was the case with his brother, the metaphysical foundation for Ernest Holmes' philosophy and practical work is found in the Swedenborgian concepts of deity, influx, correspondence, and Christ-Power. "The physical universe," we read, "is the Body of God—the invisible Principle of All Life. Our physical being is the body of the unseen man."[30] This "First Cause, Spirit, Mind" or "invisible Essence" is "The Thing Itself"[31]; it is the "origin of everything"[32] and "the Universal Energy."[33] It is the "One Central Life, from Whose Self-Existence all draw their livingness...."[34] God is the unmade, co-eternal substance of the Universe which is governed by immutable law.[35] He is the Creative Intelligence[36] which exists in everything.[37] There is only one Mind, which is God and is in me, and there is one spiritual body, which is also mine. Within me is the mind of Christ and my body is the Body of God.[38] We live, as it were, surrounded by a sea, which is God,[39] our substance and supply.[40] In virtually Swedenborgian terminology, we learn that since we are made of the same stuff as the Central Fire of the Universe, we are the offspring of the Supreme Spirit.[41] We read that "the *sun* stands for the inner Spiritual Principle," which always shines when we remove the obstructions of unbelief.[42] The Creator is the immutable, inexorable, and impersonal manifestation of the Mother-Father God.[43]

God is the triune principle[44]; he is the physical universe manifested as body[45]; he is also the "invisible Life Essence of all that is, the intelligent Energy running through all."[46] Being infinite, God is indeed greater than man,[47] who is a finite form; but the mind of man is part of the mind of God[48]; man is God objectified.[49] Actually, the divinity which constitutes man's inner life is the only knowable God.[50] Man is the microcosmic image of the macrocosmic deity.[51]

The Christ-concept of Holmes is scarcely less central than his theology. Since we are the offspring of the Supreme Spirit, mankind enjoys a universal sonship, which is the Christ within,[52] the Christ-Mind,[53] the immanent savior.[54] This Power is always present, to a lesser or greater degree, in every human being.[55]

The man "Jesus became the Christ through a complete realization of the Unity of Spirit...."[56] He "became the embodiment of the Christ, as the human gave way to the Divine Idea of Sonship."[57] We must comprehend that "Christ is God in the soul of man."[58] "As the external Jesus gave way to the Divine, the human took on the Christ Spirit and became the Voice of God to humanity."[59] Christ is the manifestation of God as universal.[60] The indwelling Christ is generic man, "The Real Man."[61]

Christ, then, is not a person or an individual; he is, rather, an omnipresent power, available to everyone without measure and existent in each of us to whatever degree we can absorb and assimilate this energy and illumination.

Holmes's theology and Christology lead directly to his concept of death and immortality, which, again, are distinctly Swedenborgian. The soul is the true human entity, which controls the body, "its legitimate effect."[62] Thus, our true bodies are eternal for they are "not made with hands."[63] No man will ever die, for the Spirit of God is within and cannot change; therefore, each life is forever.[64] The soul needs a physical body temporarily, but when this is no longer adequate, it is discarded and the soul continues to function, but more subtly.[65] Actually, we are spirits now, as much as we ever shall be.

This Swedenborgian doctrine is repeated over and over: if the soul can project a body here, there is no reason to doubt that it will create another for the eternal life.[66] The future body will resemble the present one, but will be free from disease, old age, or any other undesirable condition.[67] Once we become unconscious of death, we will easily pass "from this life to the next" without even being aware of the transition.[68] Thus, we prepare, not for death, but for eternal life, a passage which will be a "glorious experience."[69] Like the eagle free from his cage, the soul will soar from its home of heavy flesh to its native heights, in the

Father's house.[70] Resurrection is nothing more or less than rising from a belief in death.[71] "The physical disappearance of Jesus after his resurrection was the result of the spiritualization of his consciousness."[72]

Since the immortal soul exists, there can be no doubt of spirit communication.[73]

Another Swedenborgian concept which animates Holmes's thinking is the Doctrine of Correspondence. "In the subjective world," he writes, "there must be a correspondent of everything in the objective...."[74] And again: "The spiritual world contains an image of the physical; the physical is a counterpart of the spiritual."[75]

One of the most pervasive ideas found in Holmes is the Swedenborgian Doctrine of Influx. The great creative force or power which is and sustains the universe is constantly and universally sending forth its beneficent stream of energy; and every vegetative, sentient, or intelligent entity draws upon this for life, illumination, and well-being. The creative mind of God flows through the universe.[76] The Divine Spirit fills me with perfect life, exclaims the author: "*I am bathed in pure spirit...*"[77] and "receptive...to the influx of perfect life...."[78] It is essential that we "open up our own ever-widening channel for this Divine Influx,"[79] a "Power which flows through you without effort...."[80]

Our spirits are part of the Universal Spirit[81] and "when we open our minds to the influx of Divine Wisdom we are allowing our lives to be guided by the Infinite."[82]

4. *Evil.* In Holmes's system, sin and evil are mere negatives and must never be regarded as entities. There can be no duality in the universe since God is All in All; the devil has no existence except in negative thought,[83] and sin is only a mistake,[84] for which punishment "is an inevitable consequence."[85] Actually, there is neither sin nor sinner[86]; since there is no God-ordained evil, it can have no existence of its own.[87]

Evil is a problem only because we believe in it; it is neither person, place, nor thing, and it will disappear as we discard destructive methods.[88] Heaven and hell are states of consciousness, and the latter is the abode of a morbid imagination.[89] Heaven is a kingdom which can exist within us; hell is a discordant state, a belief in cosmic duality, a sense of separation from God.[90] Since there is no evil in the universe, such things as hell or a devil can exist nowhere except in our delusions.[91]

5. *The Theory and Technique of Healing.* The preceding leads

directly to Holmes's often-expressed theory of disease and healing, which is simply applied Christianity.[92] However, we should note that the metaphysician is not yet sufficiently advanced to set bones or to walk on water[93]; nor does he reject *materia medica*, pills, drugs, or the ministrations of a medical doctor whenever these will be of help.[94]

There is no doubt that the medical profession would agree with Holmes that there are many self-induced diseases and that extreme worry,[95] suppressed desire,[96] or unexpected grief may eventuate in death[97]; and that metaphysical and psychological methods have an important field of their own,[98] especially in the treatment of emotional disturbances.[99]

Holmes, however, does not hesitate to venture into areas where the more conventional healers may not follow. He declares categorically that "since the Law of God is Infinite, from the spiritual viewpoint, there is no *incurable disease....*"[100] And he declares "that man is a spiritual being now as much as he ever shall become" and "the spiritual man has no disease."[101] "Sickness is not a spiritual Reality; it is an experience—an effect and not a cause."[102]

What, then, is disease? It is "an impersonal thought-force operating through people which does not belong to them at all."[103] *"Disease is not an entity."*[104] It is "the mesmeric effect of race-thought...a heritage of the ages believed in by so many persons that it seems to be true."[105] It is "human experience...operating from the subconscious reaction of the whole race."[106] Since there is no material body to be healed, there can be no material disease.[107]

Only by discarding all valid testimony can we deny that bodily healing by mental and spiritual means is a fact.[108] This treatment "is a consciousness of the Unity of all Life and the spiritual nature of all being. Man's life is rooted in the Universal and the Eternal..."[109]

Holmes does not say categorically but certainly implies that resurrection from death will one day be possible and that even cancer will one day yield to one sufficiently endowed with spiritual power.[110] Since colds have no part in life, we can rid ourselves of them by simply declaring our disbelief in them.[111] Nor is there any need to grow old[112] or to suffer from advancing years.

The practitioner heals through the operation of impersonal, immutable, and universal law.[113] He employs the Law of Life, which is simply to affirm its truth[114] and to accept its operation for himself and his patient.[115] His treatment consists in declarations to the effect that the patient is a spiritual being who lives and moves in the Divine Wisdom and who is receptive to the inexhaustible energy of the universe, the influx of perfect life.[116] Or, again: "There is no thought of failure that can operate through this person's mind. He is open to the influx of new ideas.... He is sure of himself, because he is sure of God."[117]

The certainty that God is everywhere omnipresent is the basis for all spiritual treatment.[118] Since thoughts are things,[119] the healing mentality of the practitioner is transferred to the patient and removes negation and error. This treatment is equally effective whether present or absent.[120] In order to heal, it is only necessary for the practitioner to convince himself.[121] Weariness, like sickness, is only an error of mind.[122]

Over and over, Holmes explains that the "practitioner consciously removes the apparent obstruction, and leaves the field open to a new influx of Spirit."[123] He permits the "stream of creative energy to take definite form."[124] He heals because he believes that there is but one Creative Intelligence in the universe and that this flows in unlimited supply through every individual.[125] The patient must cooperate by permitting the Life Essence to flow freely through him.[126] If the victim of asthma will declare his body to be a receptive channel for the operation of the God-Life, the obstruction will pass away.[127]

This beneficent flow and influx is as effective to create success as it is to restore health. The practitioner declares that "there is no thought failure that can operate through this person's mind."[128] Again: "He allows the Divine Wholeness to flow through him.... There is a new influx of inspiration into his thought."[129] As this mental affirmation opens the consciousness to a new influx of life, success is certain to ensue."[130] Even one who has missed his golden opportunities can still enjoy an open, rich, full, abundant life.[131]

6. *Psychoanalysis*. Holmes often approaches the Freudian method or technique of psychoanalysis. Just as the surgeon sets a broken bone with no ethical opinion about his patient,[132] so must the practitioner refrain from any moral judgment concerning this patient's emotional disturbances.[133] He may not agree, but he must never be unsympathetic. "The slightest sense of condemnation or judgment about the patient" makes healing impossible.[134] Holmes discusses at length the case of an eminent architect who was on the verge of insanity because of his subconscious hatred for a brother and who was healed when the

cause of his distress was revealed to him.[135] As in Freud, the explanation is the cure. Holmes describes the treatment and healing of alcoholics[136]; that of a woman who was going mad with abdominal pains resulting from emotional stress[137]; of a child who had traumatic experiences because of parental conflicts[138]; of a cultured woman of sixty who was tormented by voices.[139] Holmes declares that psychoanalysis "is making a splendid contribution in teaching us how to rebuild consciousness. But it will remain incomplete unless spiritual values are added."[140] And this was precisely what the Church of Religious Science was designed to accomplish: a marriage between religion and the Freudian technique.

Thus, the practitioner deals with the problem posed by Macbeth:

> Cans't thou not minister to a mind diseas'd,
> Pluck from the memory a rooted sorrow,
> Raze out the written troubles of the brain,
> And with some sweet oblivious antidote
> Cleanse the stuff'd bosom of that perilous stuff
> Which weighs upon the heart?

7. *Health, Happiness, and Prosperity.* This carries us to the culminating aspect of New Thought, which is, above all, a religion of well-being, and which is intended to redeem us from sickness, hate, morbidity, and poverty.[141] Supply is sufficient to cover every need and only awaits the demands of all those who believe.[142]

III. ADDITIONAL TEACHINGS OF ERNEST HOLMES

In addition to the above, we should summarize the concepts found in some of the other publications authored by Holmes.

1. *The Concept of Deity.* This is all-pervasive. Spirit, Mind, and Substance are universal—"pure energy becoming tangible through Law in the form provided for it by thought and idea. It makes no difference whether we think of Law as being spiritual, mental, or physical, providing we realize that the three work together in perfect unity, being but different functions of the great Laws of God."[143]

All creation exists as the expression of God[144]; in fact, the universe itself is God[145] and constitutes unlimited abundance.[146] God is a spirit with innumerable incarnations.[147] Thus "intelligence is manifest in everything from the blade of grass to our own theoretical speculations about the nature of the universe."[148] God is a law written in the vegetable, animal, and human kingdoms.[149] God is Good or Harmony[150]; the divine essence which fills all space[151]; the impersonal Life Principle which animates the universe.[152] Since this is true, he is available to all persons at all times[153]. Since God is energy, He is also everything that exists as an expression or manifestation of Himself.[154] He is Universal Intelligence, Spirit, Absolute Cause, Existence, or Reality which fills and constitutes the universe.[155] The Trinity, we read, is the Spirit that directs, the Law which executes, and the creation which results.[156]

2.   *God and Man.* Since God is everything and man is his highest manifestation in creation, their interrelation is highly significant. God is an inner light in man,[157] which is the essence of his being, the Eternal God, the everlasting Spirit or Father.[158] Humanity is cradled, as it were, in the Infinite and all men are the offspring of the Most High.[159] There is a divine unity binding us all together.[160] We are all children of God[161]; and therefore we are God in the germ.[162] Man is the center of all self-conscious life and God is the Principle which animates him.[163] Holmes declares that every human being is an incarnation and individualization of deity.[164] The realization of this fact should remove from everyone all sense of inferiority, every such complex, and the need for psychological adjustment—and would alleviate all the physical diseases in the world.[165] From this it follows that man can be his own savior.

The concept of divine influx is pervasive in Holmes. There is, he declares, an influx of divine ideas which stimulates the human will to a divine purposefulness.[166] There is a river of life flowing from the Mind of God which renews our vigor, remakes our strength, and enables us to heal our bodies and our fortunes and bring peace into our hearts.[167]

3.   *Jesus and the Christ.* It is interesting to note that in addition to calling Jesus the *Wayshower*, as was first done in Christian Science, Holmes also uses other appellations very similar to those used by the early Christian Ebionites. He is called the Exemplar, the Teacher, the Enlightened One, the Great Revelator, the Man of Wisdom, the Great Physician, a Spiritual Genius. Elsewhere he is called the Cosmic Man.[168]

However, there is a sharp differentiation between Jesus and the

Christ, who is not a historic person, but simply that which lives and moves and breathes in every human being.[169] Jesus was a man like all other men, both as to his humanity and his divinity[170]; what distinguished him was the fact that he had laid hold on the power of spirit.[171] By at-one-ment we mean merely that if we misuse the Law of God, we must suffer until justice has been done.[172]

4. *Hell, the Devil, Etc.* As in New Thought generally, Holmes denies all such concepts with scorn. Hell, the devil, etc., are only myths[173]; since God is all, there can be no duality in the universe.[174] Heaven and hell are simply states of mind.[175] To believe in a physical hell is to be tied to ignorant superstitions.[176] We are not punished because of our sins, but *by them.*[177]

However, since we create our own hells, they are certainly real enough for those who believe in them; but when we transpose our thought to heaven, their supposed flames are at once extinguished.[178]

5. *The Power of Mind and Thought.* Again and again, Holmes explains the intimate relationship between our conscious thinking and our deep, unconscious, or subjective motivations.[179] Since the former acts as a feeder to the latter and since we have free will or choice, we can change our negative mental states to positive[180]; our subjective state of thought produces our psychosomatic ailments and problems.[181] By changing the conscious thought-pattern, we can transform our lives.[182] Thought, therefore, is creative, for both good and evil[183]; negative thought is a terrible scourge.[184]

6. *The Conscious and the Subconscious Mind.* The mind, declares Holmes, operates on three planes: (1) the material, (2) the mental, and (3) the spiritual.[185] "The subjective [subconscious] state of our thought constitutes ninety percent of our thought-content.... All these unconscious thoughts and thought-patterns—motivations, conflicts, impressions, whatever you want to call them—are beneath our conscious threshold, but they also help to constitute our entire thought."[186] Only the conscious mind has the power to change the subconscious mind.[187]

7. *Spiritual Mind-Healing.* Thus, the conscious mind exerts a profound influence upon the subconscious, a fact which leads directly to the efficacy of Spiritual Mind-Healing. People are sick, poor, and unhappy chiefly because their conscious minds are choked with wrong words and concepts.[188] Science of Mind enables us to use the conscious mind to build into the subconscious functions that operate benefi-

cently; and for this reason, psychosomatic medicine is effective.[189] When the right ideas are poured into the subconscious by the conscious mind, they will eliminate negative ideas of discord, worry, hatred, disease, and limitation.[190]

The healer or practitioner deals with disease, not as an unreality of experience, but as a wrong arrangement resulting from wrong thoughts.[191] To an ever-increasing degree, psychosomatic medicine is demonstrating that the power of thought can make us sick or can heal us.[192] This is based on certain and scientific knowledge. In successful treatment, we first determine the good we desire, declare it specifically, accept it as our own actual experience, and *know* that it will be manifested in accordance with Law.[193]

Science of Mind never denies that people really *are* sick. Furthermore, it is right and good, when necessary or effective, to use drugs, surgery, sanitation, and proper exercise. Hospitals are necessary[194]; the sick should by all means seek regular medical assistance when it will help.[195] God speaks every time a scientist discovers a new invention.[196] Science of Mind simply offers a bridge from all such things to the achievement of perfect and permanent health. Its treatment includes psychosomatic medicine as well as that of the regular physician. It proclaims the unity of all things; and, as a result, many leading physicians have now adopted its principles.[197]

8. *The Nature and Efficacy of Prayer.* There is a true science of prayer, which can be followed by anyone.[198] Mere supplication, however, is a contradiction.[199] Effective prayer consists of affirmations, expressed in four steps: (1) recognition; (2) identification; (3) declaration; and (4) acceptance of those facts and conditions which we desire and already know to exist.[200] Thus prayer becomes a creative process,[201] as is the Lord's Prayer. The words *Our Father which art in Heaven* mean merely that we possess an inner and accessible divine power.[202]

Holmes provides many model prayers, one of which reads as follows:

> I now accept my divine birthright. I now consciously enter into my partnership with love, with peace, with joy, with God. I feel the infinite Presence close around me. I feel the warmth, the color, and the radiance of this Presence like a living thing in which I am enveloped.
>
> I am no longer afraid of life. A deep and abiding sense of calm and of

poise flows through me. I have faith to believe that the Kingdom of God is at hand. It is right where I am, here, now, today, at this moment.

I feel that there is a Law of Good which can, and does govern everything. Therefore, I feel that everything in my life is constructive, everything in my thought that is life-giving is blessed and prospered. It blesses everyone I meet. It makes glad every situation I find myself in. It brings peace and comfort to everyone I contact. I am united with everything in life, in love, in peace, and in joy. And I know that the Presence of Love and Life gently leads me and all others, guiding, guarding, sustaining, upholding, now and forever.[203]

Thus, "affirmative prayer, or spiritual mind-treatment, is the recognition of this universal creative Presence and Power which surrounds us and is responsive to us."[204]

9. *The Successful Life.* In order to achieve true success in life, we must banish all feelings of hatred, bitterness, and fear[205]; we must carry no grudge[206]; only love, which also brings happiness, can make us attractive.[207]

Although poverty is no virtue,[208] success does not necessarily consist in making money.[209] We are not struggling for wealth, as such[210]; prosperity is a state of mind.[211] In order to achieve a successful life, ten steps are essential:

(1) overcome all negative mental attitudes;
(2) stop worrying;
(3) overcome a sense of inferiority;
(4) think about your own personality;
(5) make your work as easy as possible;
(6) count your blessings;
(7) forgive yourself and others—do not carry grudges;
(8) learn how to get along with others;
(9) use prayer and affirmative meditation in personal achievement;
(10) get the most out of your religion.[212]

10. *Specific Religious Concepts.* Religion, declares Holmes, is a belief in an invisible, superhuman power or powers—in a God or gods—any system of faith, doctrine, or worship.[213]

The new religion now dawning on mankind will be a spiritual psychology, an idealist philosophy, and a system of metaphysics designed consciously to create in the mind a recognition and realization that the eternal is one with man; that this creative intelligence is available to all humanity; that the dynamic and purposive Power which urges everything forward is latent in man, who can discover the Divine Presence within himself.[214]

The tribute and monument to Ernest Shurtleff Holmes is found and expressed in the many churches which espouse and proclaim his teachings and the tens of thousands of individuals who have found peace and surcease from sorrow in his reviving gospel.

Chapter X

THE CHURCHES OF RELIGIOUS SCIENCE

I. RELIGIOUS SCIENCE INTERNATIONAL

1. *Name and Headquarters.* Although the name International Association of Religious Science Churches (IARSC) is still a trademark to designate it, its name was changed officially to the Church of Religious Science International in 1972. Its headquarters is housed in a handsome and spacious building at 3130 Fifth Avenue in San Diego, where its monthly periodical, *Creative Thought*, is published and which serves as the center of its activities.

2. *Growth.* The IARSC was, as we have noted, created in 1949; and in 1953, with nineteen member churches, it began operation as a separate entity from the Religious Science Institute. In an official statement, the International declares that the IARSC simply went on as before but that a number of churches withdrew from it—meaning

those which became the United Church of Religious Science with headquarters in Los Angeles.

Since then, the growth of the International has been steady and rapid, especially in recent years, as shown in the following table:

Year	Bodies	In U.S.	In Calif.	Foreign
1954	19	18	13	1
1960	30	29	14	1
1965	42	40	19	2
1970	47	44	21	3
1975	65	61	34	4
1980	80	74	43	6
1985	100	92	44	8

We note, therefore, that, although California remains as the stronghold of the Church, its members have spread to other areas in the United States and even abroad to a degree and in a proportion quite beyond what existed at the beginning, when thirteen of the nineteen churches were in the area of origin. In 1982, in addition to eighty-six churches which had ordained ministers, there were nine societies headed by Leaders, three of them located in foreign countries.

3.   *The Magazine* Creative Thought. This has been issued monthly since 1953; it consists of sixty-four pages in a rather small format, 4½ x 6 inches, comparable in size to the *Daily Word* of Unity, which it resembles in other ways as well. The present editor, Catherine Hubbell, has a statement called "Thoughts," printed on the inside of the front cover. Then follow several short articles by well-known Religious Science writers, usually occupying ten pages; then comes the reading or meditation for each day of the month—also by well-known New Thought authors—which have such titles as "I Am Inspired"; "I Use Time Effectively"; "I Am Health"; "I Learn Quickly"; "I Am At Peace with Myself"; "I Have Spiritual Authority"; "I Listen to My Inner Self"; "I Am Opportunity Conscious"; "My Inner World Perfects the Outer"; "I Dwell in the Wisdom of Spirit"; "I Am Well, Strong, and Happy"; "My God Is My Self-Expression"; "My Business World Is the Dominion of God"; "I Am Prosperity and I Prosper"; "I Am Rich"; "I Live a Healthy Life"; "Life Is Completed"; "I Am Free and Mighty"; "I Am Rooted in Divine Power." These are affirmative

prayers of almost infinite variety, all dedicated to a life of health, happiness, and prosperity. In the centerfold of every issue is a Lesson numbered by the month of issue: for example, in that for September 1982, we find Lesson Nine, by Carl Ray Ambrose; the subject is Intuition, which is regarded as a form of divine guidance and which, in everyday living, "reveals to you what you need to know in order to keep your life peaceful." Each number also includes a complete roster of all churches, societies, and practitioners. On the back cover we find a quotation from such men as Raymond Barker, Robert Bitzer, Kahlil Gibran, Ralph Waldo Emerson, and Walt Whitman.

4. *Three Aspects of Approach.* The Church publishes a brochure which states that anyone may approach Religious Science through any one of three aspects and thus discover a new, dynamic, and creative way of thinking:

> As a *philosophy* Religious Science presents a practical, down-to-earth way of thinking about the nature of the universe and man's relationship to it. It considers man's place in the scheme of things and how he can better live up to and express the potentialities within him. Such an increased understanding broadens his scope of activity and releases him from limitation and fear. As a creation of God expressing His nature, he discovers his rightful position as a co-creator with God.
>
> As a *religion* Religious Science is something to believe and have faith in. Not in an abstract manner, but as a belief and a faith that have significance and value in every aspect of life. As a religion it brings to your understanding truths which have been announced by prophets of the world's religions. It presents a sound way of thinking and not questionable concepts subject to doubt and speculation.
>
> As a *science* Religious Science presents specific and definite ideas which each can demonstrate for himself in his own life and experience. No formula is involved, but there are offered certain methods, techniques, and procedures which, if properly used, enable a person to discover and experience a better way of life. The procedure is called spiritual mind treatment—the elevation of prayer out of a routine ritual to its highest and most effective point. Spiritual mind treatment brings together and uses basic religious ideas and scientific knowledge of mind-body relationships.

5. *Democracy in Organization.* During a visit to the headquarters in San Diego, we received important help and information from the

Assistant to the President. The Church has an elaborate set of bylaws which spell out the details of its organization and operation. One element stressed therein is the spiritual necessity for democratic procedures, individual responsibility, the autonomy of the member churches, and the control over the national organization by representatives duly elected by them. The Preamble of the Bylaws declares:

> We hold that spiritual unity among men can most effectively be manifested under a democracy, wherein the inherent freedom and divine individuality of all members may express for the good of all in understanding, brotherly love, justice, and equality....
>
> We declare that the future good of Religious Science can best be maintained in the consecrated hands of the many, under a spiritual democracy, rather than in the hands of even the most capable few.

6.   *Membership*. The Bylaws provide that membership may consist of churches, societies, and centers, which shall be required to meet certain qualifications to be established by the Board of Directors. Societies have no voting power; churches must have duly qualified and ordained ministers; every church must use Articles of Incorporation and a set of Bylaws approved by the International. Any church, society, or center has the right to withdraw from membership at any time; but if it does so, it may no longer use a name or trademark belonging to the Corporation.

7.   *Government*. All legislative power is vested in a Congress which consists of accredited representatives of the member churches and centers and of all pastors or leaders of these. This Congress, which meets at least once annually, has the power to determine its own membership and to admit or expel, by a two-thirds vote. It elects the Board of Directors and levies and collects contributions for the support of the International.

The Board of Directors, which acts as the executive and judicial body of the organization, consists of nineteen members, of whom thirteen are ordained ministers and six are lay members in good standing who have completed basic courses of study in Religious Science. All Directors are elected by Australian ballot for a period of three years. Any such Director may be removed by a two-thirds vote of the Board, but he has a right to appeal such action to the entire Congress at its next annual convocation. The Board, which elects its own officers, meets at least twice between Congresses; and it is its duty and function to carry on and manage the business of the Corporation.

When any vacancy occurs on the Board, except by expiration of term in office, this is filled for the interim period by the Board itself.

The Board has broad powers to establish general standards of procedure for the International, its churches, centers, and societies. It determines the qualifications for approval and licensing of ministers, teachers, leaders, and practitioners; and can expel any such individual for just cause by certain procedures which entail provisions of appeal.

The Board can also grant or rescind charters for any church, center, or society; it establishes salaries for personnel; administers all funds necessary for the welfare of the International; controls all publications; manages its finances; and appoints or creates any committee or department deemed necessary to carry on its work.

The President of the Congress also presides over all meetings of the Board of Directors and performs such other functions as normally pertain to such executive office.

All churches and centers select and send voting representatives to the annual Congresses; each sends one for every fifty active members, in addition to the pastor; however, no church may have more than twenty delegates.

At the Annual Congress, a Nominating Committee prepares a slate of candidates for office; however, any number of additional nominations may be made from the floor; election is by Australian ballot.

8. *The Board of Education.* One of the most important bodies in the International is the Board of Education, which consists of five members appointed by the Board of Directors for a term of five years, with one expiring annually. The President serves as an ex-officio member of the Board of Education.

This Board establishes the curriculum to be followed for all Religious Science International class-instruction, the conditions under which credit will be granted for the successful completion of the accredited class-instruction, and the criteria for granting transfer credits from other organizations. It also recommends to the Board of Directors minimum tuition charges for instruction, additional requirements for the qualification of practitioners and ministers, and the requirements for the accreditation of teachers.

All instruction is given in the local churches by accredited teachers under the general supervision of the local ordained pastor; however, there are occasional seminars held in San Diego or elsewhere under the general sponsorship of the International in which ministers and leaders can deepen their understanding of Religious Science.

For licensing a minister, four-year courses of study are prescribed; in addition to this, after receiving a license, the minister serves at least two years in a local congregation before ordination.

Practitioners must take three years of instruction before receiving licenses, and these must be renewed annually.

All licenses and ordinations are determined and issued at the headquarters by the Board of Directors.

9. *The Operation of the Churches.* As noted, the local organizations enjoy a great degree of autonomy. The headquarters has prepared a model for Articles of Incorporation which is to be used as the basis in whatever state the branch may be located. This provides that should a church dissolve—that is, terminate all activity—its assets must revert to the International. This is a requirement for membership in the association.

In the model By-laws prepared for the member-churches, a similar provision is mandatory; however, should a going congregation decide to disaffiliate, it can do so and take its property with it; but it may not thereafter use any name or trademark which would indicate membership in the International. And before taking such action, it agrees to discuss the issue with a representative from headquarters, who will meet with the Board of Trustees and the membership for a full discussion of the reasons for the proposed separation.

Churches are administered by a Board of Trustees with a suggested membership of seven but not more than nine, elected to staggered three-year-terms.

No person can serve as the pastor of an International church unless he has been licensed and ordained by the Board of Directors.

Regular procedures are set forth by which the congregation can expel undesirable members, and even for the removal of the minister.

10. *Practitioners.* While the United Church of Religious Science has many more churches than the International, it lists no more than 82 practitioners in 175 churches, while the issue for May 1985, of *Creative Thought* lists 454, or an average of nearly 5 per church. The Reverend Lola Mays, minister of the Mesa Church, stated that she trains more of these than any other church in the denomination except

that in New York. We do not know the precise reason for this disparity unless it is that the International emphasizes the need and importance of this service and activity more than the other denomination.

We learned from one minister that practitioners generally devote their efforts more or less equally to three kinds of counselling; (1) for those with physical ailments; (2) for those with emotional problems, such as alcoholism or neuroses; and (3) for those who need help in achieving proper adjustment with others in family or other personal relationships, or in achieving desirable economic objectives.

One brochure states that the Practitioner should be a person of high spiritual consciousness, skilled in mind-treatment, dedicated to the cause of helping others, and licensed to practice professionally. Such treatment, it declares, consists in healing the mind, body, and affairs through the use of Scientific Prayer, which can change the individual's consciousness and thereby accomplish an improvement in body and outward relationships—a change not done *for* you, but *through* you. The Practitioner is simply a teacher and the patient is a student.

You need a Practitioner, we are told, if you are too close to your problem to see the situation clearly; if you lack the experience and understanding necessary to remove your difficulty; and if you feel a real need for help and instruction.

Most of the practitioners operate out of their own homes, although some list office numbers and addresses. Thus, some engage in this as a part-time, others as a full-time profession or career.

The brochure, published in 1982, quotes the following fees for treatments: $20.00 for a single lesson; $50.00 for a week; and $150.00 for a whole month.

11. Psycho-Cybernetics *by Maxwell Maltz.* Since we have already analyzed the teachings of Ernest Holmes, this requires no repetition, although it is equally applicable to both divisions of Religious Science. As the readers of this volume know, we have already dealt with the writings of Joseph Murphy, Thomas Troward, Emma Curtis Hopkins, Emmet Fox, and others whose works are very popular in the New Thought Movement. However, since *Psycho-Cybernetics* by Maxwell Maltz is used perhaps more intensively by teachers and ministers in the International than elsewhere in the preparation and instruction of practitioners, we present here a brief analysis and summary of this very significant volume.

This book, first published in 1960, has been so popular that it has sold more than a million copies. It does not belong strictly in the New Thought cycle, because it advances no opinions concerning the deity or other specifically metaphysical concepts, although it refers sometimes to Jesus and passages in the Bible; nor does it advance beliefs in immortality or claim remarkable healings for organic diseases. However, in other areas its ideology is so similar to that found in Quimby, Emma Curtis Hopkins, Charles Fillmore, Ernest Holmes, and many others as to make the author a favorite among their adherents, as well as with a great many who belong to other denominations or to none at all. The fact is that Maltz's analysis of human beings and their problems, as well as his solution for success and happiness, differs more in semantics than in the basis upon which it is founded.

The dictionary defines cybernetics as a science dealing with the comparative study of the operation of complex electronic computers and the human nervous system. Maltz refers to the subconscious mind simply as the unconscious. This, he declares, is a vast storehouse in which records are kept of all experiences (pages 20, 228); although individuals have no conscious memory of these, they are ever present and exercise a dominating influence. The brain, therefore, and the nervous system constitute a computer-like machine which directs the conscious organism into the pathways it will seek and traverse (pages 19-23).

Man, we are told, is not a machine, but he uses one—the creative, impersonal servo-mechanism, which is the brain and the nervous system, the computer in which all past experience is stored, as in a tape-recorder (pages xx, 12, 14, 17, 20, 37, 71, 226). However, this mechanism has no imagination of its own, and it can only receive, retain, and direct (page 22); and it cannot tell the difference between real and imagined failure (page 206).

Maltz agreed with Fillmore and other New Thought writers in so many details that he appeared as one of their disciples. He declares, for example, that you should never criticize yourself (pages 61, 62, 170); you must accept yourself as you are (pages 114, 116); never carry a grudge or a grievance (pages 130, 147, 152); forgive others as well as yourself (pages 146, 149); never take counsel from your fears (page 216); overcome evil with good (page 219); think positive thoughts only (page 70); treat other people well (pages 112, 170); and compliment at least three persons every day (page 171).

The most important thing in the world is for a person to create the best possible self-image through self-esteem (pages xix, 1, 91). In order to improve, we must create this self-image through the constructive use of our subconscious servo-mechanism (pages 38, 45).

Among all the areas in which Maltz finds himself in complete agreement with other writers, none is more pervasive than the influence of thought upon a person's behavior, health, success, and happiness, which are normally the great objectives in life. In order to achieve these, it is necessary to program the servo-mechanism—i.e., the subconscious—into the proper basis for accomplishment. When a proper self-image has been created, the battle for all these is half won. Every person, says the author, is engineered for success (pages 25). Our bodies are equipped to maintain health, cure diseases, and remain youthful (page 228). In other words, health is the normal and disease the abnormal state of man. He tells the story of a comparatively young man who, because of discouragement, aged twenty years in a few weeks; but when the cause of this was revealed to him and removed, he regained his former appearance and zest in an equally short time (pages 47-49). Negative ideas will cause inferiority complexes which, in turn, cause any number of dire results (page 50, 54). Your imagination can make you fail or succeed, according to its influence (page 51). In order to succeed, we must think success (page 113); we must also have a feeling and desire for it (page 68); it is necessary that a goal be set (page 70); if we picture ourselves as failures, we will become failures (page 206). It is possible to make an old man of one who is only thirty by the power of thought (page 238); on the other hand, it is possible to maintain a youthful capacity and appearance well beyond the seventies (pages 237-39). Placebos have proved effective because the patient thinks he has received an effective curative substance—which exists solely within his own organism (page 237). Conscience can make us into cowards even when we have nothing to fear (page 164). By thinking pleasant thoughts, we can achieve happiness (page 91); fear and negative thoughts must therefore be avoided and banished (page 97). A person's hand can be burned by a cold poker if he believes it is hot (page 29); a man will be terribly frightened of a stuffed image if he thinks it is a wild boar (page 31).

On the other hand, the power of thought can help you overcome bad habits such as alcoholism (page 28). In order to achieve health and happiness, there are certain things you must do. "The method consists in learning, practicing, and experiencing new habits in thinking, imagining, remembering, and acting, in order to (a) develop an adequate and realistic self-image, and (b) use your creative mechanism in achieving particular goals" (page 13). That is to say, as Fillmore and Murphy also declared, that your conscious mind must pour into your subconscious the elements which will transform the latter into a creative force for the achievement of your objective. Maltz declares that he was propelled into this realm of constructive thought as a result of his experiences as a plastic surgeon; he found that cosmetic surgery helped some to reshape and glorify their lives; but for others, no matter how successful the facial operation, there was no regeneration or improvment. The secret lay within the patient; with or without the surgery, if he developed self-confidence and a good self-image, his problems were solved; but if this did not happen, nothing else availed (pages 10-11).

From his long experience and observation, Maltz found that some people have a Failure Mechanism in the subconscious and are, therefore, constant failures. The formula for this consists of (1) frustration, hopelessness, futility; (2) misdirected aggressiveness; (3) insecurity; (4) loneliness, which is lack of "oneness"; (5) resentment against others and oneself; and (6) emptiness—a feeling of worthlessness (page 119). On the other hand, he had also observed the formula for success and happiness: (1) a sense of direction; (2) understanding; (3) courage and faith; (4) charity toward others and oneself; (5) self-confidence; and (6) self-acceptance—the development of the best possible self-image (page 104).

Although Maltz does not refer to God as Universal Spirit or Intelligence, there are a few passages which hint at something similar. He says, for example, "I believe there is One Life, one ultimate source, but that this One Life has many channels of expression and manifests itself in many forms" (page 245). "Life and power," he declares, "is not so much contained in us, *as it courses through us* " (page 227). And he concludes his treatise with these words:

> Finally, let us not limit our acceptance of Life by our own feelings of unworthiness. God has offered us forgiveness and the peace of mind and happiness that come from self-acceptance. It is an insult to our Creator to turn our back upon these gifts and to say that his creation—man—is

so "unclean" that he is not worthy, or important, or capable. The most adequate and realistic self-image of all is to conceive of yourself as "made in the image of God." "You cannot believe yourself the image of God, deeply and sincerely, with full conviction, and not receive a new source of strength and power."

II.   THE UNITED CHURCH OF RELIGIOUS SCIENCE

A. *The Headquarters Complex*

1. *A Visit There.* In 1983, this writer spent some time at the headquarters of the Church located on West Sixth Street, Los Angeles. Mr. William Lynn and Mr. Mark H. Shaw, the Chief Executive Officers, were most gracious in supplying information and documents concerning the operation of the Church. Others were also very helpful.

The headquarters occupies an entire block consisting of 3.5 acres with frontage on Sixth Street and extending 600 feet back on New Hampshire to Fifth Street. Buildings include the Church offices with 21,155 square feet at 3251 West Sixth; the Magazine Building next to it; the World Ministry of Prayer at 3261-65; and, on the corner of Berendo, the magnificent Founders Church, begun in 1958 and dedicated in 1960, with 1,487 seats. This has 8,000 members and two services are held each Sunday. At the corner of Fifth and New Hampshire are facilities housing the Department of Education, the Youth Center, and the Library, containing eight to ten thousand volumes of New Thought literature.

The replacement value of this property was estimated at more than $12 million in 1983. The Church budget for 1980-81 exceeded $4 million. There were at least 100 full-time employees at the complex, in addition to many others who worked part-time or on a contract basis, such as most of the teachers who constitute the faculty in the Department of Education.

More than 300,000 people pass through the doors of this headquarters each year for ongoing activities or to obtain help of some kind.

2. *History.* As already noted, the Institute of Religious Science broke with the International Association of Religious Science Churches

in 1953-54 and new Bylaws were prepared for it as the Church of Religious Science. In 1967, the name was changed to United Church of Religious Science; and in 1968, it was decided to establish a single corporation as an umbrella or association of churches, which could extend all church advantages to the member congregations. In 1982, Articles of Incorporation were filed with the Secretary of State in California to establish the Science of Mind International, controlled by the United Church of Religious Science.

The growth of the Church, especially in recent years, has been spectacular. Consulting back issues of *Science of Mind*, we found the information set forth in the following table:

| Year | Listed Practitioners | | Organizations | | Churches | | Study Groups | Foreign Organizations |
	In Calif.	Outside	Total	Domestic	In Calif.	Total		
1955	155	95	50	50	40	50	None	None
1958	187	33	59	57	45	58	1	2
1960	199	31	76	74	51	71	5	2
1965	122	29	82	76	55	76	6	6
1970	119	32	103	96	58	79	24	7
1978	60	19	147	139	79	125	22	8
1983	45	36	355	319	89	175	180	36

The November, 1986, issue of *Science of Mind* lists 197 churches.

The number of churches since 1955 has increased from 50 to 197, the study groups from none to 180. Whereas 40 of the churches were in California in 1955, only about half of them—89—were there in 1983. Strangely enough, the number of listed practitioners declined from 230 in 1960 to 81 in 1983; however, Mr. Lynn explained that one reason for this is that a charge has been made for the listing in the magazine. Actually, there were 555 in 1980 and 603 in 1983.

He stated that the active membership was then between 35,000 and 40,000. A document called "Profile: United Church of Religious Science" contains the following statistics for March 1, 1981: membership, 36,025; chartered churches, 146, of which 38 were established during the two previous years; and fellowship churches, 8. There were at that time 150 study groups, of which 89 had been in existence less than a year; 603 active and 33 retired practitioners; 187 active and 117 retired or inactive clergy; and 47 candidates.

3.   *Study Groups.* Marjorie Staum, Assistant Director of Member

Churches, in charge of Study Group Development, explained that every such listed organization has a leader called a Director, but that there is no formal requirement for its establishment or operation. A group can come into existence wherever individuals interested in Science of Mind meet, but not in sufficient numbers to form a church or hire a minister. Any individual can organize it; and it usually meets in a private home for the purpose of studying the principles of Science of Mind. All such classes or groups receive materials for study, which consist of a variety of cassettes, pamphlets, and texts. Each group, to maintain its status, makes two Progress Reports a year.

Most of the groups are small and Ms. Staum estimated the average number at seven or eight persons. However, many of these have grown rapidly, and most of the fifty churches established since 1978 developed from these groups.

4. *Science of Mind Publications.* On the second floor of a building owned by the Church at 600 New Hampshire are the offices of the Science of Mind publications, which include the monthly magazine of the same name, with a circulation of 100,000. Although some of the books available from this office are issued by other publishers, it prepares, prints, and distributes an enormous quantity of literature. Its 1983 catalog listed thirty-nine titles under its own copyright, in addition to about thirty under that of others.

5. *The Ministry of Prayer.* This is an operation basically similar to that of Silent Unity—but on a smaller scale. It had nine full-time practitioners in 1983 who operated several phone lines on a twenty-four-hour basis. It sent out about 9,000 letters monthly; answered 1,800 telephone calls from people in distress; answered 1,200 requests received by mail for personal help or counsel. It had about 900 contributors and its monthly income was about $18,000. By installing computers, it was expected that its capacity for service would double without increasing the personnel. As in Unity, this Ministry is supported entirely by voluntary contributions from those who have been helped.

6. *The Holmes Center for Holistic Healing.* On the third floor of the building on New Hampshire are located the offices of the Holmes Center for Holistic Research and Healing. Barbara Waldron, Executive Secretary, explained its purpose and operation.

It holds annual symposiums attended by about a thousand people in

Los Angeles; the ninth was held on April 17, 1982, at which several speakers with national reputations presented the results of their research. There was also a Round Table with several scientists and physicians who answered questions from the audience.

Ms. Waldron emphasized that the Center itself does not engage in healing; its purpose is to encourage and help finance research projects by qualified scholars in medical schools and universities. In an average year, it operates on a budget of about $150,000; and grants may total anywhere from $40,000 to $100,000, depending on available funds—all of which derive from interested and philanthropic donors.

We should note that the basic objective of the Center is to establish a scientific validation for the phenomena of healing methods outside the world of traditional medicine—in short, to correlate the spiritual or mental process with the physical. It seeks this result through scientific investigation and evaluation; its purpose is to establish and demonstrate the interrelationship between the mind and the body of man.

The fact that literally scores of leading medical doctors and university scholars now endorse and cooperate with the Holmes Center indicates the extent to which it has penetrated thinking in the highest intellectual circles; in fact, it has risen to a position and a status which elevates it quite beyond the need to fear attacks from any source, such as those which were hurled at Christian Science, especially during its early years.

B. *The Church Structure*

1.   *The Bylaws.* These are rules and regulations enacted by the delegates from the autonomous member churches, which are granted affiliation and charters after meeting certain qualifications.

The country is divided into four districts, each of which has approximately the same number of churches and active members. Each district elects a Steering Committee consisting of six persons who serve three-year staggered terms, of whom at least three must be laymen, one an ordained minister, and one a licensed practitioner who is not also a minister. Each district holds a convention in odd years, while the United Church holds one in every even-numbered year. The same delegates meet in both the district and the general conventions.

Since the member churches elect the delegates to both the district and the general conventions, and since these have power to amend, revise, or repeal any provision in the Bylaws, it is obvious that the principle of democratic control is well established. However, the Institute, which is an independent corporation organized in 1927 and reincorporated in 1935, exercises a significant degree of control; from this we can only conclude that the member churches not only accept this authority but also believe that it is highly desirable. Others might prefer to place greater authority and responsibility in the individual churches; however, the rapid growth of the United Church would indicate that most people prefer a central source of educational and ecclesiastical direction.

2.   *Member Churches and Study Groups.* A 120-page document called *Church Code* describes the operation of member churches and study groups. This contains the Rules, first prepared in 1974, later amended and ratified in their present form in 1980. Included are sections dealing with Charter Requirements; Federal and Income Tax Laws; A Clergy and Employees' Retirement Plan; Study Groups; Annual Reports to the Department of Member Churches; and Miscellaneous Exhibits, including Models of Agreement of Affiliation, Bylaws, and several others.

Under Charter Requirements, we find that twenty-five persons may qualify to obtain a charter—however, this was later increased to fifty. In order to obtain membership, a congregation must submit an Affiliation Agreement; copies of proposed bylaws; a filing fee; resolutions for tax-exemptions; an Insignia Agreement; articles of incorporation (where necessary); and certain other formal documents.

Bylaws are suggested which provide that, upon dissolution, termination, or disaffiliation, all the assets of the church shall revert to the United Church. However, Mr. Lynn assured me that this—especially the provision in regard to disaffiliation—is purely voluntary, and is not included in most agreements or Bylaws; he declared that not only can member churches take their property with them upon disaffiliation, but that several have done so. However, the member church agrees that should it wish to separate, it will arrange a conference with a representative from headquarters; and that such action will be taken only if two-thirds of the membership of the church determine upon such a course.

Finally, the bylaws provide that should a member church violate its Agreement of Affiliation in such a manner as to bring the church into disrepute, the Commission on Church Affairs may forfeit its charter and terminate its affiliation.

C. *The Department of Education*

The educational department operates under two divisions: The Institute of Religious Science and the School of Ministry, which are cognate but separate organizations.

1. *The Institute.* Established in 1927, this had by 1983 trained or educated more than 160,000 persons in the principles of Science of Mind in extension courses. A brochure describing this work states that it has been reaching leaders in the fields of religion and philosophy and that it is now known throughout the world as the foremost institution of its kind; that it has enabled people from all walks of life "to experience more happiness, better health, and greater success.... The testimony of thousands demonstrates that the principles of the Science of Mind are not theoretical, but very practical...and have proved their worth and are opening the doorway to new and wonderful experiences for those who use them daily."

The classes, which are conducted entirely at the local level, present a "synthesis and summation of basic religious thought, and modern metaphysical, philosophical, and scientific concepts."

Each person who enrolls in the Basic Science of Mind course receives a copy of the textbook, *Science of Mind*; a metaphysical dictionary; forty-eight weekly lessons in four separate mailings of twelve each; and weekly letters to supplement, explain, and clarify the studies being pursued. At the conclusion of each twelve-lesson course, the student takes a written examination; upon the satisfactory completion of all lessons, the graduate is given a Certificate of Completion.

The forty-eight segments are based on pages 63 to 307 of the official textbook. Each week, the students study very carefully several pages; at the weekly class-session, this material is discussed and explained.

Completing this extension course is a prerequisite for most advanced work both in the Institute and the School of Ministry.

In 1980-81, 4,000 students graduated from the two-year Basic Course in the Science of Mind. Classes were conducted in 112 churches; and there were 50 offering study leading to Certificates of Recognition as practitioners in the Church—an activity also under the direction of the Institute.

2. *The School of Ministry.* This institution is one of the most important activities in the Church complex. Its resident enrollment rose from 32 in 1976 to 114 in 1980; in 1981, it was 110; in the spring quarter alone it was 93. The enrollment varies during different parts of the year; in February 1983, it was 55. In 1976, it graduated 16 ministerial candidates, who received the Religious Science Fellowship Recognition (RScF). The number of graduates during recent years has averaged about 28.

The School offers two principal courses of study; in addition to that leading to the ministry, there is a General Studies program intended for practitioners and others who wish to develop their understanding and expertise "in metaphysics, communication, and leadership for the New Age...."

The Dean is the only full-time employee; generally, there are eight or nine other members, sometimes more, who serve on the faculty at any given time. There are religious authorities, such as Marcus Bach; prominent ministers in the United Church of Religious Science; and professors who hold positions in colleges or universities, chiefly in the Los Angeles area.

A full three-year course of study is required for the RScF recognition. In order to qualify for such advanced study—that is, to become a candidate for the ministry—certain prerequisites, such as the completion of the two-year Basic Course in the Science of Mind, are mandatory.

Each year of study consists of at least three ten-week quarters, in each of which not less than fifteen hours of credit are to be earned. The 1981-82 catalog includes a typical course which would be pursued. Seven courses were offered in administration, eight in communication and homiletics, six in general and five in Science of Mind metaphysics, six in psychology, and six in Directed Independent and Advanced Study.

D. *The Practitioners and Their Code*

The training and education of practitioners is carried on entirely by teachers—usually ministers—on the local level under the direction of the School of Continuing Education, which is a division of The Institute of Religious Science. The prerequisite for the two years of Professional Practitioners Studies—leading to certification as a licensed practitioner in Spiritual Mind Healing—is the basic two-year course in Science of Mind Metaphysics, already described.

A leaflet called "You and Your Practitioner" states that:

> Spiritual Mind Treatment is based upon the belief that we are surrounded by a Universal Mind, which reacts to our thoughts according to Law. Through the use of scientific techniques, Spiritual Mind Treatment (which is really scientific prayer), the individual's consciousness (his belief about himself) is changed, thereby causing a change in his body and affairs.... As an individual's faith in his ability to use this Law of Mind grows stronger, his capacity to know the Truth of his being develops, bringing happier self-expression.

The leaflet continues:

> A licensed Religious Science Practitioner is one who has been trained to help people use the art and skill of Spiritual Mind Treatment to solve problems and to correct conditions. He has the understanding to impersonally assist clients to handle their personal problems. A Practitioner lives, demonstrates, and practices Spiritual Truth.

The Professional Practitioner Studies cover two years, each consisting of three ten-week courses. These classes, which meet for three hours weekly, are taught by ministers or accredited instructors. Thus, there are thirty sessions each year, totalling 180 hours before the completion of the studies. The Special Textbook for Term I includes elaborate explanations covering hundreds of pages of curriculum, to be followed in developing practitioner candidates into full-fledged professionals. Term I begins the process of changing consciousness, which is the goal of this term. The first year then goes on with two more terms, or twenty sessions, in which the practitioner-candidate develops his capacity to understand the Science of Spiritual Mind Healing.

The second year of these Professional Studies is an Accredited Course, also of thirty three-hour sessions, in which the candidates become practitioners-in-training. In other words, during this advanced curriculum, each student learns to make practical application of what he or she has learned or is learning. The goals of Year II are set forth as follows:

(1) to have students actually experience life as a licensed practitioner;

(2) to make them proficient in communication skills;

(3) to improve their skills in written and oral mind treatment;

(4) to have them learn how to write and deliver meditations;

(5) to provide them with opportunities to enunciate spiritual principles with ease;

(6) to deepen their spiritual consciousness;

(7) to move their awareness from the relative to the absolute;

(8) to assist them in knowing that a practitioner's responsibility is to maintain an active awareness that *the spiritual man is perfect*;

(9) to have them develop a personal Practitioner's Manual; and

(10) to enable them to understand the role of the Practitioner, his privileges, duties, obligations, Code of Ethics, and his many spiritual and ecclesiastical relationships.

For each of the six terms covering these studies, there is a large manual, consisting altogether of about 1,500 pages. We can only conclude that when all of this has been fully understood and digested, the student-candidate has absorbed an education which is probably without parallel in the religious field.

Mr. Lynn stated that a great many testimonials have been received attesting that help has been given and that cures have occurred even in cases of organic disease. Even if these cannot be verified by medical proof, it is certain that clients *believe* they have been aided or cured—which, in a sense, amounts to the same thing. Practitioners treat every kind of personal difficulty, whether emotional, physical, neurotic, spiritual, financial, or involving family dissensions or troubles at places of work. Many of these, of course, are psychosomatic.

Some practitioners have business offices where they pursue full-time work and where clients with appointments are treated; however, most of their work is part-time, out of their own homes.

The Church publishes a pamphlet called *Practitioner's Code*, which sets forth Practitioners' functions and the nature of their work, which is under the supervision of the Commission on Church Affairs, which establishes the policies for granting Recognition Certificates and grants licenses for the practice of Spiritual Mind Healing according to the principles enumerated in the textbook *Science of Mind*. Candidates must be members of the United Church of Religious Science; they must complete satisfactory interviews, oral and written examinations, and must pass psychological tests and meet proficiency standards, as prescribed by the Commission. They must agree to practice faithfully and exclusively the principles and techniques taught in the *Science of Mind* textbook; to abide by the Practitioners' Code, to devote a definite portion of their time to professional practice, and to maintain a telephone and suitable quarters for their work.

Licenses must be renewed annually and renewals must be approved by the minister of the church to which the practitioner belongs. Licenses can be terminated for anyone found not in compliance with the Code.

The Code of Ethics under which the practitioner operates stipulates that he must not give advice in matters of law, finance, or the use of drugs or medicines; he must not prescribe diets or vitamins or employ or advise any therapy except Spiritual Mind Treatment. It is considered unethical for him to criticize anyone or speak in a derogatory manner to a client or about his work. He is expected to cooperate fully with the Religious Science activity of the church of which he is a member. (The *he* is used generically throughout.)

The relationship between the practitioner and his client must be completely confidential, as is that of a medical doctor or psychiatrist with his patient. Nor may he offer any guarantee of success to his client as a result of treatment.

The practitioner is expected to support his church financially in an identifiable manner; he is also expected to help in the preparation of a newsletter, in the Dial-a-Prayer ministry, by calling on the aged and infirm, by attending and working in healing workshops, and in other areas of church activity. Whenever his minister asks him to do so, he should agree to perform any service which will be of benefit to the church and the congregation.

The practitioner must never criticize or attack any other branch of the healing profession; on the contrary, he must hold the regular medical doctors in the highest esteem by recognizing them as representatives of the healing power in the Universe. He must also at all times cooperate with the legal authorities in such matters as reporting communicable diseases and any accidental death which comes to his attention.

The practitioner may conduct funeral or christening services, but may not perform wedding ceremonies.

He must at all times conduct himself with dignity so as to bring respect to his profession and his church.

He must realize that he represents the healing arm, that he is an important ecclesiastical representative, and that his work is crucial in accomplishing the objectives of the United Church of Religious Science. "The eyes of his fellow church members, as well as the public at large, are on" him. "The future growth of the Church...to a great extent, depends upon the manner in which the Practitioner performs his professional activities and...his work with the United Church of Religious Science and the Member Church to which he belongs."

E. *The Ministerial Code*

The Commission on Church Affairs—an agency of the Ministerial Senate—formulates and recommends the specific policies governing the conditions prerequisite for licensing and ordaining ministers in the Church, who are established in three categories: Novitiate, Licentiate, and Ordained.

Any person, upon payment of application and examining fees, who meets the requirements of the Code and who has received a call from a member church, may apply for ministerial status to the Department of Member Churches and file a formal application with the Director of that Department.

A graduate of the School of Ministry who has received his RScF Recognition shall have the right to make such application to the Department, which will then review the applicant's qualifications; in addition to meeting established requirements, he must show evidence of moral and emotional fitness; upon the successful completion of all requirements, he will receive a license which places him on the eligible list of approved ministerial candidates.

A minister from another denomination who desires to apply for a license as a minister in the United Church of Religious Science may do so by taking and passing the Ministerial Licensing Examinations and Motivational Tests required by the Commission on Church Affairs; the results of this will determine the category of licensing to which he may be eligible.

Whenever the Commission deems it in the best interests of the Church, it may grant Novitiate status for a period of one year to any applicant who passes all examinations successfully. Such ministers must make quarterly reports to the Department of Member Churches, and the license must be renewed before the expiration of the year.

A Novitiate Minister may become a Licentiate applicant provided he is a Licensed Practitioner and has satisfactorily completed all interviews, written and oral examinations, motivational tests, and met the proficency standards prescribed by the Commission on Church Affairs.

In order to become an Ordained Minister, the Licentiate must first serve at least two years in a member church or in some other ecclesiastical capacity. Once ordained, he cannot lose this status; however, his privileges, affiliations, and associations may be revoked if he is found to be in flagrant violation of the Ministerial Code.

Any applicant for ministerial status in any category must show that he holds an exclusive membership in the United Church of Religious Science; must make the principles and techniques presented in the *Science of Mind* textbook the basis of his teaching and practice; and must declare that he is willing to abide by the Ministerial Code and be governed by the laws of the United Church of Religious Science.

Articles VIII and IX of the Ministerial Code provide elaborate procedures by which a minister may be removed from his pulpit and have his license suspended or revoked.

The Code declares that every minister in the Church is in a unique profession; he is a teacher, a counselor, a Practitioner; he should exercise a healing influence on all who come into contact with him; he is a spiritual therapist of the highest order; and he commits himself to the following ideals:

(1) to lead those who seek guidance into an assurance and acceptance of wholeness and well-being;

(2) to reflect an image and a breadth of heart which expresses a great desire to serve;

(3) to abide by the Truth that the Kingdom of Heaven is within us;

(4) to love mankind, be generous and unselfish with all others, and to be free from fear and superstition;

(5) to use warmth and compassion in relation to all members of his congregation;

(6) to engage in no activities involving moral turpitude;

(7) to remain true always to the principles and ideals of Religious Science;

(8) to know always that God is over all, through all and in all, and that the mind in each of us is that which was in Christ Jesus;

(9) to center his thought upon the Universal Divine Presence;

(10) to let the peace of God abide in his heart, through love forever;

(11) to vow allegiance to the Church of Religious Science;

(12) to give unqualified support to the Church;

(13) to dedicate himself to the spiritual needs of those who call upon him for help;

(14) to continue in faithful meditation and diligent study in order to expand his consciousness and ministry;

(15) to dedicate himself to the Truth of word and action; and

(16) to abide by the policies and regulations set forth by the Board of Trustees of the United Church of Religious Science and by the local Church of which he is the Minister.

Chapter XI

THE SCOPE OF NEW THOUGHT

I. LITERATURE AND PUBLICATIONS

The most important source of New Thought Literature is De Vorss and Company of Marina del Rey, California, whose 1985 catalog lists 1,240 authors and about 2,500 titles dealing with a great variety of subjects and written by authors from many countries and differing periods of time. New Thought literature is very well represented; however, the catalog also covers a broad spectrum of psycho-analytical material, among which we find H.B. Blavatsky. *The Aquarian Gospel of Jesus Christ* is featured as a best-seller; and many titles by such New Thought exponents as Jack Addington, Joel Goldsmith, Raymond Barker, Catherine Ponder, Emmet Fox, Ernest Holmes, Thomas Troward, Robert Schuller, and Joseph Murphy are given special prominence.

Another source is the Rare Book Company of Freehold, New Jersey, which, for many years, has supplied scholars with rare books long out of print. Many of these were necessary for the preparation of this study, especially in the field of Christian Science.

In a volume called *Who's Who in New Thought*, published in 1977 by Tom Beebe, we find 171 authors and the titles of 774 books. Eighty-four of these were still living and 284 volumes are credited to them. Among the historical figures are Horatio W. Dresser, Emmet Fox, Ernest and Fenwicke Holmes, Emma Curtis Hopkins, Ralph Waldo Trine, Ella Wheeler Wilcox, and Emanuel Swedenborg. Considerable space is also devoted to such authors as Frederick Rawson, Ursula Gestefeld, and Joseph Murphy. Beebe attempted to compile a complete roster of New Thought organizations and leaders, which included 815 churches and 1,360 prominent individuals; however, since he received responses from only seventy-five percent of the 1,400 to whom he addressed a request for information, and since many well-known churches are not even mentioned, we know that there were, even in 1977, hundreds in addition to those he enumerates. There are now, including the Christian Science churches, probably not less than 3,000 New Thought organizations in the United States alone.

Almost every New Thought church has its own newsletter and its own book room or library in which reading materials of great variety are available. The International New Thought Alliance (INTA) publishes a slick quarterly called *New Thought*; and Jack Addington has a very popular periodical called *Abundant Living*.

Since we discuss the publications of the different denominations in our chapters dealing with them, we need not repeat this information here. For a partial list of New Thought publications, the reader may consult various titles listed in this work at its close. Several New Thought magazines give a complete roster of ministers, practitioners, and organizations.

It may be interesting to note that the volume entitled *Yearbook of American and Canadian Churches*, published by the National Council of Churches, completely ignores all New Thought churches, including those of Christian Science, as if they did not exist. However, it includes Jehovah's Witnesses, as well as others which surely do not belong among the conventional religious bodies. Are New Thought churches, then, considered nonreligious by the mainstream denominations?

II. EXTENT AND INFLUENCE OF THE MOVEMENT

We cannot estimate accurately the total membership of New Thought churches and organizations, nor yet the influence of their philosophy beyond their own specific boundaries. If we include those in Japan and other foreign countries, the number would vastly exceed the 3,000 or so in the United States. If those in this country average 200 members, they would total about 600,000, which makes it obvious that the movement is very substantial.

Even within its own confines, therefore, New Thought has now become a very significant phenomenon; and the outreach of its ideology—the influence of its philosophy—has penetrated many conventional church congregations (although they do not admit it) to such an extent that they have become definitely different from the predecessors whose names they still bear; in fact, many of them now resemble New Thought in their sermons more than they do those of Calvin, Luther, or even John Wesley. What, we might ask, has become of everlasting torture in hell for the great majority of people because they were not predestined for salvation?

This, in fact, is the true measure of its role, as well as that of Swedenborg, Emerson, Parker, Warren Felt Evans, Ralph Waldo Trine, and a host of others who beckon to us from the realms of the departed.

III. THE PERIPHERAL MOVEMENT

1. *Outstanding Independents*. New Thought has penetrated the old-line churches; and, in addition, there are a number of outstanding personalities who now come very close to the New Thought syndrome. Among these, two of the most popular are Robert Schuller and Norman Vincent Peale.

Peale became the minister of the Marble Collegiate Reformed Church of New York in 1932; and has received the Distinguished Salesman's Award, the Horatio Alger Award, the Human Relations Award, and various others. In addition to conducting radio and television programs, he has written more than a dozen bestselling books, of which *The Power of Positive Thinking* has probably been the most popular; other titles include *The Art of Living*, *You Can Win*, *A Guide to Confident Living*, *The Tough-Minded Optimist*, *The Healing of Sorrow*, *You Can If You Think You Can*, and *Dynamic Imaging*. We cannot analyze these here; but suffice it to say that all are intended to bring peace of mind to troubled emotions and to help people achieve happiness and success, all in the New Thought tradition.

After Robert Schuller served as pastor in the Reformed Church of America for five years, he founded the independent Garden Grove Community Church in 1955 in California. He conducts one of the most popular religious television programs in the country, called "The Hour of Power"; his church has built the magnificent Crystal Cathedral, in which thousands gather every week; some of the most distinguished citizens of his state are members or supporters. He has written a number of popular books, such as *God's Way to the Good Life*; *Your Future Is Your Friend*; *Self-Love: The Dynamic Force of Success*; *The Greatest Possibility Thinker Who Ever Lived*; *You Can Become the Person You Want to Be*; *Turning Your Stress into Strength*; *Daily Power Thoughts*; *Tough-Minded Faith*; and the recent best seller *The Be Happy Attitudes*—all of which are intended to help the reader in achieving well-being and a successful life.

Jack Addington, of the Abundant Living Foundation, who publishes *Abundant Living*, and is headquartered in San Diego, California, was once a minister in the Church of Religious Science, but now operates as an independent; he has a national radio program which is heard on some forty or fifty stations. He is extremely popular and successful, and his message is pure New Thought. And we must especially note Johnnie Coleman's Christ Universal Temple in Chicago, in which 3,500 worshippers gather every Sunday to hear her inspiring, pure New Thought message. The Church has 10,000 black members, who imbibe from her the principles of a happy and self-reliant life.

2. *The Omega.* I receive a twenty-four-page newspaper called *Omega: The New Age Directory*. Although this may not be described as a New Thought publication, it certainly belongs in its periphery. The May 1985 issue, has a "Great Invocation" which reads:

> From the point of Light within the Mind of God
> Let Light stream forth into the minds of men—
> Let Light descend to earth.

From the center where the Will of God is known
Let purpose guide the little wills of men—
The purpose which the Master knows and serves.

Let Light and Law and Power restore the Plan on Earth.

What first caught my attention was the fact that the *Directory* lists every New Thought Church and organization in Arizona, of which there are at least twenty. It also includes Counselors, Psychics, Astrologers, and Readers. It lists 260 churches, organizations, and individuals who are engaged in this work, including the Swedenborgian Church of the New Jerusalem, the Infinite Way group (featuring the teachings of Joel Goldsmith), a Psycho-Cybernetics group, as well as the Spiritual Church of Aquarian Science, the Theosophical Study group, the Church of Scientology, and the A-Bundant Life Center. All these have something—more or less—in common with New Thought; and all seek to help people undergoing emotional stress to achieve peace of mind and happiness—in short, a solution of their psychic or psychosomatic ailments.

If similar organizations exist throughout the United States in the same ratio, they would number in the thousands.

3.   *The Huna Movement.* Many years ago, Max Freedom Long established a movement based on the teachings of the Kahunas of Hawaii; after he died, the direction of this world-wide movement was assumed by Dr. Otha Wingo, who now publishes a newsletter called *Huna Work* and who organizes meetings and seminars held every year in different parts of the world. The movement features books written by Max F. Long, all of which are available from De Vorss: *Growing into Light*, *Huna Code of Religions*, *Psychometric Analysis*, *Recovering the Ancient Magic*, *Secret Science at Work*, and *Secret Science Behind Miracles*, all of which have some relationship to New Thought and which explain in detail the three-level operation of the human psyche.

In the Spring 1985 issue of *Huna Work*, there is a very interesting article called "Profile of a Huna Healer" written in the pure New Thought tradition and reminding us of Phineas Quimby. Its author is Clarence "Lloyd" Youngblood, who operates an apartment building in St. Petersburg, Florida. He stated that he had been using Huna techniques since 1981, after he stumbled onto some of the writings of Max Freedom Long.

His healings are conducted and effected through conversations with the afflicted; he declared that he had been successful as a Huna practitioner with many different kinds of illness; and he described a large number of cases in which cures had been accomplished. Recently, he said, he healed a diabetic in twenty minutes; and he found that his work was as successful in a telephone conversation as in a face-to-face confrontation. What he did was to assure, persuade, and convince the subject that there are infinite powers in the universe upon which he can draw and which, when properly utilized, can restore the body to health by a spiritual process.

He said that he is successful in about seventy-five per cent of his cases; the reasons for failure are to be found in the psyches of the patients who really do not want to be helped. The Low Self (the *Id* or the subconscious) can retain illness for various reasons, even though the Middle Self (the conscious reason) may strongly desire healing. Some retain their maladies because of the attention it brings them from friends and relatives. Some receive charity, which they are afraid of losing. Some retain their maladies as an excuse to avoid labor. Some simply do not feel worthy of good health. And there are other secret motivations.

In a long article published in the 1985 autumn issue of *Huna Work*, he discusses at length the reasons why prayers sometimes are not answered and why recovery does not occur. He declares that he has been very successful in healing several serious diseases and injuries and in his business investments. The basic reason why healing does not occur in various cases is that the Low Self of the patient has stored away in its computer a menagerie of outlaw or renegade beliefs or emotions—such as fears, hates, worries, guilt complexes, and other corrosive and destructive forces—which have surfaced as psychoses or other derangements or illness. Even though these may have been forgotten by the Middle or Conscious Self, they continue to exercise power and influence. Before healing can take place, these outlaw thoughts or emotions must be brought into the conscious understanding of the Middle Self. The High Self can then exercise its healing power over the patient and he may achieve health, sometimes within an hour—or it may require treatment over a period of time.

Thus, recovery is a scientific process which occurs when the High, the Middle, and the Low Self achieve complete peace and harmony within the human three-level psyche.

Youngblood declares that, since he is economically independent, he practices Huna healing without charge, and only suggests that grateful recipients of healing make some contribution to *Huna Work*.

4. *The Spiritual Advisory Council*. This organization was first established in 1974 by Paul V. Johnson, with the help of co-founder Robert D. Ericsson; it has its headquarters in Longwood, Florida, which houses a sanctuary, a bookstore, meeting rooms, offices, and a research library. It has a nucleus of more than 1,000 members and a contributing membership of 8,000.

Mr. Johnson was reared in the Swedish Lutheran Church in America, an offshoot of the state church in the Mother Country. But he found its doctrines and practices highly restrictive, abandoned it entirely, and for some time had no religious interest or commitment. However, what may be called his Illumination began in 1971 when he attended a lecture by Dr. Marcus Bach at the Bismarck Hotel in Chicago; and this ignited an interest which caused him to embark on a career in search of esoteric and metaphysical truth.

Shortly thereafter, he held a seminar at the Unity Church in Oak Park, Illinois, attended by 160 people, more than four times the number expected. This extraordinary success prompted the establishment of the Spiritual Advisory Council, which was incorporated in Illinois in 1975 and in 1979 in Florida, when it absorbed the Spiritual Research Society; the Council has had a gradual but steady growth ever since. It conducts seminars, workshops, classes, development groups, and festivals, and places special emphasis upon counseling and healing. It has a school which prepares laymen and ministers for work in the organization.

Although the Council is not an integral part of the New Thought movement *per se* , its objectives and teaching are strikingly similar. As a statement of faith or belief, it declares:

As we become aware of our oneness with the universe, our senses open to the inflow of infinite powers—powers that create a greater harmony and balance within ourselves and in our relationships to others. As we expand our consciousness and develop our human potential more fully, we begin to live happier, more productive lives and are better able to reach out to help and express our love.

A brochure issued by the Council declares that as it "continues to grow and evolve, it takes on new, more expansive goals, and expects to achieve the maximum potential provided by Divine Guidance.... We place emphasis upon direct, personal experience and knowledge of the divine order created by God."

IV. THE FOREIGN OUTREACH

Although New Thought is distinctly an American phenomenon, it has of late years spread to virtually all parts of the globe, except for communist nations and those under the domination of the Catholic Church. Unity, for example, in its 1984 *Yearbook of Association Churches*, lists fifty-four study classes and sixty-two churches outside the United States, including thirteen churches in Canada, eighteen in Africa, eight in Australia, and seven in England. The United Church of Religious Science lists forty-four study groups or churches in foreign lands.

However, the foreign New Thought churches which are branches of American denominations total only a small portion of those which are to be found, especially in Japan, which has developed a tremendous movement of its own and on its own initiative. The founder of this is Dr. Masaharu Taniguchi, who was born in 1893, and about whom Roy Eugene Davis wrote a book, *Miracle Man of Japan*, published in 1970. When still a very young man, Taniguchi was a determined seeker after truth; but his great illumination came when he discovered and absorbed Fenwicke Holmes's *The Law of the Mind in Action*, which made such a profound impact on his mind that it set the course which he was to pursue for the remainder of his life. As soon as it became possible, he began the publication of a magazine, *The Truth of Life*, in which he revealed his mission to the world. As happened with other New Thought founders and promoters, he soon began receiving letters stating that the writers had been healed of various ailments. In time, such readers met in groups, and the New Thought movement in Japan was under way. But it was not until after World War II that the movement grew by leaps and bounds and became a great force in the country.

Davis declares that when his book was written, the movement, known as Seicho-No-Ie, had 3 million adherents, 300,000 tithers, and 2,000 centers or temples in Japan alone. Taniguchi's principal work, *The Truth of Life* (in twenty volumes), had then sold about 20,000,000 copies worldwide. When the author travelled and lectured in the United States, he was welcomed in Unity, Divine Science, and Religious Science churches, with whose teachings his own were in very close agreement. He was met everywhere with overflow audiences; and he lectured to as many as 20,000 at one time.

Davis's book includes pictures of the great headquarters building in Tokyo; its main temple on the outskirts of the city, which seats more than 6,000; its American headquarters at Gardeno, California; and its headquarters in Sao Paulo, Brazil. The author estimated that the movement then embraced more than 60,000 members in South America alone.

Seicho-No-Ie emphasizes the use and importance of Affirmative Prayer; and practices spiritual healings, of which 74 examples are described in a book entitled *Recovery from All Diseases*. We find that the ailments were psychosomatic, although some had taken on the definite appearance of organic disease.

For its Japanese-American membership, Seicho-No-Ie distributes each month a handsome forty-page magazine in English which is also named *Truth of Life*. This includes not only New Thought articles, but also an inspirational text or message for each day of the month, similar to those found in publications by Unity, Divine Science, and Religious Science.

Throughout, Taniguchi emphasizes the spiritual over the material nature of humanity and the extreme importance of ridding the psyche of corrosive emotions such as fear, worry, and hatred.

Millions have come under the direct influence of Dr. Masaharu Taniguchi and the movement he founded, which summarizes its basic position and teachings in its Seven Declarations of Truth:

1.   We should not be prejudiced in favor of any religious sect for we

believe in the spiritual nature of man as he lives in accordance with the spiritual truths of life.

2.   We believe that to bring the Great Life Principle into full manifestation is the way to infinite power and plenty; and that the personality of every individual is immortal.

3.   We study and make known the law of the Creative Spirit so that mankind may follow the right way to infinite growth.

4.   We believe that love is the best nourishment for life and that prayer and words of love, along with praise, are the creative ways to use the Word in order to bring love and harmony into manifestation.

5.   We believe that we, as sons of God, have infinite power and plenty within ourselves and can attain absolute freedom by following the principles of the creative way of life.

6.   We publish monthly magazines and other books and booklets filled with helpful messages so that all men may follow the creative way of life through the printed word and live happy lives.

7.   We organize movements in order to conquer all the pains and troubles of humanity, by the means of right understanding of life, right living, and right education, so that, at last, the kingdom of Heaven will be manifest on earth.

Dr. Taniguchi died June 17, 1985, at the age of ninety-two.

Chapter XII

THE INTERNATIONAL
NEW THOUGHT ALLIANCE

I. HISTORY, ORGANIZATION, AND MEMBERSHIP

The International New Thought Alliance (INTA) was established at a convention held in St. Louis in 1915. It was preceded by the International Divine Science Association of 1892 and the International Metaphysical League of 1900. These two had come into existence under the leadership of several outstanding New Thought exponents, among whom were Horatio W. Dresser and Charles Brodie Patterson. INTA's first regular congress was held in San Francisco in 1916 and such convocations have been held every year—with only two exceptions—since that time.

Presently, INTA has its national headquarters in Scottsdale, Arizona; its president is Blaine C. Mays, pastor of the Phoenix Unity Church of Christianity; he is also the editor of the quarterly magazine *New Thought*.

INTA is the most important attempt to assemble all New Thought groups under a single umbrella. It lists all its members in its quarterly, and in the Autumn 1986 issue are the names, addresses, and ministers of 359 entities, of which 325 are in the United States. Of these, 86 belong to the Unity School of Christianity, 140 to Religious Science and Science of Mind, 16 to Divine Science; and 117 are what may be called miscellaneous or Independents. Of these, 46 became members since January 1985.

All these, however, constitute only a fraction of all New Thought congregations; for example *Spirit* lists 33 Divine Science churches; *Science of Mind* lists 347 churches and study groups; *Creative Thought*, published by the International Church of Religious Science, lists 85 churches and 485 practitioners; in 1985, Unity had 619 churches and study classes, of which 122 are in foreign countries and 419 are churches in the United States. Of course, there are also hundreds of independent New Thought churches, of which Robert Schuller's is one of the largest and most important.

II. STATEMENTS AND DECLARATIONS

There are, of course, specific differences among New Thought organizations, both in statements of faith and in techniques of operation. However, there are certain basic principles on which they all agree; and these are concerned primarily with the nature of God and the Christ-Spirit, both of which are universal entities. They are also united in the conviction that the purpose of religion should be to achieve the good life in the here and now; in short, that our highest objective ought to be the attainment of health, happiness, success, prosperity, and freedom from guilt and worry, all of which is intended to place the communicant in profound rapport with all living creatures, especially his fellow human beings.

In previous chapters, we have attempted to delineate and particularize the teachings and practices of the most important New Thought groups or denominations. Here we simply summarize what INTA says concerning its history, its goals, its purposes, and its faith. We quote from one of its brochures:

1. *Its History*

The term "New Thought" has been applied to the metaphysical movement which began with P.P. Quimby more than a century ago. The meaning of the words in this context was given by Judge Thomas Troward, one of the great leaders in the movement. It comes from the creative law of mind or Spirit and refers to the fact that a new thought embodied in consciousness produces a new condition. New Thought was taken as the name of an alliance which held its first conference in 1915. On January 20, 1917, the Alliance was incorporated as the International New Thought Alliance, familiarly known as INTA.

Through its service, the Alliance has proven its spiritual integrity. It does not depend on personalities, but demonstrates the truth. Many people want to take steps to insure the continuance of this ministry, not only through their financial support while here, but through bequests which will insure that their financial help will continue to assist this divine ministry.

The International New Thought Alliance is incorporated under the laws of the District of Columbia as a religious, educational, non-profit organization.

2. *Its Goals*

To unify all churches, centers, and schools in the New Thought field in a spiritual framework that provides for, and encourages, full freedom of expression and function.

To marshall the potential strength of the many groups, and focus it into coordinated power directed for the whole individual.

The healing of all nations.

3. *What It Can Do*

It can enlarge and enrich your way of life. It can universalize your vision and consciousness and increase your wealth of fellowship with kindred souls.

It can make you aware that you are a part of a great spiritual movement and a tremendous power for good.

It will reveal to you that the greatest secret in living life with blessings abundant, is in serving with wisdom and understanding.

4. *What It Is*

INTA is a free and open alliance of truth-motivated individuals and organizations who desire to unfold and practice a positive life-style of spiritual maturity and who are dedicated to the universal propagation of these principles as described in the Declaration of Principles. INTA is an alliance uniting individuals and organizations with common determination to bring out the best in individuals through an understanding of these eternal verities.

The International New Thought Alliance is a year-round working organization, democratic in structure, and serves as the means through which metaphysical schools, churches, and centers of like mind can work together.

INTA does not function as a church, school, policy-making organization, publishing house, promoter of certain doctrines, sectarian creeds or dogmas. INTA does not promote or engage in spiritualism or other occult phenomena. INTA is not a political, social, or economic group, nor does it authorize such groups. It does not ordain or train individuals to become authorized or New Thought ministers, practitioners, teachers, or counselors. It does not engage in denominational practices, favor any particular group, or recognize any hierarchy.

New Thought is a synonym for growth, development, perpetual progress. It deals not with limitations; it sets no bounds to the soul's progress, for it sees in each soul transcendental faculties as limitless as infinity itself.

New Thought may be said to possess a fixed ideal, that of an eternal search for Truth. The adherents of New Thought worship the omnipotent God, the indwelling God, in whom we live, and move, and have our being.

5. *Its Purpose*

To teach people to come into a conscious realization of the divinity within, and the unity of God and man, so that out of the sublimity of our souls we can say, "I and the Father are one," is the supreme purpose and meaning of New Thought....

Because no church or school, regardless of its strength, can lift the world consciousness alone, the INTA is to serve as the spearhead combining the united strength of all units to move forward dynamically in the discharge of its great mission. It is not absorbing but expressing the good of all groups that each will remain autonomous and make its individual contribution....

To encourage newly formed centers with interest and attention and assist whenever and wherever possible.

To invite and encourage the training of leaders and ministers and to raise all teaching to an accredited academic level.

To encourage the teaching of New Thought at all levels, paying more attention to the children, youth, and adult groups.

To maintain a flow of materials into the archives of the New Thought movement.

6. *Statement of Principles, Adopted in 1954*

We affirm the inseparable oneness of God and man, the realization of which comes through spiritual intuition, the implications of which are that one can reproduce the Divine perfection in his body, emotions, and in all his external affairs.

We affirm the freedom of each person in matters of belief.

We affirm the Good to be supreme, universal, and eternal.

We affirm that the Kingdom of Heaven is within us, that we are one with the Father, that we should love one another, and return good for evil.

We affirm that we should heal the sick through prayer, and that we should endeavor to manifest perfection "even as our Father in Heaven is perfect."

We affirm our belief in God as the Universal Wisdom, Love, Life, Truth, Power, Peace, Beauty, and Joy, "in whom we live, move, and have our being."

We affirm that our mental states are carried forward into manifestation and become our experience through the Creative Law of Cause and Effect.

We affirm that the Divine Nature expressing itself through us manifests itself as health, supply, wisdom, love, life, truth, power, peace, beauty, and joy.

We affirm that the universe is the body of God, spiritual in essence and governed by God through laws which are spiritual in reality, even when material in appearance.

As we have noted, Michael Servetus Villanovus was burned at the stake by John Calvin for having declared in his book, *De Erroribis*

Trinitatis, that God, instead of being a Trinity of persons, is, rather, one of manifestation; in it, as Father, he constitutes the substance of the universe, as Word or Son, its energizing force, and as Holy Spirit or Christ, its vitalizing and illuminating element. This concept crept into the theology of John Milton and was basic in Swedenborg's reconstruction of Christian doctrine. And here we see that it constitutes the base on which New Thought ideology is constructed.

III. THE CONGRESSES

The 67th Congress of INTA was held in San Diego, California, July 25-30, 1982, where, as usual, it convened at one of the very best hotels. The charge for attending all meetings was $100 for members and $125 for others. Presiding over it was the Reverend Blaine C. Mays and Robert Stevens, Executive Director of the Decanso, California, Unity Retreat. The theme of the convention was "Anchoring in the Sea of Life," with different portions of the program dedicated to doing so in Prosperity, Wholism, Meditation, Love, and Happiness. There were about sixty sessions, including workshops and general meetings and at least a thousand were in attendance. The second day was devoted to the memory of Joseph Murphy, the ex-Catholic priest who died in 1980 and whose books and cassettes are among the most popular in New Thought. We should note that at least sixty individuals played key roles of one kind or another in the program, which was certainly far more elaborate than most conventional churches could duplicate.

One remarkable feature at all INTA congresses is the vast array of books offered for sale and written by a variety of authors. Table after table is loaded down with this literature, which is transferred into the hands of the readers avid for information and inspiration.

The 68th Congress, at which Blaine C. Mays again presided, was held at the Hyatt-Regency in Phoenix from July 31 to August 5, 1983. There were about 500 full-time registrations, mostly from out of town, with people in attendance from some foreign countries and from practically every state in the Union. At some of the general evening meetings, there were 800 or 900 in attendance; and it is certain that well over 1,000 individuals took some part in the proceedings. The theme of the Congress was "Let Your Son Shine"—which was a cryptic reference to the Son-Christ which permeates universal essence. Pictures and brief biographies were printed in the General Announcement of ninety principal participants.

The six-day program was filled from early morning until late in the evening. Each day began with a Hatha-Yoga exercise. On each day except Sunday, there was an Intensive Dialogue from 9 to 11 A.M.; there was a business meeting for INTA members only from 11:30 to 12:30. Every day, except Sunday and Wednesday, there were three workshops from 1 to 2 and from 2:30 to 3:30 P.M., followed by two workshops and a general meeting in the Ballroom from 4 to 5. From 7 to 8, there were two workshops and a Demonstration in the Ballroom, followed by a final general session from 8:30 to 9:30. Not counting the INTA business sessions or the Hatha-Yoga exercises, there were about sixty workshops and general meetings. Admission was free—with a love offering—at the general meetings; but there was a fee for participation in any of the workshops. A schedule of fees is published in the program for each Congress.

There was a great banquet in the Ballroom on Wednesday evening with more than 500 present; at this, awards were presented and a great many persons were introduced. A roll call of the states showed how many had come from all parts of the country.

It would be impossible here to summarize what was said at the many meetings. However, we might note that the first speaker was Marcus Bach, who appeared on the afternoon program of July 31st. The evening session was addressed by the actress Anne Francis and by the Futurist Barbara Marx Hubbard.

At the afternoon programs in the Ballroom, outstanding speakers discussed such New Thought progenitors as Quimby, Emerson, Troward, Emma Curtis Hopkins, Ernest Holmes, Charles Fillmore, and Nona Brooks, and such topics as Modern-Day Mystics.

As in the past years, the literature tables were loaded with educational material; in a cursory examination, we counted about 900 different items. We found, however, very few hardcover books—those which may be described as books as opposed to pamphlets were for the most part in paperback. And we noted a marked development since the 62nd Congress, held in the same place in 1977: the enormous number of cassettes now being offered. Dozens of prominent ministers have prepared single tapes or albums containing anywhere from two to eight in a collection. Thus, people can go home and listen to New Thought expositions in the comfort and leisure of their own living rooms.

I conversed with several individuals—mostly women—who said they would not miss the experience of attending the Congress for anything in the world. And consider this: if forty or fifty new churches join INTA every year, who can envision the size and the quality of the Congress in the year 2000?

What was perhaps the largest and most successful congress ever held (the 69th) occurred on July 22-27, 1984, at the magnificent Hotel Riviera in Las Vegas, with the watchword "You Are Born a Winner."

We should note that all speakers and leaders, of whom there were eighty-five and whose biographies were printed in the Announcement, paid for their own expenses, including travel, meals, and hotel rooms. Only the winner of the Humanitarian Award received his actual expenses from INTA. Of course, many speakers and leaders had books and/or cassettes on sale, from which they received a portion of the sales price; however, many others came simply for the pleasure of partaking in such a glorious experience and to meet and mingle with kindred souls, not only from all parts of the United States, but also from abroad.

The program format, in general, followed that of previous years. Each morning, Monday through Friday, there were early exercises and meditation from 8:30 to 9:30 in four concurrent sessions. These were followed by intensive dialogues daily from ten to noon. In the afternoon on Monday there were twelve workshops, each lasting an hour from 1:30 to 2:30, from 3 to 4, and from 4:30 to 5:30 P.M. The day concluded with a large meeting in the Main Ballroom from 7 to 8 o'clock.

On Tuesday, there were eight workshops in the afternoon and another large assembly in the evening. All such meetings featured outstanding and popular speakers.

On Wednesday afternoon, there were again twelve workshops, and in the evening, a meeting similar to that of the previous day.

The great event on Thursday was the evening banquet, at which the Humanitarian Award was presented as well as the Joseph Murphy Award for Outstanding Service, which went to Carmelita Trowbridge.

The Congress concluded on Monday with eleven workshops in the afternoon and another large convocation from 7:30 to 8:30 P.M.

The themes and presentations of the speakers were as varied as their personalities, interests, and numbers. One very interesting feature consisted of a series of workshops which explored the contributions of several important forerunners or proponents of New Thought. These covered Swedenborg, P.P. Quimby, the Fillmores, Emma Curtis Hopkins, Nona Brooks, and Ernest Holmes, to all of whom we have devoted considerable space in this work.

To describe the content of all the workshops and lectures would require a volume of some size. We simply note again that several long tables were heavily loaded with books and cassettes, thousands of which were carried away by happy searchers for truth, happiness, success, and peace of mind in a troubled world.

In 1985, the Congress was held in Calgary, Canada; and in 1986 in Houston, Texas. Those for future years have already been scheduled, and will occur in various parts of the United States, as follows: for 1987, in Portland, Oregon; for 1988, in Washington, D.C.; for 1989, in San Jose-San Francisco, California; for 1990, in Orange County, California; and for 1991, in New York City.

Chapter XIII

A NEW THOUGHT
SERVICE AND MESSAGE

Attending a service in a New Thought church is usually an inspirational experience and, at least for a stranger, very different from what occurs in an old-line church, an evangelical denomination, or even in Christian Science. There is a pervasive sense of affection and camaraderie; the newcomer is welcomed, sometimes with a hug or a warm, vigorous handclasp; and sometimes, either at the beginning or during the meeting, everyone stands and turns to those in front of, behind, or beside him or her and introduces himself or herself with an expression of goodwill.

The stranger is impressed with the prevailing sense of joy and happiness which exudes from everyone. It is obvious that these people intend to enjoy life to the utmost and make the most of every moment.

If one asks those in attendance how or why they happen to be there, the reply usually involves some experience which created a special interest in New Thought. They were disappointed with the religious organizations in which they were reared; their questions were never resolved satisfactorily; they received no help for personal problems; they suffered intensely from condemnation or a sense of guilt or from frustration; or they felt useless, worthless, or rejected. Some may explain that they received help by healing from emotional distress or physical malfunctions in New Thought. Others declare that it helped them overcome and eliminate such addictions as smoking or alcoholism. Some even say they have been cured of organic diseases.

One cannot spend a couple of hours listening to New Thought services and mingling with the congregation without imbibing a sense of pleasure at simply being there, breathing the fresh air, and experiencing a vibrant vitality.

At every service I have attended, there is a soloist—and a good one—who sings a lilting and happy melody. The congregation, which is completely uninhibited, sometimes breaks into applause in response to anything which it believes merits such appreciation. There is a sense of freedom totally absent in the ordinary church service elsewhere.

At many services, the Lord's Prayer is sung by the congregation; as the organ orchestrates its accompaniment, the voices of the people roll forth in powerful consonance; and, as the climax approaches, the words *For thine is the Kingdom, and the Power, and the Glory, Forever* rise in such a crescendo that one can literally feel the auditorium vibrate; and, as the anthem concludes with its *Amen*, peace and calm descend upon the congregation.

Although most New Thought churches have hymnals of their own, songs sung by the congregation often come from other sources.

It is obvious that these people are not oppressed by thoughts of sin or condemnation; they are not worried about possible punishment from some unseen source or power. They regard the universe as basically beneficent, and they intend to make the best possible use of it. Instead of looking for trouble, they are seeking success, harmony, happiness; and they mean to do whatever they can or is necessary to achieve them. This does not mean, however, that their moral standards are lower or less strict than those of people who belong to the conventional churches; quite the reverse, for they believe that they will be punished for any wrongdoing or act of aggression committed against another. There is no such thing as forgiveness or atonement for our sins by an external agency. Any "sin" against another will be eradicated only by complete restitution and forgiveness. And is there any higher possible form of morality?

Ministers in New Thought churches are usually well-educated and capable speakers. Many of them have come from other denominations, where they were prepared in conventional seminaries; their sincerity can scarcely be questioned, for, in most cases, they left more lucrative positions because of conscience or intellectual convictions. When the old faith proved inadequate to meet their spiritual needs or their intense craving for personal integrity, they came into New Thought; and, since they were already trained and experienced in pulpit techniques and parish ministry, the transition was not very difficult or lengthy. Actually, such ministers usually do not need any substantial re-education, for they have already adopted a New Thought attitude and orientation; it was only necessary to train them in certain specific techniques and in the basic texts of their new affiliations.

The "sermon"—usually called a lesson or a message—is almost always an inspirational discourse on any one of a multitude of topics, as varied as are the articles to be found in *Spirit, Creative Thought, Science of Mind, Daily Word,* or *Unity* magazine. This is always intended as a help for or an explanation of personal problems, which are to be solved or at least reduced in intensity. It may be a discussion of the relation of the conscious to the subconscious mind, and the way in which the individual can gain mastery over his own life by the proper use of both. I have never heard any discussion of orthodox dogmas in a New Thought church. One minister once remarked that his people rarely mention sin—for this is something more akin to error than to evil.

The talk usually lasts about thirty minutes—rarely more than thirty-five. For those who desire further study, most churches provide lessons during the week, in some cases several between one Sunday and the next.

The minister may use a theme as a text taken from Holmes's *Science of Mind;* in the Church of Divine Science, some passage from the writings of Nona Brooks or Emma Curtis Hopkins may be combined with some quotation from the Bible. In Unity, there is a vast storehouse consisting of literature emanating not only from headquarters but from the world of New Thought writers, all of which can supply material. The possibilities are limitless; and a minister could go on for years with a variety of themes without ever repeating himself. For example, in one series of "lessons," Reverend Blaine C. Mays of the Phoenix Unity Church spoke on the following subjects: "How to Enjoy Your Trip to the Top," "Your Right to Peace of Mind," "How to Love Your Neighbor," "How to Get Results through Prayers," "How to Move Up in Life," "Self-Esteem Is God-Intended," "Life's Greatest Benefits Are Yours," "A Spectacular You," "Your Place in the Success Plan," "Heavenly Flavor," "Your Uniqueness," "Get Involved with Life," "How to Add New Zip to Living," and "Overcoming Fear of Criticism." We could go on and on for pages.

Reverend Tom Johnson of the Church of Religious Science in Canoga Park, California, offers a great number of tapes from message-lessons, of which the following are typical: "Love Is Always There," "You Are the Doctor," "The Law and the Word," "Feeling Good," "Does Success Mean Happiness?" "The Power within Us," "The Gold Mine of You," "Our Business Is to Create," "Prosperity/ Love," "Peace of Mind/Health," "How to Get Loose," "The Search for Significance," "The Power of Guilt," "Be Free of Envy," and "Think Big." There are dozens or hundreds of others. Many ministers create a series of their own.

New Thought groups and organizations express their beliefs in somewhat differing terms. But, after interviewing many New Thought ministers and studying all the available Statements of Faith published by New Thought groups or churches, I have concluded that the following sets forth in simple language what all accept as the basis of their thought and action:

STATEMENT OF NEW THOUGHT PRINCIPLES

That God is Universal Essence or Existence, the substance of all things tangible and intangible, material or spiritual;

That this God-Essence is impersonal, yet beneficent, and works for the good of all who realize this and utilize the blessings offered;

That man is an individualized expression of the divine essence in an inseparable oneness; and therefore has unlimited potential for perfection in his body, his emotions, and in all his activities;

That, since all human beings are parts of this divine essence, they constitute a universal brotherhood and should and can learn to live in peace and harmony with each other;

That this divine essence expresses itself in humanity as health, wisdom, life, truth, peace, beauty, joy, well-being and prosperity;

That, since every human being is an embodiment of the divine essence, each one should look upon himself or herself as a being of great worth;

That we should banish all thoughts of guilt or self-condemnation;

That we should likewise refrain from the condemnation of others;

That the Christ is a universal Power available to everyone and all can partake of this to whatever extent they apply themselves to do so;

That Jesus was the Great Wayshower or Exemplar who had absorbed greatly of this Christ-Spirit and was therefore empowered to perform his mission, which was to show humanity the way to the abundant life;

That, since this was the mission of Jesus, each person should seek his Great Good in the attainment of health, happiness, and prosperity in the here and now;

That we should seek truth wherever it may be found; that we should examine and analyze the various "truths" offered, and accept for ourselves only that which meets our personal needs and can serve as our own guide;

That hell and heaven are conditions of mind and not physical places to which souls may be at some future time consigned;

That a personal heaven and salvation are attainable through a consciously self-directed process of moral regeneration;

That there is a divine influx from the divine essence into man and throughout all creation, which serves as the basis of universal well-being;

That this divine influx or intelligence is present in every material or spiritual manifestation throughout every portion of the universe;

That the Bible is the Word of God, but that it can be understood correctly only though spiritual interpretation;

That the mind has power to heal or cause physical ailments;

That human thought has creative power over the physical body;

That the latter transmits ideas and motivations into the subconscious which then exercises control over our emotional lives, and, to a large extent, determines the health or degeneration of the physical body;

That the mind and the body are so interrelated that a host of illnesses are psychosomatic; that the way to physical health is through a healthy mind, which will be reflected in a healthy body;

That healing can be accomplished through Affirmative Prayer;

That advancing age should retain vigor and vitality and should not bring mental or physical senility or debility;

That the human psyche operates on three levels: the conscious, the subconscious, and the superconscious.

We should note that certain subjects are not dealt with by New Thought ministers. In the first place, they do not discuss disease, either organic or psychosomatic, in their pulpits, since this is a field pre-empted by practitioners and counselors.

In the second place, I have never heard a lesson or message refuting the creeds or dogmas of historical religion, although it is well known and firmly established that these have been rejected; they are left to lie in oblivion. (Incidentally, the same is now true of many old-line churches, but there is a vast difference: New Thought ignores them because they have been outgrown; the other churches ignore them because they no longer fervently embrace them.)

In the third place, there is no discussion of politics; perhaps this is true because New Thought churches wish to avoid any confrontation with the Internal Revenue Service; possibly, knowing what danger persecution might entail because of their positions in theology and religious practice, they walk a straight and narrow path in this highly sensitive field. Nothing could be further removed from New Thought objectives, for example, than those pursued by Jerry Falwell and his Moral Majority. New Thought focuses on the daily emotional and subjective needs and problems of the average American.

In the fourth place, New Thought never ventures into the field of economics or taxation. These, again, are sensitive areas which could result, not only in serious controversy, but also in disputes with the government over tax-exempt status. And, more important, such dis-cussion would not be permitted unless in accord with media propa-ganda, which no honest man can accept.

In all this, we believe that the course of wisdom is being followed.

New Thought has carved out for itself a large and important field of endeavor; to venture into others would only dilute and reduce the force of its impact upon modern society.

In most New Thought churches the following song and hymn is sung by the congregation at the conclusion of the service:

> Let there be peace on earth, and let it begin with me;
> Let there be peace on earth, the peace that was meant to be.
> With God as our Father, brothers all are we,
> Let me walk with my brother in perfect harmony.
>
> Let peace begin with me, let this be the moment now,
> With every step I take, let this be my solemn vow;
> To take each moment, and live each moment, in peace eternally;
> Let there be peace on earth, and let it begin with me.

At the beginning of the song, all the members of the congregation rise and clasp hands; as their voices rise in unison, there is a sense of goodwill and affection; as the last line approaches its end, all raise their arms above their heads in token of triumphant and pervading peace, which is to include all mankind.

Those who have never attended a New Thought service should do so, if merely for the healing and elevating experience. And this applies not only to those in need of comfort and solace, but to persons of any religious persuasion or orientation as well as to those who have no such commitment at all.

BIBLIOGRAPHY AND CITATIONS

Chapter II
EMANUEL SWEDENBORG

The symbols at the left are used in the citations, where numbers refer to sections in Swedenborg's writings, or to pages in those of other authors. Wherever other works are cited, their names are given. The works of Swedenborg are published by the Swedenborg Foundation of New York.

SELECTED WORKS ABOUT SWEDENBORG

Noyes	*History of American Socialisms*, John Humphrey Noyes, 1962
Park.	*Collected Works*, Theodore Parker, 2 Vol., 1979
Emer.	*Swedenborg: The Mystic*, An Essay, Ralph Waldo Emerson
Dufty	*Swedenborg: The Scientist*, J.G. Dufty, 1938
Grat.	*The Three Jameses*, G. Hartley Grattan, 1962
Sig.	*The Swedenborg Epic*, Cyriel Odhner Sigstedt, 1952
USE	*Emanuel Swedenborg: The Spiritual Columbus*, U.S.E. (Undated)

Yng.	*The Philosophy of Henry James, Sr.*, Frederic H. Young, 1951
Tro.	*Swedenborg: Life and Teaching*, George Trobridge, 1938.
Block	*The New Church in the New World*, Marguerite Block, 1984

SWEDENBORG'S PRINCIPAL WORKS

JD	*Journal of Dreams*, 1744
WLG	*The Worship and the Love of God*, 1745
SP	*The Spiritual Diary*, 5 Vol., 1749-65
AC	*Arcana Coelestia*, 12 Vol., 1749-56
AE	*The Apocalypse Explained*, 6 Vol., 1759
H&H	*Heaven and Its Wonders and Hell*, 1758
DNJL	*Doctrine of the New Jerusalem Concerning the Lord*, 1763
DNJHS	*Doctrine of the New Jerusalem Concerning the Holy Scriptures*, 1763
DLNJ	*Doctrine of Life for the New Jerusalem*, 1763
DNJF	*Doctrine of the New Jerusalem Concerning Faith*, 1763
DLW	*The Divine Love and Wisdom*, 1763
DP	*The Divine Providence*, 1764
AR	*The Apocalypse Revealed*, 2 Vol., 1766
CL	*Conjugial Love*, 1768
TTCR	*The True Christian Religion*, 2 Vol., 1771
MATC	*The Messiah about to Come*, Bryn Athyn, 1949

MTW   MISCELLANEOUS THEOLOGICAL WORKS, New York, 1959

NJHD	*The New Jerusalem and Its Heavenly Doctrine*, 3-205
BE	*Brief Exposition of the Doctrine of the New Church*, 207-313
WH	*The White Horse Mentioned in the Apocalypse*, 354-84
LJBD	*The Last Judgment and Babylon Destroyed*, 507-88
CCLJ	*Continuation Concerning the Last Judgment*, 58-608
CCSW	*Continuation Concerning the Spiritual World*, 609-34

PTW I   POSTHUMOUS THEOLOGICAL WORKS, Vol. I, New York, 1956

DeCor	*Coronis: Or the Appendix to the True Christian Religion*, 17-97
INC	*Invitation to the New Church*, 115-43
CNC	*Canons of the New Church*, 165-226
DNJCC	*Doctrines of the New Jerusalem Concerning Charity*, 227-81
LJ	*The Last Judgment*, 379-477
CSW	*Concerning the Spiritual World*, 478-514
5 MR	*Five Memorable Relations*, 521-32
JGW	*Justification and Good Works*, 537-46
CWC	*Conversations with Calvin*, 547-54
DNC	*The Doctrine of the New Church*, 555-60
PTW II	*Marriage*, 433-66

1   Tro. 287
2   Park. II 8, I 222
3   Emer.
4   Published by Sweden-
    borg Press of Chicago
5   Sig. 117, 490
6   *Ib.* 107-117
7   *Ib.* 133-140
8   *Tro. 227-241; Sig.*
    133-164
9   Sig. 321-324
10 *Ib.* 408
11 *Ib.* 401-403
12 *Ib.* 389
13 *Ib.* 390
14 *Ib.* 393
15 *Ib.* 395
16 *Ib.* 395, 398, *404-408*
17 *Ib.* 404-405
18 *Ib.* 405
19 *Ib.*
20 *Ib.* 405-407
21 *Ib.* 408
22 *Ib.*
23 *Ib.* 44-46
24 *Ib.* 42-43
25 *Ib.* 57-58
26 *Ib.* 86-91
27 *Ib.* 124-125
28 W LG 9-25
29 IN C 55
30 J D 25, Sig. 184
31 J D 22 ff.; Sig. 185
32 J D 33, Sig. 186
33 PTW I 590-591
34 Sig. 199
35 Ib. 203, 207
36 Ib. 209
37 Sig. 179, 181, 308;
    PTW I 591
38 AR 531, Sig. 318
39 USE 166
40 S D 1092-1101
41 BE 98
42 A C 7502

43 *Ib.* 3833
44 *Ib.* 10, 137
45 *Ib.* 2310
46 MTWT 62, DNJHS
    94, SD 5179
47 AE 544
48 SD 434
49 CL 494
50 AC 4766
51 AC 3993, AR 959
52 AE 1179
53 Ib. 1180
54 DNC 3
55 AR 537
56 *Ib.* 605
57 *Ib.* 634
58 AE 1079-1080
59 IN C 46
60 Tro. 52
61 A C 9020
62 AR 802
63 TT CR 94
64 A C 9410
65 LJB D 57
66 AE 1065
67 *Ib.* 1091
68 *Ib.* 1071
69 *Ib.* 1049
70 AR 802
71 *Ib.* 796
72 AR 784
73 *Ib.* 759
74 *Ib.*
75 *Ib.* 770
76 *Ib.* 802
77 AC 3636; DLW 300
78 DLW 157
79 DP 1
80 TTCR 70
81 *Ib.*
82 AE 349 a
83 *Ib.* 349 b
84 Sig. 134
85 CN C V iii 5
86 *Ib.* V iii 2

87 AE Vol. VI, 513, 520
88 BE 64
89 CN C V ii 1
90 A C 9866
91 TT CR 26
92 A C 2083
93 *Ib.* 1124
94 TTCR 364
95 DLW 353
96 *Ib.* 355
97 AC 3884
98 *Ib.* 5937
99 AE 936
100 DeCor. 19
101 AC 3634
102 AE 969
103 DP 328
104 AC 313, DP 328
105 AC 2308
106 *Ib.* 6495, 6488
107 AE 805 b (7)
108 *Ib.* 800
109 A C 10, 026
110 AE 806
111 *Ib.* 726
112 TT CR 489
113 AC 3854
114 AR 875
115 INC 6
116 DP 129 (1) (6)
117 AC 2881
118 TTCR 356
119 BE 65
120 AE 948
121 DLNJ 63
122 H&H 533
123 AC 4063
124 AE 940
125 TTCR 580
126 AC 248
127 TTCR 412
128 DNJCC 72
129 *Ib.* 126
130 DLNJ 1
131 AC 3776

[132] TTCR 425
[133] IAE 932
[134] H&H 364
[135] Ib.
[136] TTCR 746
[137] AC 6934
[138] Ib. 7038
[139] AE VI 379
[140] DNJCC 167
[141] Ib. 164
[142] Ib. 158
[143] AC 7318
[144] H&H 360, 361
[145] AC 1673
[146] Ib. 2027
[147] CSW 316
[148] Ib.
[149] AE 537 a

[150] 5 MR II 4
[151] CCSW 32
[152] AC 2481, 2483
[153] SD 662, 804-805, 808, 2347
[154] CL 45 (3) (4) (5) (7)
[155] MAR 55, 68
[156] Ib. 5
[157] H&H 489
[158] Published 1875, p. 540
[159] AC 6221
[160] AE 322, 447
[161] USE 131, SD 4348
[162] AC 5711, 5712
[163] SD 4592, 2439, 2716
[164] Ib. 2299
[165] AC 5726
[166] Sig. 375

[167] TTCR 768
[168] Revelation 12:1
[169] AR "Spiritual Sense" Ch. XII 533
[170] Ib. 534
[171] AE 707
[172] Ib. 758
[173] Ib. 762; AC 10249
[174] BE I; AR 914; DNJL 63, 65; AE 431 b; TTCR 107
[175] CNC V x 4
[176] TTCR 788
[177] CeCor. Sum. LII
[178] Ib. 24
[179] Ib. Sum. LV; AE 948
[180] AE. 865
[181] Ib. 730 a
[182] PTW I 587

Chapter III
PHINEAS P. QUIMBY

FAM   Goldsmith, Margaret, *Franz Anton Mesmer*, Doubleday, 1934
PoPPQ   Dresser, Annetta Gertrude, *The Philosophy of P.P. Quimby*, 1895
THMS   Dresser, Julius A., *The True History of Mental Science*, 1887
QMSS   Quimby, P.P., *The Quimby Manuscripts*, Edited by Horatio W. Dresser, 1921 (includes the letters from Mary Baker Patterson to Quimby)
MH   Zweig, Stephan, *Mental Healers*, New York, 1932

[1] Q MSS 269
[2] Published in Boston
[3] THMS 10-11
[4] Ib. 12-13
[5] QMSS 40
[6] Ib. 54, 38
[7] Ib. 43
[8] Ib. 47
[9] Ib. 47-8
[10] Ib. 48
[11] Ib. 38
[12] Ib. 67
[13] Ib. 53, 57

[14] Ib. 57
[15] Ib. 150-51
[16] Ib. 277
[17] Ib. 70
[18] Ib. 324
[19] Ib.
[20] Ib. 323
[21] Ib. 330
[22] Ib. 408
[23] Ib. 409
[24] Ib. 422
[25] Ib. 128
[26] Ib. 389

[27] PoPPQ 109
[28] Ib.
[29] Ib. 110, QMSS 324
[30] QMSS 323, 337
[31] Ib. 324
[32] PoPPQ 91
[33] QMSS 327
[34] Ib. 185
[35] Ib. 196
[36] Ib. 243
[37] Ib. 403
[38] Ib. 422
[39] Ib. 340

40 *Ib*. 122
41 *Ib*. 320
42 *Ib*. 344
43 *Ib*. 346
44 *Ib*. 185
45 *Ib*. 215
46 *Ib*. 217
47 *Ib*. 210
48 *Ib*. 214
49 *Ib*. 150
50 *Ib*. 120
51 *Ib*. 208
52 *Ib*. 228
53 *Ib*. 178
54 *Ib*. 126-27
55 *Ib*. 283
56 *Ib*. 312
57 *Ib*. 143, 170
58 *Ib*. 228
59 *Ib*. 242
60 *Ib*. 388
61 *Ib*. 143
62 *Ib*. 176, 369, 407
63 *Ib*. 201, 370
64 *Ib*. 346-7
65 *Ib*. 422
66 *Ib*. 189
67 PoPPQ 112, 113
68 QMSS 209
69 *Ib*. 216, 246
70 *Ib*. 353
71 *Ib*. 369-373
72 *Ib*. 273
73 *Ib*. 340
74 *Ib*. 326
75 *Ib*. 283
76 *Ib*. 224
77 *Ib*. 355-6
78 *Ib*. 339
79 *Ib*. 369-70
80 *Ib*. 398
81 *Ib*. 379
82 *Ib*. 408
83 *Ib*. 379
84 *Ib*. 255-6

85 *Ib*. 345
86 *Ib*. 338, 271
87 *Ib*. 294, 269
88 *Ib*. 295
89 *Ib*. 299
90 *Ib*. 336-7
91 *Ib*. 289
92 *Ib*. 332, 261
93 *Ib*. 329, 242
94 *Ib*. 384
95 *Ib*. 378
96 *Ib*. 169
97 *Ib*. 270, 241
98 *Ib*. 230, 241
99 *Ib*. 276, 287
100 *Ib*. 278
101 *Ib*. 288
102 *Ib*. 205, 142
103 *Ib*. 318
104 *Ib*. 232, 271, 277
105 *Ib*. 215
106 *Ib*. 210, 259
107 *Ib*. 271
108 *Ib*. 231-2
109 *Ib*. 325
110 *Ib*. 338
111 *Ib*. 276
112 *Ib*. 277, 262
113 *Ib*. 331
114 *Ib*. 267
115 *Ib*. 328
116 *Ib*. 262-3
117 *Ib*. 334
118 *Ib*. 277
119 *Ib*. 259
120 *Ib*. 231-2, 173, 328, 416
121 *Ib*. 306
122 *Ib*. 76
123 PoPPQ 100
124 QMSS 204
125 *Ib*. 259
126 *Ib*. 78-9
127 *Ib*. 55
128 *Ib*. 277
129 *Ib*. 337, 123

130 *Ib*. 362
131 *Ib*. 352
132 *Ib*. 360
133 *Ib*. 105-6
134 *Ib*. 106
135 *Ib*. 346
136 *Ib*. 347
137 *Ib*. 398
138 *Ib*. 396
139 *Ib*. 350
140 *Ib*. 287
141 *Ib*. 277, 283
142 *Ib*. 360
143 *Ib*. 363
144 *Ib*. 190
145 *Ib*. 387, 388, 393, 394
146 *Ib*. 394
147 *Ib*. 395
148 *Ib*. 72
149 *Ib*. 71
150 *Ib*. 351
151 *Ib*. 353-4
152 *Ib*. 284
153 *Ib*. 288
154 *Ib*. 260
155 *Ib*. 277
156 *Ib*. 15
157 *Ib*. 43
158 *Ib*. 418
159 PoPPQ 33
160 QMSS 179, 180, 222, 227, 421
161 *Ib*. 61
162 *Ib*. 334
163 *Ib*. 167, 275
164 *Ib*. 118, 141, 167
165 *Ib*. 194
166 *Ib*. 222-3
167 *Ib*. 413
168 *Ib*. 257
169 *Ib*. 50-1
170 *Ib*. 278
171 *Ib*. 73, 327
172 *Ib*. 336; PoPPQ 107
173 *Ib*. QMSS 397

174 *Ib.* 246
175 *Ib.* 403; cf. PoPPQ 70
176 QMSS 213
177 PoPPQ 23
178 *Ib.* 24
179 QMSS 270, 271
180 *Ib.* 285
181 *Ib.* 134, 214
182 *Ib.* 234, 368
183 *Ib.* 61, 367
184 *Ib.* 269
185 *Ib.* 300
186 *Ib.* 118
187 *Ib.* 311
188 *Ib.* 220
189 *Ib.* 174
190 *Ib.* 280
191 *Ib.* 80
192 *Ib.* 296-7
193 *Ib.* 180
194 *Ib.* 182
195 *Ib.* 177
196 *Ib.* 179
197 *Ib.* 194

198 *Ib.* 223
199 *Ib.* 402
200 *Ib.* 80
201 *Ib.* 270
202 *Ib.* 52-3
203 *Ib.* 253-4
204 *Ib.* 277
205 *Ib.* 154
206 *Ib.* 63
207 *Ib.* 104-5, 110
208 *Ib.* 117
209 *Ib.* 129
210 *Ib.* 139-40
211 *Ib.* 217-18
212 *Ib.* 376
213 PoPPQ 86
214 QMSS 169
215 *Ib.* 319
216 *Ib.* 204
217 *Ib.* 286
218 PoPPQ 20-1
219 QMSS 143
220 *Ib.* 369
221 *Ib.* 370

222 *Ib.* 407
223 *Ib.* 372
224 *Ib.* 327
225 *Ib.* 406
226 *Ib.* 227
227 *Ib.* 177
228 *Ib.* 171-2
229 *Ib.* 412-3
230 *Ib.* 379-80
231 *Ib.* 344-5
232 *Ib.* 369-70
233 *Ib.* 400
234 *Ib.* 405
235 *Ib.* 375
236 *Ib.* 203
237 *Ib.* 200-1
238 *Ib.* 215
239 *Ib.* 250
240 *Ib.* 344
241 *Ib.* 327
242 *Ib.*
243 *Ib.* 202
244 PoPPQ 48

Chapter IV
WARREN FELT EVANS

MC	*The Mental Cure*, 1869
MM	*Mental Medicine*, 1872
SB	*Soul and Body*, 1876
DLC	*The Divine Law of Cure*, 1881
PMC	*The Primitive Mind-Cure*, 1884
EC	*Esoteric Christianity*, 1886

1 HI 119
2 CD, HI
3 PMC 77
4 NA 7
5 *Ib.* 8
6 SB 97
7 *Ib.* 16
8 DLC 120

9 EC 134
10 Schaff-Herzog Encyclopedia IX 354
11 MC 20
12 DLC 22-23
13 *Ib.* 26
14 MC 238
15 DLC 223

16 PMC 148
17 EC 24
18 DLC 63
19 *Ib.* 260
20 *Ib.* 190
21 EC 17
22 MC 21; MM 93; PMC 123

23 EC 87, 92, 96, 102-103
24 MC 22
25 MM 170
26 PMC 170
27 DLC 72
28 EC 74
29 MC 349
30 EC 66-67
31 DLC 53
32 EC 70
33 SB 58
34 MC 240
35 DLC 237, 238
36 *Ib*. 134
37 *Ib*. 137
38 *Ib*. 79, 108
39 PMC 175
40 DLC 80
41 PMC 35
42 DLC 125; PMC 158
43 *Ib*. 238
44 EC 32
45 MM v
46 DLC 43
47 MC 76-77
48 EC 95
49 SB 42-43
50 MC 237-239
51 *Ib*. 216-217, 224
52 DLC 59
53 *Ib*. 167
54 EC 103
55 MC 36
56 *Ib*. 29
57 MM 18-19
58 *Ib*. 25
59 EC 171
60 MC 228
61 *Ib*. 65

62 DLC 245
63 *Ib*. 163-165
64 MC 153
65 *Ib*. 284
66 DLC 51
67 MC 175
68 EC 31
69 MM 14
70 *Ib*. 13-14
71 DLC 78
72 *Ib*.
73 MM 92
74 DLC 253
75 *Ib*. 217
76 MC 104-105; MM 102
77 SB 41
78 PMC 22-27
79 *Ib*. 28
80 *Ib*. 35
81 MM 174
82 MC 163
83 *Ib*. 113
84 SB 140-141
85 MM 97-102
86 MM iv
87 PMC iv
88 *Ib*.
89 MM 12
90 EC 170
91 DLC 55
92 MM 85
93 *Ib*. 140
94 PMC 97
95 MM 23
96 *Ib*. 26
97 *Ib*. 135
98 EC 132
99 MM 148
100 DLC 44

101 *Ib*. 56
102 SB 56
103 DLC 126-127, 42; MM 12
104 SB 3-4; MC 98
105 EC 5
106 DLC 167
107 *Ib*. 177, 268
108 PMC 84
109 MM 21-24
110 SB 52-53
111 PMC 85
112 EC 149
113 *Ib*. 150
114 *Ib*. 58-59
115 MM 17
116 MC 318
117 EC 55
118 PMC 86
119 MM 16
120 PMC 60
121 *Ib*. 104
122 EC 170
123 *Ib*. 4
124 MC iii, 63, 98, 153, 155, 168, 215, 350
125 *Ib*. 107
126 *Ib*. 63
127 MM 163-164
128 *Ib*. 42
129 *Ib*. 47-49
130 *Ib*. 44, 45
131 *Ib*. 90-91, 113-114
132 *Ib*. 52-53
133 *Ib*. 148
134 PMC 102
135 EC 131
136 DLC 268
137 MM 142

Chapter V
CHRISTIAN SCIENCE

THE WORKS OF MARY BAKER EDDY

S&H   *Science and Health*
             Citations from first and second editions, shown as follows: (*S&H* 1 213); those for the third to the fifteenth, which are two-volume editions, citations shown thus: (*S&H* III, 167).
             Science and Health with Key to the Scriptures includes all later editions, through the 226th, shown thus: (*S&H* 16 497); and citations for the definitive edition (F 459).
SoM   1876   *Science of Man*, 1876 edition
SoM   1883   *Science of Man*, 1883 edition
CM   Church *Manual*
CC   *Christ and Christmas*
CSH   *Christian Science Hymnal*
JCS   *Journal of Christian Science*
CSJ   *The Christian Science Journal*

THE PROSE WORKS, INCLUDING THE FOLLOWING

Misc.   *Miscellaneous Writings*
Ret.   *Retrospection and Introspection* (the autobiography)
Un.   *Unity of Good*
Pul.   *Pulpit and Press*
Rud.   *Rudimental Divine Science*
No   *No and Yes*
Pan.   *Christian Science vs. Pantheism*
'00   *Message to the Mother Church, 1900*
'01   *Message to the Mother Church, 1901*
'02   *Message to the Mother Church, 1902*
Heal.   *Christian Healing*
Peo.   *The People's Idea of God*
My.   *The First Church of Christ, Scientist, and Miscellany*

OTHER IMPORTANT SOURCES

Beasley   Beasley, Norman, *The Cross and the Crown*, Duel, Sloan, and Pearce, 1952.
Dakin   Dakin, Edwin Franden, *Mrs. Eddy, the Biography of a Virginal Mind*, Scribners, 1930
Dickey   Dickey, Adam H., *The Memoirs of Mary Baker Eddy*, Merrymount Press, 1927

Ditt.	Dittemore, John V., and Bates, *Mary Baker Eddy*, Alfred Knopf, 1932
Kimball	Kimball, Edward. A., *Lectures and Articles on Christian Science*, Watt, 1921
Milmine	Milmine, Georgine, *The Life of Mary Baker Eddy, and the History of Christian Science*, Doubleday, 1909
Olston	Olston, Albert E., *The Facts and Fables of Christian Science*, Author, Chicago, 1912
Peabody	Peabody, Frederick W., *The Religio-Medical Masquerade*, Fleming H. Revell Co., New York, 1910
Powell	Powell, Lyman P., *Christian Science, the Faith and Its Founder*, G.P. Putnam's Sons, New York, 1908
Studdert	Studdert-Kennedy, Hugh A., *Christian Science and Organized Religion*, The Farallon Foundation, Los Gatos, Calif. 1930
	—*Mrs. Eddy*, The Farallon Foundation, Los Gatos, Calif., 1947
Tomlinson	Tomlinson, Irving C., *The Revelations of St. John: An Open Book*, The Open Book, Dorchester, Mass., 1922
	—*Twelve Years with Mary Baker Eddy*, CSPS, 1945
CS	Twain, Mark, *Christian Science*, Harper and Brothers, New York, 1900
Wilbur	Wilbur, Sibyl, *The Life of Mary Baker Eddy*, CSPS, 1907

SELECTED GENERAL BIBLIOGRAPHY
(not specifically cited in the text)

Anonymous, *The Faith and Works of Christian Science*, MacMillan Co., New York, 1909

Bancroft, Samuel Putnam, *Mrs. Eddy As I Knew Her in 1870*, The Rare Book Co.

Bill, Annie C., *Christian Science vs. Plagiarism*, Beauchamp, 1921

Braden, Charles Samuel, *Christian Science Today: Power, Policy, and Practice*, SMU Press, Dallas, Texas, 1958

Brown, W. Gordon, *The Evolution of the Christian Science Organization*, Foundational Book Co., 1970

Brown, William Lear, *Christian Science, Falsely So-Called*, Fleming H. Revell Co., New York, 1921

Buckley, J.M., *Faith Healing, Christian Science, and Kindred Phenomena*, Century Co., New York, 1892

Buskirk, James Dale, *Religion, Healing, and Life*, MacMillan Co., New York, 1952

Chester, John, *Ruth, the Christian Scientist*, H.H. Carter & Karrick, Boston, 1888

Christian Science Hymnal, The, CSPS, 1909

Coppage, L.J., *Christian Science in the Light of Reason*, Standard Publishing Co., Cincinnati, Ohio, 1914

Corey, Arthur E., *Christian Science Class Instruction*, The Farallon Foundation, Los Gatos, Calif., 1950

—*Class Notes*, The Farallon Foundation, Los Gatos, Calif., 1950, 1956, 1962

—(With Robert E. Merritt) *Christian Science and Liberty*, De Vorss & Co., Los Angeles, 1970

Directors, Christian Science Publishing Society, *Christian Science Wartime Activities*, CSPS, 1947

Doorly, J.W., *God and Science*, Frederick Miller, Ltd., London, 1949

—*The Pure Science of Christian Science*, Foundational Book Co., London, 1946

Dresser, Annetta Gertrude, *The Philosophy of P.P. Quimby*, The Church of the Truth, Boston, 1895

Dresser, Horatio W., *Christ or Science*, Willing Publishing Co., San Gabriel, Calif.

Dresser, Julius, *The True History of Mental Science*, Alfred Midge & Sons, Boston, 1887

Eddy, Mary G. Baker, *Historical Sketch of Metaphysical Healing*, Author, Boston, 1885

Fisher, H.A.L., *Our New Religion*, Jonathan Cape and Harrison Smith, New York, 1930

Flynn, W. Earl, *Christian Health Science vs. Christian Science*, W.F. Black & Co., Minneapolis, 1910

Gestefeld, Ursula, *How to Control Circumstances*, The Exodus Publishing Co., Chicago, 1908

—*Jesuitism in Christian Science*, The Exodus Publishing Co., Chicago, 1888

—*The Joyous Birth*, The Exodus Publishing Co., Chicago, 1910

—*The Science of the Larger Life*, William Rider & Son, London, 1909

Gifford, M.W., *Christian Science against Itself*, Jennings & Page, Cincinnati, Ohio, 1902

Gray, James M., *The Antidote to Christian Science*, Fleming H. Revell Co., New York, 1907

Haldeman, I.M., *Christian Science in the Light of the Scriptures*, Fleming H. Revell Co., New York, 1909

Hanna, Septimus J., *Christian Science History*, CSPS, 1890

Hopkins, Emma Curtis, *Christian Mental Practice*, High Watch Fellowship, Cornwell Bridge, Conn., 1958

Humiston, Charles E., *The Faith, Falsity, and Failure of Christian Science*, Fleming H. Revell Co., New York, 1925

Huse, Sibyl Marvin, *Twelve Baskets Full*, G.P. Putnam's Sons, New York, 1922

Kimball, Edward A., *Teaching and Addresses*, Kratzer Publishing Co., 1917

Laird, Margeret, *All Is One*, Laird Foundations, Los Angeles, 1957

—*Government is Self-Government*, The Portal Press, Evanston, Ill., 1952

Larson, Christian Daa, *The Good Side of Christian Science*, E.J. Clode, New York, 1916

Lord, Frances, *Christian Science Healing*, Lily Publishing Co., Chicago, 1888

McCabe, Joseph, *The Absurdities of Christian Science*, E. Haldeman Julius, Girard, Kansas

Mangasarian, M.M., *What Is Christian Science?* Author, Chicago, 1921

Merritt, Robert E. and Corey, Arthur E., *Christian Science and Liberty*, De Vorss & Co., Los Angeles, Calif., 1970

New York City Christian Science Institute, *Vital Issues in Christian Science*, G.P. Putnam's Sons, New York, 1914

Orgain, Alice L., *Distinguishing Characteristics of Mary Baker Eddy's Progressive Revisions of Science and Health*, Rare Book Co., 1933
—*The Story of the Christian Science Church Manual*, Rare Book Co., 1934

Peabody, Frederick W., *The Complete Exposure of Christian Science*, Fleming H. Revell Co., New York, 1901
—*The Religio-Medical Masquerade*, Fleming H. Revell Co., 1913

Peel, Robert, *Christian Science: Its Encounter with American Culture*, 1964
—*Mary Baker Eddy: The Year of Discovery*, 1966

Quimby, P.P., *Christ or Science*, Willing Publishing Co., San Gabriel, Cal.
—*Manuscripts*, Thomas Y. Crowell Co., New York, 1921
—*Manuscripts*, The Julian Press, New York, 1961

Ramsay, E. Mary, *Christian Science and Its Discoverer*, CSPS, 1935

Riley, Woodbridge, Peabody, Frederick W., and Humiston, Charles E., *The Faith, the Falsity, and the Failure of Christian Science*, Fleming H. Revell Co., New York, 1925

Searle, George M., *The Truth about Christian Science*, Paulist Press, New York, 1916

Sheldon, Henry C., *Christian Science So-Called*, Eaton & Mains, New York, 1913

Smith, Hanover P., *Writings and Genius of the Founder of Christian Science*, 1886

Snowden, James H., *The Truth about Christian Science*, Westminster Press, Philadelphia, 1921

Springer, Fleta Campbell, *According to the Flesh*, Coward-McCann, New York, 1930

Stetson, Augusta E., *My Spiritual Aeroplane*, G.P. Putnam's Sons, New York, 1919
—*Reminiscences, Sermons, and Correspondence*, G.P. Putnam's Sons, New York, 1917
—*Vital Issues in Christian Science*, G. P. Putnam's Son's, New York, 1914

Sturge, M. Carta, *The Truth and Error of Christian Science*, E. P. Dutton & Co., New York, 1903

Zweig, Stephan, *Mental Healers*, The Viking Press, New York, 1932

1 Christian Science 355	14 Ditt. 67	27 *QMSS* 147-158
2 *Ib.* 285-286	15 Milmine 33	28 Ditt. 116-117
3 *Ib.* 72	16 *Ib.* 34	29 Dakin 52-58; Ditt. 123
4 *Ib.* 73	17 Dakin 33-34	
5 *Ib.* 82	18 Milmine 38	30 Milmine 70
6 I Powell v	19 *Ib.* 39-41	31 *Retrospection* 24
7 II Powell 103	20 *Quimby MSS* 146-147	32 Wilbur 127
8 Milmine 10-13	21 Milmine 56	33 Beasley 5
9 *Ib.* 21-22	22 *Ib.* 58	34 Milmine 84-86
10 Ditt. 41-42	23 *Ib.* 58-59	35 *Retro.* 24
11 *Ib.* 10-20	24 *Ib.* 59	36 Milmine 118
12 Milmine 29-30	25 *Ib.* 60	37 *Ib.* 119
13 *Ib.* 32	26 *Ib.* 92	38 *Ib.* 132

39 *Ib*. 134

40 *Ib*. 135-137

41 Ditt. 138

42 Milmine 140-141, 146, 153

43 *Ib*. 150-151; Ditt. 143-144

44 Milmine 152-153

45 *Ib*. 153-154

46 *Ib*. 176-177

47 *S&H* I 373-374

48 Milmine 176-178, 232-235

49 Ditt. 163-164

50 *Ib*. 164

51 Milmine 269-270

52 Ditt. 163, 177-178; Milmine 174-175

53 Milmine 276, 277-278

54 *Ib*. 281-283; Ditt. 217

55 Milmine 285

56 *S&H* Final xii: Ditt. 463-473

57 Milmine 313-314

58 *My*. v

59 Ditt. 205, 206

60 Milmine 307

61 *Ib*. 341, 399

62 *Ib*. 400-404

63 *Ib*. 301, 357-360

64 Beasley 185

65 Ditt. 291-293

66 *Retro*. 78

67 Milmine 398

68 *Ib*. 405-406

69 *My*. 303

70 Dakin 462-465, Ditt. 420-421

71 New York *Sun*, June 26, 1911; Olston 128-131

72 Ditt. 228-232, 445-449; Dakin 525-530

73 Ditt. 389

74 *Mis*. 248-249

75 Dickey xv

76 *S&H* I 343, II 104

77 *S&H* III, I 156

78 *Ib*. 11

79 *S&H* VI, I 3-4

80 J. Dresser 25

81 Milmine 102

82 Powell II 110

83 Dakin 225-226

84 *S&H* 16 508

85 *S&H* Final 30, 497

86 Milmine 335

87 *S&H* I 52

88 *S&H* Final 330, 331

89 *Heal*. 3

80 *No* 39

91 *S&H* I 284

92 *S&H* Final 92

93 *Mis*. 18

94 '01, 7

95 '00, 5

96 *Pan*. 15

97 '01, 10

98 *S&H* I 45

99 *Ib*. 143, *My*, 218

100 1883 *SoM* 6; *S&H I* 41; *S&H* Final 313

101 *S&H* I 208

102 *Ib*. 301-302

103 *Ib*. 312

104 *Ib*. 284

105 *Ib*. 292

106 *No* 35; *Mis*. 123

107 1876 *SoM* 5; *S&H* I 267

108 1876 *SoM* 6

109 *Un*. 31

110 *S&H* Final 257

111 *Ib*. 349-350

112 *Ib*. 215

113 *Mis*. 206

114 1883 *SoM* 11

115 *S&H* I 14-15

116 *Ib*. 17-18, 20

117 *S&H* Final 120

118 *Ib*. 181

119 *S&H* I 14

120 *Ib*. 337

121 *Ib*. 355

122 *Ib*. 366

123 *Ib*. 240-241

124 *Ib*. 244

125 *Ib*. 404

126 *Ib*. 405

127 *Ib*. 438

128 *S&H* I 347

129 *Ib*. 355

130 *S&H* Final 154

131 *S&H* I 89

132 *Ib*. 102

133 *Ib*. 214, Final 245

134 *S&H* I 37

135 *Mis*. 174

136 *S&H* Final 207

137 *Mis*. 58

138 *Ib*. 42

139 *S&H* Final 291

140 *My*. 140

141 *Un*. 2

142 1883 *SoM* 14

143 *S&H* I 303

144 *Ib*. 262

145 *S&H* Final 549

146 *S&H* I 262, 336

147 *Mis*. 288

148 *My*. 5

149 *Mis*. 289

150 *Ib*. 298

151 *Ib*. 286

152 *Ib*.

153 *S&H* I 322

154 *Mis*. 2

155 *S&H* Final 239

156 *Mis*. 82

157 *S&H* Final 114

158 *Ib*. 176

159 *Ib*. 177

160 *Ib*. 311

161 *Un*. 23

162 Milmine 209

163 *S&H* 1 251, 255
164 *Ib*. 255
165 *Ib*. 251
166 *Ib*. 171
167 *S&H* Final 241
168 *Mis*. 169
169 *S&H* Final 579-599
170 *S&H* 1 124
171 *Mis*. 24
172 *S&H* Final 79
173 *Ib*. 324-325
174 *Ib*. 146, 328
175 *Mis*. 91
176 *Ib*. 145
177 *S&H* 1 181-182
178 *Ib*. 289
179 *Peo*. 2-3

180 *S&H* Final 158
181 *Ib*. 150-151
182 *Ib*. 180
183 *Ib*. 198
184 *S&H* 1 330, 51
185 *Ib*. 400
186 *S&H* Final 464
187 *My*. 219, 344-345
188 *S&H* Final 447
189 *Ib*. 169, 184
190 *S&H* 1 187-188, 341;
Final 155, 174, 370;
My. 107
191 *S&H* Final 158
192 *S&H* 1 437
193 *S&H* Final 175
194 *Ib*. 197

195 *S&H* Final 377
196 *Ib*. 385
197 *No* 31
198 *S&H* Final 404
199 *My*. 349
200 *S&H* Final 377
201 1883 *SoM* 16
202 *Retro*. 26
203 *S&H* Final 147
204 *'01*, 31
205 *Retro*. 70
206 *S&H* Final 55, 134
207 *S&H* 16 511-527
208 *Ib*. 511
209 *S&H* Final 568-569
210 *Ib*. 558
211 *Ib*. 559
212 Ditt. 311

Chapter VI
THE GREAT POPULARIZERS

I. THE UNITARIAN SWEDENBORGIANS

1 *Representative Men*, Caldwell Co. 125, 132
2 The Divinity School Address
3 *Ib*.
4 *Ib*.
5 *Ib*.
6 *Representative Men* 96
7 *Ib*. 99

8 *Ib*. 118-119
9 *Ib*. 128, 137-138
10 *Works*, Trubner & Co. Vol. II 73
11 *Ib*. 191
12 *Ib*. 51, 119, 156
13 *Ib*. 88
14 *Ib*. 195
15 *Prayers*, Trubner 15, 21, 39, 45, 51, 61, 77, 88, 102, 109, 125, etc.
16 *Works* 72
17 *Prayers* 8, 35
18 *Works* 215
19 *Ib*. 217
20 *Ib*. 222
21 *Prayers* 98
22 *Ib*. 122

II. HENRY JAMES, SR.

1 C. Hartley Grattan, *The Three Jameses* 47-48
2 *Ib*. 52-53
3 *Christianity: The Logic of Creation*, 81-83
4 *The Three Jameses* 53
5 *The Church of Christ Not an Ecclesiasticism* 81-82, 87-88, 122-123
6 *Substance and Shadow* 230
7 *Moralism and Christianity* 81-82
8 Young 319
9 *Ib*. Ch. Four, 29-69
10 *The Three Jameses* 106-107
11 *Literary Remains* 388-390

III. HENRY DRUMMOND

1 *Natural Law in th Spiritual World* 19
2 *Ib.* 20
3 *Ib.*
4 *Ib.* 21
5 *Ib.* 56-57
6 *Ib.* 5
7 *Ib.* 28
8 *Ib.* 29
9 *Ib.* 32, 59-60
10 *Ib.* 32, 55
11 *Ib.* 69, 70
12 *Ib.* 33-34
13 *Ib.* 40
14 *Ib.* 41
15 *Ib.* 43
16 *Ib.* 45
17 *Ib.* 47
18 *Ib.* 50
19 *Ib.* 51
20 *Ib.* 68
21 *Ib.* 72

22 *Ib.* 78ff.
23 *Ib.* 81
24 *Ib.* 82
25 *Ib.* 83
26 *Ib.* 87
27 *Ib.* 88
28 *Ib.* 89-90
29 *Ib.* 93
30 *Ib.* 94
31 *Ib.* 95
32 *Ib.* 96
33 *Ib.* 99
34 *Ib.* 103
35 *Ib.* 126
36 *Ib.* 109ff.
37 *Ib.* 122
38 *Ib.* 126
39 *Ib.* 127
40 *Ib.* 138
41 *Ib.* 139
42 *Ib.* 164, 181
43 *Ib.* 173

44 *Ib.* 259
45 *Ib.* 284
46 *Ib.* 191
47 *Ib.* 196
48 *Ib.* 215
49 *Ib.* 246
50 *Ib.* 307ff.
51 *Ib.* 314-315
52 *Ib.* 320-322
53 *Ib.* 323
54 *Ib.* 324
55 *Ib.* 336-337
56 *Ib.* 345
57 *Ib.* 346
58 *Ib.* 347
69 *Ib.* 348
60 *Ib.* 362
61 *Ib.* 373
62 *Ib.* 377
63 *Ib.* 379-382
64 *Ib.* 387-393

IV. EMMA CURTIS HOPKINS

1 *Spirits in Rebellion* 143
2 *Mary Baker Eddy* 265
3 *Ib.* 272
4 *Spirits in Rebellion* 144
5 Scientific Mental Practice Lesson Three

69-70
6 Lesson Two 46
7 *Ib.*
8 Lesson Five 107; Lesson Seven 138
9 *Ib.* 110
10 Lesson Seven 148
11 Lesson Nine 182

12 *Understanding the Scriptures* 11-12
13 Lesson Ten 200
14 Lesson Eleven 231
15 Lesson Five 112-113
16 *Ib.* 114
17 *Ib.* 112
18 No. Twelve 261-262

V. THOMAS TROWARD

1 For example, in his acceptance of the Law of Biogenesis
2 *The Hidden Power* , Robert McBride & Co. 9, HP

3 *Edinburgh Lectures,* Dodd, Mead & Co. 55, E L
4 *The Doré Lectures,* Dodd, Mead & Co. 1, D L

5 *Ib.* 3
6 *Ib.* 6
7 *Ib.* 7
8 *Ib.* 10
9 *Ib.*
10 *Ib.* 15

11 *Ib*. 16-17
12 *Ib*. 16
13 *Ib*. 20
14 *Ib*.
15 *Ib*. 23
16 *Ib*. 26
17 *Ib*. 27
18 *Ib*. 29
19 *Ib*. 35
20 *Ib*. 38
21 *Ib*. 44
22 *Ib*. 45
23 *Ib*. 50
24 *Ib*. 51
25 *Ib*. 53
26 *Ib*. 55
27 *Ib*. 57
28 *Ib*. 65
29 EL 9; cf. *The Law and the Word* 52-53,
30 *Ib*. 20
31 *The Creative Process in the Individual* 55,
32 EL 15
33 *Ib*. 17
34 *Ib*. 18
35 *Ib*. 19
36 CP 67
37 LW 50
38 EL 45
39 HP 7
40 CP 6
41 EL 46
42 *Ib*. 59
43 *Ib*. 14
44 *Ib*. 15
45 *Ib*. 47
46 *Ib*. 9
47 *Ib*. 13
48 HP 52
49 EL 42
50 *Ib*. 48-49
51 *Ib*. 42
52 LW 109
53 EL 48

54 *Ib*. 50
55 CR 38
56 *Ib*. 80
57 EL 11
58 *Ib*. 8
59 LW 68
60 CP 79
61 *Ib*. 52-53; EL 4
62 CP 136
63 EL 37
64 CP 30
65 *Ib*. 31
66 *Ib*. 36
67 EL 53
68 *Ib*. 52
69 HP 174
70 *Ib*. 177
71 *Ib*. 51
72 CP 141
73 EL 35
74 CP 10
75 *Ib*. 39
76 *Ib*. 167
77 HP 182
78 EL 100
79 HP 188
80 EL 91
81 CP 45
82 HP 207
83 EL 128
84 *Ib*. 22
85 *Ib*. 23
86 *Ib*. 24
87 *Ib*. 25
88 *Ib*. 30
89 *Ib*. 26
90 *Ib*.
91 *Ib*. 28
92 *Ib*. 27
93 *Ib*. 74
94 *Ib*. 75
95 *Ib*.
96 *Ib*. 69
97 *Ib*. 79
98 *Ib*. 77

99 *Ib*. 78
100 *Ib*. 32
101 LW 154
102 *Ib*. 1
103 CP 91, 18
104 HP 83
105 EL 44
106 *Ib*. 42
107 *Ib*. 65-66
108 *Ib*. 58
109 *Ib*. 105
110 *Ib*. 16
111 *Ib*. 15
112 LW 73
113 EL 12
114 *Ib*. 49
115 *Ib*. 50
116 CP 131
117 LW 87-88
118 *Ib*. 87
119 EL 67
120 CP 58-59
121 LW 100
122 EL 80
123 LW 97
124 HP 36
125 *Ib*. 145
126 CP 38, 41
127 *Ib*. 132
128 HP 42
129 EL 36
130 HP 65-66
131 CP 37
132 HP 142
133 EL 96
134 *Ib*. 105
135 *Ib*. 78
136 HP 167
137 LW 113, 139
138 CP 86
139 *Ib*. 86, 88
140 LW 195
141 *Ib*. 204
142 CP 145
143 *Ib*.

144   HP 119   146   CP 157   147   EL 70
145   LW 110

VI. CHARLES BRODIE PATTERSON

1   *What is New Thought*
    35-36
2   *Ib*. 7
3   *Ib*. 11, 14, 84, 220,
    235
4   *The Will to Be Well*
    41, 53, *The Will* 12
5   *What Is* 56; *The Will*
    12
6   *The Will* 24
7   *Ib*. 117
8   *Ib*. 118; 12, 23
9   *Ib*. 166. 22
10 *Ib*. 52; *What Is* 3
11 *What Is* 22
12 *Ib*. 35
13 *The Will* 101
14 *Ib*. 166
15 *Ib*. 187
16 *Ib*. 246-247
17 *Ib*. 37
18 *What Is* 43
19 *Ib*.
20 *Ib*. 93
21 *Ib*. 151
22 *The Will* 124
23 *What Is* 37
24 *Ib*. 58

25 *Ib*. 91
26 *Ib*. 94
27 *Ib*. 119
28 *The Will* 35
29 *Ib*. 131
30 *Ib*. 122
31 *Ib*. 13
32 *Ib*. 123
33 *Ib*. 108
34 *Ib*. 243
35 *Ib*. 244
36 *What Is* 13
37 *Ib*. 33
38 *Ib*. 148
39 *Ib*. 149
40 *The Will* 101
41 *What Is* 131
42 *Ib*. 15
43 *The Will* 217
44 *Ib*. 219
45 *What Is* 130
46 *Ib*. 156
47 *Ib*. 161
48 *Ib*. 61
49 *The Will* 182
50 *Ib*. 101-102
51 *What Is* 84
52 *The Will* 86

53 *What Is* 223
54 *Ib*. 224
55 *Ib*. 225
56 *The Will* 87
57 *Ib*. 91
58 *Ib*.
59 *Ib*. 90
60 *Ib*. 97
61 *What Is* 163
62 *Ib*. 165
63 *The Will* 85
64 *Ib*. 253
65 *Ib*. 70
66 *What Is* 74
67 *The Will* 223
68 *Ib*. 226
69 *Ib*. 228
70 *Ib*. 200
71 *Ib*. 134
72 *The Will* 55
73 *What Is* 155
74 *Ib*. 15
75 *Ib*. 53
76 *The Will* 126
77 *Ib*. 123
78 *Ib*. 27
79 *What Is* 152

VII. ELLA WHEELER WILCOX

1   *The Heart of New*
    Thought 6
2   *Ib*. 36
3   *Ib*. 11-12
4   *Ib*. 16
5   *Ib*. 79
6   *Ib*. 76
7   *Ib*. 20

8   *Ib*. 51
9   *Ib*. 25
10 *Ib*. 49
11 *Ib*. 28
12 *Ib*. 39
13 *Ib*. 79
14 *Ib*. 76
15 *Ib*. 33

16 *Ib*. 34
17 *Ib*. 60
18 *Ib*. 51
19 *Ib*. 54
20 *Ib*. 40-41
21 *Ib*. 41
22 *Ib*. 44
23 *Ib*. 63-65

24 *Ib.* 66
25 *Ib.*
26 *Ib.* 69

27 *Ib.*
28 *Ib.* 70
29 *Ib.* 71

30 *Ib.* 91
31 *Ib.* 92

VIII. RALPH WALDO TRINE

1 *What All the World's A-Seeking* 16
2 *Ib.* 20, 30, 34, 162
3 *Ib.* 50
4 *Ib.* 58-59
5 *Ib.* 87
6 *Ib.* 95
7 *Ib.* 111
8 *Ib.* 112-113
9 *Ib.* 116-117
10 *Ib.* 146, 150-152
11 *Ib.* 154-155, 160-161
12 *Ib.* 185
13 *In Tune with the Infinite* 199

14 *Ib.* 11-12
15 *Ib.* 17
16 *Ib.* 38-39
17 *Ib.* 142-143
18 54
19 57
20 58
21 *Ib.* 61
22 *Ib.* 82-83
23 *Ib.* 83
24 *Ib.* 121
25 *Ib.* 122
26 *Ib.* 95
27 *Ib.* 137

28 *Ib.* 146
29 *New Alignment* 197
30 *In Tune* 205-209
31 *Ib.* 204-205
32 *Ib.* 29
33 *Ib.* 198
34 *Ib.* 176-177
35 *Ib.* 192
36 *Ib.* 178
37 *Ib.* 181
38 *Ib.* 187
39 *Ib.* 190
40 *The New* 212
41 *Ib.* 224-225

IX. JOEL GOLDSMITH

1 *Conscious Union with God* 243
2 *God, the Substance of All Form* 19
3 Cf. discussion of Buddha's Illumination in *God, the Substance* 95-99
4 *The Art of Spiritual Healing* 123, 137; also *Conscious* 251
5 Cf. *Spiritual Interpretations of Scripture*
6 Cf. Bunyan's *Grace Abounding*
7 *The Art of SH* 27
8 *Ib.* 63; *Conscious* 158
9 *Conscious* 79
10 *The Art of SH* 25, 141, 185

11 *Conscious* 48
12 *Ib.* 65
13 *God, the Substance* 15
14 *The Art of SH* 40
15 *Living the Infinite Way* 33
16 *The Art of SH* 149, 184; *Conscious* 125, 126, 148
17 *Art of Meditation* 152; *The Art of SH* 12
18 *Conscious* 187; *Living* 47, 64; *God, the Substance* 108
19 *The Art of SH* 76, 100; *Living* 38
20 *God, the Substance* 53-54; *Conscious* 12; *Art of Meditation* 84

21 *Art of SH* 26; *Living* 81
22 *Art of SH* 28; *Living* 47
23 *Conscious* 12, 15; *God, the Substance* 12, 17, 116, 125, 126, 158
24 *Conscious* 21; *Living* 83-84, 85, 87; *God, the Substance* 42, 73
25 *Art of SH* 28, 41
26 *Conscious* 181
27 *Ib.* 192
28 *Art of Med* 37
29 *Ib.* 39
30 *Ib.* 76
31 *Ib.* 84
32 *Ib.* 127; *God, the Substance* 53-54
33 *Conscious* 41

34 *Ib*. 16
35 *Living* 93, 103
36 *God, the Substance* 68
37 *Ib*. 72
38 *Ib*. 62
39 *Living* 110
40 *Conscious* 37; *Art of Med* 77
41 *Art of Med* 19
42 *Conscious* 127
43 *Ib*. 185, 186
44 *Ib*. 191
45 *Living* 40, 110
46 *Conscious* 12
47 *Art of SH* 112-113
48 *Conscious* 78
49 *Ib*. 17
50 *Art of SH* 118, 119; *Conscious* 45, 203
51 *Conscious* 76
52 *Ib*. 202; *God, the Substance* 82, 84
53 *Art of SH* 122
54 *God, the Substance* 86
55 *Living* 75
56 *Art of SH* 59
57 *Ib*. 61, 63; *Conscious* 85
58 *God, the Substance* 75
59 *Art of SH* 33; *Conscious* 92
60 *Ib*. 94; *Conscious* 84
61 *God, the Substance* 83

62 *Conscious* 43
63 *Ib*. 63, 146, 163
64 *Ib*. 138, 162
65 *Ib*. 143
66 *Ib*. 44
67 *Ib*. 213
68 *Ib*. 136
69 *Art of SH* 102
70 *God, the Substance* 61, 121
71 *Art of SH* 54
72 *Art of Med* 96
73 *Ib*. 94
74 *Ib*. 134
75 *Ib*. 116
76 *Art of SH* 48
77 *Ib*. 51
78 *God, the Substance* 15
79 *Art of SH* 11
80 *Ib*. 32
81 *God, the Substance* 129
82 *Conscious* 143
83 *Ib*. 135
84 *Art of SH* 13
85 *Art of Med* 118
86 *Ib*.
87 *God, the Substance* 71, 172, 173
88 *Ib*. 56
89 *Living* 32
90 *Ib*. 22
91 *Art of Med* 137
92 *Ib*. 138
93 *Art of SH* 54

94 *Ib*. 19
95 *Ib*. 136
96 *Art of Med* 54
97 *Ib*.
98 *Conscious* 18
99 *Ib*. 19
100 *Ib*. 29
101 *Ib*. 25
102 *Ib*. 23
103 *Art of SH* 147
104 *Ib*. 171; *Art of Med* 20, 92; *Conscious* 105; *God, the Substance* 15
105 *God, the Substance* 15
106 *Ib*. 37
107 *Conscious* 227
108 *God, the Substance* 26
109 *Art of Med* 52-53
110 *Art of SH* 98
111 *Art of Med* 53
112 *God, the Substance* 39
113 *Living* 116, 120, 35
114 *Art of Med* 8
115 *God, the Substance* 93
116 *Living* 19
117 *Ib*. 12-13
118 *Art of SH* 145
119 *Ib*. 137-138
120 *God, the Substance* 64
121 *Ib*. 37
122 *Living* 66
123 *Ib*. 51
124 *Ib*. 44
125 *Ib*. 41
126 *Conscious* 151
127 *Ib*. 121
128 *Ib*.

X. EMMET FOX

1 *Spirits in Rebellion* 353-355
2 *Power through Constructive Thinking* 12, 170,
3 *Ib*. 92
4 *Alter Your Life* 119-148
5 *Power* 13-40
6 *Ib*. 101-109
7 *Alter* 7-30
8 *Ib*. 34-61
9 *Ib*. 62-83
10 *Power* 100

11 *Ib*. ix
12 *Ib*. 118
13 *Ib*. 75, 84, 105
14 *Ib*. 10
15 *Ib*. 96
16 *Ib*. 102-103
17 *Sermon* 82-83

18 *Alter* 8
19 *Ib.* 55
20 *Ib.* 64
21 *Ib.* 71
22 *Ib.* 153; *Power* 2, 110, 173, 174
23 *Power* 259
24 *Ib.* 265
25 *Ib.* 137
26 *Ib.* 113, 140
27 *Alter* 70
28 *Ib.* 123
29 *Power* 178
30 *Ib.* 131, 163
31 *Ib.* 250
32 *Alter* 64
33 *Power* 143
34 *Ib.* 91
35 *Ib.* 201-230
36 *Ib.* 203
37 *Ib.* 205
38 *Ib.* 207

XI. CHRISTIAN DAA LARSON

1 *Pathway of Roses* 17-18,
2 *The Ideal Made Real* 251,
3 *Pathway* 300
4 *Ib.* 312
5 *Ib.* 326
6 *Ib.* 178
7 *Ib.* 25
8 *Ib.* 28
9 *Ib.* 87
10 *Ib.* 29
11 *Ib.* 35
12 *Ib.* 42
13 *Ib.* 49
14 *Ib.* 83
15 *Ib.* 129
16 *Ib.* 141
17 *Ib.* 154
18 *Ib.* 165
19 *Ib.* 169
20 *Ib.* 186
21 *Ib.* 188
22 *Ib.* 213ff.
23 *Ib.* 217
24 *Ib.* 225
25 *Ib.* 240, 242, 287
26 *Ib.* 354
27 *The Ideal* 66
28 *Ib.* 35
29 *Ib.* 25
30 *Ib.* 26
31 *Ib.* 27-28
32 *Ib.* 160-169
33 *Ib.* 160
34 *Ib.* 162
35 *Ib.* 161-162
36 *Your Forces and How to Use them* 25-34
37 *Ib.* 170-171
38 *Ib.* 171
39 *Ib.* 58
40 *Ib.* 219
41 *Ib.* 220
42 *Ib.* 229
43 *Ib.* 18
44 *Ib.* 20
45 *Ib.* 24
46 *Ib.* 26
47 *Ib.* 39
48 *Ib.*
49 *Ib.*
50 *Ib.* 41-42
51 *Ib.* 49
52 *Ib.* 53
53 *Ib.* 61
54 *Ib.* 67
55 *Ib.* 31
56 *Ib.* 74
57 *Ib.* 75
58 *Ib.* 89
59 *Ib.* 94
60 *Ib.* 139
61 *Ib.* 164
62 *Ib.* 165
63 *Ib.* 63
64 *Ib.* 62

XII. HORATIO W. DRESSER

1 *Spirits in Rebellion* 530-532
2 *Ib.* 160
3 *In Search of a Soul* 36
4 *Ib.* 90
5 *Ib.* 108
6 *Ib.* 113
7 *Ib.* 120-121
8 *Ib.* 21
9 *Ib.*
10 *Ib.* 192
11 *Ib.* 196
12 *Ib.* 168
13 *Ib.* 187-188
14 *Ib.* 213-221
15 *Methods and Problems of Spiritual Healing*
16 *Ib.* 37
17 *Ib.* 34
18 *Ib.* 39
19 *Ib.* 24-25
20 *Ib.* 75-76
21 *Health and the Inner Life* 118-119

22   *Ib.* 244
23   *Ib.* 135
24   *Ib.* 137
25   *Ib.* 223
26   *Ib.* 87
27   *Ib.* 226
28   *Ib.* 142

29   *A Physician of the Soul* 99
30   *Ib.* 39
31   *Ib.* 19
32   *Ib.* 20-21
33   *Ib.* 25

34   *Ib.* 34
35   *Ib.* 22-23
36   *Ib.* 12-13
37   *Ib.* 48-49
38   *The Philosophy of the Spirit* 114

Chapter VII
THE CHURCH OF DIVINE SCIENCE

PP   *Divine Science: Its Principles and Practice*
M   *Mysteries*

The following are by Joseph Murphy

RAYR   *Riches Are Your Right*, 1952
HTAM   *How to Attract Money*, 1955
PWY   *Peace within Yourself*, 1956
QMWG   *Quiet Moments with God*, 1958
MMD   *The Miracle of Mind Dynamics*, 1962
ALCMP   *The Amazing Laws of Cosmic Mind Power*, 1965
T   *Telephysics*, 1973
TCE   *The Cosmic Energizer*, 1977
WYIP   *Within You Is the Power*, 1977
PSM   *The Power of the Subconscious Mind*

1   *Mysteries* 6
2   *Ib.* 17
3   *Ib.* 19
4   *Ib.* 39
5   *Ib.* 31
6   *Divine Science: Its Principles and Practice* 203
7   *Ib.* 136
8   *Ib.* 86
9   *Ib.* 126
10   *Ib.* 127
11   *Ib.* 139-140
12   *Ib.* 127
13   *Ib.* 143
14   *Ib.* 46
15   M 22

16   P&P 192
17   *Ib.* 190
18   M 72
19   P&P 172
20   M 48
21   *Ib.* 48-49
22   P&P 48
23   *Ib.* 99-100
24   *Ib.* 105
25   *Ib.* 102
26   *Ib.* 62, 70
27   M 46
28   *Ib.* 47
29   P&P 145-146
30   *Ib.* 417-418
31   *Ib.* 150-151
32   *Ib.* 51-52

33   *Ib.* 152
34   *Ib.* 154
35   *Ib.* 154-155
36   M 143
37   *Ib.* 60
38   *Ib.* 61
39   *Ib.* 67
40   *Ib.* 69
41   P&P 235
42   *Ib.* 86-97
43   *Ib.* 92
44   *Ib.* 88-92
45   *Ib.* 91
46   *Ib.* 92
47   M 73
48   *Ib.*
49   *Ib.* 71

50 *Ib.* P&P 98
51 *Ib.* 100
52 *Ib.* 102
53 *Ib.* 103
54 *Ib.* 104-105
55 M 53
56 *Ib.*
57 *Ib.* 54
58 *Ib.* 55
59 MMD 6
60 *Ib.* 7
61 ALCMP 97-98
62 *Ib.* 92
63 *Ib.* 149; WYIP 57
64 MMD 192
65 WYIP 9
66 *Ib.*
67 *Ib.* 168
68 *Ib.* 197
69 *Ib.* 42; T 83
70 *Ib.* 36
71 *Ib.* 75
72 *Ib.* 82
73 MMD 156, 193
74 QMWG 15
75 *Ib.* 22
76 *Ib.* 24
77 *Ib.* 45
78 *Ib.* 50; RAYR 56
79 MMD 52; QMWG 13, 27
80 QMWG 33
81 WYIP 33; TCE 61; MMD 143
82 QMWG 26, 41, 48
83 *Ib.* 29

84 *Ib.* 39
85 *Ib.* 51
86 *Ib.* 54
87 *Ib.* 16, 19
88 *Ib.* 25
89 *Ib.* 32
90 *Ib.* 35
91 WYIP 159
92 PWY 18
93 *Ib.* 19
94 *Ib.* 205
95 *Ib.* 238-239
96 HTAM 44
97 PWY 57
98 *Ib.* 126
99 *Ib.* 179
100 HTAM 9
101 *Ib.* 10
102 TCE 88
103 HTAM 11
104 *Ib.* 15
105 *Ib.* 27, 26
106 *Ib.* 14
107 *Ib.* 13
108 *Ib.* 30
109 *Ib.* 16, 43
110 *Ib.* 39
111 MMD 58
112 *Ib.* 50
113 *Ib.* 185
114 *Ib.* 144
115 *Ib.* 148
116 *Ib.* 147
117 WYTP 47, 199
118 T 53
119 *Ib.* 212, 217

120 WYIP 132
121 QMWG 75
122 *Ib.* 72
123 *Ib.* 68
124 *Ib.* 59
125 ALCMP 30
126 T 95
127 HTAM 60
128 MMD 149
129 T 21
130 *Ib.* 39
131 ALCMP 31
132 RAYR 23
133 ALCMP 91, 192
134 *Ib.* 171-172
135 MMD 107
136 *Ib.* 46
137 *Ib.* 103
138 RCE 51
139 *Ib.* 56-58
140 *Ib.* 136-137
141 T 163
142 *Ib.* 150-151
143 WYTP 36-37
144 *Ib.* 112-113
145 *Ib.* 24-25
146 *Ib.* 64
147 *Ib.* 130
148 *Ib.* 40
149 MMD 47
150 T 92-93
151 ALCMP 45-46
152 *Ib.* 35
153 TCE 125

Chapter VIII
THE UNITY SCHOOL OF CHRISTIANITY

The Story of Unity by James Dillet Freeman
Lessons in Truth by Emilie Cady

The following are by Charles Fillmore

ASPM   *Atom-Smashing Power of Mind*

CH   Christian Healing
JCH   Jesus Christ Heals
KTL   Keep a True Lent
MBD   Metaphysical Bible Dictionary
MG   The Mysteries of Genesis
MJ   The Mysteries of John
P   Prosperity
TT   Talks on Truth
TPM   The Twelve Powers of Man

1   Story of Unity 24
2   Ib.
3   Ib. 132-133
4   Story of Unity 5
5   Ib.
6   Ib. 81
7   Ib. 82
8   Ib. 105
9   Ib. 131
10 Ib. 218
11 Lessons in Truth 43-45
12 MJ 18
13 TT 99
14 J CH 25
15 CH 10
16 J CH 29
17 TPM 35
18 J CH 18
19 Ib. 60
20 Ib. 24
21 J CH 21; KT L 25
22 MJ 59; TPM 18
23 TPM 34
24 J CH 23-27
25 P 24
26 MG 23; MJ 74; TT 99
27 TT 149
28 CH 19
29 TT 134; MJ 136
30 J CH 63
31 Ib. 121-122
32 KT L 14-17
33 J CH 11; ASPM 100
34 TPM 4, 35, 70, 136

35 P 36, TT 167; KTL 197
36 TPM 158
37 MG 39
38 TT 17
39 MJ 87, 128
40 Ib. 64
41 J CH 178; ASPM 100
42 MJ 92
43 KT L 131
44 J CH 54; KT L 26
45 TPM 15
46 KT L 53
47 Ib. 185
48 TT 164
49 Ib. 166
50 ASPM 162
51 MG 8
52 CH 29-30
53 MG 26
54 KT L 97
55 CH 112
56 Ib. 113 KT L 116
57 TT 112
58 Ib. 129
59 JGH 151-153
60 MG 69
61 MJ 145
62 ASPM 78
63 TT 31
64 MG 48
65 Ib. 45
66 P 59
67 Ib. 96

68 MG 77
69 Ib. 104
70 CH 23
71 MG 159
72 KT L 87
73 TPM 3
74 ASPM 76
75 TPM 144
76 ASPM 20
77 CH 62
78 Ib. 101
79 TT 118
80 Ib. 149
81 CH 64
82 Ib. 96-97
83 J CH 108
84 CH 52
85 P 112
86 MG 135
87 P 102
88 Ib. 103
89 CH 126
90 P 110
91 ASPM 72
92 P 123
93 TT 49
94 Ib. 45
95 Ib. 56
96 ASPM
97 J CH 37-38, 44
98 CH 72
99 Ib.
100 Ib. 70
101 J CH 67

[102] *Ib.* 72
[103] MJ 181
[104] ASPM 148
[105] MJ 90
[106] J CH 59
[107] TT 140
[108] *Ib.* 143
[109] J CH 136
[110] TT 120
[111] *Ib.* 56
[112] MJ 76
[113] CH 41
[114] *Ib.* 39
[115] J CH 4-5
[116] *Ib.* 14
[117] ASPM 131-132
[118] *Ib.* 89
[119] *Ib.* 142
[120] CH Preface
[121] TT 153
[122] CH 48
[123] *Ib.* 49
[124] *Ib.* 101-102

[125] *Ib.* 132-133
[126] *Ib.* 132
[127] ASPM 84
[128] TT 124
[129] ASPM 129
[130] MG 66
[131] JCH 157
[132] *Ib.* 25
[133] TT 148
[134] KTL 84
[135] CH 40
[136] *Ib.* 7-8
[137] P 125
[138] *Ib.* 129
[139] TT 50
[140] *Ib.* 95
[141] P 64
[142] TT 57
[143] CH 124-125
[144] TPM 23, 37, 56-57, 165, 166, 167, 168, 169, MG 47
[145] MG 124

[146] P 19
[147] MG 52
[148] P 167
[149] TPM 152-155
[150] KT L 101
[151] P 89, 90
[152] *Ib.* 107
[153] *Ib.* 113
[154] *Ib.* 186
[155] *Ib.* 21
[156] *Ib.* 80
[157] *Ib.* 138
[158] *Ib.* 133
[159] *Ib.* 141
[160] *Ib.* 167
[161] *Ib.* 69
[162] CH 99
[163] MJ 27
[164] *Ib.* 37-38
[165] CH 24
[166] KT L 98
[167] TT 158-159
[168] J CH 13, 49

Chapter IX
ERNEST HOLMES
AND RELIGIOUS SCIENCE

The Law	*The Law of the Mind in Action*
The Faith	*The Faith That Heals*
Sc. of Mind	*Science of Mind*
How to Use	*How to Use the Science of Mind*
This Thing	*This Thing Called Life*
WTHT	*Words That Heal Today*
DRL	*Discover a Richer Life*
PASM	*Practical Application of Science of Mind*
KY	*Know Yourself*
FFS	*Freedom from Stress*
FTL	*Freedom to Live*
IUY	*It's up to You*
IFL	*Ideas for Living*
ICHY	*It Can Happen to You*

1 This material found in Braden, pp. 285-311
2 *Ib.*
3 *The Law* 1
4 *Ib.*
5 *The Faith* 69
6 *The Law* 166
7 *Ib.* 167
8 *Ib.* 20, 22, 46, 74, 86, 166
9 *The Faith* 18
10 *Ib.* 17
11 *Ib.* 25
12 *The Law* 93
13 *Ib.* 124
14 *Ib.* 139
15 *Ib.* 170
16 *Ib.* 174
17 *Ib.* 188
18 *Ib.* 195
19 *Ib.* 15
20 *Ib.* 40
21 *Ib.* 76
22 *Ib.* 100, 206
23 *Ib.* 150
24 *Ib.* 159
25 *Ib.*
26 *Ib.* 104
27 *Ib.* 105
28 *Ib.* 152
29 *Ib.* 115
30 *Sc. of Mind* 98-99
31 *Ib.* 26
32 *Ib.* 35
33 *Ib.* 48
34 *Ib.* 67
35 *Ib.* 70
36 *Ib.* 611
37 *Ib.* 77
38 *How to Use* 87; *This Thing* 139
39 *This Thing* 60; *Science of Mind* 98, 246
40 *Sc. of Mind* 405
41 *Ib.* 484-485

42 *This Thing* 121
43 *Sc. of Mind* 583
44 *Ib.* 80, 81
45 *Ib.* 373
46 *Ib.* 480
47 *Ib.* 392
48 *Ib.* 390
49 *Ib.* 608
50 *Ib.* 599
51 *Ib.* 106, 113, 134
52 *This Thing* 61
53 *Ib.* 107
54 *How to Use* 76
55 *Sc. of Mind* 366
56 *Ib.* 337
57 *Ib.* 603
58 *Ib.* 413
59 *Ib.* 422
60 *Ib.* 578-579
61 *Ib.* 601
62 *Ib.* 100
63 *Ib.* 491
64 *Ib.* 546-547
65 *Ib.* 375
66 *Ib.*
67 *Ib.* 376
68 *Ib.* 492
69 *Ib.* 388
70 *Ib.*
71 *Ib.* 630
72 *Ib.* 104
73 *Ib.* 377, 379, 385
74 *Ib.* 105
75 *Ib.* 483, 581
76 *How to Use* 1, 4
77 *Ib.* 35
78 *Ib.* 45; *Sc. of Mind* 363
79 *This Thing* 112
80 *Ib.* 129, 135
81 *Sc. of Mind* 11
82 *Ib.* 585
83 *Ib.* 584
84 *Ib.* 383
85 *Ib.* 623, 633

86 *Ib.* 516
87 *Ib.* 337
88 *Ib.* 590
89 *Ib.* 124
90 *Ib.* 598
91 *This Thing* 28, 30
92 *How to Use* v
93 *Sc. of Mind* 219
94 *Ib.* 320
95 *Ib.* 145
96 *Ib.* 237
97 *Ib.* 240
98 *How to Use* 115
99 *Ib.* 141
100 *Sc. of Mind* 215-216
101 *How to Use* 88-89
102 *Sc. of Mind* 177
103 *Ib.* 585
104 *Ib.* 589
105 *How to Use* 102; *Sc. of Mind* 624
106 *How to Use* 103
107 *Sc. of Mind* 409
108 *Ib.* 137-38
109 *Ib.* 163-164
110 *Ib.* 365, 175
111 *Sc. of Mind* 252
112 *This Thing* 68
113 *Ib.* 143
114 *Ib.* 42
115 *How to Use* 11
116 *Ib.* 44-45
117 *Ib.* 97-98
118 *Ib.* 69-70, 119
119 *Sc. of Mind* 183; *How to Use* 65
120 *Sc. of Mind* 178; *This Thing* 47
121 *This Thing* 130
122 *Sc. of Mind* 226
123 *Ib.* 59
124 *Ib.* 194
125 *Ib.* 228
126 *Ib.* 233, 443
127 *Ib.* 243-244

128 *How to Use* 97
129 *Ib.* 107
130 *Ib.* 110
131 *Sc. of Mind* 305
132 *How to Use* 140
133 *Ib.* 141
134 *Ib.*
135 *This Thing* 78-80
136 *Ib.* 82-86
137 *Ib.* 132-135
138 *Ib.* 99-100
139 *Ib.* 102-105
140 *Ib.* 105
141 *Sc. of Mind* 620
142 *Ib.* 635-636
143 DRL 17
144 *Ib.* 42
145 *Ib.* 47
146 *Ib.* 54
147 *Ib.* 81
148 ETL 11
149 *Ib.* 12
150 *Ib.* 30
151 *Ib.* 40
152 PASM 58
153 IUY 87
154 FFS 76
155 KY 92
156 *Ib.* 24-25
157 *Ib.* 22

158 *Ib.* 25
159 FTL 94
160 FFS 23
161 *Ib.* 70
162 *Ib.* 95
163 KY 28
164 DRL 43, 51; IUY 37;
    KY 92
165 KY 93
166 *Ib.* 21
167 *Ib.* 91
168 *Ib.* 94
169 DRL 41
170 IUY 36
171 FTL 27
172 IFL 52
173 DRL 12
174 *Ib.* 24
175 IFL 52
176 FTL 18
177 PASM 34
178 *Ib.* 13
179 KY 45
180 PASM 9, 20, 21
181 KY 45
182 DRL 47
183 FTL 34
184 *Ib.* 35
185 KY 9
186 DRL 33

187 PASM 15
188 KY 42
189 *Ib.* 44
190 *Ib.* 85
191 DRL 53
192 *Ib.* 56
193 PASM 84
194 DRL 89
195 ICHY 23
196 KY 23
197 DRL 85
198 ICHY 90
199 *Ib.* 91
200 ICHY 93-94
201 KY 75
202 DRL 63
203 *Ib.* 71
204 IUY 76
205 IFL 54
206 PASM 33
207 IUY 47
208 FFS 42
209 IUY 19
210 *Ib.* 22
211 *Ib.* 21
212 *Ib.* 89-94
213 DRL 11
214 *Ib.* 12-13

ADDITIONAL BIBLIOGRAPHY

The following books and authors, in addition to those listed in connection with Swedenborg, and Christian Science, have been studied or consulted in the preparation of this work.

Addington, Jack Ensign, *Introduction to the Science of Mind*, 1954
Allen, James, *Eight Pillars of Prosperity*, Thomas Y. Crowell Co., New York, 1911
Anderson, Wing, *Health, Wealth, and Happiness While You Sleep*, The Kosmon Press, Los Angeles, 1948
Andrews, Edward Deming, *The People Called Shakers*, The Dover Publications, New York, 1963
Atkinson, W.W., *The Inner Consciousness*, Advanced Thought Publishing Co., Chicago, 1908
____*The Law of New Thought*, Psychic Research Co., Chicago, 1902
____*Reincarnation and the Law of Karma*, Yogi Publication Society, Chicago,
____*Mind Power: The Secret of Mental Magic*, Yogi Publication Society, Chicago, 1912
Bach, Marcus, *They Have Found a Faith*, Bobbs, Merrill Co., Indianapolis, 1946

—*The Unity Way of Life*, Prentice-Hall, New York, 1962

Bailes, Dr. Frederick, *The Secret of Healing*, Scrivener & Co., Los Angeles, 1962

—*The Spiritual Foundation of Freedom*, 1951

—*What Is This Power That Heals?* 1950

Barker, Raymond Charles, *How to Change Other People*, Author, New York, 1947

—*Money Is God in Action*, New York, 1960

Barney, Laura Clifford, *Some Questions Answered of Abdul-L-Baha*, Bahai Publishing Committee, Wilmette, Illinois, 1930

Baxter, Betty, *The Betty Baxter Story*, Published by Rev. Don Heidt, 1951

Beebe, Tom, *Who's Who in New Thought*, CSA Press, Lakemont, Georgia, 1977

Besant, Annie, *Esoteric Christianity*, Theosophical Publishing Home, Los Angeles, 1901

Blavatsky, H.P., *Isis Unveiled*, The Theosophy Co., Los Angeles, 1931

—*The Secret Doctrine*, The Theosophical Publishing Co., London, 1888

Braden, Charles S., *Spirits in Rebellion*, SMU Press, Dallas, Texas, 1963

—*These Also Believe*, MacMillan Co., New York, 1960

—*Varieties of American Religion*, Willett, Clark, and Co., 1949

—*War, Communism, and World Religions*, Harper & Brothers, New York, 1953

—*The World's Religions*, Abingdon Press, New York, 1954

Brooks, Nona L., *Mysteries*, Divine Science Federation International, Denver, 1924

Buskirk, J. Dale, *Religion, Healing, and Health*, MacMillan, New York, 1952

Butterworth, Eric, *Unity: A Quest for Truth*, Robert Speller & Sons, New York, 1965

Cady, Emilie, *God a Present Help*, Unity School of Christianity

—*How I Used Truth*, Unity School of Christianity

—*Lessons in Truth*, Unity School of Christianity

Carnegie, Dale, *How to Stop Worrying and Start Living*, Simon and Schuster, New York, 1951

—*How to Win Friends and Influence People*, Simon and Schuster, 1936

Clark, Glenn, *How I Found Health through Prayer*, Harper and Brothers, New York, 1940

Collier, Robert J. *The Secret of the Ages*, 7 vol., R. Collier, New York, 1926

Collins, Mabel, *Light on the Path of Karma*, The Theosophical Press, Wheaton, Illinois, 1944

Cramer, Malinda E., and James, Fannie B., *Divine Science: Its Principles and Practice*, Divine Science Federation International, Denver, 1957

Curtis, Donald, *How to Be Happy and Successful*, The Science of Mind Church of Religious Science, Los Angeles, 1960

D'Andrade, Hugh, *Charles Fillmore, Herald of a New Age*, Unity School of Christianity, 1974

Delme, Corinne, *Healing Miracles of Christ Jesus*, The New Age Press, Los Angeles, 1950

DeWaters, Lillian, *How to Have Health*, Stamford, Conn., 1919
—*The Time Is at Hand*, Stamford, Conn. 1930

Dinnet, Ernest, *What We Live By*, Simon and Schuster, New York, 1932

Douglas, Lloyd, *Magnificent Obsession*, Willet Clark & Co., Chicago, 1933

Dresser, Annetta Gertrude, *The Philosophy of P.P. Quimby*, The Church of Truth, Boston, 1895

Dresser, Horatio, W., *Health and the Inner Life*, G.P. Putnam's Sons, 1906
—*A History of New Thought*, Thomas Y. Crowell Co., New York, 1919
—*In Search of a Soul*, G.P. Putnam's Sons, New York, 1907
—*Methods and Problems of Spiritual Healing*, G.P. Putnam's Sons, 1899
—*The Philosophy of the Spirit*, G.P. Putnam's Sons, New York, 1908
—*A Physician of the Soul*, G.P. Putnam's Sons, New York, 1908
—*The Spirit of New Thought*, George G. Harrap and Co., Ltd., London, 1917

Dresser, Julius A., *The True History of Mental Science*, Alfred Midge and Son, Boston, 1887

Drummond, Henry, *The Greatest Thing in the World*, Collins, London

—Natural Law in the Spiritual World, H.M. Caldwell Co., New York

Eddy, Mary Baker, *Concordance to Miscellaneous Writings*, Trustees under the Will of Mary Baker Eddy, Boston, 1915

—Historical Sketch of Metaphysical Healing, Author, Boston, 1885

Evans, Warren Felt, *The Divine Law of Cure*, H.H. Carter, Boston, 1881

—Esoteric Christianity and Mental Therapeutics, H.H. Carter and Karrick, Boston, 1886

—Mental Cure: Illustrating the Influences of the Mind on the Body, H.H. Carter, Boston, 1869

—Mental Medicine: A Theoretical Treatise on Medical Psychology, H.H. Carter, Boston, 1872

—The Primitive Mind-Cure, H.H. Carter, Boston, 1884

—Soul and Body: Or The Spiritual Science of Health and Disease, Colby & Rich, Boston, 1876

Esslemont, J.E., *Baha-U'Llah and The New Era*, Bahai Publishing Trust, Wilmette, Illinois, 1950

Favorite Radio Talks: A Compilation, Unity School of Christianity, 1950

Fillmore, Charles, *Atom-Smashing Power of Mind*, Unity School of Christianity, 1949

—Christian Healing, Unity, 1941

—Jesus Christ Heals, Unity, 1939

—Keep a True Lent, Unity, 1953

—Mysteries of Genesis, Unity, 1936

—Mysteries of John, Unity, 1965

—New Ways to Solve Problems, Unity, 1947

—Prosperity, Unity, 1960

—Talks on Truth, Unity, 1965

—The Twelve Powers of Man, Unity, 1964

—You Can Be Healed, Unity, 1937

Fillmore, Charles, and Cora, *Teach Us to Pray*, Unity

—Christ Enshrined in Man, Unity

Fillmore, Lowell, *Things to Be Remembered*, Unity

—The Prayer Way to Health, Wealth, and Happiness, Unity, 1964

Fillmore, Myrtle, *How to Let God Help You*, Unity, 1956

—Letters, Unity, 1936

Fosdick, Harry Emerson, *Adventurous Religion*, Grosset and Dunlap, New York, 1946
___*Living under Tension*, Harper and Brothers, New York, 1941
___*The Man from Nazareth*, Harper and Brothers, New York, 1949
___*The Meaning of Service*, Association Press, New York, 1920
___*The Modern Use of the Bible*, MacMillan Co., New York, 1924
___*On Being Fit to Live With*, Harper and Brothers, New York, 1914
___*What is Vital in Religion?* Harper and Brothers, New York, 1955
Fox, Emmet, *Alter Your Life*, Harper and Brothers, New York, 1931
___*Around the Year with Emmet Fox*, Harper and Brothers, 1952
___*The Four Horsemen of the Apocalypse*, Harper and Brothers, 1942
___*The Golden Key*, Harper and Brothers, 1931
___*Life As Consciousness*, Unity School of Christianity, 1955
___*Make Your Life Worth While*, Harper and Brothers, 1942
___*Power through Constructive Thinking*, Harper and Brothers, 1932
___*Reincarnation*, Harper and Brothers, 1939
___*The Sermon on the Mount*, Harper and Brothers, 1934
___*The Seven Days of Creation*, Harper and Brothers, 1945
___*The Seven Main Aspects of God*, Harper and Brothers, 1942
___*Sparks of Truth*, Grosset and Dunlap, New York, 1937
Freeman, James Dillet, *The Household of Faith*, Unity School, 1951
___*The Story of Unity*, Unity School, 1951
___*The Story of Unity*, Unity School, 1978
Gatlin, Dana, *Prayer Changes Things*, Unity School
Gestefeld, Ursula, *How to Control Circumstances*, Exodus Publishing Co., Chicago, 1908
___*The Joyous Birth*, Exodus Publishing Co., Chicago, 1910
___*The Science of the Larger Life*, William Rider & Son, London, 1909
Goldsmith, Margaret, *Franz Anton Mesmer*, Doubleday, Doran, & Co., Garden City, New York, 1934
Goldsmith, Joel, *The Art of Meditation*, Harper and Brothers, New York, 1956
___*The Art of Spiritual Healing*, Harper and Brothers, 1959
___*Business and Salesmanship*, Willing Publishing Co., San Gabriel, Calif., 1947

—*Conscious Union with God*, The Julian Press, New York, 1962

—*God, the Substance of All Form*, University Books, New York, 1962

Grattan, C. Hartley, *The Three Jameses*, New York University Press, New York, 1962

Green, Arthur Jay, *Not Anything Happens by Chance*, Church of Divine Truth and College of Mental Science, Seattle, Wash.

Hall, Manly Palmer, *The Adepts: The Arhats of Buddhism*, Philosophical Research Society, Los Angeles, 1957

Hamblin, Henry Thomas, *Divine Adjustment*, Science of Thought Press, Chichester, 1937

Harrison, John F.C., *Quest for the New World: Robert Owen and the Owenites*, Charles Scribner's Sons, New York, 1969

Hart, H. Maryn., D.D., *A Way That Seemeth Right*, James Ratt & Co., New York, 1897

Hawkins, Ann Ballew, *Phineas Parkhurst Quimby, Revealer of Spiritual Healing to This Age*, DeVorss, Los Angeles, 1951

Holley, Horace, *Bahai Scriptures*, Brentano's, New York, 1923

—*Bahai: The Spirit of the Age*, Brentano's, New York, 1921

Holliwell, Raymond, *Working with the Law*, Author, 1939

Holloway, Mark, *Heavens on Earth: Utopian Communities in America*, Dover Publications, New York, 1966

Holmes, Ernest, *Alcoholism, Its Cause and Cure*, Institute of Religious Science, Los Angeles, 1941

—*The Bible in the Light of Religious Science*, Robert M. McBride Co., New York, 1929

—*Creative Mind*, Dodd, Mead & Co., New York, 1957

—*Discover the Richer Life*, Science of Mind Publications, Los Angeles, 1978

—*Freedom from Stress*, Science of Mind Publications, 1964

—*Freedom to Live*, Science of Mind Publications, 1969

—*How to Develop the Faith That Heals*, Robert M. McBride Co., New York, 1925

—*How to Use Science of Mind*, Dodd, Mead & Co., New York, 1948

—*Ideas for Living*, Science of Mind Publications, 1979

—*It's Up to You*, Science of Mind Publications, 1980

—*Know Yourself*, Science of Mind Publications, 1982

__*Science of Mind*, Dodd, Mead & Co., New York, 1961

__*This Thing Called Life*, Dodd, Mead & Co., New York, 1953

__*This Thing Called You*, Dodd, Mead & Co., New York, 1948

__*What Religious Science Teaches*, Institute of Religious Science, 1944

__*Words That Heal Today*, Dodd, Mead & Co., New York, 1949

__*Your Invisible Power*, Church of Religious Science, 1940

Holmes, Ernest, and Kinnear, Willis, *A New Design for Living*, Prentice-Hall, Englewood Cliffs, N.J., 1959

__*Practical Application of Science of Mind*, Science of Mind Publications, 1958

__*It Can Happen to You*, Science of Mind Publications, 1959

Holmes, Fenwicke L., *The Law of the Mind in Action*, Robert M. McBride, New York, 1930

__*Twenty Secrets of Success*, Robert M. McBride, 1927

__*Ernest Holmes: His Life and Times*, Dodd, Mead & Co., 1970

Hopkins, Emma Curtis, *Esoteric Philosophy in Spiritual Science*, High Watch Fellowship, Cornwall Bridge, Conn.

__*High Mysticism*, High Watch Fellowship

__*Scientific Christian Mental Practice*, High Watch Fellowship

__*Understanding the Scriptures*, High Watch Fellowship, 1940

Hornaday, William H.D., *Life Everlasting*, De Vorss & Co.

__*Success Unlimited*, De Vorss, Santa Monica, Calif. 1952

Hyde, Lawrence, *Isis and Osiris*, E.P. Dutton & Co., New York, 1948

Ingraham, E.V., *Meditation in the Silence*, Unity School of Christianity

James, William, *Human Immortality*, Houghton, Mifflin & Co., New York, 1898

__*The Meaning of Truth*, Longmans, Green & Co., New York, 1909

__*Pragmatism*, Longmans, Green & Co., 1948

__*Selected Papers on Philosophy*, E.P. Dutton, New York, 1917

__*Varieties of Religious Experience*, Longmans, Green & Co., 1908

__*The Will to Believe*, Longmans, Green & Co., 1907

Jones, E. Stanley, *Abundant Living*, Abington-Cokesbury, New York, 1922

__*The Way to Power and Poise*, Abington-Cokesbury, 1926

Keller, Helen, *My Religion*, Bard Books, Avon Book Division, New York, 1927

Kinnear, Willis, and Holmes, Ernest, *A New Design for Living*, 1982

—*The Creative Power of Mind*, Prentice-Hall, New York, 1957

Krishnamurti, Jedda, *The Kingdom of Happiness*, Boni and Liverwright, New York, 1927

Laird, Margaret, *All Is One*, Laird Foundation, Los Angeles, 1957

—*Government Is Self-Government*, Portal Press, Chicago, 1952

Larson, Christian Daa, *The Creative Power of Mind*, L.N. Fowler Co., London

—*The Great Within*, L.N. Fowler, London

—*The Ideal Made Real*, Thomas Y. Crowell Co., New York, 1912

—*Leave It to God*, De Vorss & Co, Marina del Rey, Calif., 1968

—*The Pathway of Roses*, Thomas Y. Crowell Co., New York

—*Your Forces and How to Use Them*, L.N. Fowler, London, 1906

Levi, *The Aquarian Gospel of Jesus Christ*, De Vorss & Co., Marina del Rey, Calif., 1981

Lewis, Edwin, *The Revival Pulpit*, Nashville, Tenn., 1944

Lichtenstein, Rabbi Morris, *Jewish Science and Health*, Jewish Science Publishing Co., New York, 1925

Liebman, Joshua Loth, *Peace of Mind*, Simon and Schuster, New York, 1946

McKenzie, John, *Two Religions: Hinduism and Christianity*, The Beacon Press, Boston, 1952

Maltz, Maxwell, *Psycho-Cybernetics*, Wilshire Book Co., North Hollywood, Calif., 1960

Marden, Orison Swett, *How to Get What You Want*, Thomas Y. Crowell Co., New York, 1917

Metaphysical Bible Dictionary, Unity School of Christianity, 1960

Militz, Annie Rix, *Both Riches and Honor*, Unity School

Miller, R. DeWitt, *You Do Take It with You*, Citadel Press, New York, 1955

Muller, Herbert J., *Religion and Freedom in the Modern World*, University of Chicago Press, Chicago, 1963

Murphy, Joseph, *The Amazing Laws of Cosmic Mind-Power*, Parker Publishing Co., West Nyack, New York, 1973

—*The Cosmic Energizer: The Miracle Power of the Universe*, Parker Publishing Co., 1974

—*How to Attract Money*, Willing Publishing Co., San Gabriel, Calif., 1955

—*The Miracle of Mind Dynamics*, Prentice-Hall, Englewood Cliffs, N.J., 1964

—*Peace within Yourself*, De Vorss & Co., Marina del Rey, Calif.

—*The Power of Your Subconscious Mind*, Prentice-Hall, Englewood Cliffs, N.J., 1963

—*Quiet Moments with God*, De Vorss & Co., Marina del Rey, Calif., 1958

—*Riches Are Your Right*, Willing Publishing Co., San Gabriel, Calif., 1952

—*Telephysics, the Magic Power of Perfect Living*, Parker Publishing Co., West Nyack, New York, 1973

—*Within You Is the Power*, De Vorss & Co., Marina del Rey, 1977

Newhouse, Flower A., *Natives of Eternity*, Lawrence G. Newhouse, Vista, Calif., 1950

Nordhoff, Charles, *The Communistic Societies in the United States*, Hillary House Publishers, New York, 1961

Noyes, John Humphrey, *History of American Socialisms*, Hillary House Publishers, Ltd., New York, 1962

Ouseley, S.G.J., *Science of the Aura*, L.N. Fowler Co., London, 1949

Page, Kirby, *How Does God Deal with Evildoers?* Author, LaHabra, Calif.

—*Living Abundantly*, Farrar & Rinehart, New York, 1944

—*Living Joyously*, Rinehart & Co., New York, 1950

—*The Meek Shall Inherit the Earth*, Author, La Habra, Calif., 1948

—*Power from the Bible*, Author, La Habra, Calif.

Palmer, Clara, *You Can Be Healed*, Unity School of Christianity, 1937

Parker, Theodore, *Collected Works*, 2 vol., Trubner & Co., London, 1879

Patterson, Charles Brodie, *The Will to Be Well*, The Alliance Publishing Co., New York, 1902

—*What Is New Thought?* Thomas Y. Crowell Co., New York, 1913

Peale, Norman Vincent, *The Art of Living*, Doubleday & Co., New York, 1938

—*A Guide to Confident Living*, Prentice-Hall, New York, 1948

—*Not Death to All*, Prentice-Hall, Englewood Cliffs, N.J., 1948

—*The Power of Positive Thinking*, Prentice-Hall, 1952

—*Sin, Sex, and Self-Control*, Doubleday & Co., Garden City, New York, 1965

—*Stay Alive All Your Life*, Prentice-Hall, Englewood Cliffs, 1957

—*The Tough-Minded Optimist*, Prentice-Hall, Englewood Cliffs, 1961

Pratt, George K., M. D., *Your Mind and You*, Funk & Wagnalls Co., New York, 1924

Quimby (From) to Christ Truth, The Christ Truth Foundation, Portland, Oregon

Quimby, P.P., *The Philosophy of P.P. Quimby*, Edited by Annetta Gertrude Dresser, The Builder's Press, Boston, 1895
—*The Quimby Manuscripts*, Thomas Y. Crowell Co., 1921
—*The Quimby Manuscripts*, The Julian Press, New York, 1961

Rabani, Ruthyyth, *Prescription for Living*, Bahái Publishing Committee, Oxford, England

Ramacharaka, Yogi, *Hatha Yoga: Or the Philosophy of Well-Being*, Yogi Publication Co., Chicago, 1932
—*Gnani Yoga*, The Yogi Publication Society, Chicago, 1906

Rawson, F.L., *Healing by the Realization of God*, Society for Spreading the Knowledge of True Prayer, 1918
—*Life Understood from a Religious and Scientific Point of View*, Crystal Press, London, 1912
—*Man's Concept of God*, London, 1935
—*The Nature of Prayer*, London, 1930
—*Plea for the Open Door*, Crystal Press, London, 1915
—*True Prayer in Business*, Crystal Press, London, 1917

Regardie, Israel, *The Romance of Metaphysics*, The Aries Press, Chicago, 1946

Rix, Harriet Hale, *Christian Mind Healing*, Master Mind Publishing Co., Los Angeles, 1914

Royce, Josiah, *The Religious Aspect of Philosophy*, Harper and Brothers, New York, 1958

Russell, Robert Alfred, *The Creative Silence*, Denver, 1961

Salisbury, Mary E., *From Day to Day with the Faithful*, Barse and Hopkins, New York, 1912
—*From Day to Day with New Thought*, Barse and Hopkins, 1912

Scott, Ernest F., *The Ethical Teachings of Jesus*, MacMillan Co., New York, 1960

Seabury, David, *Help Yourself to Happiness*, Garden City Publishing Co., Garden City, New York, 1942
—*How Jesus Heals Our Mind Today*, Little, Brown & Co., Boston, 1940
—*How to Get Things Done*, Little, Brown & Co., New York, 1949

Seale, Ervin, *Learn to Live: The Meaning of the Parables*, Science of Mind Publications, Los Angeles, 1965
___*Ten Words That Will Change Your Life*, William Morrow & Co., New York, 1954
Sears, William, *Thief in the Night*, George Ronald, London, 1961
___*The Wine of Astonishment*, George Ronald, Garden City Press, Great Britain, 1965
Seton, Julia, *Concentration: The Secret of Success*, E. J. Clode, New York, 1912
___*The Key to Health, Wealth, and Life*, E.J. Clode, New York, 1917
Shanklin, Imelda, *Selected Studies*, Unity School of Christianity, 1926
Schenck, Ruthane, *Being Prospered*, Unity School of Christianity, 1928
Simpson, James Y., *The Spiritual Interpretation of Nature*, Hodder and Stoughton, London, 1912
Spaulding, Baird, T., *Life and Teachings of the Masters of the Far East*, 2 vol., California Press, San Francisco, 1924
Swedenborg, Emanuel, *Heavenly Doctrine*, The Swedenborg Society of London, 1911
___*Religion and Life*, The Swedenborg Society, London, 1961
Swanada, Swami, *Divine Life*, Swanada Publication League, Himalaya, 1950
Sykes, John, *The Quakers*, J.B. Lippincott Co., New York, 1959
Tonge, Mildred, *A Sense of Living*, Pendle Hall, Pa., 1954
Towne, Elizabeth, *Practical Methods for Self-Development*, The Elizabeth Towne Co., Holyoke, Mass., 1904
Townshend, George, *Christ and Baha'U'llah*, George Ronald, London, 1957
Trine, Ralph Waldo, *The Higher Powers of the Mind and Spirit*, Dodge, 1913
___*In Tune with the Infinite*, Thomas Y. Crowell & Co., New York, 1897
___*The New Alignment of Life*, Dodge Publishing Co., New York, 1913
___*What All the World's A-Seeking*, Thomas Y. Crowell & Co., 1896
Trobridge, George, *Swedenborg: Life and Teaching*, The Swedenborg Foundation, New York, 1955
Troward, Judge Thomas, *The Creative Process in the Individual*,

Robert McBride & Co., New York, 1932

—*The Doré Lectures*, Dodd, Mead & Co., New York, 1909

—*The Edinburgh Lectures on Mental Science*, Dodd, Mead & Co., 1909

—*The Hidden Power*, Robert McBride & Co., New York, 1921

—*The Law and the Word*, Robert M. McBride & Co., New York, 1925

Tweedle, Violet, *The Cosmic Christ*, Rider & Co., London, 1930

Vining, Elizabeth Gray, *The World in Tune*, Pendle Hall, Pa., 1952

We Knew Mary Baker Eddy, Series of Three Volumes by Admirers, Christian Science Publishing Society, Boston, 1943, 1950, 1953

Wilcox, Ella Wheeler, *The Heart of New Thought*, Psychic Research Co., Chicago, 1902

—*New Thought and Common Sense*, W.B. Conkey, Chicago, 1908

Wilson, Ernest C., *The Great Physician*, Unity School of Christianity, 1935

—*Have We Lived Before?* Unity School

Wilson, Margary, *Believe in Yourself*, J.B. Lippincott, Philadelphia, 1948

Witherspoon, Thomas E., *Myrtle Fillmore: Mother of Unity*, The Unity School of Christianity

Wood, Henry, *The New Thought Simplified: How to Gain Harmony and Health*, Lee Shepherd, Boston, 1904

—*The Symphony of Life*, Lee Shepherd, Boston, 1904

Young, Frederick Harold, *The Philosophy of Henry James, Sr.*, College and University Press, New Haven, Conn., 1951

Zweig, Stefan, *Mental Healers*, The Viking Press, New York, 1932

INDEX

367